SAINT THOMAS MORE

Dialogue concerning Heresies

SAINT THOMAS MORE
Dialogue concerning Heresies

RENDERED IN MODERN ENGLISH
BY MARY GOTTSCHALK

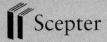 Scepter

The publisher acknowledges with thanks the work of Mary Gottschalk
in preparing this rendition of Thomas More's *Dialogue*. The quotations
from the Holy Bible herein are a rendition of More's text, as well.

Library of Congress Cataloging-in-Publication Data

More, Thomas, Sir, Saint, 1478–1535.
   [Dyalogue]
   Dialogue concerning heresies / Thomas More; rendered in modern
     English by Mary Gottschalk.
     p. cm.
   Includes bibliographical references.
   ISBN 13: 978–1–59417–044–7 (alk. paper)
   1. Catholic Church—Apologetic works. I. Gottschalk, Mary. II. Title.

BX1752.M673 2006
273'.6—dc22   2006051172

Published by Scepter Publishers, Inc.
P.O. Box 211, New York, N.Y. 10018
www.scepterpublishers.org

ISBN-10: 1–59417–044–4
ISBN-13: 978–1–59417–044–7

Printed in the United States of America

Contents

PART ONE

The letter of introduction sent from the author's friend by a trusty, discreet messenger; the letter from the author answering the same; and the messenger's explanation of the letter of introduction, on which the content of the whole entire work is based.

Here is summarily stated the order in which the author intends to discuss the issues brought before him. Because the first of these was an opinion conceived in some people's heads that a certain person recently forced to abjure heresy for having preached against pilgrimages and images and prayers made to saints was therein done a great injustice, the author briefly speaks his mind concerning the confuting of those terrible and pernicious opinions.

The objections made by the messenger against praying to saints, venerating images, and going on pilgrimages; and the author's answers to those objections. Also, the messenger's incidental comment that there would seem to be no need for Christian folk to go to any churches—that it is one and the same thing to pray there or elsewhere—and the author's answering and confuting of that opinion.

The author explains, in defense of pilgrimages, that it is the pleasure of God that he be specially approached and worshipped in one place in preference to another. And, granted that we cannot arrive at a knowledge of God's reason for this, the author yet proves by great authority that God by miracles testifies it is so.

Because the licitness of making pilgrimages is attested by miracles (among other proofs), the messenger makes objections against those miracles, noting that they could be faked and not real, or could be done by the devil, if they are done at all.

Because the messenger thinks that he can rightly doubt and deny the miracles on the basis that reason and nature tell him that they cannot be done, the author therefore first shows what unreasonableness would ensue if folk were to take that rigid a stance against giving credence to any such thing as reason and nature might seem to go against.

Because the messenger had in the beginning shown himself to be avidly focused on the text of Scripture, little interested in the old Fathers' interpretations, and disparaging of philosophy and almost all seven of the liberal arts, the author therefore mentions in passing what harm has at times happened to befall some of those young men whom he has known to devote their study to Scripture alone, disdaining logic and other secular disciplines and showing little regard for the old interpreters. By reason of which harm the author asserts that in the study of Scripture the safe course is to use, with virtue and prayer, first the judgment of natural reason, for which secular literature is very helpful; secondly, the commentaries of holy theologians of the Church; and thirdly, above all else, the articles of the Catholic faith received and believed throughout the church of Christ.

The messenger objects to the counsel of the author that the student of Scripture should rely on the commentators and on natural reason, which he calls an enemy to faith. And then the author answers those objections, proving in particular that reason is a servant to faith, and not an enemy, and must necessarily be consistent with faith and interpretation of Scripture.

The messenger objects to the counsel of the author that the student of Scripture should bring along the articles of our faith as a special rule to interpret Scripture by. And the author confirms his counsel given in this regard, showing that without that rule, one could easily fall into great errors in the study of holy Scripture.

The author, taking the occasion of certain statements made by the messenger, affirms the preeminence, necessity, and profitability of holy Scripture, pointing out, nevertheless, that many things have been taught by God not in writing. And that many big things still remain that way—unwritten—about truths it is necessary to believe. And that the new law of Christ is the law so written in the heart that it will never not be in his church. And that the law there written by God is a right rule by which to interpret the words written in his holy Scripture. Which rule, along with reason and the old interpreters, the author shows to be the really safe way by which to wade in the great stream of holy Scripture.

The messenger says that it seems to him he should not believe the Church if he observes the Church saying one thing and holy Scripture another thing, because Scripture is the word of God; and the author shows that the faith of the Church is as much the word of God as is Scripture, and therefore as much to be believed. And that the faith and Scripture, rightly understood, never contradict one another. And he further shows that with regard to any question arising from holy Scripture concerning any essential point of the faith, anyone who, from all that they can hear on both sides of the question, cannot tell which view is better and more correct, has a sure and unquestionable refuge provided them by the goodness of God, to bring them out of all perplexity, in that God has commanded them in all such unclear things to believe his church.

PART TWO

question which is the true church of Christ, pointing out that those whom we call heretics will perhaps say that they are the Church, and we not. Of which the author states the contrary, explaining how we can know that they cannot be the Church.

The author points out that no sect of those whom the Church takes for heretics can be the Church, since the Church was in existence before any of them, as the tree from which all those withered branches have fallen.

The messenger submits that the true church is perhaps not the people that we take for it, but a hidden, unrecognized class of those only who are predestined by God to be saved. To which the author responds, explaining why this cannot be so.

The messenger submits that even if the Church is not the number of only the folk predestined to Paradise, it yet could perhaps be the number of good and right-believing folk here and there, unrecognized as such, who could perhaps be those whom we condemn as heretics for holding opinion against images. Of which the author proves the contrary.

The author states and proves that this common, known multitude in Christian nations, not cut off or fallen off by means of heresies, is the true church of Christ—good people and bad together.

The messenger submits that since the Church is this known multitude of good people and bad together, of whom no one knows which are the one class and which are the other, it could perhaps be that the good class in the Church is those who believe the venerating of images to be idolatry, and the bad class those who believe the contrary. Which objection the author answers and refutes.

The author does some defending of the truth against the heresies holding against images, and, summarizing somewhat briefly what has been proved, thus finishes and ends the proof of his side of the argument.

The author commences the answer to the objections previously made by the messenger against venerating images, praying to saints, and going on pilgrimages. And first he answers, in this chapter, the objections made against praying to saints.

The messenger yet again objects to the use of relics, and expresses a great deal of doubt regarding canonization. To which the author responds.

PART THREE

to criticize a common law. And he shows also the reason why the law admits less weighty testimony in heinous criminal cases than in less weighty cases, having to do with deals or contracts.

The author makes known upon what ground and cause the man was convicted. And also several other things not brought up then, at the trial, which make it quite evident that he was greatly guilty. And thus, in passing, he shows why in a heresy trial it would not be reasonable to allow, after the slated witnesses have given their testimony and the charge has been well proved, any new witnesses to be received for the accused party.

The author proves that the ecclesiastical judges did the man a marvelous favor, and one almost more than licit, in admitting him to such an abjuration as they did, instead of leaving him to the secular authorities.

The author shows, with regard to this person who abjured for his own worldly reputation and for the more fruit from his preaching (should he be allowed to preach in time to come), that it would be much better for him if he openly and voluntarily confessed the truth. And that now, by stubbornly persisting in the denial, he both shames himself and would, if he preached, bring the word of God into discredit.

The messenger poses a question: If someone is sworn by a judge to tell the truth about himself concerning a crime that he is suspected of having committed, whether he may not legitimately swear on his oath to an untruth when he thinks that that truth cannot be proved against him. To which the author responds that he is bound upon pain of perjury to tell and confess the truth. And the much more of a sin and folly it was, then, for this man, who thus abjured, to perjure himself about something that he well knew would be proved; and a shameless folly to stubbornly stand by his perjury when he saw the case so clearly proved in fact. And with this he finishes the discussion of that abjuration.

The author explains why Tyndale's translation of the New Testament was burned, giving examples of words changed badly and for a bad purpose.

The author points out another great indication that the translation was dangerously devious and done for a bad purpose.

The author states that Tyndale's translation was too bad to be corrected.

The messenger finds fault with the clergy, in that he says they have made a synodal decree that no Bible in English will be allowed. And in this chapter

*them and ashamed even to appear so foolish as to hold them. And the author
gives several examples, some of which are newly set forth in the English
books of Tyndale, who in some respects is even worse than his master Luther
is himself.*

*The author shows by what occasion Luther first got into the devising of these
heresies. And that the occasion was one that makes it quite evident that he
was driven thereto by malice and just kept going from bad to worse, not
knowing where to stop; and that he refuses to submit to the judgment of
anyone on earth concerning the truth or falsehood of his opinions, except
only himself.*

*The author shows how Luther, in the book that he himself wrote about his
own deeds in the city of Worms in Germany, so madly forgets himself that
he unwittingly discloses certain foolish things about himself that one will
really laugh at and be very surprised to see.*

*The author shows the perpetual inconstancy of Luther, and his inconsis-
tency and contradiction with himself.*

*The author shows how Luther has been forced, for the defense of his indefen-
sible errors, to renounce and forsake the whole procedure of examining and
proving which he initially promised to adhere to. And how, like a man
shameful and shameless, he now has no proof in the world but his own word,
and calls that the word of God.*

*The author tells what things caused people to fall into Luther's foolish and
absurd sect. And he mentions also what harm the followers of that sect have
done in Germany, Lombardy, and Rome.*

*The messenger says that the malicious conduct of individuals is not to be
imputed to the sect itself, since some in every sect are bad. And the author
shows that in the case of the Lutherans, the sect itself is the cause of the
malicious conduct that the members engage in.*

*The author asserts that it is a great sign that the world is nearly at an end
when we see people so far fallen from God that they can stand it to be
accepting of this pestilent, insane sect which no people, Christian or heathen, could have tolerated before our day.*

*The author inveighs against this detestable article of this ungodly sect
whereby they take away the liberty of people's free will and ascribe everything to destiny.*

Introduction

C. S. Lewis' striking judgment that the *Dialogue concerning Heresies* is a "great Platonic dialogue, perhaps the best in English,"[1] is bound to surprise most readers today, simply because this great work has not been available in a popular edition for more than four hundred years—even though it was so popular in More's lifetime that it went through two editions in three years and More took time to revise it during his tumultuous tenure as Lord Chancellor of England (1529–1532). The present, modernized edition intends to make this "classic controversy of the Reformation"[2] available again to contemporary readers, in the hope that they may see why the *Dialogue* has been celebrated as the "wittiest" work of the English Reformation, with a "relaxed charm" and "potential to persuade" singular among Thomas More's later works on the theological controversies of his day.[3]

This introduction draws upon chapter 15 of Gerard B. Wegemer's *Thomas More: A Portrait of Courage*, rev. ed. (New York: Scepter Publishers, 2005).

[1] C. S. Lewis, *English Literature in the Sixteenth Century Excluding Drama* (Oxford: Clarendon Press, 1954), 172.

[2] So this book has been described in the original *Dictionary of National Biography*, vol. 19 (New York: MacMillan Company, 1909), 1354.

[3] *The Oxford Dictionary of National Biography*, vol. 39 (Oxford: Oxford Univ. Press, 2004), 69–70. When one considers that the first full scholarly edition of Thomas More's extensive writings was not completed until 1997, centuries later than those of any other comparable author of the English Renaissance, the strange neglect of More's writings seems somewhat more understandable, though the full story remains to be told. Of More's writings (some 15 volumes strong in the Yale Univ. Press edition), only his famous *Utopia* and *History of Richard the Third* are more widely known. References to the Yale edition of *The Complete Works of St. Thomas More* (New Haven: Yale Univ. Press, 1963–1997) are here abbreviated CW, followed by volume number and page numbers. The definitive scholarly edition of *The Dialogue concerning Heresies* is the Yale edition, edited by Thomas Lawler, Germain Marc'hadour, and Richard Marius, CW, vol. 6 (New Haven: Yale Univ. Press, 1981).

The *Dialogue* was composed in 1528 at the request of Bishop Cuthbert Tunstall of London, who commissioned Thomas More to defend publicly the doctrines of the Church and to respond to the Reformers' new opinions on a variety of controversial matters.[4] Masterfully conceived by a seasoned humanist and statesman, the *Dialogue* is a series of six conversations, taking place over four days, between Sir Thomas and a young university student and tutor, who has been influenced by all the new ideas of the age, especially the theological controversies enkindled by Martin Luther and William Tyndale. In the course of these lively exchanges, More discovers the roots of the youth's confusion by asking probing questions and by artfully addressing his concerns in classic Platonic fashion.[5] These conversations take place in the study and in the garden of More's home in Chelsea. More's hospitality is so great that he entertains his young

---

[4] See CW 6.2, 455–72, and Peter Ackroyd, *The Life of Thomas More* (New York: Nan A. Telese, 1998), 276–79, for helpful discussions of the historical context of the work. The historian John Guy also points out in his recent book *Thomas More* (New York: Oxford Univ. Press, 2000) that the composition of the *Dialogue* marks More's transition from "theological councilor" to the Crown, to "public defender of the faith" (119). As with many of More's later public works, it is important to note that he was writing swiftly at the request of the authorities, while under the incredible strain of his many other duties. Such working conditions explain, for example, occasional errors in Scriptural quotations and citations made from memory.

[5] In his earlier writing career, e.g., in the humanist masterpiece *Utopia* (1516), Thomas More had used the Platonic dialogue form and the Socratic method of cross-examination to tremendous effect—indeed, the dialectical character of *Utopia* is one key to its enduring power to prompt reflection and draw the reader into serious thought over the most important questions facing the human being. More's later theological writings do not represent a break from his humanist approach, but rather a development of it that has not been sufficiently studied or understood. As British scholar Brendan Bradshaw has persuasively argued, "the key to interpretation of More's career as a Catholic controversialist lies in his continuing commitment to Christian humanism." See "The Controversial Sir Thomas More," *Journal of Ecclesiastical History* 36 (1985): 23–43. Such commitment is evident in More's choice of the Platonic dialogue, with its emphasis on reasoned discussion and debate, to address such grave matters as the Reformation controversies.

guest at lunch or dinner four times, in addition to conducting these engaging conversations. Their serious discussions
do not, of course, take place at the family meals—a small yet
significant detail that reveals More's sensitivity to the human
requirements of different times and places and suggests one
reason why he gained the reputation as "a man for all
seasons."

In addition to the artful, Socratic character of More's
writing, another basis for C. S. Lewis's high praise of this
book is surely the subtlety of its characterization. The young
man, for example, is no stock character; he is unusually
bright and articulate, and moreover he has highly complex
motives and a very merry wit.[6] Throughout the *Dialogue* he
is called "the Messenger," because he has been sent by a
friend of More's to seek counsel regarding the many confused ideas of the time. Despite the press of business, More
makes time for this young man and cares for him as he would
for the longtime friend who sent him. As the great More
scholar Germain Marc'hadour relates, these details from the
Dialogue are quite true to life—Thomas More in fact enjoyed
receiving such visitors from the universities at his home,
where "he loved to debate with them" while taking "great
care not to crush them under the weight of his learning or
office."[7]

More's art of conversation in exploring and answering the
Messenger's many difficult questions is highly instructive. In
the course of replying to the pointed attacks against the
common culture of Christendom and Church doctrine—
attacks the Messenger relates energetically without endorsing
fully—More in turn emerges as a spirited yet modest conversation partner, despite his great advantages in learning and
experience. Indeed, the reader may be surprised to discover

[6] More's success with this vivid characterization has led some to wonder if
William Roper, More's spirited son-in-law and eventual biographer, was the
model for the character of the Messenger.

[7] CW 6.2, 456.

the image More presents of himself in the *Dialogue*. For those aware of the genius and stature of More's mind, it can be quite moving to behold England's only true genius (as the great Dutch humanist Erasmus claimed) consistently arguing on behalf of docility, obedience, and humility, and freely submitting his considerable judgment and understanding to the teaching authority of the Church, the true nature of which seems to be one of the most important of all contested issues in the *Dialogue*. That said, More's famous good cheer and mother wit are also evident in the opening chapters on saints, pilgrimages, and miracles. For example, he calls attention to the great human wonder that people are slow to believe others who testify by solemn oath to the truth of a miracle, yet those same folks will instantly believe a gossip who relates something startling and apparently evil about a neighbor simply on the strength of the gossip's word alone.

The book opens with the Messenger's arrival at More's home in Chelsea. More welcomes him and reads carefully his letter of introduction. In the original edition, this letter is called "the letter of credence," and it is important to note that the *Dialogue* begins with a simple yet significant human action: More's acceptance of his friend's letter and his willingness to trust him by taking the Messenger into his confidence. As More points out later in the *Dialogue*, "agreement and unanimity can never be where no one gives credence to anyone else," words that shed light on why More the artist begins the *Dialogue* as he does, by showing credence in the possibilities of good conversation. After this introduction, More then listens for a long time as the Messenger presents his many complaints and questions about the state of the Catholic Church. The young man is concerned about the nature of such devotional practices as making pilgrimages and praying to saints, but he is particularly disturbed by the harsh way heretics are treated. It seems to him "that the clergy, out of malice and ill will, are falsely accusing" many good people whom they call heretics (I.1). By relying upon law and public burnings, they act "contrary to the mildness and merciful mind of [Christ] their Master, and against the example of all the old holy Fathers." The Messenger is also convinced that all studies except Latin and Scripture are a waste of time for the spiritually minded believer.

Faced with these many involved issues, More does not want to give an immediate, "unpremeditated response." Instead, he simply gives the young man a hearty welcome and asks him to return the next morning. More then reflects on the young man's difficulties and works out a four-step plan to address the array of issues raised. In such planning and in the long hours lavished on conversation with this youth, More resists giving easy answers or quick "one-liners" that are easier to repeat than to understand and defend. Instead, More patiently listens and responds in ways helpful to this particular youth and appropriate to the difficult questions raised in the *Dialogue*.

The next day, More devotes the entire morning and most of the afternoon to the young Messenger. Their discussion begins just before 7:00 A.M. in More's study. Although it appears to follow the rambling course of any lively and spontaneous conversation, More actually focuses the whole morning's discussion upon the most basic question the youth raised the night before: How do we know what is true? Sir Thomas helps the Messenger develop a more thoughtful appreciation of the complexities of the world, including the complexities of how we know. To deny the very possibility of miracles, for example, is to oversimplify the concepts of nature and of God and to place the limitations of the human mind upon the liberty and bounty of God. Or to subscribe to the principle of *sola scriptura* is to overlook the difficulties involved in reading and interpreting any text, be it sacred or secular, and to place too much confidence in human judgment without adequately recognizing its tendency to err—and the consequent need for good counsel, something More dramatizes in the earlier

Utopia and the later *Dialogue of Comfort against Tribulation*, as well.

After much discussion, More asks the Messenger if he thinks a person should "better trust his eyes than his mind." The youth is surprised at the question, having always assumed that his eyes are perfectly reliable witnesses. More then gives this earthy and vivid rejoinder to counter the Messenger's naivete: "The eyes can be deceived and think they see what they do not see, if reason gives over its hold. Unless you think the magician . . . cuts your belt, in front of your face, in twenty pieces and makes it whole again, or puts a knife into his eye and sees never the worse. And turns a plum into a dog's turd in a boy's mouth" (I.23). At this point the servant comes in and asks, of all things, if he should get dinner ready! More and the youth share another good laugh (they have had many a good laugh already) while the bewildered servant is told to prepare a better meal than the one the magician proposed for the young boy. . . .

This combination of realism and humor characterizes much of Sir Thomas's conversation with the youth. In fact, some of More's best "merry tales" are in these pages. They are composed and arranged to encourage people to take a less simplistic view of life—and to take their own theories less seriously. As More explains in *Dialogue of Comfort against Tribulation*, one of several great works he composed while imprisoned in the Tower of London, "a merry tale with a friend refreshes a man much and without harm lightens the mind and amends the courage and his stomach so that it seems but well done to take such recreation."[8] Furthermore, the merry tales are an example of More's lifelong habit of speaking the truth through laughter and revealing that a great author "may sometimes say full truth in jest."[9]

Just as we learn from experience that our eyes do not perceive everything accurately, so, says More, we eventually

[8] CW 12, 82.
[9] *The Apology*, CW 9, 170.

22

must come to realize that one cannot accurately read and interpret everything by the light of one's wit alone. For the youth to argue, therefore, that all one must know is Scripture and grammar is absurd in the light of experience. Besides a particular language, many other things are needed—especially a well-trained reason and access to the vast collective learning of the Church—if one is to read Scripture according to the mind of its Author. The youth, again surprised, concludes that the Scriptures must not have been written very well if they cannot be easily understood (I.25). Arguing that the complexities of Scripture are actually part of God's high wisdom, More once again opens to this youth whole new horizons formerly not seen or understood because of unexamined hostility toward reason and an underlying lack of self-knowledge.

The other key discussion in part one of the *Dialogue* unfolds over several chapters and involves subjects of great interest to More: namely, the art of reading and interpreting Scripture; the perils of pride in reading and judgment; and the place of liberal education and cultivation in the life of a Christian. More opens by speaking in defense of thinking with the Church, which he believes has "the right understanding of holy Scripture," whereas the Messenger studies "the text alone, paying little heed to the old Fathers' interpretations or any of the liberal arts" (I.22). In this discussion, the reader sees more clearly the differences between More's judgment and the Messenger's. More, for example, presents his own judgment as the product of two kinds of education, one involving his serious study of the liberal arts and the other involving his docile relationship with the Church, in whose doctrine and teaching the human being finds the ultimate, authoritative conversation partner. The Messenger, on the other hand, confesses that he is not educated in the liberal arts (save grammar) and that he abides alone with the text of Scripture as his dialectical partner. More opposes the Messenger's approach of reading and interpreting Scripture simply by his own lights on the grounds (among other reasons) that such a reader will prove easy prey for the "spirit of pride" that unbeknownst lurks in the heart of every human being. More then offers this assessment of such readers for the Messenger's careful consideration:

> "I have known some quite good minds that have set all other learning aside, partly out of laziness, shunning the effort and pains to be sustained in that learning, and partly out of pride, by reason of which they could not endure the refutations that would sometimes come down on their side in debates. Which dispositions their inward, hidden partiality toward themselves caused them to cover and cloak under the pretext of simplicity, and good Christian devotion borne to the love of holy Scripture alone." (I.22)

More's emphasis here on pride (a favorite subject of his throughout his life)—and on the Messenger's apparent unwariness about its pesky and perilous presence at the roots of human judgment and action—suggests that the Messenger's approach to reading and interpretation is not grounded sufficiently on self-knowledge or on an adequate understanding of human nature, with the consequence that his individual, private judgment will likely be "persuaded a wrong way" by pride despite his good intentions. Rather than follow this way of reading, More argues for two safeguards for the study of Scripture, and especially for the exercise of good judgment: first, the "light of natural reason," strengthened through education in the liberal arts; and second, the light of sacred tradition in the Church through which God gives "the grace of understanding" according to Christ's promises (I.22). If these natural and supernatural safeguards are put in place and strengthened, More argues, then the reader stands a much better chance of judging well and avoiding the twin dangers of ignorance and pride, particularly in the interpretation of Scripture. On the whole, the conversation warns the Messenger of the perils involved in proudly styling oneself "judge over the Church" rather than taking the opposite approach (I.28).

On this crucial subject of pride, the *Dialogue* also contains one of More's most striking images of the tragic errors to which human judgment is prone on account of the pest of pride. Drawing on the ancient author Aesop, More remarks:

> "[Aesop says in a fable that everyone] carries over his shoulder a double wallet, and in the bag that hangs at his breast he puts other folks' faults, and this one he picks up and peers into often. In the other he stores up all his own, and it he swings at his back. This one he himself never cares to look into, but others who come after him cast an eye into it now and then." (III.11)

In a brilliant interpretation of this little fable, More scholar W. E. Campbell puts his finger on one crucial goal of Thomas More's conversation with the Messenger when he observes that "the reversal of these two wallets on a man's shoulders [is] an important and necessary spiritual experience, a kind of conversion that would benefit every man," first in terms of humility and self-knowledge, and second through an increase in charity toward others, perhaps because it is easier to be understanding with others when one has seen the truth about oneself better, or for the first time.[10] Without seeing personally the need for such a conversion, any reader, More implies, is bound to prove the plaything of his own misjudgments and skewed view of himself and others, and to distort rather than clearly understand things. While the Messenger claims that philosophy is "the mother of heresies," More demonstrates that pride, not reason, is truly the great "enemy" of faith. So engaging is their conversation that they are reluctant to break for lunch. However,

[10] "An Essay on the Spirit and Doctrine of the *Dialogue*," in *The Dialogue concerning Tyndale by Sir Thomas More*, ed. W. E. Campbell and A. W. Reed (London: Eyre and Spottiswoode, 1927), 81–82.

since they do not want to upset Lady Alice, they do leave More's study, talking and laughing as they go.

After lunch they go for a walk in More's garden and find a pleasant place to sit, under an arbor. Starting right where they had left off, More tactfully directs their afternoon discussion to a second important issue, one closely related to the first: the nature and necessity of the Catholic Church, especially the clear promises of Christ never to abandon his Bride and to send his Spirit to guide the Church—promises that should stir believers to real faith in the Church, More maintains, despite whatever controversy may be at hand (I.18, 20, 28–30). Only when this central issue is clarified and when the Messenger's trust in Christ seems to be restored does More return to the unresolved questions about pilgrimages and the veneration of images, relics, and saints. By midafternoon, we are told, the Messenger "so fully felt himself answered and satisfied with all this that he thought himself able to satisfy and convince with it anyone he should happen to meet with who would hold the contrary" (II.12).

More bids him farewell, but he prudently sets up another time to discuss the issues he has not yet answered. Sure enough, in two weeks' time the Messenger's euphoria has worn off, and he returns with many more questions that are bothering him. These perplexities have increased, at least in part, because of talks he has been having with his university friends.

Somewhat reticent before the authority and intelligence of Chancellor More, the Messenger at first says that he and his friends at the university have only one question about all that More said before, and it has to do with the status of Scripture. This opening question leads into a long discussion about William Tyndale's translation of Scripture, which had been banned from England. The Messenger and his friends have assumed that the clergy simply want to keep the laity under their control by denying them access to Scripture in their native language; More, however, shows that the prob-

Introduction

lem is in fact with Tyndale's objectionable translations, influenced as they are by the new Lutheran interpretations.

Sir Thomas strongly defends the importance of Scripture, and he too favors an English translation—provided that the translation is faithful to the text and approved by the Church, and not the work of a lone and questionably motivated translator (III.16). Modern readers may wonder why More disputes Tyndale's translation choices for certain key words in the New Testament (III.8). Why, for example, does More object to Tyndale's decision to translate the Greek word *agape* as "love" instead of "charity," or to Tyndale's rendering of *ecclesia* as "congregation" instead of "church"? What is the problem with translating *presbuteros* as "elder" or "senior" instead of "priest"? As More maintains, charity in "Englishmen's ears" signifies something much more precise than "love"—charity is "not every common love, but a good, virtuous, well-ordered love" with the first object being God, and the second, one's neighbor as oneself for love of God (see Matthew 22:36–40). As the Yale editors point out, More's dispute over this key word is also connected to his larger objection to the "faith alone" (*sola fide*) principle of the Reformers: "More's endeavor is to reassert the queenly status of charity, which solafideism tends to treat as a stepchild." [11] The dispute over *ecclesia* is perhaps more obvious given Reformation concerns over ecclesiology. "Congregation" suggests a gathering or assembly of people simply, whereas "church" signifies something more formal, structured, and organized—and reminiscent of the institutional Church. [12] Finally, More argues that Tyndale's choice to translate *presbuteros* as "elder" instead of "priest" reveals the translator's objectionable adherence to Luther's opinions that, in More's summary, "all ordination is nothing," and

[11] CW 6, 515. More makes this case again in the *Confutation of Tyndale* (CW 8, 199–203).
[12] *Oxford Encyclopedia of the Reformation* (New York: Oxford Univ. Press, 1996), 190–91.

Introduction

that a priest is "nothing else but a man chosen among the people to preach," positions that muddle and endanger the sacramental system of the Church (III.8). By deliberately removing "charity," "church," and "priest" from the Bible—and, by extension, from the vocabulary of its readers—Tyndale deliberately distorts and obscures the original texts and meanings through his new translations, More maintains.

At this point in the conversation, the Messenger agrees with More's arguments, and they again break for lunch. Afterwards, they proceed into the garden to tackle the difficult issues which Sir Thomas has deliberately kept for last. But More does not even have to bring them up. Now that the Messenger is more relaxed, he speaks freely about the concerns that bother him the most. Over the last three discussions, the Messenger has come to agree that Luther's and Tyndale's views are indeed heretical—that is, that the two men chose to set up a sect representing what More had called a "detour" or side way taken from the common belief of the whole Church.[13] But why treat them so harshly? the Messenger wonders. The Messenger believes the clergy have maliciously outlawed the Reformers' writings in self-defense, so that the laity will not read about the many clerical abuses.

[13] See part one, chapter 2. As the helpful article on heresy in the *Oxford Dictionary of the Christian Church* (Oxford: Oxford Univ. Press, 1983) elaborates, heresy is "the formal denial or doubt of any defined doctrine of the Catholic faith. . . . From the earliest days the Church has claimed teaching authority and consequently condemned heresy, following Christ's command: 'If he refuse to hear the Church, let him be unto thee as the Gentile and the publican' (Mt 18:17)" (639). The *Oxford Dictionary* also offers a helpful distinction between formal and material heresy: "The former, which is heresy properly so-called, consists in the willful and persistent adherence to an error in matters of faith on the part of the baptized person. . . . 'Material heresy,' on the other hand, means holding heretical doctrines through no fault of one's own, 'in good faith,' as is the case, e.g., with most persons brought up in heretical surroundings. This constitutes neither crime nor sin, nor is such a person strictly speaking a heretic, since, having never accepted certain doctrines, he cannot reject or doubt them."

28

More does not deny that much reform is needed, but he does argue that the Church, as Christ's bride on earth, deserves due respect and indeed faith, especially on account of Christ's clear promises that he would never abandon the Church and that the Holy Spirit would be present and active in the Church until the end of time. An important part of giving that respect and of exercising genuine faith is to use legitimate means to bring about the Church's reform—not to recklessly champion revolutionary ideas that reject "the unanimous accord and agreement of all Christian people these fifteen hundred years" (IV.1).

More also leads the Messenger to realize how little he actually knows about the teachings of Luther and Tyndale and how much faith he is placing in hearsay. The Messenger is attracted by their call for reform in the Church and for the popular use of Scripture. More agrees with these aims, but shows that Luther and Tyndale actually propose something quite revolutionary and harmful to society through the means of violent and exaggerated rhetorical "railing" that misleadingly appeals to passion rather than reason.[14] He therefore asks the youth to take a careful and calm look at what these men have actually written and to think about the implications of their positions for spiritual and civil life.

Not only do Luther and Tyndale deny the Church's authority and the validity of most of the sacraments as understood and practiced by the Church, not only do they consider "all the world wild geese" except themselves, but they also deny free will and thus ascribe responsibility for evil

---

[14] See 3.13 and 4.2 for examples of More's consistent use of the verb "rail" to describe the rhetorical style of Tyndale and Luther, respectively. See also Gerard B. Wegemer, *Thomas More on Statesmanship* (Washington, D.C.: Catholic Univ. Press, 1998), 161–82, for a full discussion of the important rhetorical differences between More's writings and the Reformers' approaches. For his part, More's fellow humanist Erasmus claimed that "no one has written more stark raving madly than Luther," powerful words cited by Marjorie Boyle in *Rhetoric and Reform: Erasmus' Civil Dispute with Luther* (Cambridge, Mass.: Harvard Univ. Press, 1983), 100.

to God, not to his creatures. By affirming such objectionable theology and teaching it to others, Luther and Tyndale endanger not only their own souls but the spiritual and civil welfare of those who give credence to their "false fables" (IV.1) and strange new statements at odds with "Scripture, natural reason, the laws and determinations of the Church, and the unanimous agreement of the holy Fathers" (IV.6). At the same time, the "one particular thing" they use to spice everything else is a doctrine of liberty which teaches that "having faith, they [need] nothing else." By claiming a personal freedom that is independent of "all governors and any kind of law, spiritual or temporal, except the Gospel," these revolutionaries were paving a sure path to war and putting themselves and the common good in peril (IV.7).

In fact, war had already erupted. As More reports, during the summer of 1525, seventy thousand Lutherans were slain in Germany before order was restored—an order that resulted in "a right miserable servitude" (IV.7). As More points out, the Lutheran doctrine "sounded so good to the common, rustic people that it blinded them . . . and could not permit them to reflect and see to what end the same would ultimately come" (IV.7). In 1526, More's friend Erasmus concluded that the "perilous business" of Reformation by Luther's radical means was shattering the world, and in a powerful letter he urged Elector John of Saxony to oppose Luther: "I am writing this, renowned Prince, not out of any desire for revenge, but because it is a matter of general public interest that Luther be forcibly reminded by law and your authority that he is not to rage with like insolence against anyone; for such conduct does no good to anybody but tends to destroy all good things." [15]

Unfortunately, the violence and dark destruction already evident in the Peasants' War and elsewhere did not cease but intensified, as angry Germans sacked Rome and tortured the

[15] *Erasmi epistolae*, ed. P. S. Allen et al. (Oxford: Oxford Univ. Press, 1906–1955), Letter 1670.

Catholic citizens who lived there, in 1527. More recounts to the Messenger what diplomats reported about that sacking of Rome. These examples of cruel behavior are, he maintains, the practical consequences of Luther's and Tyndale's theories:

> Like veritable beasts [the German soldiers] violated the wives in the sight of their husbands, and slew the children in the sight of the parents. And, to extort the bringing out of more money, when the men had already brought out absolutely all they had in order to save themselves from death or further pain, and were negotiating pacts and promises of peace without further disturbance, then the wretched tyrants and cruel tormentors, as though all of that counted for nothing, did not desist from putting them from time to time to intolerable tortures. . . . Too distressing and too disgusting would it be to relate the villainous pain and tortures that they came up with for the helpless women. . . . (IV.7)

Even the young did not escape the cruel inventiveness of these "abominable beasts," as More relates disturbingly:

> Some failed not to take the child and bind it to a spit and lay it to the fire to roast, the father and mother looking on. And then begin to talk about a price for the sparing of the child, asking first a hundred ducats, then fifty, then forty, then twenty, then ten, then five, then two, when the poor father had not one left, but these tyrants had them all already. Then would they let the child roast to death. And on top of that, they would in derision, as though they pitied the child, say to the father and the mother, "Ah, tut-tut, shame on you! What wonder is it if God sends a vengeance among you? What unnatural people you are, who can find it in your hearts to see your own child roasted in front of your face, rather than part with one ducat to deliver it from death." (IV.7)

More reports these examples in all their horrifying detail to remind the young Messenger what happens when people are not encouraged to respect law and virtue—and when an elect group dehumanizes whole classes of people.[16]

The young Messenger objects that such cruelty cannot be blamed specifically on Luther and his followers, since all wars engender cruel behavior. More counters (as Erasmus had argued earlier) that Luther's denial of free will "plainly direct[s] everyone to wretched living" (IV.8). After all, if the way we act is not within our control, what incentive is there to struggle against one's passions and temptations? Furthermore, if our actions make no difference to God, why should they make any difference to us?

More considers Luther's denial of free will to be "the very worst and most harmful heresy that ever was thought up, and on top of that, the most insane" (IV.11). "Assuredly," he says, "it is so far against all holy Scripture rightly understood, so far against all natural reason, so utterly subversive of all virtue and all good order in the world, so highly blaspheming of the goodness and majesty of Almighty God in heaven, that it is more than a wonder how anyone on earth who has either one spark of intelligence in his head or toward God or man one drop of good will in his heart would not shudder to hear it" (IV.12).

Yet, objects the Messenger, even if one agrees that such teaching is madness, why treat the mad teachers so cruelly? Why not just help reasonable people come to see how foolish the teaching is?

---

[16] More had explored such dehumanizing tendencies earlier in the *Utopia*, where it is disturbingly revealed that the Utopians long for the genocidal annihilation of a neighboring people, the Zapoletes. See Thomas More, *Utopia*, trans. George Logan (Cambridge: Cambridge Univ. Press, 2002), 88–89, for a full statement of the Utopian policy. As the narrator, Raphael Hythloday, relates in one particularly memorable sentence, the Utopians "think they would deserve very well of mankind if they could sweep from the face of the earth all the dregs of that vicious and disgusting race" (89).

More tries to help the Messenger realize that getting someone (even oneself) to be reasonable is no easy matter, especially when strong passion or personal pride is involved. By appealing to strong passion, Luther has stirred thousands to angry violence against individuals and institutions protected by law. In such a situation, the law has the duty to step in and treat such offenders, not cruelly, but with the force necessary to safeguard peace and justice. Historically, More points out, the heretics themselves have regularly been the first to use violence. Only after this has occurred have responsible princes been driven to use force for the "preservation not only of the faith, but also of the peace among their people." While More was evidently hoping that reason would prevail, he recognized that the use of force was legitimate and just in such a situation (IV.13).

To substantiate this reading of history, More goes back a thousand years and recalls the problems Augustine had with the Donatists. For most of his long life, Saint Augustine "had with great patience borne and endured their malice, only writing and preaching in refutation of their errors, and not only had done them no temporal harm but also had hindered and opposed others who would have done it." Finally, however, "for the peace of good people," Augustine found it necessary to exhort "Count Boniface and others to suppress them with force and threaten them with corporal punishment" (IV.13).

Augustine's experience was confirmed by "holy Saint Jerome and other virtuous Fathers." Yet none of these Church Fathers allowed the Church itself to use physical force against heretics; this was a matter for the civil government, a means sometimes needed in the effort to avoid "general sedition, insurrection, and open war"—all of which could "at the outset be quite easily prevented, by punishment of those few that [were] the first" (IV.15).

Such punishment, More explains, can be a civil and moral obligation in defense of the common good against seditious activity, since "nature, reason, and God's behest bind, first of all, the ruler to protect his people" and then also bind "everyone to help and defend his good, innocent neighbor against the malice and cruelty of the wrongdoer." In this context, More affirms Augustine's position on just war: that a just war is "not only excusable but also commendable" because it is undertaken "in the defense of [one's] country against enemies that would invade it." In such a war "everyone is fighting not for the defense of himself, out of personal regard for himself, but, out of Christian charity, for the protection and preservation of everyone else" (IV.14).

What makes heresy such a difficult social disorder, says More, is the hardened pride which is inevitably involved. Since pride is "the very mother of all heresies," heretics can come to a point where only the frantic pleasure of their own will can satisfy and content them. These proud fantasies arise among the learned "because they [want] to be singular among the people," and they arise among the not-so-learned because such souls "long to seem far more learned than they are." In either case, the reward for their labor is the "delight of beholding what pleasure the people have in their preaching." In More's judgment, the heretical soul is tragically centered upon its own self-image rather than upon God, the common good, or other souls.

This involved discussion comes to a halt when supper is announced; but before going, More gives the Messenger several passages to read and compare by the time they meet again the next morning. One of these, from the *Decretum* (the official book of Church law, the one recognized throughout Christendom), demonstrates that current procedures regarding heretics are no different from those that were in force at the time of the "old Fathers and holy theologians and saints." Other passages are from "certain works of Saint Cyprian, Saint Augustine, and some other holy theologians"; finally, there are some from Luther's and Tyndale's books. The Messenger retires with quite a homework assignment!

When they meet again the next day, the Messenger announces that these readings have persuaded and changed him (IV.18). Luther and Tyndale are, he says, "so plainly confuted by the old holy Fathers . . . that if I had seen so much before, it would likely have shortened many parts of our long conversation" (IV.18). In fact, the youth wonders how so many Germans can follow Luther and so many Englishmen can follow Tyndale.

More responds by pointing out that the appeal of these men is not to reason, but to "foolish" passion for impossible liberties (IV.18). By conjuring up such "false enchantments," they have understandably gained many followers. The number of these followers could increase, More warns, while the number of true Christians could be reduced to a small sect— but this sect will nevertheless be a church that will always "remain and be well known" by the profession of a faith that can be traced back to Christ. Regardless of what might happen in any one hour of darkness, Christ's church will, without fail, grow large again (IV.18).

After these challenging and yet comforting words, More sits down to lunch with the young Messenger for the last time. But first he prays that all might be one flock again, so filled "with charity in the way of good works in this wretched world that we may be partakers of the heavenly bliss which the blood of God's own Son has bought us unto" (IV.18). Good-willed and patient conversation between friends, the warm and attractive image of which the *Dialogue* as a whole presents to the reader, seems in More's mind to be one trustworthy and hopeful means of bringing about such unity again.

Gerard B. Wegemer and Stephen Smith

THE CENTER FOR THOMAS MORE STUDIES
DALLAS, TEXAS
July 6, 2006

A NOTE ON THE TITLE

Thomas More did not use the word "heresies" in the title of this work. In both the 1529 and 1531 editions, the title remained unchanged:

> A dialogue of Sir Thomas
> More, knight: one of the
> counsel of our sovereign lord the king and chan-
> cellor of his Duchy of Lancaster. Wherein be
> treated divers matters / as of the venera-
> tion & worship of images & relics /
> praying to saints / & going on pil-
> grimage. With many other
> things touching the pesti-
> lent sect of Luther &
> Tyndale / by the
> one begun
> in Saxony
> & by
> the other labored
> to be brought into England.
>
> Newly overseen by the said Sir Thomas More
> Chancellor of England
> 1530.

This long title (long titles were common in the early days of printing) gives prominence first to More's responsible position as knight, counselor, and chancellor, and then, to the "divers matters" that were of pressing concern to his fellow citizens. Only in the 1557 edition of More's *English Works* did the editor, William Rastell, invent the shorter title *Dialogue of Heresies*.

SAINT THOMAS MORE
Dialogue concerning Heresies

Part One

There is an old saying that one business begets and brings
forth another. Which proverb, as it happens, I find very true
with regard to myself, who have been forced first by the
occasion of one business to undertake a second, and now,
right after the second, to undertake a third.

What happened was this. A very distinguished friend of
mine one day sent to me a trusted, reliable friend of his with
a letter of introduction to be read to me, concerning many
matters that are actually very certain and beyond doubt, but
that have, nevertheless, recently been called into question by
wicked people, the specifics whereof appear so extensively in
chapter 1 of this part that we need not mention them here.
At first I thought it enough to speak my mind orally, to the
messenger; I figured that after our conversation ended I
would never need to do anything further in this regard. But
afterward, when the messenger had left and I was feeling
very relieved in my mind in that I considered all my work
done, I reflected on it for a little while and found that my
business that I had taken for finished was very far from that
point—in fact, little more than begun. For when I considered what the matters were, and how many big things had
been treated of between the messenger and me, and in what
kind of fashion, although I did not doubt his good will and I
very well trusted that his intelligence and education would
serve him well in the understanding and reporting of our
conversation, I yet found our discussion to have been so
diversified and so long, and sometimes so intricate, that I
myself could not without great effort call it to mind in right
order. And so it seemed to me that I had not done well in not
putting it in writing, in trusting his memory alone, especially since some parts of the subject matter are in themselves

such things as need to be attentively read and reflected upon, rather than cursorily heard and gone over. And, moreover, I realized that even if I am not at all suspicious of the messenger, which in all honesty I am not—to tell the truth, I am by nature so little mistrusting that a person would probably have to prove very plainly to be downright evil before I would take them for bad—yet, since no one can look into someone else's heart, then just as it is therefore good to think the best, so also it would not be much amiss to prepare in such a way for the worst that if a person happens to be worse than we take them for, our good opinion will not occasion us any harm. For this reason it seemed to me that, for the more security, it would behoove me to send our conversation to my said friend in writing. That way, if it did happen that the messenger, out of any furtive favor borne toward the wrong side, purposely distorted what was said, his employer could not only know the truth but also have occasion to be more wary of his messenger, who otherwise might happen to do harm, as long as he was mistaken for good.

Now, when I had, upon this deliberation taken with myself, written out the whole thing and sent it to my friend, then I had, it seemed to me, everything done, and my mind fully set at rest. But that rest did not last long. For soon after, it was told to me that of everything I had written, several copies had been made, and one of them even carried overseas. And when I recalled what a bad bunch of our apostates have assembled there, some of them having run away from religious life and all of them having run away from the right faith, it seemed to me that great danger could arise if some of that lot who have confederated and are conspiring together in the sowing and spreading of Luther's pestilent heresies in this realm should maliciously change my words for the worse and thus put in print my book, refashioned according to their delusional ideas.[1] If I should afterward point out and

---

[1] Originally an Augustinian monk and priest, Martin Luther (1483–1546) eventually took the leading role in the Reformation in Germany. On

criticize the differences, I might perhaps seem to be trying to make my case look better by amending my own upon the sight of theirs. For the avoidance of which I am now driven, as I say, to this third business of publishing and putting my book in print myself, whereby their scheme (if they should have any such in mind) will, I trust, be forestalled and thwarted. And this I have done not just of my own carefulness, but in accord with the counsel of more than one other person—whose advice and counsel, because of their wisdom and learning, I asked in that regard, and who, at my request, agreed to read the book over before I published it. For although I to some extent dare take the liberty to converse in an informal manner with individuals who, because of those delusional ideas, want to ask me any question on these subjects—this being in accord with the counsel of Saint Peter, who bids us be ready to give everyone an explanation of, and to show them a reasonable basis for, the faith and hope that we have [1 Pt 3:15]—I yet would not presume to print and

---

October 31, 1517, he posted his 95 theses on indulgences on the door of Wittenberg's castle church; in 1520, major written works urging reform followed, including *To the Christian Nobility of the German Nation Regarding the Improvement of the Christian Estate,* and the more famous *On the Babylonian Captivity of the Church* and *On the Freedom of a Christian.* Forty-one of Luther's theses were officially censured by the Church in 1520, and then Luther himself was excommunicated in 1521. After discarding his Augustinian habit in 1524, Luther married the former nun Katharina von Bora in 1525 and continued to attempt to direct efforts at reformation, though sharp differences in opinion were already emerging among the various reformers (*Oxford Dictionary of the Christian Church,* 1014). Luther and Thomas More first came into contact with one another indirectly though powerfully, through writing. After Luther publicly and vituperatively attacked Henry the Eighth's *Defense of the Seven Sacraments,* More defended the insulted and incensed King with his vigorous *Response to Luther,* written under a pseudonym (see CW 5). Later, More argued that Lutheran rhetoric had played a decisive role in both fomenting the Peasants' War and bringing it to an unhappy and bloody close in 1525. Luther also clashed in writing with the Dutch humanist Erasmus over free will in 1525; Luther argued for the utter bondage of the will, while Erasmus argued in defense of free will and personal responsibility, despite the wound of sin. [Biographical notes by Stephen Smith.]

publish any book, about anything having to do with our faith, unless men more learned than myself should consider it either profitable or, at least, harmless.

To their examination and judgment I did the more conscientiously submit this work because of two things in particular, among several others. The one was the sweeping allegations made by the messenger on behalf of the wrong side, which were expressed so unrestrainedly that I myself was halfway in doubt as to how appropriate it would be to relate anyone's words that were so down-home and sometimes so disrespectfully spoken against God's holy saints and their hallowed memories. The other was certain stories and jesting comments which he mixed in with his contentions, and some such on my own part, now and then, as the occasion came up in our conversation. Although I saw no harm in them, I nevertheless was somewhat worried that to dignified people they might seem too light and frivolous, given the weight and gravity of any such serious matter. So on these two points, although I had already seen some examples of quite holy men who, in their books responding to the contentions of heretics in their time, did not refrain from relating the exact words of those whose writings they were refuting (some of which words were of such a style and kind as probably no good person would find acceptable), and who also did not refrain from making a jesting comment themselves in a quite serious work—of which two things I could, out of godly men's books and holy saints' works, gather a good stack—I nevertheless decided that in my own work I would not allow or defend anything that the judgment of other virtuous and intelligent men would in any way be against. And then, after such men had read it and independently given their advice, I found that, as often happens, something which one wise and very learned man wanted out, two of equal wisdom and learning particularly wanted in, neither side lacking good and valid reasons for their stance. So, since it would not have become me to be judge over the judgment of those whom I had chosen and taken for my judges, they personally being such that it would be hard for anyone to say which of them had any edge in terms of erudition, intelligence, or prudence, I had no choice but to go along with the majority. Which I have done to such an extent that, just as I took out or changed several things by their good advice and counsel, so I let stand in this book nothing but what two explicitly advised me to let stand, for every one who made to me any suggestion to the contrary.

And this much I have thought necessary to give by way of explanation and excuse to all of you who will happen to read this rough, simple work. I ask your patience and pardon. May God, as a special grace, grant you as much profit in the reading as my poor heart has meant you and intended in the writing.

I.

The letter of introduction sent from the author's friend by a trusty, discreet messenger; the letter from the author answering the same; and the messenger's explanation of the letter of introduction, on which the content of the whole entire work is based.

THE LETTER OF INTRODUCTION

Master Chancellor, as heartily as I possibly can, I commend myself to your kindly remembrance, not without a thousand thanks for your good company when we were last together. Since it was your pleasure to spend some of your time with me in free and easy conversation—some part of which I trust so to remember that I myself will be the better for it, and some others no less so, who will have cause (and already do) to give you great thanks for it—I am at this time taking the liberty of sending to you my close personal friend, this bearer, to speak with you somewhat further, partly on the same matters and partly on some other things that have happened there since, about which there is a lot of talk and rumor circulating here. This way you will have the opportunity to deal more at length (if your free time permits) with certain difficulties brought up since, on the matters discussed between us before. Were it not for your other activities, I would presume upon your goodness and ask you to take a good amount of time with him. And I even do, nevertheless, earnestly ask you to answer him to his full satisfaction, as your free time permits. For he will, no matter how long he has to stick around for this, spend with you whatever days and hours you can spare him, which time cannot in these things be but well spent, considering that the matters are such, and have so much to do with God, that they would be well worth setting worldly activities aside for, especially with the need being so great. For I assure you, some folk here are talking very strangely about the things that he will bring up to you. Not just on account of the spoken statements they relate that come from there, but also, most especially, through the occasion of some letters vilely written and sent here from London by a priest or two whom they take here for honorable. But no matter what anyone may say or write, I shall, for the confidence and trust that I have in you, surely take and spread as the real truth whatever you affirm to my friend, whom I am sending to you not so much because I cannot come myself (though it is that, too) as because I really want to have him talk with you. Whatever you say to him, consider it said to myself. I trust that not only because of his uprightness and discretion, but also because of his memory, you will not dislike conversing with him. For either my affection blinds me or you will find him intelligent and (as say others who can judge this better than I) of more than average learning, with one thing added that you are likely to be very happy with: a great sense of humor. He is by nature not the least bit tongue-tied. And I have with regard to these matters encouraged him to be frank, not do any holding back out of politeness. The rituals of formal debate distort much of the content because of that concern, when one focuses more on how to conduct oneself than on what

Background letters, to and from the author

one will say. I have, I say, therefore encouraged him to mind his matter more than his manners and to come out freely not only with whatever he thinks, but with whatever he likes, yielding not one foot out of respect for you, but only when he is borne back by reason.

Thus, as you can see, I presume on your goodness, putting you to work and trouble, even sending someone to accost you in your own house! But so much the bolder am I because I know you to be a ready and sure defender in such challenges. And of such labor you in your wisdom well see° that God is the rewarder. May he long preserve you and all yours.

THE LETTER THAT THE AUTHOR SENT WITH THE BOOK

Most honorable sir:

(After most hearty greetings.) Although I recently sent you my poor mind by the mouth of your trusty friend, to whom you asked me in your letter to give no less credence than to yourself concerning all such things as he brought up and discussed with me on your behalf; and although (because of the confidence that you have in him, the intelligence and learning that I found in him, and the uprightness that I so much the more think him to be of in that I perceive you, a man of such wisdom and virtue, to hold him in such special trust) I do not and cannot believe otherwise than that he has faithfully made to you a straightforward and full report of our entire conversation, yet, since I naturally suppose that if you and I could have conveniently gotten together, you would have chosen to hear my mind by my own mouth rather than by the mediation of someone else's, I have since then, within these last few days (in which I have been at home), put the thing in writing, so that you can not only hear it by the mouth of your friend, but also (which is better than it would be to hear it once and quickly by my own mouth) read it (if you wish) more often, at your best leisure, and reflectively, from my own pen. Which is something that

45

I truly thought myself so much the more obliged to do since, on account of your special liking and affection for me, it pleased you to hold my opinions and answers on those subjects in such high regard and esteem that none of the rumors circulating there, or tales told in your part of the country, or letters sent there, or reasonings or arguments there made to the contrary, would be any hindrance or obstacle, but that you would (as you wrote) take as undoubtable truth whatever I should (through your friend) assure you of.

And certainly, sir, of this you can rest assured: that I will never deliberately betray your trust. And lest I might happen to do so accidentally, unawares, albeit I said nothing orally to your friend that I was not quite well informed of the truth about, yet since I understood from him that some folk suspected that many things were being imputed not only to that man you wrote of, but also to Luther himself, that could not be proved, I did so much there that I even obtained permission to see, and to show him as well, the books of the one and the actual court records concerning the other, so that both of us could with that much the more certitude guarantee you of the truth. If you find any man who yet doubts whether what he told you and I write you is the truth or not, I will (if he can understand Latin) find at your pleasure the means for him so to see the books himself that no matter how full of doubt he was, he will not fail to be fully convinced and satisfied. And this guarantee I will make you as far as concerns anything done here.

Now, as for the things discussed and debated between us, the conclusions themselves are such certain truths that they are not debatable. But as for whether the arguments made by me for them are effective or insufficient (albeit your friend, saying so either because he truly thought so or just out of politeness, accepted them as good), you yourself, without prejudice to the principal matters, can be the judge of that.

And so I ask that you take for what it is worth the little labor and great good will of him whom in anything that may give you pleasure, you may to the utmost of his little power good and boldly command. And may our Lord grant you, with my good lady your spouse, and all yours, to fare as exceedingly well as you would all wish.

————————

Your friend first, after your letter was read and I asked him to introduce himself, explained to me that you had sent him to me not because of any doubt that you yourself had concerning many of those things that he would mention to me, but because of the doubt that you perceived in many others, and in some folk plain persuasion to the contrary, whom you would be eager to answer with the truth—although some things, he said, were also being talked about there in such a way that you did not really know yourself which side you should believe. For it was not only being spoken there, but was also being written to there by several reputable priests in London, that the man you write of was falsely accused of many things and treated so terribly in that affair that he was forced to forswear and abjure certain heresies, and was publicly put to penance for them, when he had never held any such heresies. And that all this was done out of malice and ill will, partly of some friars (against whose wrongdoings he had preached) partly because he preached boldly against the pomp and pride and other uncalled-for conduct (which more men talk about than preach about) engaged in by the clergy. And they take as a great indication that he meant no ill the personal knowledge and experience that people have had of him—that he lived uprightly and was a good, honorable, virtuous man, far from any ambition or desire for worldly honor; chaste, humble, and charitable; free and liberal in almsgiving; and a really splendid preacher by whose devout sermons the people were greatly edified. And therefore the people say that all this stuff is being done only to stop people's mouths and put to silence everyone who would say anything about the misdeeds of the clergy. And they think it was for no other reason that there also was burned, at the pulpit cross of St. Paul's, the New Testament translation recently done by Master William Hutchins, otherwise known as Master Tyndale, who was (it is said) well known, before he went overseas, for a man of quite good living who had studied Scripture and was well versed in it, and who in several places in England was very well liked and did a great amount of good with preaching.[2] And people mutter among themselves that that Bible was not only free of error but also a very good translation, and that the burning of it was ordered so that no one would be able to prove that those errors declared (at the pulpit cross of St. Paul's) to have been found in it were never actually found there, but were falsely alleged. And such as they were (some say), those things would have been no errors at all even had they actually been translated thus, but blame was put upon, and fault found with, things not at all blameworthy, only to discredit and defame that holy work, to the end that they might seem to have some just cause to burn it.

And this for no other intent but to keep out of the people's hands all knowledge of Christ's Gospel, and of God's law, except only so much as the clergy themselves care now and then to tell us. Which, little as it is and seldom as it is imparted, is not even well respected and accurately

---

[2] The English Reformer and biblical translator William Tyndale sometimes went by the name "Hychyns" ("Hutchins" in this edition), a name his ancestors had occasionally used (CW 6.2, 604). Tyndale was educated at Oxford, became a Catholic priest, and then left England and settled in Germany in 1524, where he worked on his translation of the New Testament and composed several other works of Reformed theology, such as *A Prologue on Romans, Parable of the Wicked Mammon* and *Obedience of a Christian Man*. These works were heavily influenced by Luther, although Tyndale eventually breaks from Luther on key points, such as justification (*Oxford Dictionary of the Christian Church*, 1660). Smuggled into England in 1526, his translation of the New Testament was a subject of great controversy, and several public burnings of it occurred (CW 6.2, 247; see also CW 8, 1149–50, 1161, and 1168–70). Thomas More critiques Tyndale's theological opinions and translations at great length in *The Confutation of Tyndale* (CW 8), his longest work. Tyndale was arrested and executed near Brussels on October 6, 1535, the same year as More's death in England.

communicated, but adulterated with false interpretations and altered from the truth of the actual words and meaning of Scripture, only for the maintenance of their authority.

And the fear that this would become obvious to the people if they were allowed to read Scripture themselves in their own language was (so it is thought) the real reason not only that Tyndale's translation of the New Testament was burned, but also that the clergy of this realm have before this time, by a synodal decree, prohibited the translating of any book of Scripture into the English language, threatening to burn as heretics all who should dare keep any—as though it were heresy for a Christian to read Christ's Gospel.

"And assuredly, sir," said he, "some folk who think this dealing of the clergy to be thus—that good men are being mistreated for speaking the truth, and that Scripture itself is being pulled out of the people's hands lest they should perceive the truth—are led in their minds to doubt whether Luther himself (with whose opinions, or at least with whose works, this whole business began) actually wrote as ill as he is being said to have written. And there are many who think that he never held such things, but that because he wrote against the indulgence abuses and spoke somewhat freely against the Roman Curia and in general against the vices of the clergy, it was on that account that he was made hated and first summoned to Rome. And that when, for fear of unjust corporal punishment (for which it would have been too late to look for redress once he had already been burned up), he did not dare to show up there, then he was anathematized and his books condemned and the reading of them forbidden under pain of great penalties. And that thing done so that it would not be known what injustice he had suffered and that he neither holds nor says such odious and abominable heresies as the people are being told he does to get them to hate him—as would perhaps become obvious if they were allowed to read his books.

"And they say that it takes no genius to make it seem that a man is a heretic, if he can be reported to have said something that he never said, or if perhaps one line is taken out from among many and misconstrued, people not being allowed to see the rest, whereby it might more clearly appear what he means. By which manner of dealing, they say, one could charge Saint Paul with heresy and find an error in Saint John's Gospel.

"And yet, they say, the worst thing of all is this: that the clergy do not stop there, holding themselves content with the condemning of Luther and the forbidding of his books, but, further, wrongly use the hatred of his name against every man who in preaching the word of God is at all what he should be—that is to say, plain and bold, without pretense or flattery—whereas, if they do find a man guilty of error, let them put the blame for his error on *him*; what need is there to call him a Lutheran? Even if Luther was a devil, a person could perhaps say what he says about something and be speaking truthfully enough. For never was there a heretic whose every statement was false. The devil himself did not lie when he called Christ God's Son [Mk 3:11]. And therefore people think that this epithet of 'a Lutheran' serves the clergy as a general cover for a false accusation; that where they lack a specific thing to charge someone with in a trial, they strive to bring him first into the infamy of that name, which comprises (as they make it seem) a confused heap of heresies, no one can tell what.

"And by such behavior they hurt their own cause in yet another way. For when they accuse of being 'Lutherans' men who are of known virtue and erudition, what do they do thereby but cause the people, who hold those men in high regard for good living and learning, to think one of these two things: either that the clergy, out of malice and ill will, are falsely accusing them, or else that Luther's doctrine must be good, if such intelligent and good men are leaning toward it?

"And therefore it would be wise not to call them Lutherans, but rather, when they teach and hold any such opinions as the people know for Luther's, either let it be ignored or else let them privately, by gentle tactics, be induced to the contrary, if the points of his that they are teaching are bad. Lest by calling good and intelligent men Lutherans, they may perhaps bring themselves into suspicion of malice and ill will, and Luther into good opinion among the people, they thinking (as they are starting to think already) either that Luther said nothing as bad as is alleged against him or else that those things that he says, as odious as they seem, are actually plenty valid."

He said also that to many people it seemed a harsh thing, and extremely unreasonable, that poor, simple, uneducated folk, when they fell into errors and were led out of the right way on account of relying on the authority of men whom they believed to be virtuous and knowledgeable, should, instead of being taught better, be beaten cruelly and subjected to abjurations and public humiliation, with danger of burning, also, if a few false witnesses should after such abjurations testify that they have heard them backslide.

Finally he said that many good and well-educated men frankly thought that the clergy seem far outside the whole good order of charity, and that they act contrary to the mildness and merciful mind of their Master, and against the example of all the old holy Fathers,[3] in causing any man, any one at all, to be put to death for any error or wrong opinion concerning the faith. For they say that the old holy Fathers only engaged in disputing with heretics, teaching them and convincing them by Scripture, and not by fagots. And that by that way the faith went forward quite well; one heretic thus converted did convert many another; whereas now, people are horrified by this cruelty in the Church. And that those who seem converted think still the things that they dare not say. And that from the ashes of one heretic spring up many. And that now we make the mode of Christendom

---

[3] I.e., the early Fathers of the Church who are recognized by the Church as saints.

DIALOGUE CONCERNING HERESIES, PART ONE

seem all turned completely upside down. For whereas Christ made infidels the persecutors and his Christian people the sufferers, we make the Christians the persecutors and the infidels the sufferers—as a result of which, people think that secretly Christ's order of things is still standing, though it is not so taken and so perceived. For the people take it that it is still those who persecute that are the unbelievers, and that those poor people who suffer the persecution are (under the false name of heretics) the true believers and real Christian martyrs.

Christ also, they say, would never have anyone compelled by force and violence to believe in his faith, or want people to fight for him or his causes. He, in fact, would not allow Saint Peter to fight for his very person, but reproved him for striking Malchus [Mt 26: 51–54 and Jn 18: 10]. Nor would he defend himself, but instead, healing the ear of Malchus, his persecutor, which Peter had cut off, and giving over his whole holy body to the patient endurance of all the painful torments that his cruel enemies would inflict on it, he showed us as well by the effectual example of his death as by his godly counsel in his life, and after that he confirmed by the continual passion and martyrdoms of his holy martyrs, that his will and pleasure is that we should not so much as defend ourselves against heretics and infidels, be they pagans, Turks, or Saracens. And much less, then, should we fight against them and kill them. Rather, we should persevere in setting forth his faith against unbelievers and infidels by such ways as he himself began it; keep it, and increase it, as it was begotten. And that was by patient endurance and suffering—by which the faith was taken abroad and spread almost throughout the world within a little while. Not by war and fighting, which way has (so they say) already come quite close to losing all that the other way won.

When your friend had thus made his introduction, he asked me, both on your behalf and on his own, with respect to those things that were perhaps not well stated, to take them for what they actually were—the thoughts of others, whom you would very much like to answer and satisfy with rational argument, which you hoped to be the better able to do with the help of my response—and not the thoughts or opinions of you or him, who did and would in all things stand and abide by the faith and belief of Christ's Catholic Church. But as for such parts of this matter as concerned not any part of our belief, but only the dealings of this world—such as the justness or unjustness of some ecclesiastical persons in their chasing after and condemning people as heretics, or their books as heretical—he thought, he said, speaking for himself, that one could without any danger of heresy, for one's own part, notwithstanding the judgment given by any man, yet quite reasonably have doubts there. For though he thought it heresy to think anyone's opinions to be good and Catholic which are in reality heresies, yet one could, he thought, without any danger of heresy, have doubts as to whether someone was a heretic or not who was by human judgment condemned as one, since it could well be the case that he never held those opinions that were put upon him, but was convicted either because of the false depositions of dishonest witnesses or by the fault or malice of unjust judges. And that sometimes, perchance, some judges would out of ignorance condemn as heresies such beliefs as the wiser and better-educated would in point of judgment accept as good and Catholic; and that the latter would discern and judge the contrary of that other judgment.

However, he said that you had in me and my learning such a special trust and confidence that with regard to any of all these things, regardless of what you had heard or should hear elsewhere, you were fully determined to give full credence to me and take for the truth whatever answer he should bring you from me, wherein you very earnestly asked that I take some pains, so that you could by his mouth know fully my mind on these matters.

After this, before making any response to what he had said, I asked him what manner of acquaintance there was between him and you. And upon learning that he serves as a tutor to your sons, I then asked him to what branch of knowledge he had most given his study, and understood him to have applied himself to Latin. As for other disciplines, he cared nothing for them. For, he told me merrily, he considered logic nothing but babbling, music to serve for singers, arithmetic suitable for merchants, geometry for masons, astronomy good for no one, and as for philosophy, the most useless thing of all. And that it and logic had destroyed all good theology with the subtleties of their questions and babbling of their disputations, building everything upon reason, which rather gives blindness than any light. For, he said, humans have no light but that of holy Scripture. And therefore, he said, besides Latin, he had been (which I much commend) studying holy Scripture, which was, he said, enough education for any Christian, the apostles having held themselves content with it. And in studying it, he said, he exerted himself not only to learn many of its texts by heart, but also to search out their sense and meaning, as far as he could see by himself. For as for interpreters, he told me that he didn't really have the time to read them, and also that he found such great sweetness in the texts themselves that he could not find it in his heart to lose any time in the commentaries. And as regards any difficulty, he said that he found by experience that the best and surest method of interpretation was to put and compare one text with another; that they do not fail to explain themselves quite sufficiently between them. And he said that he used this method, which he found sufficient and surest, because thus would something most surely stick: when one found it out and learned it by one's own effort. And this, he said, everyone was able enough to do with the help of God, which is never lacking to those who faithfully trust in his promise. He has promised that if we seek we shall find, and that if we knock we shall have it opened to us [Mt 7: 7–8]. And what is it that shall be opened but that book which, as Saint John says in Revelation [3: 7 and 5: 1–7], is so sealed with seven seals that it cannot be opened except by the Lamb—that when he shuts it, then no one else can open it, and when he opens it, then no one else can shut it?

When I heard these statements and other similar ones, and realized how assiduously your friend was studying Scripture, and although I now have a very good opinion of him, and did not even at that time have completely the contrary, yet (to be frank with both you and him) by reason of his having presented the case with such enthusiasm, he made me wonder somewhat whether he had (since young students are sometimes susceptible to new delusional ideas) fallen into Luther's sect. And whether you perhaps, somewhat fearing the same, did with good intentions the rather send him to me with such a message because you hoped that he would be somewhat refuted and convinced by me. I therefore thought it not suitable, on matters so numerous and so weighty, to give him an unpremeditated response; and so, just welcoming him with nice words for the time being, and pretending a lack of free time due to other present business, I asked him to return on the following day, in anticipation of which time I would so order my affairs that we could confer at length on everything he had been sent to talk over. And he thus having departed, I began to put together in my mind the whole purport, as my memory would serve me, of all that he had presented. And because I wanted it easier to look at, so that I could the more fully and effectively respond to it, leaving no part unanswered, I briefly committed it to writing, in the order in which he presented it; which is to say, in the way that I have related it above.

2.

Here is summarily stated the order in which the author intends to discuss the issues brought before him. Because the first of these was an opinion conceived in some people's heads that a certain person recently forced to abjure heresy for having preached against pilgrimages and images and prayers made to saints was therein done a great injustice, the author briefly speaks his mind concerning the confuting of those terrible and pernicious opinions.[4]

On the next day, when he came back (this was at a little before seven o'clock, the appointment I had given him), I took him with me into my study, and—having told my servants that if anyone else should happen to want to speak with me, other than certain individuals whom I mentioned to them, they should put them off until another time—I set him down with me at a little table. And then I said to him that since he had, on your behalf, presented in short statements many long things, the enumeration of which would be a waste of time to someone who so well knew them already, I would, dispensing with all superfluous summarizing, tell him my thoughts on them all as briefly as I appropriately could. First, I would begin where he began—with the abjuration of the man he had spoken of. Secondly, I would address the condemnation and burning of Tyndale's translation of the New Testament. Thirdly, I would say something about Luther and his sect in general. Fourthly and finally, the thing he mentioned last: that is, the warring and fighting against infidels, along with the condemning of heretics to death; which two points he himself had combined and tied together.

---

[4] The "certain person" discussed anonymously here, and later in part three, chapters 1–7, is the English priest Thomas Bilney. Bilney's career was a controversial one. Bilney began by preaching against Church abuses but strayed into heresy when he preached against prayers to saints, pilgrimages, and the veneration of images; he then abjured heresy publicly, after a much-discussed and -debated investigation in 1527, only to relapse into heretical opinions once again in 1531, the year of his trial and execution (CW 6.2, 603). See also *Confutation of Tyndale* (published 1532–1533), in which More discusses Bilney's case again (CW 8, 23–26, 1170–71). For a full treatment of Bilney, see P. R. N. Carter's article in the *Oxford Dictionary of National Biography*, vol. 5 (Oxford: Oxford Univ. Press, 2004), 734–36.

"So, first," said I, "as regards the matter of the man's abjuration—where it is reported that the clergy did him wrong, and in order to make that seem likely, it is claimed that they bear hostility, malice, and ill will toward him for preaching (so you say) against their immoral conduct, and he, on the other hand, is credited with a great deal of wisdom, virtue, and goodness—I will go into neither the praiseworthiness of them nor the unpraiseworthiness of him, since the substance of this matter does not in any way lie there. For if it did, I would not pass over any part of that so quickly.

"But, now, for this matter, even if all of the clergy (wherein no one doubts there to be many a very virtuous and godly man) were in their conduct far worse than devils, yet if they did that man no wrong, then in this matter no one has any cause to complain against them. And furthermore, even if that man were in all the rest of *his* conduct as innocent as a saint, yet if he was infected with and guilty of these heresies, then in this matter he was done no wrong. And even besides all this, if he not only were in all other things very virtuous but also were utterly clear and innocent of all these heresies of which he was accused, yet if it was by sufficient witnesses—people who, no matter how untruthful they were in reality, seemed honest and likely to be telling the truth—proved in open court that he was guilty of them, then even though in such a case the witnesses would have done him wrong, his judges would yet have done him nothing but right. And therefore, letting pass, as I say, the praiseworthiness or unpraiseworthiness of either his judges or him as things beside the point, I will show you that they not only did him no wrong, but actually showed him, to my mind, the greatest favor, extending to him the most charitable mercy I have ever known to be extended to anyone in such a case.

"And first, as for any wrong that his judges did him, I very much wonder where those who report it could pinpoint it.

For if any were done him, it would have to have been in one of these two things: either in that he was incorrectly judged to have preached those doctrines that he was accused of preaching, when he had in fact preached none of them, or else in that some of the doctrines that he did preach were judged and condemned as heresies when they in fact were not. Except if anyone would say that even though he was proved guilty and convicted of heresy, he yet should have been given no punishment at all, or else not such as he was. And on that subject, in case anyone does think that way, I shall speak in the fourth part, where we shall discuss (in general) the procedure that the Church uses in the convicting of heretics.

"But as for the other points: First of all, if any priest wrote from London into your part of the country that any article of his preaching that was by his judges declared heretical was in fact valid and not against the faith of Christ's church, let him name what article. And either you will find that he will name you something that the man was not charged with, or else you will find that what he will name you is indeed something that you yourself will recognize as heresy when you hear it. For the articles with which he was charged were that we should do no venerating of any images or pray to any saints or go on pilgrimages—which things, I suppose, every good Christian will agree are heresies. And therefore we shall let that point pass and thus go on to the second, and see whether or not it was well proved that he preached them."

"Sir," said your friend, "I would for my part well agree that they are heresies. However, I have before now heard some who would not do so. And therefore when we call them heresies, it would be good to tell why, since some would, I think, if they could safely be heard, adamantly say no, who now hold their peace and bear themselves very coolly. They would speak on this matter more heatedly if it wouldn't get their lips burned!"

"Now, actually," said I, "whoever will say that these are

not heresies will not have this disputed by me, who have no expertise in such matters. Rather, as it best becomes a layman to do in all things, I lean and adhere to the common faith and belief of Christ's church. And thereby I do clearly know it for a heresy, if a heresy is a heterodoxy, a detour (taken by any sector of those who have been baptized and bear the name of Christian) from the common faith and belief of the whole rest of the Church. For this I am very sure of and perceive well, not only by experience in my own time, and the places where I myself have been, together with the consistent talk of other respectable people from all other places of Christendom, but also by books and memoirs left from long ago, together with writings of the old Fathers, now saints in heaven: that from the apostles' time to now, this way has been practiced, taught, and approved, and the contrary consistently condemned, throughout the whole flock of all good Christian people.

"And as for the texts that these heretics cite against venerating images, praying to saints, and going on pilgrimages—such as the law given to the Jews, 'Non facies tibi sculptile,' 'You shall not make for yourself a graven image' [Ex 20: 4], and the psalm 'In exitu Israel de Egipto' ['When Israel went forth from Egypt': see Ps 114: 1–2 and Ps 115: 3–9], and 'Soli Deo honor et gloria,' 'Only to God be honor and glory' [1 Tm 1: 17], and 'Maledictus qui confidit in homine,' 'Accursed is he that puts his trust in man' [Jer 17: 5], along with many other similar ones which heretics have from long ago always barked against Christ's Catholic Church—I am quite sure that Saint Augustine, Saint Jerome, Saint Basil, and Saint Gregory [the Great], along with so many a godly and intelligent man as has been in Christ's church from the beginning to now, understood those texts as well as did those heretics. Especially having as good intellects, being far better educated, exercising in their study more diligence, being a heap to a handful, and (most important of all) having (as God by many miracles bears witness), besides their learning, the light and clarity of his especial grace, by means of which they were inwardly taught by his Spirit alone to understand that the words spoken in the Old Law—to the Jews, people prone to idolatry, and not even to all of them either, for the priests then had images of cherubim in the inner sanctuary of the Temple [1 Kgs 6:23-29]—would have no place to forbid images among his Christian flock, where his pleasure would be to have the image of his blessed body hanging on his holy cross held in honor and reverent remembrance; where he would vouchsafe to send to the king Abgar the image of his own face; where he was pleased to leave the holy veronica, also an express image of his blessed face, as a keepsake to remain in honor among those who loved him, from the time of his bitter Passion to this day. Just as by the miracle of his blessed, holy hand it was imprinted and left on the sudarium, so by a similar miracle has it been, in that thin, corruptible cloth, kept and preserved uncorrupted these fifteen hundred years, fresh and easy to make out, to the inward comfort, spiritual rejoicing, and greatly increased fervor and devotion of the hearts of good Christian people.

"Christ also taught his holy evangelist Saint Luke to have another kind of attitude toward images than these heretics have, when he put it in his mind to copy and reproduce in a picture the lovely face of our blessed Lady, his mother. He also taught Saint Amphibalus, the mentor and teacher of the holy first martyr of England, Saint Alban, to carry around and venerate the crucifix. Who also showed Saint Alban himself, in a vision, the image of the crucifix, but God? Which thing worked on that holy man so strongly that he, with a few words from Saint Amphibalus, at the sight of that blessed image (which our Lord had previously shown him in his sleep) was completely converted to Christianity. And in the venerating of that same image he was arrested and brought forth to trial, and afterward to martyrdom.

"I would also like to know whether these heretics will consent to having the blessed name of Jesus held in honor and reverence, or not. If not, then we need no more to show what wretches they are, who dare denigrate that holy name that the devil trembles at hearing [James 2:19]. And on the other hand, if they agree that the name of Jesus is to be reverenced and held in honor [Phil 2:9–11], then since that name of Jesus is nothing else but a word which, in written form or by voice, represents to the hearer the person of Christ our Savior, I would like to know from these heretics this: If they give honor to the name of our Lord, which name is but an image representing his person to the human mind and imagination, how and with what reasonableness can they denigrate a carved or painted figure of him which represents him and his acts far more simply and directly?"

"Sir," he replied, "on the subject of the expenditures made on the ark of the covenant, the Temple, and the priests' apparel by the commandment of God, there is an excellent and very thought-provoking book written in English, entitled *The Image of Love,* which was authored, as it seems, by some very virtuous man, contemplative and well-educated, in which book that argument of yours is not only well refuted but even turned back against you. For in it that good, holy man makes a strong attack on these carved and painted images, giving them little praise and explicitly least commending those that are the most expensively, elaborately, and skillfully made. And he states outright that images are but the books for the illiterate; and therefore that men in religious orders, and other folk of more perfect life who are better instructed in spiritual wisdom, should let go of all such inanimate images and labor only for the dynamic, live image of love and charity. And very strongly he speaks out there against all these costly trappings of the Church, whose money would, he says, be better bestowed on poor folk. And he claims that the saints and theologians of olden times would allow no such extravagance in the furnishings of the church, but only see that they were clean and free of defect, and not costly. And on that basis he says that in their time they had wooden chalices and golden priests, and now we have golden chalices and wooden priests."

"To be sure," said I, "I have seen that book. Who the author of it was, I don't know. But the man might perhaps mean well and have just flown so high in his spiritual contemplation that while thinking he sat in the bosom of God Almighty up on high in heaven, he scorned and set at naught all earthly things and all temporal worship done to God here below by poor, pitiful people on earth. And, truly, with his intention and motivation I will not much concern myself. For a very good man can at times happen, in the indiscretion of fervor, to say something, and write it too, which when he later considers more carefully he would very much like to change. But this much I confidently dare say: that his words go somewhat beyond what he is able to defend. For I do not doubt that in the days of those holy saints, the furnishings in Christ's churches were not only free of defect and clean, but also very costly. And it could well be, and I have read that it has been so in some great dearth of grain and famine of people, that some good, holy bishops have relieved poor people with the sale of some church vessels and utensils. But I think he will never find (except when some such great, urgent cause came up on some occasion) that those holy men ever refused to have God served in his churches with the best and most precious of such metals as he in his goodness gives to us humans. For it is very right and reasonable that we in turn serve him with the best, and not do as did Cain, who kept for himself everything that was worth anything and served his Master and Maker with the worst. [See Gn 4: 2–7 and 1 Jn 3: 12.]

"And (since he mentions Saint Ambrose) I believe there is no one who will suspect of the emperor Theodosius, a man as devoted to God as he was, that he would have had himself served in goblets of gold and have allowed his and our savior Christ, in the church of Milan where he himself attended Mass and Saint Ambrose was stationed as bishop, to be

served in chalices of wood. And I truly can scarcely believe
that any Christian people, even if they were very poor,
would at this day allow the precious Blood of our Lord to be
made present and received in wood, where it would cleave to
the chalice and sink in, and not be completely received out
by the priest. But that statement I believe he put in for the
pleasure that he took in that splendid comparison between
the wooden chalices and golden priests of old and today's
golden chalices and wooden priests. And actually I think that
what he says is true—the chalices *were* made of wood when
the priests were made of gold—and that he will find that
there were then, in the olden times, many more chalices
made of gold than he finds now priests made of wood. If he
takes a good look at Platina's *Lives of the Popes,* I think he will
well see that Christ was served with silver and gold in the
vessels, utensils, and decorations of his churches a long time
before Saint Ambrose, or the oldest of those old theologians
that this man speaks of, was born. And I dare venture to
guarantee that they themselves did not ordinarily say Mass
using chalices of wood. And it seems to me that God's pleasure on this point cannot better appear than by his own
words written in holy Scripture, such as those regarding the
ark of the covenant and the vestments of the priest, and the
funds and riches spent on the temple of Solomon." [See Ex
25—28.]

"Why," said he, "that is the thing that, as I was about to
tell you, is very well and clearly answered in the *Image of Love*
book."

"In what way?" said I.

"Why," said he, "to begin with, when the ark was made
there were no poor people to bestow those riches upon; for
when the children of Israel were in the desert they were fed
with manna, and their clothes never wore out or became any
the worse in that whole forty years. And as for the opulence
of the temple built by Solomon, that could not have been of
any concern to the people, for there were no poor folk then

either. For, as the very words of Scripture inform us, there was in his day 'such a great abundance of gold that silver was not valued.'" [See Ex 16: 15, Dt 8: 2–4, and 1 Kgs 10: 21.]

"Actually," said I, "the man makes a splendid answer for the ark. But this I would like to know from him: Even if there were no poor folk among them at the time that it was made, were there never any among them later, in all the time that it was kept? I think he will not say no. And if there were, then since God would by this man's reasoning have commanded that that gold be given to the poor, if there had been any, rather than put into the making of the ark, he would by the same reasoning afterward, when there were some, have then commanded that it be broken off and given to them rather than kept in the ark. And as for the wealth spent on the temple of Solomon, whereas he says that there were then no poor people because there was such a great abundance of gold that silver was not valued, everyone may be quite certain that if everyone in the time of Solomon had been rich, he would not have had so many manual laborers. But does he suppose that because there was in his day so much gold, that therefore all the people had enough of it? I, rather, am afraid that because he was so rich, his people were the poorer. For, granted that he had great gifts sent him, and also that he did not use his own people, the children of Israel, as slaves and bond servants, it yet is likely that he imposed on them huge, harsh taxes whereby he gathered great wealth and they grew to be in great poverty. And if anyone thinks the contrary, let them see whether after Solomon's death, in the beginning of his son's reign, all the people did not complain about this so sorely that (because they could not get the promise of amendment that sober, mature men were advising the king to give, but were, by the ignorant counsel of young lads who were then leading the young king to folly, with a proud, harsh answer put in fear of worse), of the twelve tribes of Israel, ten completely fell away from him, leaving him no more than two [1 Kgs 12: 4–20]. And therefore to prove by the richness and magnificence of the prince that there were no poor people in his realm is a very poor proof. For it can so happen that the prince can be the most rich when his people are the most poor, and that the richness of the one is causing the poverty of the others, if the people's resources are gathered into the prince's purse. And, in conclusion, there can be little doubt that Solomon could have found plenty of poor folk to have given his gold to, that he expended on the temple of God. And therefore that answer does not well answer the matter."

"Well," said your friend, "that book yet has one answer that does resolve the whole entire matter. For, as it is said there, all those things that were used in the Old Law were but material and physical, and were all, as it were, a shadow of the law of Christ, and therefore the worshipping of God with gold and silver and other such corporeal things ought not be practiced among Christian people, but leaving all that shadow, we should draw ourselves to the spiritual things and give our Lord worship service only in spirit and with spiritual things. For he says so himself—that God, since he himself is spiritual, therefore seeks such worshippers as will worship him 'in spirit and in truth' [Jn 4:24]—that is, in faith, hope, and charity of heart, not in the hypocrisy and ostentation of outward observance, bodily homage, showy and costly altar furnishings, nice statues, magnificent music, fleshly fasting, and the whole slew of such unsavory rituals, all of which are now gone as a shadow. And our Savior himself, our faith in whom is our justification, appeals to our souls, and to our good, faith-filled minds, and sets at naught all those corporeal things."

"That book," said I, "does not go quite as far as you are saying it does, though many other people do indeed. But these people who make themselves so spiritual, God send them the grace that some evil spirit not inspire in their hearts a diabolical scheme whereby, under the cover of a special zeal for spiritual worship service, they attempt first to destroy all such devotion as has always, up till now, shown itself, and expressed the good affection of the soul, by good and holy works wrought to God's honor with the body. These people are coming into so a high point of perfection that they pass all the good people who worshipped God in the times of old. For as for that good, godly man Moses, he thought that to pray not only in mind but with mouth also was a good way [Ex 15: 1–18]. The good king David thought it pleasing to God not only to pray with his mouth but also to sing and dance, too, to God's honor, and rebuked his foolish wife, who did at that time as these foolish heretics do now, mocking that bodily worship [2 Sm 6: 14–23]. Holy Saint John the Baptist not only baptized and preached, but also fasted, watched, prayed, and wore a hair garment [Mt 3: 4]. Christ our Savior himself prayed not only in mind but also with the mouth [see Mt 6: 9–13 and Jn 17: 1–26], which kind of prayer these holy, spiritual heretics now mockingly call lip service. And the fasting which they set at naught, our Savior himself set so much by that he continued it for forty days in a row [Lk 4: 2]. Now as for images, which you call one of the shadows—"

"No, by our Lady," said he, "I called showy altar furnishings, and other such outward observances and physical rituals, what *The Image of Love* calls them. Such things I called, as the book does, shadows of the Old Law. But as for images, the book advises people either to completely let go of them and give them up, or, if we will needs have some, to not care how simply they are made. For the roughest and most simply made image can as well put us in mind of Christ, or our Lady or any other saint, as can the most expensive and most elaborate one that any painter or sculptor can produce.

"And actually, to tell the truth, as for statues, they are not shadows of the Old Law, but rather things clearly and obviously forbidden in it, in several other passages of Scripture as well as the texts recently mentioned by you yourself. By 'Non facies tibi sculptile,' 'You shall not carve for yourself, or chisel for yourself, any image,' and by the whole entire psalm 'In exitu Israel de Egipto,' they are with great execration and malediction prohibited."

"Well, first of all," said I, "you may not take those pronouncements for such strict prohibitions as would forbid utterly the making of any sculptures, for as I mentioned to you before, they had in the Temple those sculptures of cherubim. But it was prohibited to make such sculptures as the Egyptians and other pagans did; that is to say, the idols of false gods. This appears right there in Psalms, where the reason for the prohibition is given: 'Quoniam omnes dii gentium dæmonia, Dominus autem cælos fecit,' 'For all the gods of the pagans are devils, but our Lord made the heavens' [Ps 96: 5]. Do not these words make quite evident what images were in that psalm forbidden—that is to say, only the images and idols of those pagan gods? For else I ask you to tell me what sense this would make, if someone were to say, 'Make no image whatsoever of Christ, nor of our Lady, nor of any Christian saint, since all the gods of the pagans are but devils.' Wouldn't this be an intelligent argument well concluded!

"There is also meant by these prohibitions that no one shall venerate any image as if it were divine. For if one did, then one would be violating the precept of God by which we are commanded to worship only one God, and forbidden to worship any false gods. And thus where it is written, 'Non facies tibi sculptile,' 'You shall not make for yourself a graven image,' what comes right before that is 'Non habebis deos alienos,' 'You shall have no false gods.' And it is also written, 'Nolite converti ad idoles neque deos conflatiles facietis vobis,' 'Do not turn to idols or make for yourselves any gods of metal cast in a mold' [Ex 34: 17 and Lv 19: 4]. And where it is forbidden to venerate any image, there is used the word that signifies the honor and devotion due only to God. And therefore neither may we give any veneration to any image or idol of any perfidious pagan, nor may we with honor and devotion given as to God venerate any image of any saint, or even the actual saint. But I believe that neither Scripture nor natural reason forbids one to do *some* reverence to an image—not ultimately fixing one's focus on the image, but directing it further, to the honor of the person that the image represents—since in such reverence done to the image, no honor is taken away from either God or good human being, but rather the saint is honored in the image and God is honored in his saint. When an intermediary man, an ambassador of a great king, has much honor done him, to whom does that honor redound, to the ambassador or to the king? When a man, upon receiving a letter from his prince, takes off his cap and kisses it, does he do this reverence to the paper or to his prince?

"Really, truth to tell, these heretics rather play games than reason in this matter. For when they say that images are but the books for the illiterate, they yet cannot deny that even if they were only that, they still would be necessary. However, it seems to me that they are good books both for the illiterate and for the learned too. For, as I somewhat said to you before, all words, either written or spoken, are but images representing the things that the writer or speaker conceives in his mind, just as the figure of the thing framed with the imagination and thus conceived in the mind is but an image representing the actual thing itself that the person is thinking about. For example, if I tell you a story about my good friend your employer, the picture that I have of him in my mind is not your employer himself, but an image that represents him. And when I mention him to you by name, his name is neither himself nor even the figure of him which is in my imagination, but only an image representing to you the imagination of my mind.

"Now, if I am too far from you to say it to you vocally, then that piece of writing is not the name itself, but an image representing the name. And, moreover, all these names spoken, and all these words written, are not natural signs or images, but are only made by people's accord and agreement to betoken and signify such things, whereas images painted, engraved, or carved may be so well executed and so true to life, so close to the reality, that they will represent the thing naturally, and much more effectively than will the name either spoken or written. For a person who never heard the name of your employer would by a well-executed, true-to-life image of him be rendered able to recognize him perfectly well if they should ever see him. And surely—except that it is not humanly possible, but otherwise, if it could conveniently be done—there is in this world no writing that is as effective as it would be to express everything in imagery.

"And, now, just as a book well written and well transcribed better expresses the subject matter than does a book written by someone uneducated (who cannot tell his tale well) and transcribed in a bad handwriting, so does an image very skillfully wrought better express the subject matter than does a thing crudely made—unless this other thing moves one for some special other reason, such as, perhaps, its great antiquity or the great virtue of the person who made it, or the fact that God gives at its location some special dispensation of his favor and grace. But, now, as I started to say, since all names, spoken or written, are but images, then if you place any value on the name of Jesus, spoken or written, why should you place none on a painted or carved image of him that recalls his holy person to your remembrance as much as, and even more than, his written name does? Even these two words 'Christus crucifixus' do not as vividly recall to us the memory of his bitter Passion as does a blessed image of him on the cross—neither to an illiterate person nor to a learned one. And this these heretics themselves realize plenty well. They speak out against images not for any furtherance of devotion, but manifestly for the malicious motive of diminishing and quenching people's devotion. For they see well enough that there is no one who loves another person and does not delight in an image of that person, or in anything of theirs. And these heretics who are so sorely against images of God and of his holy saints would yet be quite angry with anyone who were to treat with disrespect an image made in commemoration of one of them, whereas the wretches do not forbear to treat vilely the holy crucifix, contemptuously throwing excrement on it, an image made in commemoration of our Savior himself, and not only of his most blessed Person, but also of his most bitter Passion.

"Now, as regards prayer made to the saints, and veneration given to them, one really has to wonder what cause these heretics have for their malice toward them. We see it commonly, in the wretched condition of this world, that one man, out of a pride in himself, has envy toward another, or because of an injury inflicted bears to someone else malice and ill will. But this has to be a diabolical hatred: to hate someone you never knew, who never did you any harm, who, even if he could now do you no good where he is, yet does—either with his good example gone before you or with his good teaching left behind him—do you (unless you are very bad-natured) great good in this world for your journey toward heaven. And this has to be an envy coming of an extreme, diabolical pride and far surpassing the rancor of the devil himself, for he only envied such as he saw and knew something about, such as when he saw the human race and the glory of God. But these heretics envy people whom they have never seen and never will see, except when they will be sorry and ashamed of themselves at that glorious sight.

"For whereas they profess a zeal for the honor of God himself—as though God (to whom alone all honor and glory is to be given) were dishonored in that some honor is done to his holy saints—they are not as mad or as childish as they make themselves appear. For if all honor were so to be given to God alone that we should give none to any creature, then where would be God's precept of honor to be given to our father and mother, to princes, governors, and rulers here on earth, and, as Saint Paul says [Rom 12: 10], from everyone to everyone else?

"And well they know that the Church venerates saints not as God but as God's good servants, and that therefore the honor that is done to them redounds principally to the honor of their Master, just as by common custom we sometimes do reverence and give a very kindly reception to some individuals for their superior's sake, whom we else would perhaps not even bid good-morning.

"And surely if any favor or charitable deed done to one of Christ's poor folk for his sake is by his great goodness regarded and accepted as done to him [Mt 25: 34–40], and whoever welcomes one of his apostles or disciples welcomes him [Mt 10: 40–42], then every wise person can well consider that likewise whoever does honor his holy saints for his sake does honor him. Unless these heretics suppose that God is as envious as they themselves are, and that he would be indignant at having any honor given to anyone else, even if it thereby redounded to himself. Of which Christ our Savior makes quite clear the contrary; for he shows himself so willing to have his holy saints be sharers in his honor that he promises his apostles that at the fearful Last Judgment, when he shall come in his high majesty, they shall have their seats of honor and sit with him upon the judgment of the world [Mt 19: 28].

"Christ also promised that Saint Mary Magdalene would be venerated throughout the world, and have here an honorable commemoration, because she bestowed that precious ointment upon his holy head [Mt 26: 13]. Which thing, when I think about it, makes me marvel at the madness of these heretics who bark against the old, ancient customs of Christ's church, mocking the setting up of candles, making silly wisecracks, asking with blasphemous mockery whether God and his saints lack light, or whether it is night with them, that they cannot see without candles. They could as justifiably ask what good that ointment did to Christ's head. But the heretics complain about the outlay now, as their brother Judas did then [Jn 12:4], and say that it would be better spent on alms for poor folk. And this say many of them who cannot find it in their hearts to spend anything on the one or the other. And some sometimes spend on the one for no other motive but that they may the more boldly criticize and rail against the other. But from the example of that holy woman, and from these words of our Savior, let them all learn that God delights in seeing the fervent heat of the heart's devotion bubble out through the body and do him homage with all such goods of fortune as God has given one.

"What riches our Lord God himself stipulated for the constructing and adorning of the Temple, and for the altar furnishings and the priests' apparel, how was he himself the better off for all this? Or for the animals that he himself ordered offered to him in sacrifice? Or for the sweet odors and frankincense? [See Exodus 25—29.] Why do these heretics more jeer at the customs of Christ's church than they do at the customs of the Jews' synagogue, unless they are Jews rather than Christians?

"If people will say that the money would be better spent among poor folk, whom he cares more about, they being living temples of the Holy Spirit [1 Cor 3:16], made by his own hand, than about the temples of stone made by human hands, this would perhaps be very true if there were so little to do the one thing with that we were driven by necessity to leave the other undone. But God gives enough for both, and gives different individuals different kinds of devotion, and all to his pleasure. Let everyone respectively, as the apostle Paul says, abound and be prolific in that kind of virtue that the Spirit of God guides them to [see Rom 12:6–8 and 2 Cor 9:6–15]. And not be of the foolish mind of Luther, who in a sermon of his expresses the wish that he could get into his hands all the pieces of the Holy Cross, and says that if he did, he would throw them where the sun would never shine on them. And for what pious reason would the wretch do such an insult to the cross of Christ? Because, he says, so much gold is now being put into the adorning of the pieces of the cross that there is none left for poor folk. Is this not a far-fetched reason? As though all the gold that is now put around the pieces of the Holy Cross would not have failed to be given to poor people had it not been put into the adorning of the cross! And as though there were nothing else lost but what is put around Christ's cross!

"Take all the gold that is expended on all the pieces of Christ's cross throughout Christendom. Granted, many good Christian princes and other godly people have, out of respect, adorned many pieces of it. Yet if all that gold were gathered together, it would appear a poor portion in comparison with the gold that is expended upon goblets—but why speak of goblets, the gold in which, though it is not given to the poor, is nevertheless saved and can be given in alms whenever people will, which they never will—how small a portion do we think the gold around all the pieces of Christ's cross would be if it were compared with the gold that is quite thrown away on the gilding of knives, swords, spurs, tapestries, and painted cloths, and (as though those things could not use up gold fast enough) the gilding of posts and entire roofs, not only in the palaces of princes and great prelates but also in the houses of many quite undistinguished people? And yet among all these things Luther could catch sight of no gold that grievously glittered in his bleared eyes, but only around the cross of Christ. For that gold, if it were gone from there, the wise man thinks, would immediately be given to poor people. And this where he sees every day that those who have their bags filled with gold give to the poor not one piece of it, but rather, if they give anything, ransack the bottom to seek out here, amidst all the gold coins, a [silver] halfpenny—or, in his country, a brass penny, four of which equal a farthing.

"Such are the impressive arguments found by those who profess holiness as a pretext for their cloaked heresies."

3.

The objections made by the messenger against praying to saints,
venerating images, and going on pilgrimages; and the author's
answers to those objections. Also, the messenger's incidental com-
ment that there would seem to be no need for Christian folk to go to
any churches—that it is one and the same thing to pray there or
elsewhere—and the author's answering and confuting of that
opinion.

At this point your friend asked me not to assume that whatever he said was voiced as his own opinion. He would, he
said, in part be telling me what he had heard some others say
on this subject, so that he might the better answer them with
what he would hear from me.

This protestation and preface made, he said that although
no good person would agree that it is right to disrespect or
dishonor saints or their images, yet not only would going on
pilgrimages to them or praying to them seem to be in vain
(considering that they all, if they can do anything, yet can do
no more for us among them all than Christ, who can do
everything, can do by himself; nor are so ready at hand to
hear us, if they hear us at all, as is Christ, who is everywhere;
nor have half the love for us and longing to help us that our
Savior does, who died for us, and whom, as Saint Paul says,
we have for our advocate before the Father [see Rom 8: 34
and 1 Jn 2: 1]), but, moreover, it seems to smack of idolatry
when we go on pilgrimage to this place and that. As though
God were not equally powerful or equally present in every
place, but, just as the devils were in olden times, under the
false name of "gods," actively present in the idols and graven
images of the pagans, so would we make it seem that God
and his saints stood in this place and that place, bound to this
post and that post cut out and carved in images. For when
we suppose ourselves to be better heard by our Lord in Kent
than at Cambridge, at the north door of St. Paul's than at
the south door, before one image of our Lady than before
another, is it not an evident sign—and practically an outright

proof—that we put our trust and confidence in the image itself, and not in God or our Lady? For she is as good in the one place as in the other, and the one image is no more like her than the other, nor is there any reason why she should favor the one over the other. But we blind people, instead of on God and his holy saints themselves, set our affections on the images themselves, and to them make our prayers, to them make our offerings, and suppose these images to be the very saints themselves, from whom our help and health will come; putting our full trust in this place and that place as sorcerers put their trust in their circles, within which they think themselves safe from all the devils in hell. And believe that if they were one inch outside, then a devil would pull them in pieces, but as for the circle, he dare not, for his ears, once put his nose over it.

And folk figure that the clergy are glad to favor these ways and to feed this superstition under the name and guise of devotion, to the peril of the people's souls, for the lucre and worldly advantage that they themselves receive from the offerings.

When I had heard him say what he wanted to, I asked if he ever thought about becoming a priest. To which he answered, "No indeed," because, he said, "it seems to me that there are too many priests already, as long as they are not better. And therefore when God sends me the opportunity, I intend to marry."

"Well," said I, "then since I have already married twice and therefore can never be a priest, and you are so set on marriage that you will never be a priest, we two are not the best suited to ponder what might be said in this matter on behalf of the priests.

"However, when I think about it, it certainly seems to me that if the thing were such as you say—so far out of kilter with right religion, and so perilous to people's souls—I cannot see why the clergy would, for the gain they get thereby, allow such an abuse to continue. For, first of all, suppose it were true that no pilgrimage ought to be made, no image left an offering, no reverence done, or prayer made, to any saint. And suppose that none of all these practices had ever been engaged in, or that they were all now done away with. Then, if that were the right way (which I well know it is not), to me there is little question that Christian people who are in the true faith and in the right way with respect to God would not on that account be at all less well disposed toward the ministers of his church, but, rather, their devotion to them would more and more increase. So that if they now get by this way one penny, they would (if this way were wrong and the other right) not fail to receive, instead of a penny now, a fourpence then. And thus no lucre given them would give them cause to favor this way, if it were wrong, when they could not fail to gain more by the right way.

"Moreover, look throughout Christendom, and I think you will find the profit from those offerings to be a very small part of the support of the clergy, and something that, though in some few places they would be glad to retain, yet the whole body could without any notable loss easily do without.

"Let us consider our own country here, and we shall find the vast majority of these pilgrimage shrines in the hands of such religious, or of such poor parishes, as have no great influence in the bishops' convocations. And besides this, you will not find, I believe, one bishop in England who receives the profit of one fourpence of any such offering within his diocese. The continuance or the breaking of this practice and custom now rests particularly, then, with people who receive no profit from it. If they believed it to be what you call it, superstitious and wicked, they would never let it continue to the perishing of people's souls—whereby they themselves would destroy their own souls—and neither in body nor in goods take any profit. And besides this, we see that the bishops and prelates themselves visit those holy places and shrines, with as large offerings and at as great a cost in coming and going as do other people, so that they not only take no temporal gain therefrom, but even spend their own therein.

"And I surely believe this devotion to be in such a way planted by God's own hand in the hearts of the whole Church—that is to say, not the clergy alone, but the whole congregation of all Christian people—that if the clergy were of the mind to drop it, the laity would yet not allow that.

"And if it were the case that pilgrimages depended solely on the greed of bad priests (since bad must they be who would out of greed help the people forward to idolatry), then good priests and good bishops would not go on them themselves. But I am very sure that many a holy bishop, exceedingly well versed in Scripture and the law of God, has had great devotion thereto.

"For whereas, as you put it, people think that it 'smacks of idolatry' to visit this place and that place, as though God were more mighty or more present in one place than in another, or as though God or his saints had bound themselves to stay at this image or that image; and that it would appear, from the way people act there, that the pilgrims put their trust in the place or the image itself, taking it as actually being God, or the saint of whom they are seeking help, and thus behave like sorcerers who put their trust in their circle: certainly, sir, holy Saint Augustine, in an epistle of his (which he wrote to both the clergy and the laity), takes pilgrimages for a more respectable and far more godly thing. He says that although the reason is unknown to us why God does miracles in some places and none in others, there yet is no doubt that he so does. And that good theologian was so very confident of this that, as he himself says, he sent two of his priests on a pilgrimage to test out the truth regarding a great matter that was in contention and debate between them. He sent them from Hippo in Africa to St. Stephen's Church in Milan (where many miracles used to be performed), to the end that God might there, by some means, cause to be revealed and made manifest by his power the truth on this subject, which he could not clearly determine by any means known to man.

"Nor do those who go on pilgrimages act anything like those sorcerers to whom you liken them, who put their confidence in the circle and circumference on the ground because of a particular belief that they have in the compass of that ground by reason of foolish charms and figures around it, with invocations of evil spirits and affiliation with devils (enemies to God), and the craft and ways of that whole business which by God himself is prohibited and forbidden, and this on pain of death [Ex 22:18]. What similarity does that have to the going of good people to holy places not dedicated to the devil by incantation but consecrated to God by his holy ordinance and with his holy words? If you would consider those two things comparable, so might you blaspheme and hold in derision all the devout rites and ceremonies of the Church, both those in the liturgy (such as incensing, the hallowing of the fire, of the font, of the Paschal Lamb candle) and, moreover, the exorcisms, benedictions, and holy, esoteric gestures used in the Consecration or in the administration of the consecrated hosts. All of those holy things—many a one of which was from hand to hand passed down in the Church from the time of Christ's apostles, and by them left to us as it was by God taught to them—people could now, by that means, make the foolish mistake of likening to the superstitious approach and idiotic procedures of witchcraft.

"Nor is the flock of Christ so foolish as those heretics make them out to be, that whereas there is no dog so mad that it does not know a real rabbit from a carved and painted one, Christian people who have reason in their heads and also the light of faith in their souls can think that statues of our Lady are our Lady herself. No, they are not, I trust, that mad. They do reverence to the image for the honor of the person whom it represents, just as everyone delights in an image and memento of a loved one. And although every good Christian has a recollection of Christ's Passion in their mind, and conceives by devout meditation a form and fashion of it in their heart, yet there is no one, I think, so good or so well-educated, or so proficient in meditation, that they do not find that they are more moved to pity and compassion upon the beholding of a crucifix than they are when they lack one. And if there should be any who, for the support of their opinion, will perhaps say that they find it otherwise within themselves, they would give me cause to fear that by neither the one way nor the other do they have of Christ's Passion more than a very faint feeling, since the holy Fathers before us did, and all devout people around us do, find and feel within themselves the contrary.

"Now, as for the argument you give," said I, "where you say that in betaking ourselves to this place and that place, this image and that image, we seem to be thinking that God is not equally powerful or equally present in every place, this argument militates no more against pilgrimage shrines than against all the churches in Christendom. For God is as mighty in the stable as in the temple. And just as he is not comprehensible nor circumscribed anywhere, so is he present everywhere. But this does not prevent heaven, be it a corporeal thing or not, from being the place of a special manner and kind of his presence, in which he is pleased to show to his blessed, heavenly company his glorious majesty, which he does not show to condemned wretches in hell, and yet he is never not there. It pleased him, in his goodness, to go with his Chosen People through the desert in the cloud by day and the pillar of fire by night [Ex 13:21–22], yet he was not 'bound,' as you liken it, like the damned spirits were to the old idols of the pagans.

"It pleased him also to choose the ark that was carried with his people—at which ark specially, by miracle, he several times made manifest his especial presence, the ark being transported from place to place.

"Was it not also his pleasure to be specially present in his

temple of Jerusalem, till he allowed it to be destroyed for
their sin? And instead of that one place of prayer (to which
he previously wanted all his people to come), he has vouch-
safed to spread himself out into many temples, and in a more
acceptable manner to be worshipped in many temples
throughout his Christian flock."

Here your friend said that the temple of Christ is, as Saint
Paul says, the human heart [1 Cor 3: 16], and that God is not
enclosed or confined in any place. And that God said so
himself, to the woman of Samaria: that true worshippers
would worship in spirit and in truth, not on the Samaritans'
mountain or in Jerusalem, or in any temple of stone [Jn
4: 21–23].

I then told him that I would well agree that no temple of
stone was as pleasing to God as the temple of the human
heart, but that this yet in no way hinders or prevents it from
being the case that God wills that his Christian people have in
various places various temples and churches, in which they
should (in addition to praying in private) assemble formally
and come in company to worship him together—those who
live so near to one another that they can conveniently go to
the same place.

"For even though," said I, "our Savior did say to the
woman of whom you spoke that the time would come when
they would worship God neither on Mount Gerizim nor in
Jerusalem—both of which places were later destroyed and
deserted, and the pagan manner of worshipping at the one,
and the Jewish manner of worshipping in the other, turned
both into the manner of worshipping of the Christian faith
and religion—yet he did not say to her that they would never
thereafter worship God in any other temple. He said that the
time would come, and had then already come, when the
real, true worshippers would worship God in spirit and
truth. And that as God is a spiritual being, so he looked for
worshippers who would in such manner worship him. In
which statements our Savior reproved all false worship—

such as the worship being done, in the manner of paganism, on that mountain in Samaria—and all such worship as was done in any place with the idea that God could not be worshipped elsewhere. Those that so believe, they are the ones who bind God to a place; which our Lord reproves, declaring that God can in heart truly and spiritually be worshipped everywhere. But this does not exclude that besides that, he will be worshipped in his holy temple, any more than does the counsel he gave that for the avoiding of vainglory, one shall not stand and pray out on the street to gather worldly praise, but rather shall pray privately in one's room [Mt 6: 5–6]. This counsel was not a command to the Jews to whom he gave it that they should never thereafter come into the Temple and pray.

"And surely, albeit some good individuals here and there, one out of ten thousand, such as Saint Paul [the Hermit] and Saint Anthony and a few such others, do live all heavenly, far removed from all fleshly company, as far from all occasion of worldly wretchedness as from the common temple or parish church, yet if churches and congregations of Christian people coming together to worship God were ever abolished and done away with, we would likely have few good temples of God in people's souls. Probably they all would, within a while, erode clean away and completely collapse. And this we know by experience: that those who are the best temples of God in their souls, they are the ones who most regularly come to the temple of stone. And those who least come there are well known for absolute lowlifes and good-for-nothings, and are openly perceived for temples of the devil. And this not in our day only; from Christ's day to ours it has been thus. I suppose no one doubts that Christ's apostles were holy temples of God in their souls, and as well understood the words of their Master spoken to the woman of Samaria, as something that their Master afterward told them himself [see Jn 4: 8]. Because how else could some of them have recorded that conversation which, as it appears from the

Gospel, none of them heard? But they—not only in their Master's day, but also after his resurrection and after they had received the Holy Spirit and had been taught by him every truth pertaining to what was necessary for their salvation—were not content just to pray privately, by themselves in their rooms, but also went to the Temple to make their prayers. And in that place, as a place pleasing to God, they did pray in spirit and in truth, as is clearly seen in the book of Saint Luke written about the acts of Christ's holy apostles [see Acts 2: 46–47]. So that there is no doubt that, still to this day and on out to the world's end, it is and shall be pleasing to God that his chosen people pray to him and call upon him in temple and church. To which he himself witnesses with the prophet: 'Domus mea domus orationis vocabitur,' 'My house shall be called a house of prayer' [Is 56: 7 and Mt 21: 13].

"Now, your argument, as I said, avails no more against pilgrimage shrines than against every church. For as God is not bound to the place, and neither is our confidence bound to the place, but to God—though we consider our prayer more pleasing to God in the church than outside it, because in his great goodness he accepts it as such—we likewise do not consider our Lord bound to the place or image to which the pilgrimage is made, though we worship God there because he himself likes to have it thus."

4.

The author explains, in defense of pilgrimages, that it is the pleasure of God that he be specially approached and worshipped in one place in preference to another. And, granted that we cannot arrive at a knowledge of God's reason for this, the author yet proves by great authority that God by miracles testifies it is so.

With this, your friend asked me what reason there was that God would assign more value to one place than to another, or how do we know that he does, especially if the one is a church and so is the other.

To which I answered that as to *why* God would do it, I could give him no answer, any more than Saint Augustine says he could. I was never that much taken into his confidence, nor would I dare be so bold as to ask him. But *that* he indeed does so, of this I am entirely sure. But it's not that he assigns more value to that place for the soil and pavement of that place, but that it is his pleasure to show more his active presence, and to be more specially approached, in some place than in some other.

Then he asked me what made me so sure of that. Whereupon I asked him this: Supposing that with regard to this thing standing in debate and question, it should please our Lord to work a miracle in proof of the one side or the other, "would you not," said I, "then consider the question decided and the doubt resolved and that side sufficiently proved?"

"Yes, of course I would," said he.

"Well," said I, "then this matter has long since been out of question; for God has proved my side at quite a few pilgrimage sites, by the working of well over a thousand miracles, one time and another. In the Gospel of John, the fifth chapter, where we read that the angel moved the water and whoever next went in was cured of their ailment, was that not a sufficient proof that God wanted them to go there for their health? Granted, no one can tell why he sent the angel there, and did his miracles there, rather than in another pool. But whenever our Lord has in any place worked a miracle— though he does it not at all for the place, but for the honor of that saint whom he wants honored in that place, or for the faith that he finds in some who pray in that place, or for the increase of faith that he finds falling and deteriorated in that place, needing the show of some miracles for the reviving— whatsoever the cause may be, I still think the inclination is to be commended, of men and women who with good devotion run there where they see or hear that our Lord is giving a sign of his special presence. And when he gives many in one place, it is a good indication that he wants to be approached and worshipped there. Many Jews there were who came to Jerusalem to see the miracle that Christ had worked on Lazarus, as the Gospel relates [Jn 11:45]. And surely we would be inferior to Jews if we were to be so lackadaisical that where God works miracles, we would not care ever to go set foot there. We marvel much that God does not perform more miracles nowadays, when it is much more of a marvel that he does vouchsafe to perform any at all among such ungrateful, lazy, lifeless people as do not care ever to lift up their heads to look at them, or that our lack of belief can allow him nowadays to work any."

5.

Because the licitness of making pilgrimages is attested by miracles (among other proofs), the messenger makes objections against those miracles, noting that they could be faked and not real, or could be done by the devil, if they are done at all.

Then your friend said, "I well see, then, that the force and effect of all the proof rests all in miracles; which I would agree to be a strong proof if I saw them done and was sure that God or genuine saints did them. But, first, since people can and perhaps do make up many a lie about miracles, we must not test this matter by those miracles unless we first prove that the miracles were real. And, moreover, if they were indeed done, yet since the angel of darkness can transform and transfigure himself into an angel of light, how will we know whether the miracle was done by God, to the increase of Christian devotion, or done by the craft of the devil, to the advancement of misbelief and idolatry, in setting people's hearts upon chunks of wood and stone instead of upon saints, or upon saints themselves (who are but creatures) instead of upon God himself?"

I answered him that the force of my argument was not the miracles, but something that I consider stronger than any miracles: the thing which, as I said in the beginning, I see as being so certain and safe, and also so clear and obvious to every Christian, that it needs no other proof. And that thing is, as I said before, the faith of Christ's church, by the common accord of which these matters are settled and it is well known that the veneration of saints and images is commended, officially approved, and adopted into custom as a bona fide Christian and meritorious virtue, and the contrary opinion not only refuted by many theologians, but also condemned as heresy by several general councils.

"And this in the beginning I told you," said I, "was and would be the force and strength of my argument—although, indeed, I did also say to you that it seemed to me that the miracles wrought by God would be sufficient evidence and backing for it even if there were no other. Which thing, since you seem to call it into question, I shall, as I can, give you an answer about."

"No, sir," said he, "I ask that you not take me that way, as though I myself called it into question. No, as I explained to you before, I related to you what I have heard some others say."

"Right!" said I. "Then, since they are not here, I ask you to defend and substantiate their side with all that you have heard them say, and also to add to that everything more that you think they may say afterward, lest you return not fully equipped for your purpose."

6.

Because the messenger thinks that he can rightly doubt and deny the miracles on the basis that reason and nature tell him that they cannot be done, the author therefore first shows what unreasonableness would ensue if folk were to take that rigid a stance against giving credence to any such thing as reason and nature might seem to go against.

"So first, whereas you say—"

"No," said he, "whereas *they* say."

"Well," said I, "so be it: whereas *they* say. For here my

tongue always trips. But now, therefore, first whereas *they* say that they have never seen any of these miracles themselves and therefore the miracles are no proof to them, since as long as they have never seen them they are not obliged to believe in them: either they would seem very remiss, if they do no investigating when they have doubts and suspicions regarding the truth in such a weighty matter, or, if they have diligently made inquiry, then it would have to be the case that they have heard of so many, told and related by the mouths and the writings of such good and credible persons, that they would seem unreasonably skeptical if they think to be altogether lies what so many honest persons, or persons likely to be honest, so seriously do report. If these people were judges, few cases would come to a conclusion at their hand, or at least the plaintiff would have a bad outcome, if they would believe nothing but what was proved and consider nothing proved but what they saw themselves.

"Every man can thus consider himself unsure of his own father, if he believes no man, or since all the proof of this rests only with one woman, and she being the one who, though she can tell the best, yet if it be wrong has the greatest reason to lie. Leave the knowledge of the father alone, then, among our wives' personal secrets, and let us see if we believe nothing but what we see ourselves. What man can consider himself sure of his own mother? For it is possible that he was exchanged in the cradle. A rich man's wet nurse may have brought home her own child as her employer's, and have kept her employer's as her own, to make her own a gentleman on the cheap. And this would not be difficult, as long as the mother has no way of identifying her own child."

"Sir," said your friend, "if I were to answer them thus, and by these examples attempt to prove to them that they are bound by reason to believe in all these reported miracles because many credible people relate them—since otherwise we would believe in nothing but what we see ourselves, and then the whole world would be full of confusion, nor could any judgment be given except on things done in the judge's sight—I would, I am afraid, very little convince them. For they would immediately say that the examples are nothing like the matter in question. Rather, just as it stands to reason that I should believe honest people about all such things as may be true and about which I see no reason why they would lie, so would it be completely against reason to believe people, no matter how many they are and how credible they seem, when reason and nature (of which two things each by itself is more credible than all of them) show me plainly that their tale is untrue, as it must necessarily be if its content is impossible, as it is with all these miracles. And in such a case, even if I can see nothing that they stand to gain thereby, yet when I clearly see that it could not be true, I must clearly see that it was not true. And thereby I must necessarily know that if they have nothing to gain by lying, then they are lying not for any greed, but purely and simply for their personal pleasure."

"Actually," said I, "that is quite an agreeable answer. And to tell the truth, for as far as we have yet gotten into the matter of these miracles, not much amiss or very far from the mark. But since this thing is very important, many big things depending on it, we shall not so shortly shake it off, but we shall come one or two steps closer to the issue. And first I will say to them that it would be hard for them, and not very safe, to believe that everyone lies who tells them as being true a tale that reason and nature seem to show them to be false and impossible. For in this way they shall in many things err and completely delude themselves, and sometimes when they assure themselves of the wrong side, if they were to contend and compete on it with wagers, they would upon their confidence in nature and reason lose everything they ever were able to bet on it.

"Suppose there is an Ethiopian man who has never come out of his country, and has never in his life seen any white man or woman. Since he sees innumerable people who are black, he might think it is against the nature of the human being to be white. Now, if he should, because nature seems to show him this, believe therefore that everyone in the world who said the contrary was lying, who would be in the wrong? He that believes his reason and nature, or they that against his persuasion of reason and nature will tell it to him as it really is?"

Your friend answered that reason and nature did not tell the Ethiopian man that all human beings must be black, but rather, he believed this against reason and against nature, since he had nothing to lead him to this conclusion except that he himself had seen no white ones, which was no reason. And he might by means of nature realize, if he had any education, that the heat makes his country black. And, by the same line of reasoning, that the cold of other countries must make the people white.

"Well," said I, "and yet he comes to his conviction by a syllogism and reasoning almost as according-to-rule as the argument by which you prove the human race to be endowed with reason. For what line of reasoning do you have for this, that first brought you to perceive it, other than that this person is endowed with reason, and this person, and this person, and this person, and so forth—all of those you see. By the example of whom, of those whom you know, presuming, thereby, no human being to be otherwise, you conclude that every human being is endowed with reason. And he thinks himself safer in his argument than he thinks you in yours. For he has never seen people who are other than black, whereas you see many people who are fools. And as for his hearing from others that there are white people elsewhere, this in no way serves your purpose if you believe no witness against the thing that your reason and experience show you. And whereas you say, 'If the Ethiopian man was educated he would realize that it is not against nature, but, rather, consonant with nature, that some other people in other countries should be white even though all his compatriots are black,' so perhaps those whose view you are sustaining, if they had some education that they lack, would well realize that according to reason they should give credence to credible persons reporting to them things that seem far against reason because they are far above reason. Of this we may perhaps have more perceiving in our conversation hereafter, before we finish what we have in hand. But in the meantime, to show you further what necessity there is to believe other people about things not only unknown to us but also seemingly impossible, the Ethiopian man that we speak of can by no kind of education know the course of the sun, whereby he would perceive the cause of his blackness, unless it be by astronomy, which science who can learn that will believe nothing that seems to himself impossible? Or who would not think it impossible, if experience had not proved it, that the whole earth hangs in the air and people walk foot against foot and ships sail bottom against bottom— a thing sounding so absurd, and seeming so far against nature and reason, that Lactantius, a very intelligent and well-educated man, in his work that he writes, *Divinæ institutiones,* takes to be impossible, and does not refrain from laughing at the philosophers for affirming, that point, which is yet now proved true by the experience of those who have in less than two years sailed all the way around the world. Who would think it possible for glass to be made of fern roots? Now, if those who think it impossible according to reason, and have never seen it done, believe no one who tells it to them, then although it is no peril to their souls, yet so much do they have knowledge the less and unreasonably persist in their error through their disbelieving of the truth.

"It is not yet fifty years ago that there came to London the first man (as far as anyone has heard) who ever separated gold from silver, quickly reducing the silver to dust with a very pure liquid. In fact, when the refiners and goldsmiths of London first heard about this, they did not at all marvel at it, but laughed at it as at an impossible lie. Had they continued still in those persuasions, they would still at this day be lacking all that knowledge.

"Now, I will not deny that one can be too unthinking in belief and by such examples be brought into belief too far. Recently a good associate and friend of mine, in talking of this matter of marvels and miracles, intending for fun to make me believe for a truth a thing that could never be, first brought up what a force the fire has that will make two pieces of iron able to be joined and cleave together and, with the help of the hammer, be made both one, which no amount of hammering could accomplish without the fire. Which thing, because I see it every day, I accepted. Then he went on to say that it was still more of a marvel that the fire will make iron run as silver or lead does, and make it take a print. Which thing I told him I had never seen, but because he said he had seen it, I thought it to be true. Soon after this, he tried to make me believe that he had seen a piece of silver of two or three inches around, and in length less than a foot, drawn by human hand through narrow holes made in iron, till it was brought in thickness to not half an inch around, and in length drawn out to 'I cannot tell how many yards.' And when I heard him say that he saw this himself, then I well knew he was being facetious."

"Indeed, sir," said your friend, "it was high time to give him up as a hopeless case, when he came to that."

"Well," said I, "what if I should tell you now that I had seen the same?"

"By my faith," he said merrily, "I would believe it eventually, when I had seen the same; and in the meantime I could not keep you from saying whatever you please in your own house. But I would think that you were being facetious, to make a fool out of me."

"Well," said I, "what if there should, besides me, ten or twenty good, respectable men tell you the same story, and that they had all seen the thing done themselves?"

"Seriously," said he, "since I am sent here to believe you, I would on that point believe you by yourself as well as I would all of them."

"Well," said I, "you mean you would believe us all alike. But what would you then say if one or two of them were to say more?"

"Goodness," said he, "then I would believe them less."

"What if," said I, "they were to tell you that they have seen this: that the piece of silver was gilded over, and, the same piece being still drawn through the holes, the gold was not rubbed off but continued to go out in length with the silver, so that the whole length of many yards was gilded with the gilding of the first piece not a foot long?"

"Assuredly, sir," said he, "those two that would tell me that much more, I would say were not even as clever in the supporting of a lie as was the companion of a pilgrim who had said in York that he had recently seen in London a bird that covered the whole churchyard of St. Paul's with its wings. The companion, upon coming to the same place on the next day, said that he had not seen that bird, though he had heard a lot of talk about it, but that he had seen in the churchyard of St. Paul's an egg so big that ten men could barely move it with levers. This fellow could have helped the story along with an apt digression. But he is no proper underpropper of a lie who would lessen his credibility by affirming all of the first lie and adding to it a more flagrant one."

"Well," said I, "then I take it that if ten should tell you so, you would not believe them."

"No," said he, "not if twenty should."

"What if a hundred would," said I, "who seemed good and credible?"

"If they were," said he, "a thousand, they would have run out of credibility with me when they told me that they saw something that I myself know from nature and reason to be impossible. For when I know it could not be done, I know well that they are all lying, no matter how many they are who say they saw it done."

"Well," said I, "since I see well that you would not on this point believe a whole town, you have put me to silence, so that I dare not now venture to tell you that I have seen it myself. But assuredly, if witness would have served me, I think I could have brought you a great many good men who would say, and even swear, that they have seen it themselves. But now I shall provide me, tomorrow perhaps, a couple of witnesses of whom I well know you will mistrust neither the one nor the other."

"Who are they?" said he. "For it would be hard to find anyone I could better trust than yourself, whom, whatever I have said in fun, I in all honesty could not but believe regarding what you should tell me seriously, upon your own knowledge. But you are in the habit, my employer says, of looking so serious when you mean something in jest that many times people think you might be joking when you are dead serious."

"In all honesty," said I, "I am dead serious now; and yet, as well as you dare trust me, I shall, as I said, if you will go with me, provide a couple of witnesses of whom you will believe either one better than two of me, for they are close relatives of yours, and you are better acquainted with them, and they are such as, I dare say for them, are not often apt to lie."

"I ask you," said he, "who are they?"

"Why," said I, "your own two eyes! For I shall, if you want, bring you to where you will see it, no further away than right here in London. And as for iron and latten being thus drawn out in length, you shall see it done in twenty shops, almost, on one street."

"Well, of course, sir," said he, "these witnesses will indeed not lie. As the poor man said about the priest—if I may be so down-home as to tell you a funny story in passing—"

"A funny story," said I, "never comes amiss to me."

"The poor man," said he, "had found the priest over-familiar with his wife, and because he said it in public and could not prove it, the priest sued him for defamation before the bishop's official, where the poor man was, under pain of excommunication, commanded that in his parish church he should on the following Sunday, at High Mass time, stand up and say, 'Mouth, you lie!' At which time, for the fulfilling of his penance, the poor soul was put in a front pew so that the people could stare at him and hear what he said. And there, quite loudly, he repeated what he had reported about the priest, and then put his hands on his mouth and said, 'Mouth, mouth, you lie!' And immediately after that he put his hands on both his eyes and said, 'But eyes, eyes,' said he, 'by the Mass, you lie not a whit!' And so, sir, indeed, if you bring me those witnesses, they will not lie a whit.

"However, sir, even if this thing is true (as in all honesty I believe and am sure that it is), I nevertheless am not any the more bound by reason to believe those who would tell me of a miracle. For even if this thing is incredible to someone who hears it, and surprising and astonishing to someone who sees it, it yet is something that can be done. But someone who tells me of a miracle tells me of something that cannot be done."

"I gave you this example," said I, "to put you in mind that in being overly resistant to believing in things that by reason and nature seem and appear impossible, where they are reported by credible witnesses having no cause to lie, there is as much danger of error as where people give their credence too readily. And this much I have proved to you as a preliminary: that if you believe no one about such things as cannot be, then it must follow that you ought to believe no one about many things that can be; for it is all the same to you, whether they can be or cannot be, if it seems to you that they cannot be. And, in fact, you cannot tell whether they can be or cannot be unless they are two such things as imply contradiction, such as that one selfsame thing is in the selfsame part both white and black at once. For else many things will seem to you to be such as all reason will resist and nature will in no way admit. And yet they will be done plenty well. And be, in some other place, in common practice and custom. But, now, because your whole dodge comes down to this—that about a miracle reported to you, you can reasonably believe that all those people are lying, because reason and nature, which are more to be believed than all of them, tell you that what they are saying is wrong, since the thing reported for a miracle cannot be done—I have shown you that nature and reason do show you that many things cannot be done which yet in fact are done. Indeed, when you see them done, you can quite rightly count them as miracles, for anything that reason or nature can tell you as to by what natural order and cause such and such could be done, except that you shall still see reason stand quite against it, as in the drawing of the silver or iron."

7.

The author shows that neither nature nor reason does deny that the miracles are real, or go against them; and that they can quite easily be done.

"Sir," says he, "we are still not hitting the point. Granted, many things are really done, and by nature, where neither my intellect nor perhaps that of anyone else can get itself so taken into nature's confidence that we can see how she does what she does. But just as some unlearned people are astonished by a clock that has the spring (which is the cause of its functioning) invisibly carried and enclosed in the case, so we marvel and wonder at her work; and yet, always, all those things differ from miracles and are unlike them. On this you yourself will agree with me: that when I believe that reason and nature definitely teach me that miracles are things that cannot be done, I am not mistaken about that, though I may be mistaken about such other things, that seem impossible and yet can be done. And therefore, concerning miracles, about which you yourself will agree that I am not led astray by any mistaking of reason and nature, you yourself cannot, it seems to me, deny that I can rightly, with reason, believe

94

the two of them against all of those who will tell me they have seen such things done as you yourself do agree that those two (that is to say, nature and reason) do really and truly tell me cannot be done."

"What kind of things are those?" said I.

"Good heavens," said he, "*miracles*—such as you yourself will agree would be done against nature."

"Give us," said I, "some example of those."

"Such as," said he, "if someone would now come tell me that at Our Lady of Rouncivalle a dead child was brought back to life."

"Let that," said I, "be one; and let another be that a bishop, during the constructing of his church, finding one beam cut a great deal too short for his building, stretched it out, between someone else and himself, to four feet (if you will) longer than it was, and thus made it serve."

"So be it, by my word," said he.

"Shall we," said I, "take for the third that a man was by miracle carried a mile off, from one place to another, in the time it takes to say an Our Father?"

"So be it," said he.

"Now, they that should tell me," said he, "that they had seen these miracles—would I be obliged to believe them?"

"Whether you would be obliged or not," said I, "we shall see later on. But now, why should you not by reason trust them, if they are credible and report it seriously and perhaps by oath testify to it, having no cause to invent it, nor being likely to lie and commit perjury for nothing?"

"I will," said he, "not believe them, because nature and reason are two witnesses more to be believed than all those that bear witness against them."

"Why," said I, "what do reason and nature tell you?"

"The two of them tell me," said he, "that those three things cannot be done which those men say they saw done."

"Do you really know," said I, "that reason and nature tell you that?"

"Yes indeed," said he, "I really know that they do, and I think you yourself will agree that they tell me that."

"No, sir, by our Lady," said I, "that I will not. For I think that neither reason nor nature tells you that, but, rather, both of the two tell you the exact opposite. That is to say, the both of them bear witness that those three things, and suchlike others, are things that can quite easily be done."

"Yes?" said he. "Goodness, this is a different tack. Then we have been off-track for a while, if you prove that."

"It seems to me," said I, "that nothing is easier to prove than that."

"For I ask you to tell me," said I, "do or do not reason and nature tell you that there is a God?"

"Faith tells me that, certainly," said he, "but whether nature and reason tell it to me or not, that I question, since great thinkers and philosophers have questioned it. And some of them have been plainly persuaded and of the belief that there is none at all, and that virtually the whole population of the world has fallen from 'knowledge' of or belief in God into idolatry and worship of idols."

"No," said I, "there is little doubt, I trust, that nature and reason give us good knowledge that there is a God. For albeit the Gentiles worshipped among them a thousand false gods, yet all that proves that there was and is in all humans' heads a mysterious natural consensus that there is a God; else they would have worshipped none at all. Now, as for the philosophers, though a very few were in doubt, and one or two thought there was no God, yet as one swallow does not a summer make, so the folly of so few makes no change of the matter, against the whole entire number of the ancient philosophers who, as Saint Paul acknowledges, learned from nature and reason that there was a God, either maker or governor, or both, of this whole mechanism of the world, the marvelous beauty and constant course of which show well that it neither was made nor is governed by chance [see Acts 17: 22–29 and Rom 1: 19–20]. But, when they had from these visible things knowledge of his invisible majesty, they then did what we do: fall from the worship of him to the worship of idols. We Christians do this now, not (as heretics lay to the charge of good people) in doing reverence to saints or honor to their images, but in doing as do those heretics themselves, making our belly or our beneath-the-belly, or our possessions, or our own blind affection for other creatures, or our own proud affection and foolish fondness for ourselves, our fetishes and idols and very false gods. But certainly both nature and reason will show and teach us that there is a God."

"Well," said he, "I will not balk at this, since Saint Paul says it."

"Then," said I, "if reason and nature tell you that there is a God, do not reason and nature tell you also that he is almighty and can do what he wants?"

"Yes," said he, "that is both natural to him as God and easy to perceive by reason."

"Then it follows," said I, "that reason and nature do not tell you that those three miracles (that we agreed should stand as examples) absolutely could not be done, but they taught you only that they could not be done by nature. But you can (as you now do) perceive that they themselves teach that they can be done by God, since they teach you that there is a God and that he is almighty. And therefore when you will in no way believe those who tell you they have seen such miracles done, you are not refusing to believe in things that cannot be done, but rather you are doubting without cause the trustworthiness and credibility of respectable people in the reporting of things that, by him that they say did them, can quite easily be done."

8.

The messenger claims that God can do nothing against the course of nature. The author asserts the contrary, and, moreover, shows that our Lord in the working of miracles does nothing against nature.

"Sir," said he, "you are indeed somewhat gaining on me now. But yet it seems to me that reason and nature still teach me that I shall in no way believe those who tell me they have seen such miracles done. For first, if you will grant me that they teach me that if they were to be done, they would have to be done by God against the course of nature, then so, too, reason tells me that God has directed all things, already from the first creation, to proceed in a certain order and course, which order and course people call 'nature,' and that he of his infinite wisdom has done so well, and arranged for that course to proceed in such a manner and fashion, that it cannot be improved. And therefore it seems that reason tells me that God will never do anything against the course which he, in his great wisdom, power, and goodness, has made so good that it could never be broken for the better. For if it could, then that would mean our Lord did not make his order and course perfect in the beginning. And therefore, as I say, reason and nature do still bear witness against those who shall say they see such miracles, since God will never work against the course of nature, which he himself has already set in so excellent an order that it could not possibly be better, and since God in his goodness will make no change for the worse."

"Assuredly," said I, "you now go very far wide of the mark. For although it cannot be otherwise than that anything of the making of God's goodness must necessarily be good, reason does not prove to you that God has therefore made everything to be of sovereign perfection (for then all creatures would have to be equal); or even that the work of his creation as a whole, though it does have in it a sufficient and quite wonderful perfection, that therefore it is wrought to the utterest point of sovereign goodness that his almighty Majesty could have made it of. For since he wrought it not by his nature but by his will, he wrought it not to the uttermost of his ability, but with such degrees of goodness as he of his high pleasure chose to allot. For else his work would be of as infinite perfection as himself. And of such infinite, equal perfection was there by God brought forth nothing but only the two Persons of the Trinity, that is to say, the Son and the Holy Spirit. Of which two the Son was first by the Father begotten, and after that, the Holy Spirit by the Father and the Son—'after,' I say, in order of origin, but not in time—produced and brought forth. And in this high generation and production the doers did work both volitionally and naturally, and according to the utterest perfection of themselves; but they did this only there, not in anything else. And therefore God could, if he wanted to, break up the whole world and immediately make a better one, and not just change in the natural course of this world some things for the better. However, God in the working of miracles does nothing against nature, but some special favor *above* nature. And someone who does someone else a good turn which you are not able to do is not doing anything against you. And therefore, since God can do what he wants, being almighty, and since in the doing of miracles he does for the better, neither reason nor nature tells you that those who say they saw such and such a miracle are relating to you a thing that cannot be done, since you have no rational argument whereby to prove that God either cannot do it or will not do it. For since he can do it and it may be that he will do it, why should we doubt good, respectable people who say they saw him do it?"

9.

The author asserts that although one may doubt some of the particular miracles, yet no reasonable person can either deny or doubt that many miracles have been done and wrought.

"True," said he, "and yet, as for miracles, I would not for all this be obliged to believe in any. For I never yet have spoken with anyone who could tell me that they ever saw any."

"It may," said I, "be your fortune to live so long that you will find no one who was present at your baptism, or when you were confirmed, either."

"Why," said he, "for all I know, I have lived that long already."

"Then why do you not doubt," said I, "whether you were ever baptized or not?"

"Because everyone," said he, "presumes and believes that I am baptized. It is a thing so commonly done that we consider ourselves certain that no one leaves it undone."

"If the common presumption," said I, "sufficiently serves you to set your mind in certainty, then although it is true that miracles are not things commonly and customarily done, and that no presumption can sufficiently serve for the proof of this miracle or that, yet there have from the beginning of the world, in every nation, Christian and heathen, and in almost every town, at one time or another, been wrought outside the common course of nature so many miracles and marvels that I think throughout the world it is as universally believed that there are miracles and marvels as anything is believed that people look at. So that if common presumption serves you, you can, as I said, as well believe that miracles are done as that you yourself were ever baptized. For I well dare say that for every one person who believes that you were ever baptized, or ever knew whether you were born or not, there are a thousand who believe that miracles have been done.

"Nor did the theologians of Christ's church ever doubt the wonders and marvels that the pagans speak and write of as having been done by their false gods, but they account them to have been done by the devil through God's sufferance, for the deluding of those who by idolatry had deserved to be deluded. And whether they be miracles (by which name we commonly call the wonders wrought by God) or marvels done by the devil, that is irrelevant to this argument of ours. For if you grant that the devil can do any such things by God's sufferance, you cannot deny that God can much more easily do them himself.

"And since you are a Christian man and accept Scripture,

I could in this matter," said I, "have silenced you long ago with the manifold miracles and marvels that are related there."

10.

The author proves that many things done every day by nature or human skill, that we marvel at not at all, are actually more marvelous and amazing than the miracles we marvel at the most and consider the hardest to believe.

"No," said he, "certainly, even though it has done me good to hear what you had to say, yet I do not doubt, nor do I suppose that any other good person doubts, that God has outside of the common course of nature worked many miracles.

"But yet, of those that people tell of as done in your time—the ones by which you would have it seem well proved that the practices of praying to saints, going on pilgrimages, and venerating images have been quite sufficiently validated, even if there were no other proof of that—I meant the ones in the talk of which, it seems to me, I need not believe a popular rumor of this miracle and that, started by some silly woman going to the shrine of Saint Zita when she is distressed over a misplacing of her keys. I'm talking about these miracles, and all those that people say are being done nowadays at various pilgrimage sites by various saints or various images; the ones where it seems to me that with regard to the things told as having been done which nature and reason say are impossible, I can justifiably disbelieve the tellers. Or else how many of them will make me a sufficient proof of an impossible occurrence? One or two, or even three, seem to me too few to trust the credibility of, concerning a thing that incredible. And if I shall not believe in them till I find many witnesses, I think I would have to wander the world over before I sufficiently proved many miracles, of the kind, I say, that you validate your pilgrimages by."

"Your few statements," said I, "have wrapped in them many things, that seem somewhat couched together. When we see them unfolded and consider each part separately, we can better examine them, and better see whereof they serve.

"First you speak of going to saints' shrines for trivial causes, such as the loss or misplacement of Kitty's keys. Then you want to know how many people you must hear say they saw a miracle before you should, according to reason, believe in it. Thirdly, you think you would be likely to travel a long way before you would find any proved true. Finally, when you say that you mean only those miracles that people tell of as done at pilgrimage sites, you seem to be tacitly asserting a difference between the miracles wrought during pilgrimages and those that are wrought by God otherwise. The reason for which I must go on to ask you later. For I do not quite understand what you mean by that.

"But first, seeing that you are still speaking as though you can legitimately disbelieve these people, be they however many, because they are telling you a thing that reason and nature say is 'impossible,' it seems to me that you should now change that word. For I have already proved that reason and nature say not that a miracle is impossible, but only that it is impossible for nature. And they acknowledge, the both of them, that miracles are possible for God; and those who report them do report them as things done by God. And therefore they are telling you no impossible tale.

"For the clearer consideration whereof, let us turn to the miracles that we agreed should stand as examples. So, first: If someone were to tell you that they saw before an image of Christ on the cross a dead man raised to life, you would much wonder at that, and so you well might. Yet I could tell you something that I have seen myself, that seems to me as great a wonder; but I have no desire to tell you, because you are so circumspect and wary when it comes to belief in any miracles that you would not believe it because of your trust in me, but would mistrust me on account of it."

"No, sir," said he, "really and truly, if something seemed to me no matter how unlikely, still, if you were to say in all seriousness that you yourself have seen it, I would not and could not doubt it."

"Very well," said I, "then you make me the more confident to tell you. And I even will be telling you nothing but what I would if need be find you good witnesses to prove."

"There will be no need of that, sir," said he, "but I beg you, let me hear it."

"All right," said I, "since we are speaking of a man raised from death to life. There were in the parish of St. Stephen's in Walbrook (which is in London, where I lived before I came to Chelsea) a man and a woman who are still alive and able to talk; and they were young, the both of them. The older one was, I am sure, not over twenty-four. It happened with them, as it does among young folk, that the one took a fancy to the other. And after many hindrances (for the girl's mother was much against it), at last they came together and were married in St. Stephen's Church, which is not greatly famous for any miracles, but yet every year on St. Stephen's Day it is somewhat sought out and visited with folk's devotion. But now, to make a long story short, this young woman (as is the custom with brides, as you well know) was at night brought to bed by reputable women. And then, after that, the bridegroom went to bed, and everybody else went their ways and left the two of them there alone. And that same night—well, wait a minute, don't let me lie; now really, to tell the truth, I am not very sure of the time; but certainly, as it appeared afterward, it was likely the same night or some other time soon after, unless it happened a little before."

"The time makes no difference," said he.

"True," said I, "and as for the thing itself, the whole parish will testify to its being true, the woman was known for so honest. But, in short, the seed of the two of them turned, in the woman's body, first into blood, and later into the shape of a man-child. And then grew animate, and she, great therewith. And was within the year delivered of a beautiful boy; and honestly, he was not then (for I saw him myself) over a foot long. And I know for a fact that he is now grown to an inch longer than me."

"How long ago was that?" he asked.

"By my faith," said I, "about twenty-one years."

"Pooh," said he, "some miracle this is."

"In all seriousness," said I, "I have never known that any man could say that he had any other beginning. And it seems to me that this is as great a miracle as the raising of a dead man."

"If it seems that way to you," said he, "then you have a surprising way of seeing things, for I think it seems that way to no one else."

"No?" said I. "Can you tell what the cause is? None other, surely, but that the acquaintance and daily beholding takes away the wondering. We, for instance, wonder not at all at the ebbing and flowing of the sea or the Thames, because we see it every day. But someone who had never seen it or heard of it would at the first sight wonder greatly at it, to see that great water come wallowing up against the wind, keeping a common course to and fro, no cause perceived that drives it. If a man born blind suddenly had his sight, how surprised he would be to see the sun, the moon, and the stars, whereas someone who has seen them sixteen years in succession marvels not as much at them all as he would wonder at the first sight of a peacock's tail. And no real reason can I see why we should by reason marvel more at the reviving of a dead man than at the begetting, bringing forth, and growing of a child into the state of a man. A cuckoo is no more amazing than a cock, though the one is seen only in summer and the other all year long. And I am sure that if you saw dead men as commonly called back by miracle as you see men brought forth by nature, you would consider it less of a marvel to bring the soul back into the body, its shape and organs remaining not much deteriorated yet, than from a little seed to make all that stuff newly, and make a new soul as well.

"Now, if you had never seen a cannon in all your days, nor heard of any before, if two men should tell you, the one that he had known a man to be by miracle conveyed and carried a mile off, from one place to another, in the time it takes to say an Our Father, and the other that he had seen a stone of more than a man's weight carried more than a mile in as little time by human skill, which of these things would you honestly take as the more incredible?"

"Certainly," said he, "both of the two would sound very absurd. But yet I could not help but think it true that God did the one, rather than that human skill could do the other."

"Well," said I, "let's turn, then, to our third example. If it were told to you that when Barking Abbey was being built, Saint Erconwald, or his sister, stretched out a piece of timber that was cut too short for the roof, should this be so incredible to you to believe, that they elongated a piece of wood by the power and help of God's hand, when we see daily a big piece of silver, brass, latten, or iron elongated into thin wire as astonishingly by human hands?"

11.

The author shows that a miracle is not to be doubted even if it is done in a small matter and on a seemingly trivial occasion.

"Now, though you would perhaps (as you seem to do) consider this cause a very slight one for God to perform such a high-class miracle, since a longer piece of timber might have been gotten without a miracle, and so you would perhaps doubt it because of the trivialness of the occasion, likening it to the misplacing of some good housewife's keys, God has, I think, so much sense on his own that he does not need our advice to inform him what thing would be a sufficient occasion to work his wonders for. And if you read the books of Cassian, Saint Gregory, Saint Augustine, Saint Jerome, and many other holy, virtuous men, you will (unless you do not believe them) learn and know that God has for his servants done many a great miracle in very small matters. And so much the more are we beholden to his goodness in that he is willing to be so down-home with us as to show us in a little thing so great a sign of his mighty Godhood. And no sense would it make to deprive him of his credit and honor because of his down-home goodness.

"And if you perhaps would not believe their writings, turn to Christ's Gospel and look at his first miracle. Could he not have provided for wine without a miracle? But such was his pleasure, to do in a small matter a great miracle, for some show of his Godhood among those he saw as fit for one; whereas on the other hand, before Herod, who would have loved to see some miracle, where his life was on the line and a miracle might have delivered him from the Jews, he nevertheless did not see fit to show the proud, curious king one miracle, or even to speak one word. [See Jn 2: 8–11 and Lk 23: 8–9.] So as for the times, places, and occasions, reason dictates that we leave them to his discretion, and not look to prescribe and appoint at our pleasure where, when, and for what purpose God shall work his miracles, and otherwise blaspheme them and say we will not believe in them."

12.

The author comments a little on the perverse mentality of the many folk who would be very slow to believe a man attesting by oath to a miracle, but very quick to believe on her mere word a woman telling a malicious tale.

"Now, where you ask how many witnesses should be requisite and suffice to make you think yourself, according to reason, to have good cause to believe such an absurd thing, it seems to me that a very few would be sufficient, of those who would say they saw a great good thing done by the power and goodness of God, unless it is hard for us to believe either that God is so mighty that he can do it or that he is so good that he would do it.

"But—since you want to know from me how many witnesses are requisite—that is a matter not so much of number as of weight. Some two may be more credible than some ten. And although I do not very well see why I should doubt anyone who seems honest and tells a good tale about God in which there appears no particular motive for lying, yet if any witness will serve you, then I want to know from you how many you yourself would agree to. For I now put the case that ten different reputable, solid men from ten different parts of the realm were to come, each of them with an offering, to the same shrine, such as, for example, Our Lady of Ipswich, and each of them affirming upon his oath a miracle done for himself in terms of some great, sudden cure quite obviously beyond the power of skill or nature. Would you not believe that among them all, at least two of those ten were telling the truth?"

"No, by our Lady," said he, "not if there were ten and twenty."

"Why so?" said I.

"Good heavens," said he, "because, be they no matter how many, having no other witness, but each man telling his tale for himself, they are all solitary, and actually less than solitary. For each miracle has but one witness, and even he is not credible in his own cause. And so no miracle is really proved."

"Well," said I, "I really approve of your wisdom, that you are so circumspect that you will believe nothing without good, sufficient, and full proof."

"I put you, then," said I, "another case: that ten young women, not very specially known for good, but come upon outdoors at random, all living in one town, were to report and relate that a friar of good repute, upon hearing their confessions at an indulgence festival, had given them all, as their penance, to let him lie with them. On your faith, would you not believe that among so many, some of them were telling the truth?"

"Yes, about that I would," said he, "by the Mass in honor of our Lady, believe they were telling the truth, all ten of them, and well dare swear for them, even if they were but two."

"Why so?" said I. "They are witnesses as solitary as those others that I mentioned to you before. For none of them can tell what was said to any other; and they are even unsworn, also. And, moreover, they are but women, who carry less weight and are less to be regarded; living all in one town, also, and thereby they could the more easily conspire a false tale."

"They are," said he, "good enough witness for such a matter, the thing being so likely in itself—that a friar will be a womanizer, however saintly the holy whoreson may look."

"You do not deny," said I, "that God can as easily do a good turn by miracle as any man can do a bad one by nature."

"That is true," said he. "If he wants."

"Well," said I, "see now what a good way you are in, you who are, of your own good, godly mind, more ready to believe two mere women that a man will do evil, than ten or twenty men that God will do good."

13.

The author shows the badness of attitude of the many people who, with regard to miracles so highly pertaining to the honor of God and the well-being of their own souls, will neither believe other folk who relate them nor deign to go investigate them themselves.

"But since this kind of proof will not suffice you, I dare say that if you were to search and inquire, you would find many done in your day, in the presence of many people."

"Where would I see that?" said he.

"You could," said I, "on Good Friday every year in these last two hundred years, till within these five years since the Turks took the town, have seen one of the thorns that was in

Christ's crown bud and bring forth flowers during Mass, if you would have gone to Rhodes—"

"That far?" said he. "No, I would even rather have God's blessing to believe what I do not see, than travel so far for that."

"I am very happy about that," said I, "for if you would rather believe than take the trouble of a long pilgrimage, you will never be so unyielding in any opinion that you will put yourself in jeopardy for obstinacy and a stubborn standing by your side of the dispute."

"No indeed," said he, "I guarantee you that I will never be so mad as to hold on till it gets too hot. For I have a similar whimsical notion of my own: that I would rather shiver and shake for cold in the midst of summer than be burned in the midst of winter."

"Facetiously said," said I, "but yet, seriously, where such an awe-inspiring yearly miracle is wrought so wondrously in the sight of the world, before so great a multitude, it is a great badness of attitude—in the case of something so highly concerning the honor of God and the well-being of our own souls—both to disbelieve all those who say they have seen it and, out of either laziness or incredulity, not deign to check it out oneself."

"Were I to have gone," said he, "and found it a lie, then some sensible journey I would have made! And on the other hand, were I to have seen there such a thing myself, I still could scarcely consider myself certain."

"No?" said I. "That would be a surprising situation."

"Not very surprising," said he. "For you are speaking of miracles done before a multitude, and one can very well be deceived there."

14.

The messenger makes the objection that miracles performed before a multitude can be faked; and the author shows, by way of one or two examples, how God in his goodness soon brings the truth of

such deceitfulness to light. And it is further shown that there are
many miracles which no good Christian can deny to be real.

"Some priest, to attract a pilgrimage to his parish, may get some dishonest fellow to disguise himself, come visit a saint's shrine in his church, and there suddenly say that he has gotten his sight. Then shall you have the bells rung for a miracle. And the gullible folk of the area soon made fools of. Then women coming there with their candles. And the parson, by buying from some lame beggars three or four pairs of their old crutches and spending twelve pennies on wax men and women thrust through in several places (some with arrows and some with rusty knives), will for the next seven years make twice as much from his offerings as from his tithes."

"This is," said I, "quite true—that such things can be, and sometimes, perhaps, are so indeed. I remember, for instance, hearing my father tell of a beggar who, in the days of King Henry VI, came with his wife to St. Alban's, and was walking there, around the town, begging, for five or six days before the king's arrival, saying that he was born blind and had never seen in his life. And that he had been informed in a dream that he should come out of Berwick (where, he said, he had always lived) to seek the help of Saint Alban; and that he had been at his shrine, and had not been helped. And therefore he would go seek his help at some other place, for he had heard some say, since he came, that Saint Alban's body was in Cologne. (And indeed, there has been such a contention. But actually, as I am reliably informed, he lies here at St. Alban's, except for some relics of him which they there display enshrined.) But, to continue telling you, when the king had arrived and the town was full, suddenly this blind man, at Saint Alban's shrine, had his sight, and a miracle was solemnly rung and a Te Deum sung, so that nothing was talked of in all the town but this miracle.

"It then so happened that Humphrey, Duke of Gloucester, a great, wise, and very well-educated man, having great joy at seeing such a miracle, called the poor man over to him. And, first showing himself joyous of God's glory so shown in the getting of his sight, and exhorting him to be meek and not take for himself any part of the credit, nor be proud of the praise of the people who would call him a good and godly man on account of it, finally he took a good look at his eyes and asked whether he could never see anything at all in all his life before. And when his wife, as well as he himself, affirmed steadfastly, 'No,' then he looked intently at his eyes again and said, 'I very well believe you, for it seems to me that you still cannot see well.'

" 'Yes, sir,' said he, 'I thank God and his holy martyr, I can now see as well as any man.'

" 'You can?' said the duke. 'What color is my gown?' Then at once the beggar told him.

" 'What color,' he asked, 'is this man's gown?' He told him that also; and so forth, without any hesitation, he told him the names of all the colors that could be shown him. And when my lord saw that, he dismissed him as an impostor and had him publicly set in the stocks. For though he could have seen at once, by miracle, the difference between different colors, he yet could not by the sight so promptly tell the names of all these colors unless he had known them before, any more than the names of all the people that he would be seeing soon after."

"Look, therefore, I say," said your friend, "who can be sure of such things, when such charades are put on before the whole town? I now recall what a production *I* have heard of. This took place in Leominster (in the days of the King's father), where the prior privately brought into the church an unknown young woman who said that she was sent there by God and would not lie outside the church. And later she was confined, within iron grates, up in the choir loft, where, it was believed, she lived without any food or drink—only by angels' food. And several times she was given Communion (as the people saw it) with an unconsecrated host, and, all the people looking on, there was a device with a thin wire that conveyed the host from the paten of the chalice, out of the prior's hands into her mouth, as though it came on its own; so that all the people, not only from the town but also from the surrounding countryside, took her for a real live saint, and daily sought so thick to see her that many who could not get near her cried out loudly, 'Holy maiden Elizabeth, help me!' and had to throw their offerings over their companions' heads, because of the jam.

"Now lay the prior with holy maiden Elizabeth nightly in the loft, till she was subsequently taken out and tested in confinement by my lady the King's mother. And by the longing for food, with the voiding of what she had eaten (which had no saintly smell), she was perceived for no saint, and confessed the whole thing."

"Really," said I, "it would have been a great act of charity if the prior and she had been burned together at one stake. What became of the prior?"

"That," said he, "I cannot say, but I believe he was put to such punishment as was the poor nun who was given for her penance to say this verse—'Miserere mei Deus, quoniam conculcavit me homo' ['Have mercy on me, O God, because man has trodden me down': Ps 56: 1]—with a big threat that if she ever did the same thing again, she would have to say the whole psalm. But as for holy Elizabeth, I heard it said that she lived, and fared well, and was, for many a fair day after, a common harlot at Calais, where she quite merrily laughed about the whole thing."

"The more of a pity," said I, "that she was thus let go."

"That is true," said he. "But now, what do you say, what trust can we have—or at least, what certainty can we have—with regard to such things, when we see them so shamefully faked in the face of the world, so openly, and so many people so badly deceived that they would not have hesitated to swear, and some to stake their lives on it, that this whole production was the work of God's own hand, till the truth came to light and the slut was driven out of the church in the devil's name?"

"Actually," said I, "there was deception on the one side, and great folly on the other side. And just as that noble duke Humphrey astutely uncovered the deceitfulness of that pseudo-blind beggar, so did that noble lady the King's mother intelligently detect and uncover that beastly filth. And to tell the truth, there was cause enough in both these parties for the people to have reasonably garnered so much suspicion that, had they made sufficient inquiry and investigation into these matters, they could never have been so badly deceived. For they might well have doubted the word of a beggar whom they had met only recently, and who was quite likely to lie in order to gain, first, favor and, later, money. And also, people might well think that a young she-saint was not appropriate to be enshrined alive in a monastery, amongst a congregation of monks. And, moreover, in the end, in order that no such faked wonders should discredit bona fide miracles done by God, he in his goodness soon brought them both to knowledge. And so does he in his special care and providence always soon bring to light such falsehood and fraud, to the shame and confusion of the perpetrators. He did, for instance, in Bern, a big city in Germany, bring to knowledge the false miracles whereby certain friars were deceiving the people; for which they were publicly burned. And so God always brings such false miracles to light."

"No, no," said he, "there are many such, I guarantee you, that never come to light and are still being taken for quite genuine."

"You cannot very well guarantee it," said I. "For since God brought to light the false, faked miracle of the priests of the idol Bel in the olden time (this appears in the fourteenth chapter of the prophet Daniel), it is more likely that among Christians he will allow no such things to lie hidden for long.

And also, how can you guarantee that many of those miracles are false? For as long as there is no doubt that many are true, and you do not know of any which you know for a fact are false, you are not sure whether any are such or not."

"Why," said he, "that reasoning holds as well on the other side. For since I do not know of any which I know for a fact are true, I do not know whether any are true or not."

"No," said I, "that argument will not thus serve you. For though no one obliges you to believe that everything is true that is told for a miracle, yet some there are of which you must of necessity consider yourself certain, and about which you cannot, if you are a Christian, have any misgiving or doubt."

"Yes?" said he. "I would love to know which ones those are."

"Why," said I, "all that are recorded in the Gospel."

"Why," said he, "that I well know; but we are not talking about them, for they were done by God himself."

"Well," said I, "aren't they all? If you will not admit to being sure of any of those that are told about saints, what do you say about the miracles of the apostles, recorded by Saint Luke?"

"No," said he, "you are still taking me wrong, for I do not mean any skepticism regarding the miracles done in days of old by God for his apostles or holy martyrs, in corroboration and propagation of the faith. I mean only those miracles that people tell and talk of nowadays as being done at those images, where these shrines are, and where we ourselves see some of them proved plainly false. And yet told for so true, and so many fraudulent scoundrels affirm it, so many simple souls trust it, so many foolish folk believe it, that one can with good reason doubt all the rest."

"You have," said I, "more often than once spoken of a difference between the miracles done by God in olden times and these miracles that are done, or said to be done, nowadays at pilgrimage sites. But surely if you grant the miracles done in olden times, we need no more for the proof of our entire case. For I believe that pilgrimage sites and miracles done at them are very old things, and not things newly begun nowadays, unless you call a thousand years ago, or fourteen hundred years ago, 'nowadays.' For I am very sure that that long ago, and even longer ago, good Christian people did pray to saints and go in pilgrimage to their holy relics, and hold images in great veneration, and our Lord did work many wonderful miracles as proof of his high pleasure, to the conservation and increase of the devotion of his Christian people therein, as we find extensively written and reported in the godly books of holy Saint Gregory, Saint Augustine, Saint Jerome, Saint Eusebius, Saint Basil, Saint John Chrysostom, and many another old holy theologian of Christ's church whose books were not untranscribed these thousand years. And where you say, about miracles, that many are nowadays faked, so may it be that some were then also; but neither then nor now, either, were (or are) all faked.

"And any that were true, even if they were very few, would be enough for our argument. For if God had but with one miracle made it clear that he is happy and pleased that this thing be in his church, it would necessarily have sufficed for the Church against all the heretics in the world who would ever bark against the Church over it. And therefore there can be no doubt in the matter, when God has made his pleasure known by so many a thousand, and has done this in every era, not only nowadays but also a thousand years, or fourteen hundred years, and even more, too, before our day. And as for faked miracles, of which you speak so much: granted that there have been some of those, I yet truly think that neither in olden times nor now would Christ, among Christian people, allow such things to happen often, nor such delusion to last long, but that he does shortly, to the shame of the perpetrators (as has appeared with some) reveal and make manifest their falsehood, as he himself said of all such: 'What you whisper, one in another's ear, shall be

proclaimed out loud upon the ridge of the house roof ' [Lk
12: 3]."

15.

*The author shows that if, of those miracles that are spoken and
written of as having been done at various shrines and are commonly believed to be quite genuine, we knew for a fact that some
were deceitfully faked, that would still be no reason to doubt the
rest.*

"But let's take it as a given that, in the midst of so many
miracles as are daily spoken and written of as having been
done at various pilgrimage sites, you allege a difference between those and others. (We shall, as I said before, know
further your mind hereafter, as to why.) And let's also suppose that of those which have long been famous and always
taken for true, you yourself knew for a fact that some were
quite false. Would you therefore think that among all the rest
there was not one true one? What if you find to be wearing
make-up some lovely woman whose color you had thought
was natural? Will you never thereafter believe that any
woman in the world has of herself a lovely color? If you find
to be treacherous flatterers some folk who long seemed
friendly, will you take ever after all the world for such? If
some that everyone in the world would have sworn were
good, godly persons turn out to be utter hypocrites, shall we
therefore be suspicious of all others because of them, and
think there are no good ones at all?"

"By my word," said he, "I once rode in good company—
and, to tell the truth, *for* good company—to Walsingham, on
a pilgrimage, during which a good fellow's horse started
halting so badly that the fellow was forced to rent another
one and let loose the one he had been riding. That horse was
so lean and so pitiful, and halted so badly, that, unladen as he
was, he could scarcely keep pace with us. And when we had
thought we should have left him behind, suddenly he caught
sight of a mare, and forth he limped on three legs so lustily

that his master's horse with four feet could scarcely overtake him. But when the fellow caught him and came back, he swore in great anger all the oaths he could swear, that he would trust the 'halting Sir Thomas' the less for as long as he lived."

"What was that 'halting Sir Thomas'?" I asked.

"Why," said he, "their parish priest, who was, so he told us, as lean and as pitiful and as halting as his horse, and as holy, too. But since he would as long as he lived trust the halting priest the less on account of his halting horse, if I find a holy whoreson hypocritically halting, I shall not fail, as long as I live, to trust all his confreres the less."

"Well," said I, "you are being facetious. I well know that you will do better, whatever you say. I am sure that even if you see some white sapphire, or beryl, so well dissembled and so set in a ring that a quite good jeweller will take it for a diamond, you yet will not, for all that, doubt that there are in many other rings already set real diamonds indeed. Nor will you mistrust Saint Peter on account of Judas. And even though the Jews were, many of them, so evil that they put Christ to death, you yet are more well-informed, I well know, than was the lady who, in talking once with my father, when she heard it said that our Lady was a Jew, at first could not believe it, but said, 'What? Surely you are joking. I beg you, tell the truth.' And when it was so fully confirmed that she finally believed it, she said, 'If she was a Jew, then so help me God and all things holy, I shall love her the less for as long as I live.' I am sure you will not do that, nor be skeptical of all on account of some, either people or miracles."

16.

The author points out that anyone who did any investigating would soon find that at pilgrimage sites many great and undisputed miracles are wrought every day, and well known about. And in particular he speaks of the great out-in-the-open miracle recently worked at Our Lady of Ipswich on the daughter of the knight Sir Roger Wentworth.

"And as for the point that we spoke of concerning miracles done in our day at various images where these pilgrimage sites are, I could even tell you of some that were done so publicly, and that are so far from all cause of suspicion, and, moreover, testified to in such a sufficient manner, that anyone could seem almost mad who, upon hearing the whole matter, would doubt the miracles. Among which I dare boldly tell you for one the wonderful work of God that was, within these last few years, wrought in the house of a very honorable knight, Sir Roger Wentworth, on several of his children, and in particular one of his daughters, a very lovely young lady of twelve years of age, who was in an astonishing way vexed and tormented by our spiritual enemy the devil, her mind alienated and raving with contempt and blasphemy of God and hatred of all blessed articles, with knowledge and distinguishing of the blessed from the unblessed, when she had been given no information as to which was which. And after that, she was moved in her own mind and enjoined by the will of God to go to Our Lady of Ipswich. Along the way of which pilgrimage, she prophesied and related many things being done and said at the same time in other places, which were proved true; and, while lying in her trance, said many things that were of such wisdom and learning that very knowledgeable men greatly marveled at hearing from such a young and uneducated lady, when she herself did not know what she was saying, such things uttered and spoken as very well-educated men might have missed with a long study. And finally, being brought and laid before the statue of our blessed Lady, she there was, in the sight of many devout people, so grievously tormented, and in face, eyes, look, countenance, so gruesomely changed, with her mouth drawn to one side and her eyes laid out upon her cheeks, that it was a terrible sight to behold.

"And after many extraordinary things at the same time

visited upon several persons by the devil (through God's sufferance), all the rest, as well as the young lady herself, in the presence of the whole band of pilgrims, were restored to their good state, cured perfectly and instantly.

"And there was in this affair no pretext of begging, no suspicion of pretense, no possibility of fakery, no naiveness in the observers. Her father and mother, being quite respectable and rich, were extremely embarrassed at seeing such occurrences in their children; the witnesses were of a great number, and many of great repute, sound sense, and good experience; the young lady herself was too young to be faking; and the behavior itself was too abnormal for anyone to fake. And the end of the affair was virtuous, the virgin being so moved in her mind with the miracle that she forthwith, for all that her father could do, forsook the world and professed religion in a very good, godly order, the Poor Clares, where she has lived a good and godly life ever since."

17.

The messenger concedes that many of the miracles done at pilgrimage sites are genuine, but nevertheless lays out objections to these. He presents reasons and arguments whereby, he says, many people are moved to believe and think that those miracles that are done there are done by the devil, to set our hearts on the idolatry of worshipping images instead of God.

"But now, although, as I said, I could swear for you to that miracle and prove it to you in such a way that I know well you would be as far out of any doubt about it as you would be deep in the marvel of the miracle, and although I could mention to you perhaps several others, done recently at various pilgrimage sites, and prove them well too, yet I would like first to hear from you what distinction or difference it is that you make, and why you make it, between the miracles done in olden times and these that are done nowadays at these pilgrimage sites."

"Sir," said he, "somewhat, a little, I touched on that in the beginning, making, as it were, a passing shot at it. But I would be loath to hit it with a full-force and direct shot, since I have seen some with such arguments split the target in two that they seemed to knock over the whole thing, support and all. Which arguments I would be loath to allege in so fierce a manner, lest I might perhaps give you some occasion to think that I either was adding in something of my own or else, at the least, really was on that side and was a favorer of that faction."

"No, no," said I, "by all means don't fear that; for I am not so suspicious as to suspect someone of thinking ill just because he defends the worse side well by way of argument and reasoning. And also I trust that all their shots shall be so far too feeble to knock over the support that few of them shall touch the mark, many too faint to pierce the paper. And some too high, and some too short. And some land a bow's length wide of the support. And therefore I ask you not to refrain from bringing up everything that ever you have heard, or that you think can be said on the subject."

"Sir," said he, "since you can hear it so dispassionately, I shall not refrain from speaking it. And certainly, to begin with, all that I think true, I will not fail to acknowledge. For although I have long persisted in arguing with you against the giving of any credence to miracles done nowadays—in which resistance I have much the longer persisted because of some I have known before who were so far from belief in any miracles at all that, in all honesty, they made me halfway wonder whether they would say they believe there is any God at all, if fear and shame did not keep them from daring to say all that they seemed to think—yet, to tell the truth, I never heard anything said there that was weighty enough ever to move me to think that any rational argument could support the relentless skepticism of those who, among so many evident miracles as are done daily in various places, would believe that none at all are true. But really, as I began to get at a little in the beginning, whether these miracles are made by God, and for bona fide saints, or by the devil, for our deception and delusion, albeit I believe, and always will, as the Church does, yet some people occasionally say such things on this subject that I am driven to do as I do with other articles of the faith: stick fast to belief, for lack of any argument I can find to answer them with. For, first, they take as a premise that the devil can do miracles. And if we wish not to allow them to be called by that name, that will not get us anywhere, for if we want called by the name of 'miracles' only things done by God above nature, we nevertheless will not deny that God suffers the devil to work wonders which the people cannot distinguish from miracles. And therefore when they see them, miracles they will call them, and for miracles they will take them. Now, since it is true that the devil can do such things, by what means shall we be sure that God does them? And since the devil can do them, and we are not sure that God does them, why can we not as justifiably believe that it is the devil who does them?"

"Goodness," said I, "you told me that you have no use for logic, but now you play the logician, straight-out. However, one can turn that argument on its other side and say that since God can do them much better than the devil can, and we are not sure that the devil does them, why should we not rather believe that they are done by God, who can do them better? And where a wondrous work is wrought, it makes much more sense to ascribe it to God (the master of all masters) rather than to the devil (who can do nothing but by sufferance), unless we see some cause not to; something disallowing that work to be considered God's."

"Well," said he, "then it makes sense that we show you some such cause."

"There is," said he, "cause enough in that we see that God has in Scripture forbidden such image veneration, and has attached to it a great curse, such as in the law which you yourself spoke of before: 'Non facies tibi sculptile.' And in the psalm 'In exitu Israel de Egipto,' where he (by the mouth of the prophet) starts describing the folly of the people who worship those images that have ears and cannot hear, hands and cannot feel, feet and cannot walk, mouth and cannot speak [Ps 115: 5–7]. All of which absurdities and irrational follies appear as well in the veneration of our images as in that of the pagans' idols. And afterward he states the curses that shall take effect thereupon: 'Equally seeing may they be to them all: those who make them, and all those who put their trust in them.' And right after that, he states who it is that good people have their trust in, and the benefit that comes of it. He says, 'Domus Israel speravit in Domino, adiutor eorum et protector eorum est,' 'The house of Israel has put their trust in our Lord; the helper and defender of them is he.' Now, when the words of God are clear, and openly and obviously on this side, what sense does it make to believe the commentaries and interpretations of men such as you brought up just now, with which you would get around the true texts of God? Why should we give credence to the example of men's doings against the plain commandment of God's writings? And when Christ alone is our savior and our mediator to bring our nature back to God, and our only agent and advocate before his Father, and can help us the best and will help us the most, why shall we make either our Lady or any other creature our advocate, or pray to them, who in all likelihood do not hear us? For none of them can be present at as many places at once as they are called upon. And if they were, they yet would be no nearer to us than is God himself, nor as desirous of seeing us do well as is he who died for us. And therefore, when we not only do them reverence (which I do not mind their being done, for God's sake, as you said before), but also pray to them, we do Christ and God great insult. For if we pray to the saints as mediators and advocates for us, we take from Christ his office and give it to them. If we ask help and health of them, then we make them downright gods and deliver to them the power of the Godhead. For it is God alone who gives everything good, as witnesses Saint James: 'Every good and perfect gift comes from above, descending from the Father of lights' [James 1:17]. And surely if we consider how we behave toward them, though you say that all the honor given to a saint redounds to God, since it is done, as you say, not for their own sake but for his, yet I would not think that God is well content that we should for his sake give to any creature like honor as to himself. For Scripture says that he will not give his glory away from himself, nor to any creature like honor as to himself. And for that reason the universities, as I hear it said, have come up with a threefold difference in honoring. They call the one kind 'dulia': the reverence or honor that one person on earth gives to another, such as the slave to the lord. The second, 'hyperdulia': what one gives to a more excellent creature, such as an angel or a saint. The third, 'latria': the veneration, honor, and adoration that creatures give only to God. Which of these categories you put the venerating of images in, I am neither well enough versed in them to tell nor curious enough to care greatly. But this I see well: if any of all these three kinds of veneration is better than the others, the images get it. For they get all that we can ever give. For what do we give to God, when we do worship him in that fashion that they call 'latria,' that is not the same as what we give both to saints and to images? Does it consist in kneeling? We kneel to saints and their images. In praying? We pray as intensely to them as to God. In incensing, and in the setting up of candles? We incense them also, and set up for some saints seven candles to God's one. So that whatever fashion of reverence 'latria' is, the same is as generally done to saints and statues as to God. And not only to statues (which, though they have no life, yet have some humanlike shape and features), but, as some believe, to pigs' bones also, sometimes. For what reverent honor is there daily done, under the name and repute of a saint's relic, to some old rotten bone that was perhaps at one time, as Chaucer says, a bone of some holy Jew's sheep! Do we not see that some one saint's head is shown in three places? And some one whole saint's body lies in different countries, if we believe the lies of the people. And in both the places is the one body venerated, when the one or the other is inauthentic and one body is mistaken for another, perhaps that of a bad person for that of a good one. And yet will the priests of both places take offerings, and lure people there with miracles, too. In which case you must say either that the miracles of one place are false, and faked, or else that miracles do not make your matter good or prove your pilgrimage sites legitimate. And yet all this stuff might be much the better borne if it were true, what you defend these things with—when you say that in the venerating of saints and images, people venerate neither the former nor the latter as gods, but the images for the saints' sake, and the saints for God's. But, now, as it seems, the case is in fact far otherwise. For the people pray to the saints for their needs, putting, moreover, the trust for their petitions in the saints themselves, as though it was they and not God who did the granting. And it is in the images that the people put their trust, instead of in the saints themselves. For although it might stand to reason, as you have answered me, that, presupposing the miracles at these pilgrimage sites to be done by God, the people might then in accord with reason go seek out and visit such places as God has by miracles made it known that he would have himself or his holy saints approached and honored in, this answer is nevertheless only partly on-target and does not take care of the whole problem. For not only do the people visit these places and there do all the reverence to the saints that they could possibly do to God (with the hope of getting from the saints themselves their cure, which they should well know can be given only by God), and thus, by this behavior, make the saints God's colleagues—that is to say, the servants matches with their master, and the creatures mates with the Maker— but also they behave in as religious a fashion and show as fervent an affection to the statues of stone or wood as either to saint or to God. And manifestly do take these statues for the saints themselves, and for God himself. And put into these images, that they make pilgrimages to, their full hope and whole trust, that they should be putting in God.

"Which, besides what I have said before, is clearly shown in this: that they will make comparisons between Our Lady of Ipswich and Our Lady of Walsingham. As if they believe that one statue is more powerful than the other; which they would never do unless they put their trust in the statue itself instead of our Lady. And the people in speaking of our Lady: 'Of all Our Lady's,' says one, 'I love best Our Lady of Walsingham.' 'And I,' says the other, 'Our Lady of Ipswich.' By which words what does she mean but her love and her affection for the statue that stands in the chapel of Walsingham or Ipswich.

"What do you say when the people speak in this fashion in their pains and perils: 'Help, Holy Cross of Bradman!' 'Help, our dear Lady of Walsingham!' Is it not quite obvious that they either trust in the statues instead of in Christ and our Lady, letting go of Christ and our Lady, or at least so take those statues that they think they are actually, the one Christ, the other our Lady herself? And so, either way, we have the faith and devotion withheld from God, who should have it, and our hearts by these images blinded and set upon the lifeless chunks of wood and stone.

"Now see also the good fruit that follows therefrom. I will let pass the fraud and deception occasionally perpetrated there, sometimes by the priests, sometimes by beggars, in the making up of false miracles. Look what devotion people come there with. With the most come those who most delude themselves—those, I mean, who have the most trust and blind faith in these blind images. But most of those who come do so out of no devotion at all, but only for good company, to babble on the way there, and drink themselves drunk there, and dance and reel home. And even that is not all. For I tell you nothing now about the many disreputable gangs, and the many a lowlife and his ladylove, that make their illicit liaisons at these wholesome sanctuaries. And many a woman who seems an honorable housewife at home has the help of a procurer to bring her to mischief as she travels abroad on her pilgrimages. I heard once, when I was a child, the good Scottish friar Father Donald—whom I definitely take for a saint, if there be any in heaven—I heard him preach at the pulpit cross of St. Paul's that our Lady was a virgin and yet many foul meetings take place at her pilgrimage shrines. And loudly he cried out, 'Ye men of London, gang on yourselves with your wives to Willesden, in the devil's name, or else *keep* them at *heme* with you! Else ye'll be sorry!' And certainly many good men think this would be best, considering that those voyages are but wandering-about vanity or superstitious devotion, and the next thing to idolatry, when people have their affections attached to blocks and stones instead of to God. And now, this stuff being such, what wonder is it if (as I said before) the devil is glad to give attendance there and do for his part what he can to help his own schemes move forward? Or what wonder is it if God, in this accursed world, when we fall from him to others, and from the honor of him to that of his saints; when we do what the pagans did, worship idols instead of God, and all this by falling into following men's explanations rather than his own texts; what wonder is it if God in return does to us what he did to them, and lets the devil delude us as he did them, and make us fall for false miracles, since we knowingly fall for false gods?

"*They* say that," said he, "those who speak on that side. And much more yet; more than I can call to mind. But, assuredly, since you wanted me to hold nothing back, I have, as I could, rather added in a little, not of my own thinking, but of my own thinking up, than leave out anything I could think of that I had ever heard anyone claim to prove that the miracles done at pilgrimage sites are open to doubt as to by whom they are wrought; or, rather, to prove that they are not God's miracles, but the devil's wonders."

18.

The author postpones responding to the aforesaid objections, and first, by Scripture, he proves that the church of Christ cannot err with regard to any essential point of Christ's faith. And in this chapter are particularly discussed those words of Christ "Super cathedram Moysi sederunt. . . . Qui dicunt vobis facite, quæ autem faciunt nolite facere," about the authority of the Church.

"Assuredly," said I, "I, for my part, very sincerely thank you for your not having defended your side halfheartedly, like a corrupt attorney who would by collusion handle his client's case feebly for the pleasure of his adversary; for your having said for it, I cannot tell whether as much as anyone could say, but certainly, I believe, as much as you either have heard anyone else say or can come up with on your own. And, at the least, much more than I have heard from anyone else or could have come up with on my own. And undoubtedly (since you spoke of shooting in the beginning) this stuff, how close it comes to hitting the bull's-eye, we shall see later. But this I promise you: in doing so, it would have to knock over the support and all. For if it could hold and be abided by, and were as well able to be proved true as I trust to prove it false, then the target we shot at would be quite gone, for any security that we could consider our faith and Christendom to have.

"But, now, to come to the point: Since it is already agreed between us that there are at these statues and shrines either miracles performed by God, for the confirmation of his pleasure therein, or else wonders wrought by the devil, for our delusion and damnation, then if it can be made clear to us that they are not done by the devil, it will naturally follow that they are done by God. Or if they are proved to be done by God, for the good of his church, then it will be clear enough that they are not wonders wrought by the devil, for the deceiving of Christian people. And since either the one or the other of these alternatives, if proved, implies the refutation of your argument, I will attempt to demonstrate, and I hope to prove quite well to you, the correctness of our side, by one of these ways or perhaps by both; that is to say, as well in proving that God does these miracles as in disproving and confuting that they are done by the devil. And I would really like to deal first with your objections and answer them right away, while they are fresh, except that it seems to me better to postpone them for the time being, seeing that there are some things it will be necessary that we first agree on. Without this agreement we would be likely to argue at cross purposes and run so wild, so loose, that our case could have no ground, order, or conclusion.

"Now, if I were in this case to dispute with a pagan who wanted to make it a question between their miracles and ours, then although I would in the end have a clear case, it yet would of necessity be a long and very involved case before it should come to a conclusion. And whole books would it take up—both the refuting of theirs and the making of our own to them—especially since they do not accept our Scripture and there is between them and us nothing in common to rely upon but reason. And if we should dispute with a Jew, we would have less difficulty, since although he would deny the New Testament, we would yet have an agreement with him on reason and the Old Testament, where we would be at variance not about the text, but about the meaning and interpretation. For there we would have him adamantly contradicting us. But, now, since we will in our case be disputing and arguing with people who identify as Christians, our disputations are so much the shorter, in that we must necessarily be in agreement on more things. For we must agree in reason where faith does not refuse it. And, in addition, we will agree upon the whole corpus of Scripture, the New Testament as well as the Old. But in the interpretation we may perhaps hit a snag. Is it not so?"

"Yes," said he.

"Well," said I, "is there any other thing on which you think we will differ besides the interpretation of Scripture?"

"Not that I can recall," said he, "except the very issues that we are talking about, such as image veneration or praying to saints—about which people think there can be no great question if Scripture is rightly interpreted."

"You do," said I, "agree that such things as are mentioned in the Gospel as having been spoken by Christ to Saint Peter and others of his apostles and disciples were said not only to them, or only for them, but to them for their successors in Christ's flock, and through them to us all; that is to say, everyone who will belong to his party."

"What things do you mean?" said he.

"I mean," said I, "such as, for example, when he said, 'Nisi abundaverit iusticia vestra plusquam scribarum et pharisiorum, non intrabitis in regnum cœlorum,' 'Unless your righteousness abounds and exceeds the righteousness of the scribes and the Pharisees, you will never enter the kingdom of heaven' [Mt 5: 20]. And where he says, 'If you would enter into the kingdom of heaven, keep the commandments' [Mt 19: 17–23]. Did he not say such things to them for all the Christians who would come later?"

"I think yes," said he, "for that second statement, concerning the commandments. But as for the first, that their righteousness should be better than the righteousness of the scribes and the Pharisees, perhaps there he was speaking specifically to his apostles themselves, saying that they should not be like the scribes and the Pharisees, who commanded others to do many things and did nothing themselves."

"That is in my opinion," said I, "well taken, and thus does holy Saint Augustine expound it. But, since you think he addressed that statement to his apostles specifically, rather than to his whole entire flock, I ask you: do you think he was saying it only to them, or also to all the others who would later come in place of them and succeed them in office?"

"Oh, before God," said he, "he was saying it to all the bishops, all the prelates and spiritual rulers of his church, that there ever will be in the Church. He was forbidding them to bind and lay upon the backs of other poor people grievous burdens to the bearing whereof they themselves will not once lift a finger."

"Very well said," said I. "What, then, do you think about this thing that he said: 'Do such things as they command you to do, but do not do as you see them do'?" [See Mt 23:3.]

"By that," said he, "our Lord meant that all the people should do all that the prelates should command, as far as was commanded by God in the Law; but he meant no further. And thus he said that they sat upon the chair of Moses, and that he wanted them obeyed for that reason [Mt 23:2–3]. And there he meant in such things only as they should command that were by God commanded of the people in the law given to Moses. And that Christians should in like manner obey the bishops and prelates commanding only such things as he himself has commanded his people in his Gospel and his own law."

"And in nothing else?" said I. "What does it mean, then, what the Lord said in the parable of the Samaritan about his carrying the wounded man into the inn of his church, and delivering him to the innkeeper after having dressed his wounds himself with wine and oil; and leaving with the innkeeper the two coins of the two testaments, promising the innkeeper, in addition, that whatever more the innkeeper would bestow upon him, he would when he came back reimburse him for? [See Lk 10:33–35.] And also, in that text that we spoke of, our Savior said that the scribes and the Pharisees did (in addition to the law of Moses, on whose seat they sat) lay and firmly bind on other people's backs burdens to the bearing of which they would not lift a finger themselves; and yet, for all that, he ordered the people to do what their prelates ordered them to, even if the burden was heavy, and not quit doing it even if they should see the orderers do the exact opposite. For which he added, 'But as they do, do not you.'"

"By our Lady," said he, "I do not agree with this interpretation. For it makes all for the bonds by which the laws of the Church make us bound to more ado, almost, than the Jews were with Moses' law. And I know well that Christ said, 'Come to me, you who are overburdened, and I will refresh you' [Mt 11:28]. And his apostles said that just the law of Moses by itself, apart from the observances added to it by the scribes and the Pharisees, was more than the Jews were ever able to bear and fulfill. And therefore Christ came to call us into a law of liberty. And that was in taking away the bond of those wearisome ceremonial laws. [See Acts 15:10, Gal 5:13, Rom 8:21, and James 2:12.] And thus our Savior says, about the law that he calls us to, 'My yoke,' he says, 'is made-to-fit and easy, and my burden but light' [Mt 11:30]. Which shows that he meant to take away the tight-fitting yoke and lay on a more comfortable one. And to take off the heavy burden and lay on a lighter one. Which he did not do if he would have us laden with a big bundle of men's laws, more than a cart can carry away."

"The laws of Christ's church," said I, "are made by him himself and his Holy Spirit, for the good order of his people; and they are not, in hardness and difficulty of keeping, anything like the laws of Moses. And of that I dare, of necessity, make you yourself the judge. For if you really think about it, I believe that if you were, at this age that you are now, to choose, you would rather be bound to many of the laws of Christ's church than to the circumcision one alone. And as much comfort as we may think Christ called us to, the laws that have been made by his church are not half as much trouble or difficult to keep as are his own—the ones that he himself imposes in the Gospel—even if we set aside the counsels. It is, I feel, harder not to swear at all than not to swear falsely; to forbear every angry word than not to kill; to watch and pray continually than to do so on a few designated days [see Mt 5:33–37, Mt 5:21–22, and Lk 18:1]. And then what an anxiety and solicitude there is with the forbearing of every idle word! What a severe threat, from an earthly point

of view, for a small matter! Almost never was such a distressing thing said to the Jews by Moses as is said to us by Christ
in that statement alone, where he says that on Judgment Day
we shall give an account of every idle word [Mt 12: 36–37].
And then what do you say about the forbidding of divorce
[Mt 19: 3–9], and the revoking of the liberty to have several
wives, where they had the liberty to wed as they pleased if
they took a fancy to any that they came across in the war?"

"One of that ware is enough," said he, "to *make* for any
one man war."

"Now that is said in jest," said I, "but even if one eye
would be enough for an archer, he is still willing to keep two
in store, and would be even if they were sometimes sore, the
both of them, and should put him in some pain. Also, what
comfort do you call this, that we are obliged—under pain of
perpetual damnation—to suffer whatever kind of affliction
and shameful death, whatever kind of martyrdom, for the
profession of our faith? Do you believe that these ease-giving
words of his easy yoke and light burden were not spoken as
much to his apostles as to you? And yet what ease did he call
them to? Did he not call them to watching, fasting, praying,
preaching, traveling, hunger, thirst, cold and heat, beatings,
scourgings, imprisonment, painful and shameful death? The
easiness of his yoke does not consist in bodily ease, nor does
the lightness of his burden consist in the slackening of any
bodily pain (unless we are so oblivious that whereas he himself did not gain heaven without pain, we expect to get there
with play), but it consists in the sweetness of hope, whereby
we experience in our pain a pleasant taste of heaven. This is
the thing, as holy Saint Gregory Nazianzen explains, that
refreshes people who are laden and makes our yoke easy and
our burden light—not any delivering from the laws of the
Church (or from any good civil laws, either) into a sorry
liberty of slothful rest. For that would be not an easy yoke,
but a pulling of the head out of the yoke. And it would be
not a light burden, but all the burden removed, contrary to

the words of both Saint Paul and Saint Peter, who as well understood the words of their Master as these men do, and as a thing consonant and quite consistent therewith do command of us obedience to our superiors and rulers, of the one kind and the other, in things not forbidden by God, even if the things are hard and distressing. [See Eph 6: 5, Titus 2: 9— 3: 1, Heb 13: 17, and 1 Pt 2: 13–21.]

"But see, for God's sake, how we have run a great way further than I thought to go when I began, and have veered off from what we should be going ahead with."

"It is no loss," said he, "for there is a good thing well gotten along the way."

"Well," said I, "let's go back again to where we veered off. You agree that Christ spoke his words not to his apostles only, for their own time, but that whatever he said to them, he meant for all who would come after them. And in some part, what he said to them was for the priests and bishops only. Such as when he said, 'Vos estis sal terre,' 'You are the salt of the earth' [Mt 5: 13]. And in some part for the whole flock, such as when he said, 'Mandatum novum do vobis ut diligam invicem sicut ego dilexi vos,' 'I give you a new commandment: that you love one another as I have loved you' [Jn 13: 34]. Tell me, then, I ask you: when Christ said to Saint Peter, 'Satan has desired to sift you like wheat, but I have prayed for you, that your faith will not fail' [Lk 22: 31– 32], did he say this to him as a promise of the faith to be by God's help perpetually kept and preserved in Saint Peter only, or else in the whole Church—that is to say, the whole congregation of Christian people professing his name and his faith and abiding in the body of the same, not being excommunicated and cut off—meaning that his faith would never so utterly fail in his church that it would not abide and remain, whole and entire, therein?"

"Indeed," said he, "this is a good thing to reflect on. For although Christ for the most part, such things as he spoke to one, spoke to all (according to his own words, 'Quod uni dico, omnibus dico,' 'What I say to one, I say to all' [Mk 13:37]), yet some things he did say and mean in a particular manner when he said them. Such as when he told Saint Peter to come upon the water to him [Mt 14:28]; he did not tell the rest to come thus. And thus it may perhaps be that this other sentence, too, was spoken and meant in relation to Peter alone."

"That," said I, "will be very hard to hold. For his faith later failed. But since, upon his first profession of the right faith (that Christ is God's Son), our Lord made him his universal vicar and, under himself, head of his church; and since this first successor of his was to be the man upon whom and whose firmly professed faith he would build his church, and (of any who was only human) make the first and chief head and ruler thereof, he therefore declared to him that his faith—that is to say, the faith professed by him—would never fail in his church [Mt 16:16–19]. And it never did, notwithstanding his denial. For the light of faith yet always stood in our Lady, of whom we read in the Gospel that she stayed continually present to her sweetest Son, without fleeing or faltering. And with all the others we find either a fleeing from him, at one time or another, or else, after his death, doubt of his resurrection. His dear mother was the only exception. For the symbolization and commemoration whereof, the Church every year, in the Tenebrae lessons, leaves her candle still burning when all the rest, that symbolize his apostles and disciples, are one by one put out. And since his faith did in fact fail, and yet the faith that he professed abode always in our Lady, the promise that God made was (as it seems) not meant for Peter except as head of the Church. And thus our Lord added to it, 'And you, being converted one of these days, confirm and strengthen your brethren' [Lk 22:32]. In which, by these words, our Savior meant and promised that the faith would stand forever. So that the gates of hell would not prevail against it.

"Otherwise you could say that these words spoken to Saint Peter, 'Feed my sheep' [Jn 21: 17], were meant only for himself, and not as a commandment to any successor of his, or any bishop or prelate. And by that stratagem you could also say that these words of Christ's promise made to his disciples—that the Holy Spirit would instruct them in all things [Jn 14: 26]—were meant only for themselves, personally, and did not mean that he would through all time instruct his church, after their days. And when he said, 'Wherever two or three are gathered together in my name, there am I myself, among them' [Mt 18: 20], we shall by this stratagem say that this applied only to his own disciples in his own time, while he was here with them, and did not mean that he would be likewise present with other such congregations in his church later. And finally, then would these words be nullified, where he said, 'Lo, I am with you all the days to the world's end' [Mt 28: 20], if he meant them only with reference to those who heard him speak them. Then it would be evident that he had intended a church only of them and for their time. And then from their death on out to this day, everything was over."

"Indeed, sir," said he, "I can well agree that all such things were spoken by Christ to assure them that the faith would never fail in his church. However, if I dare express a doubt on that point, there is one thing that somewhat nags at my mind."

"Doubt on," said I, "between the two of us, and do not hold back. Don't hesitate to tell me what is bothering you."

"Sir," said he, "I think that God does not place any higher a value on faith than on charity. But as for charity and good works, they will, along with virtuous living, cool and decline in the Church, as our Savior says in the twenty-fourth chapter of Matthew: 'Because iniquity will abound, the charity of many will cool.' And it certainly seems to me that it is well nigh all gone already."

"God forbid," said I. "For albeit that it is greatly declining day by day, and a lot of people are bad, yet there are many good ones around, and always will be, even if they are few in relation to the multitude. And furthermore, it is not entirely the same with other virtues as it is with faith; that is to say, with knowledge and belief of the articles of our faith. I mean those articles that we are of necessity obliged to believe. For although the flock of Christ will never lack good, devout, virtuous people, yet both will the best be sinners and also much more of the multitude will always have the faith that I speak of than will have the goodness in way of living."

"Why so?" said he.

"For two reasons," said I. "One, the perversity of the people, on account of which they will not be as ready to live right as to believe right. For the people themselves will keep better the faith than other virtues, since it is less trouble to know what one should believe, and also to believe it when one knows it, than it is to do right. For though the knowledge and belief bring many to the labor of good works, yet the world in general and the frailty of our flesh, with the enticements of our spiritual enemies, make us willingly and wittingly, well knowing and believing in the right course, yet choose the wrong one, as does sometimes the sick man who, believing his physician, and also having had, plenty often, good proof by his own experience to his grief before, that some certain food or drink will do him harm, does yet of an importune appetite fall, for his little pleasure, to his great grief and harm."

"Another reason is," said I, "the goodness of God, who, no matter how far his people fall from the practice of virtue, yet will not, as he himself has promised, allow them to fall from the knowledge of virtue—not only for the manifestation of his justice (so that their own consciences may condemn them when they do the things that they themselves know to be bad), but also to the intent that they may still have among them a perpetual occasion of amendment. For if ever the faith were gone, and the church of Christ fallen into that error of believing vice to be virtue, and idolatry the right way to worship God, then they would have no norm to guide them to anything better. And therefore as long as we are not in error of understanding and faith, then no matter how we fall or how often we sin, we see the way to turn back, by grace, to God's mercy. But if faith were gone, everything would be gone, and then God would have here no church at all."

19.

The author points out that if the venerating of images were idolatry, then the Church, in believing it to be legitimate and pleasing to God, would be in a wrong belief and a fatal error; in which case the faith would have failed in the Church, whereas Christ has promised the contrary, as is shown in the previous chapter.

"Surely, sir," said he, "that God made his church to last not for a while but till the end of the world, with that there is no Christian who will not well agree. And since his church cannot stand without faith, which is the entry into Christendom (for as Saint Paul says, 'Accedentem ad Deum oportet credere,' 'Whoever would come to God must needs believe' [Heb 11: 6]), no one will deny that faith is and always will be in his church. And that his church, not only with regard to faith and the knowledge of the truths that need to be known for our soul's health, but also with regard to the doing of good works and avoiding of evils, is, has been, and always will be specially guided and governed by God and the secret inspiration of his Holy Spirit."

"Well," said I, "then if the Church has faith, it does not err in belief."

"That is true," said he.

"It would err," said I, "if it did not believe all the truths that we are obliged to believe."

"What else?" said he.

"What if we believed," said I, "all that is true, and, in addition to that, some other thing which is not only false, but displeasing to God? Did we not then err in our necessary belief?"

"What kind of thing do you mean?" said he.

"Such as," said I, "if some man believed in all three Persons of the Trinity—the Father, the Son, and the Holy Spirit—and, together with that, was convinced that there is a fourth Person besides, equal and one God with them."

"He must," said he, "necessarily be erring in his necessary belief, by which he is obliged to believe in the Trinity. That fellow believes in a Quaternity."

"That is," said I, "the whole Trinity plus one more."

"But we are not only not obliged," said he, "to believe in any more, but also obliged not to believe in any more."

"Very well," said I. "Then those who believe in too much err as much, and are as much lacking in right belief, as those who believe in too little; and those who believe something that they should not, as those who do not believe something that they should."

"What else?" said he. "And what then?"

"Good heavens," said I, "this: If we believe that it is a legitimate and good thing to do to pray to saints, and to reverence their images and do honor to their relics and visit shrines, and then, when we do these things, they in fact are not a good thing to do, but are displeasing to God, and regarded by him as a diminishment and taking away of the honor due to himself, and therefore are, before his Majesty, blameworthy and odious and taken as idolatry, is not this belief a deadly, pernicious error in us, and a plain lack of right faith?"

"Yes, before God," said he.

"But you grant," said I, "that the Church cannot err in the right faith that it is necessary to believe, which is given and always kept in the Church by God."

"True," said he.

"Then it follows," said I, "that in believing that saints are to be prayed to, relics and images to be venerated, and shrines to be visited and resorted to, the Church is not mistaken, and is not in error, but rather, the Church's belief there is correct. And along with that it also follows that the wondrous works done above nature, at such statues and shrines, at holy relics through prayers made to saints, are not done by the devil to delude the church of Christ with, since the thing that the Church is doing is a good thing to do, and not idolatry. Rather, by the great honor done to saints, God himself is the more highly honored, in that his servants receive so much honor for his sake. And from there it follows that he himself does the miracles, to show his approval thereof.

"Also, if this that you have granted is true—that God keeps and ever shall keep in his church the right faith and right belief by the help of his own hand that has planted it— then it cannot be that he will allow the devil to work wonders like unto his own miracles to bring his whole church into a wrong faith. And then if those things are not done by the devil, I trust you will not then deny that they are done by God.

"And thus is our case yet again doubly proved. First, in that you grant that God will not allow his church to err in regard to his right faith, and secondly (which follows therefrom), by the fact that he has by many visible miracles made it known that this faith and manner of observance is very pleasing and acceptable to him; miracles which, since they are proved to be done upon good ground and cause, are clearly shown to be done by God and not by our spiritual enemy."

20.

The messenger claims that the perpetual being and active presence of Christ with his church to keep it out of all condemnable errors is nothing else but his being with his church in holy Scripture; and the author asserts the contrary.

"What do you think?" said I. "Is there anything amiss in this argument?"

"I cannot really tell," said he, "what I could say in answer to it. But yet it seems to me that I have come to this point by some inadvertence in granting."

"Well," said I, "people say sometimes, when they want to say or do something and cannot quite get at it, but miss it and trip themselves up in the attempt, 'It doesn't matter,' they say, 'you can start over and amend it, for it is neither Mass nor Matins.' And although in this matter you have granted nothing that is not to my mind as true as the Matins, or the Mass either, yet if you consider yourself to have been overly swift in granting, I give you permission to go back and bring up again whatever you wish."

"In all honesty," said he, "it would in my own view be very hard to think otherwise than that God will always keep the right belief in his church. But yet, since we come to this conclusion by the granting of that point, let's take another look at it. What if people were to say what I myself once did hear someone say: that God perhaps does *not* always keep faith in his church, to give them information with as to when they do right and when the contrary? That, rather, since he has given them, and left with them, Scripture, in which they can sufficiently see both what they should believe and what they should do, he leaves them alone with that, without any other special tending of his to their faith and belief? For in it they can see all that they need to, if they will look at and study it. And if they will not, there is nothing but their own laziness and foolishness to blame. And whoever is willing to improve and be better can always get light to see how by having recourse to the reading of holy Scripture, which will stand a person in like stead as did, as you said before, the way that God safeguarded the faith before: by his special intermediaries in his church."

"If," said I, "it were thus, then to what avail would be Christ's promise 'Ego vobiscum sum omnibus diebus usque ad finem sæculi,' 'I am with you all days, to the end of the world'? [See Mt 28:20.] Why would he be here with his church if his being here would not keep his right faith and belief in his church?"

"Good heavens," said he, "these words are quite compatible with that. For God is, and will be until the world's end, with his church in his holy Scripture. Just as Abraham answered the rich man in hell by saying, 'They have Moses and the prophets' [Lk 16:29], meaning not that they had them all at that time present with them, but only that they had their books, so Christ, since Scripture has his faith contained in it (according to his own words, 'Scrutamini scripturas, quia scripturæ sunt quæ testimonium perhibent de me,' 'Search you the Scriptures, for they bear witness to me' [Jn 5:39]), therefore said, 'Ego vobiscum sum usque ad finem sæculi,' 'I am with you to the end of the world,' because his holy Scripture will never fail as long as the world endures. 'Heaven and earth,' he says, 'will pass away, but my words will never pass away.'

"And therefore in his holy writing is he with us still, and therein he keeps and teaches us his right faith, if we care to look for it; and otherwise, as I said, our own fault and folly it is."

"If God," said I, "is with us in no other way but in holy Scripture, then those words of Christ, 'I am with you to the world's end,' are somewhat strangely spoken, and are not like the words of Abraham to which you liken them. For Christ did not leave behind him one book of his own authorship, as Moses did, and the prophets. (And he was spoken of in their books, as he was in the Gospel.) And so if he had been speaking of and referring to Scripture, he would have said that they would have with them always his evangelists, the writers of his Gospels, just as Abraham said 'they have' Moses and the prophets, who were the writers of the books that the Jews had. Also, Christ said, 'I *am* with you till the end of the world'—not 'I shall be,' but 'I am,' which is the expression appropriated to his Godhead. And therefore that expression 'I am' is the name by which our Lord would, as he told Moses, be named to Pharaoh [see Ex 3:9–15], this being a name which from all creatures (since they are all subject to time) clearly distinguishes his Godhead, which is ever being and present, without difference of time past or to come. In which way he was not in his holy Scripture, for that had a beginning, and when those words were spoken, was not yet all written. For of the chief part, which is the New Testament, there was as yet, at that time, not one word written. And also we are not assured, by any promise made, that Scripture will endure to the world's end, albeit I truly think the substance will. But yet, as I say, we have no promise about that. For where our Lord says that his words will not pass away, nor one iota thereof be lost, he is speaking of his promises made, indeed, as his faith and doctrine were taught: by mouth and inspiration. He did not mean that of his holy Scripture in writing there would never be lost one iota. Of that, some parts are already lost; more, perhaps, than we know of. And of that we have the books in some part corrupted, through miscopying. And yet the substance of those words, what he meant, is known, even where some part of what was written is unknown. He says also that his Father and he will send the Holy Spirit, and also that he himself will come [see Jn 14:16–18 and 15:26]. To what end, all this, if he meant nothing more than that they would leave the books behind them and go their way?

"Christ is also present among us bodily, in the Blessed Sacrament. And is he there present with us for nothing? The Holy Spirit taught, I think, many things not in writing, and of which some part was never incorporated into Scripture, even to this day, such as this article which no good Christian will doubt: that our blessed Lady was perpetually a virgin, as well after the birth of Christ as before.

"Our Savior also said to his apostles that when they should be accused and brought to trial, they would not need to worry about their answer, it would right then be put in their minds. And by that he meant not only the remembrance of holy

Scripture (any quoting of which would have left the pagan judges cold and unaffected), but such words newly given them by God, inspired in their hearts, so effectual and confirmed with miracles, that their adversaries, even if they were angry at what they said, would nevertheless not be able to resist it [Lk 21:12–15]. And thus, with secret help and inspiration, is Christ with his church—and will be to the world's end—present and active. Not just spoken of in writing."

21.

The author shows that even if what the messenger said were indeed true—that is, that Christ remained with his church in no other way, but only by leaving to it his holy Scripture, and also that all of the faith is only therein—it still would then follow that as far as the requirements for our salvation make necessary, God gives the Church the right understanding of it. And from there it further follows that the Church cannot err regarding the right faith. From which is again inferred all that the messenger wanted to escape from before. And from which it also follows, in particular, that all the texts of holy Scripture which heretics cite against the venerating of images, or against any other point of the universal belief of Christ's Catholic Church, can in no way serve their purpose.

"But now I would like to know, since you suppose him to be in no other way present than in holy Scripture, does he or does he not give his church the right understanding of holy Scripture?"

"What if he does not?" said he.

"Good heavens," said I, "then you yourself well see that they would be as well off without it. And that the Scripture would stand them in as good a stead as a pair of spectacles would stand a blind friar in."

"That is quite true," said he. "But to take care of that problem, he has, in his wisdom and goodness, provided that Scripture be written in such a way that it can be rightly understood by the comparison and consideration of one text with another."

"Could it not also be," said I, "that some of those who do diligently read it, and diligently compare and consider every text, how it may accord with another, could yet, for all that, misinterpret and misunderstand it?"

"Yes," said he, "that could be. For else there would not have been as many heretics as there have been."

"Very true," said I. "But, now, if all the faith is in holy Scripture, and no part of it anywhere else in such a way as to negate that it must be learned altogether therein, would it, then, be sufficient to understand some parts rightly, and some other parts wrongly, in the essential points of our faith? Or must we, as far as the essentials of it are concerned, misunderstand no part?"

"We must," said he, "take wrongly no part as far as the essentials of our faith are concerned. Indeed, we must have so right an understanding of *all* of it that we conceive no condemnable error."

"Well said," said I. "Then if we must, we can. For if we cannot, we do not have to. For our Lord binds no one to an impossibility."

"We can," said he.

"If we can," said I, "then we can either by good luck fall into the right understanding, or else by natural reason come to it, or else by supernatural grace be led into it."

"That is true," said he. "It must necessarily be one of these ways."

"Well," said I, "we will not yet try to figure out which. No, I first want to know whether Christ has a church in the world continually, and will so have it to the world's end, or else has one sometimes, and sometimes none at all. We might, for instance, think that he had one while he was here himself and perhaps a while after, and maybe none at all ever since, and will not have one again till we know not when."

"No," said he, "that cannot in any way be. He must necessarily have his church continue uninterruptedly somewhere. For else how could he be with it continually to the world's end, in Scripture or otherwise, if it (the church with which he promised to be and continue to the world's end) should not continually last that long? Or how could those words of Christ be true, 'Lo, I am with you all days, to the world's end,' if before the world's end he should be away some days, since he would indeed be away from the Church some days if in some days he had no church?"

"Well," said I, "I want to know still one thing more. Can he have a church without faith?"

"No," said he, "that would be impossible."

"Indeed," said I, "so it would. For his church is a congregation of people gathered into his faith. And faith is the first substantial difference distinguishing Christians from heathens, just as reason is the difference dividing humankind from all the species of brute beasts. Now, then, if his church is and always will be continual, without any in-between times (in which there will be none), and without faith it can never be, and no part of the faith is, as you say, to be gotten elsewhere than in holy Scripture, and all of it must be had, and also, as we agreed a little while ago, there must be no error adjoined thereto, and therefore, as far as the essentials of the faith are concerned, no part of Scripture may be taken wrongly, but all of it must be understood rightly, and can be understood rightly by either luck, reason, or the help of grace, then it necessarily follows that by one or another of these ways the church of Christ has always, and never misses, the right understanding of Scripture, as far as pertains to what is required of us."

"That follows indeed," said he.

"Well," said I, "let pass, for the time being, what follows further? And since the Church does have it, let's first establish by which of these three ways the Church has it: whether by luck, reason, or grace."

"By luck," said he, "would be a poor having. For thus it might happen to have it and happen to lack it."

"Then," said I, "since it has it always, it cannot be by luck. What, then, do you think of reason?"

"As little," said he, "as anyone does. For I take reason for an obvious enemy to faith."

"You take it perhaps wrong," said I. "But we shall look further into that later on. But now, since that is what you think, you leave only the third way, which is the help of grace."

"No, surely," said he.

"Truly," said I, "it being the case that reason may between different texts stand in great doubt as to which way to lean, I think that God with his Holy Spirit leads his church into the consensus of the truth. For he himself said that the Holy Spirit (whom he would send) would lead them into all truth [Jn 16:13]. He said not that the Holy Spirit would at his coming *write* them all truth, or tell them the whole entire truth orally, but that he would by secret inspiration *lead* them into all truth. And therefore, surely, for a correct conclusion effected in such intermediaries by God himself, by the help of his grace (as you yourself grant) the right understanding of Scripture is ever preserved in his church from any such mistaking from which could follow any condemnable error concerning the faith. And from this there does immediately follow that besides Scripture itself, there is another present assistance and special tending that God gives his church, perpetually, to keep it in the right faith, that it not err by a misunderstanding of holy Scripture—contrary to the opinion that you expressed when you said that Christ's being with his church was only the leaving of his holy Scripture to us. And furthermore, supposing that God *were* present in no other way than you speak of, yet since it is proved that his church for all that does have the right understanding of Scripture, we are back at the same point that you were so much wanting to escape from. For if Scripture (and nothing but Scripture) does contain everything that we are obliged to believe, and to do, and to refrain from doing; and if God also therefore provides his church with the right understanding thereof, concerning everything necessary for us that is contained in Scripture, then from this there must necessarily follow the thing that you feared you had gotten wrong and rashly granted: that God always keeps the right faith in his church. And alongside of that, there follows further the rest of all that is in question between us: that the faith of the Church in the veneration that it believes to be legitimately given to saints, relics, and images is not erroneous but right. And alongside of that it also follows that the miracles done at such places are not delusions from damned spirits, but the mighty hand of God showing his pleasure in corroboration thereof, and in the excitation of our devotion thereto."

"Indeed," said he, "we have gotten back here by going forward, as one walks in a maze."

"Yet you have not," said I, "wasted all that effort. For though you have half a check on this point, you yet have (if you perceive it) mated me on another point, by one thing that is now settled between us."

"What is that?" said he.

"This," said I, "that I as well as you have assented to: that God has given his church the right understanding of Scripture as far as pertains to the essentials for salvation."

"On what point," said he, "has that mated you?"

"Why," said I, "you do not see that? No? Then I will not tell you, unless you pay me; or if I tell you, you yet will not win the game thereby. For since you do not see it yourself, it is but a blind-mate."

"Let me know it anyway," said he, "and I agree to take no advantage of it."

"On that bargain, all right," said I.

"You well know," said I, "that against this thing of venerating images and praying to saints, you laid certain texts of Scripture, to prove it forbidden by God and regarded by him as idolatry. And when, in answer to that, I laid the claim that people must go along with the meanings that the Church and holy theologians of the Church give to those texts, you said they were but men's false interpretations, that go against God's true texts. And now, since you grant, and so do I, that the Church cannot misunderstand Scripture to the detriment of the right faith, in essential things, and since you also acknowledge this thing to be such that it must be either the right belief and an acceptable way of worshipping God or else a wrong, erroneous opinion and downright idolatry, it necessarily follows that the Church does not misunderstand those texts that you or anyone else can cite and bring forward for that purpose, but rather that all these texts are to be taken and understood in such a way that they go not at all against the Church, but all against your own opinion in this matter.

"And thus have you suddenly made answer yourself to all those texts, out of hand, with a commentary of your own which is as true as any text in the Bible, and which no one in the world will ever be able to refute unless they would make Scripture serve the Church for nothing, or rather to its hindrance than furtherance in the faith. For that would be the case if it could be that God does not give the Church the correct understanding of it, but allows the Church to be deceived and deluded in errors by a mistaking of the literal meaning of the text."

"Goodness," said he, "this is indeed a blind-mate."

"Those two points," said I, "certainly seem to me to be two points as true and intelligible to a Christian as any axiom of Euclid's geometry is to anyone able to reason. For as true as it is that every whole thing is more than its own half, it is indeed just as true—and to every Christian, faith makes it just as certain—first, that Christ's church cannot err in any such article as God wills that we, upon pain of loss of heaven, believe; and from there it necessarily follows that there is no text of Scripture, rightly understood, by which Christian people are commanded to do something which the Church believes they can legitimately leave not done; nor any text whereby we are forbidden anything which the Church believes that one can legitimately do."

22.

Because the messenger had in the beginning shown himself to be avidly focused on the text of Scripture, little interested in the old Fathers' interpretations, and disparaging of philosophy and almost all seven of the liberal arts, the author therefore mentions in passing what harm has at times happened to befall some of those young men whom he has known to devote their study to Scripture alone, disdaining logic and other secular disciplines and showing little regard for the old interpreters. By reason of which harm the author asserts that in the study of Scripture the safe course is to use, with virtue and prayer, first the judgment of natural reason, for which secular literature is very helpful; secondly, the commentaries of holy theologians of the Church; and thirdly, above all else, the articles of the Catholic faith received and believed throughout the church of Christ.

"And, since we are speaking of Scripture now, and of the fact that the Church with regard to things necessarily requisite to salvation has the right understanding of holy Scripture, wherein I understand that you are studying the text alone, paying little heed to the old Fathers' interpretations or any of the liberal arts (all seven of which, except grammar, you consider good for almost nothing)—I have such a good opinion of you that I trust that all your studying will benefit you. But to some folk I have certainly seen so much harm come of it that I would never advise anyone else to take that approach to the study of Scripture."

"Why not?" asked he.

"Because," said I, "I have known some quite good minds that have set all other learning aside, partly out of laziness, shunning the effort and pains to be sustained in that learning, and partly out of pride, by reason of which they could not endure the refutations that would sometimes come down on their side in debates. Which dispositions their inward, hidden partiality toward themselves caused them to cover and cloak under the pretext of simplicity, and good Christian devotion borne to the love of holy Scripture alone.

But within a little while after, the damnable spirit of pride that (unbeknownst to themselves) lurked in their hearts has begun to put out its horns and show itself. For then have they longed under the praise of holy Scripture to show off their own study. Which, to have it seem the more to be esteemed, they have started off with a disparaging and deriding of all other disciplines. And because in speaking of such things as are common knowledge to all Christians, they could not seem superior, nor make it appear and seem that in their study they have performed any wonderful feat, to show themselves therefore extraordinary they set out paradoxes and surprising opinions against the common faith of Christ's entire church. And because they have there the old holy theologians against them, they resort to contempt and disparagement of them, either pitting their own idiotic glosses against the interpretations of the old astute and blessed Fathers, or else basing themselves on some words of holy Scripture that seem to speak for them against the many more texts that plainly speak against them, without accepting, or even giving ear to, any reasoning or authority of anyone alive or dead, or of the entire church of Christ, to the contrary. And thus, once proudly persuaded a wrong way, they take the bridle in the teeth and run forth like a headstrong horse, so that all the world cannot pull them back. Rather, with their sowing of sedition, their setting forth of errors and heresies, and their spicing of their preaching with denunciations of the priesthood and prelacy for the people's pleasure, they bring many to ruin, themselves included. And then the devil deceives them in their blind passions.

"They take for a good zeal for the people their malicious envy. And for a great virtue their ardent propensity to preach, in which they take such great pride on account of the people's praise that preach I think they would even if God by his own mouth were to command them the contrary."

"Why should you think so?" said he. "And how can you be sure that you are not misconstruing their good intentions? Oftentimes it is hard to judge a deed of someone else's that has some appearance of being bad, because the purpose and intent may make it good. So how dangerous is it, then, where the deed appears good, there to judge as bad the thought and intent, which who can see but God? As Scripture says, 'Only God sees the heart' [1 Sm 16: 7]. And therefore says our Savior [see Mt 7: 1 and 1 Cor 4: 5], 'Do not judge before the appointed time.'"

"I do not judge," said I, "except upon quite clear and obvious things. For I am speaking only of those whose erroneous opinions in their preaching, and whose obstinate pride in the defense of their worldly reputations, well make known their intentions. And some I have seen who, when they have for their terrible preaching been forbidden by their prelates to preach, have, that notwithstanding, proceeded on still. And who for the defense of their disobedience have amended the matter with a heresy, boldly and stubbornly maintaining that since they had the ability to preach, therefore they were by God bound to preach; and that no man, or law that was made or could be made, had any authority to forbid them. And this they thought sufficiently proved by the words of the Apostle, 'Oportet magis obedire Deo quam hominibus' ['We must obey God rather than men'—Acts 5: 29]. As though these men were apostles now expressly sent by God to preach heresies and sow sedition among Christians, just as the true apostles were in actuality sent and commanded by God to preach his true faith to the Jews. One of this sort, of this new kind of preacher, when asked why he was going around saying in his sermons that nowadays men were not really preaching the Gospel, answered that he thought this because he did not see any preachers being persecuted, or any conflict or commotion ensuing from their preaching. Which things, he said and wrote, were the fruit of the Gospel, because Christ said, 'Non veni pacem mittere sed gladium,' 'I have not come to bring peace into the world, but a sword' [Mt 10: 34]. Was this not a pious understanding, that because Christ would make a division among infidels, from the rest of them to win some, therefore these apostles would sow some cockle of dissension among the Christian people whereby Christ might lose some of them? For the fruit of conflict among the hearers and persecution of the preacher cannot easily grow among Christian people except by the preaching of some alien novelties, and bringing in of some newfangled heresies, to the contamination of our old faith.

"One I knew who, for all his pertinacity in that opinion (that he could and would and was bound to preach, any prohibition notwithstanding), when he was, after several bold and public defenses of it, finally reasoned with by a few honorable folk and not only shown the law that runs counter to his opinion, which law was made at a general council, but also proved to by plain authority of holy Scripture that his opinion was erroneous, considered himself so satisfactorily answered that he meekly acknowledged his error and offered to abjure it and submit himself to penance. But on the next day, when he came out in public, in the presence of the people, and saw there many who had often heard him preach, because of his secret pride he fell into such an obvious feeling of shame at the thought that they would be hearing him go back on his word, these persons who had previously held his sermons in high esteem, that at the first sight of the people he revoked his revocation and said loudly, so that he could well be heard, that his opinion was correct and that he had on the day before been mistaken in that he had confessed it to be wrong. And thus he held his own, stubbornly and irrationally, till the books were shown him again and he himself read them before all the people, and perceived the audience that stood about him to feel and understand the proud foolishness of his defense of his indefensible error. And then, at last, he gave himself up again. Such secret pride had our spiritual enemy conveyed into the heart of this man, who, I assure you, seemed in all the rest of his outward manner to be as meek and simple a soul as one could have seen in a summer's day.

"And some of them do not forbear to defend themselves with lies and even perjury, and some to stand firm in defense of their errors, or in mendacious denying of their own deeds, to their great danger of being burned, should their judges not show them more mercy than their malice merits. And all this they do because, as they themselves eventually admit, they think that if they recant, they will afterward be allowed to preach again. Such a scabby itch of vainglory do they get in their preaching that even should all the world be the worse for it and their own life lie on it, they would still long to be pulpited. And this, I say, is what has become of some who have with contempt of all other learning given themselves to Scripture alone—some who have not in the beginning perceived as such their passions of pride and sloth, but have accounted their vices as devoutness."

"Would you, then," said he, "condemn that manner of study by which a person has such a great passion for Scripture alone that he, for the delight thereof, feels little satisfaction in anything else? Would you have us waste our time on philosophy—the mother of heresies—and leave Scripture alone?"

"No," said I, "I am not of that mind. There was never a thing written in this world that is in any way comparable to any part of holy Scripture. And yet I think the other liberal arts also to be gifts from God, and not to be thrown away, but worthy to wait and give attendance upon theology, as handmaids. And on this point I am not alone in my thinking. For you will find Saint Jerome, Saint Augustine, Saint Basil, and many of the other old holy theologians clearly and obviously of the same opinion. And of theology I consider the best part to be contained in holy Scripture. And this I say for him who will have the time for it, and who is heading for the priesthood from young adulthood, and wanting to make himself, with God's help, fit for the office of a preacher.

However, if any man happens to be starting so late that he will perhaps not have the time for it, or if any young man has that intense an appetite for Scripture that he cannot find it in his heart to read anything else (which passion one is very fortunate to be given, if with grace and meekness one guides it well), then I would counsel him to study mainly for the virtuous ordering of his own passions, and to exercise great moderation and restraint in his preaching to others. And in all things to flee the desire of praise and showing off of knowledge, ever mistrusting his own inclinations, and live in fear and dread of the devil's subtle tricks and strategies. For though the devil continually lies in wait upon every preacher to reel him into pride if he can, yet his highest enterprise and proudest triumph consist in the bringing of a person to the worst misuse of that thing that is of its own nature the best. And therefore he makes a great effort, and a great boast if he brings it about, to have a good mind misuse its efforts spent on the study of holy Scripture.

"For the sure avoidance of which, my poor advice would be that in the study of holy Scripture one pay special heed to the commentaries and other writings of old holy Fathers. And also that before tackling either the one or the other, a person needs before all else (after grace and the help from God to be gotten with abstinence and prayer and cleanness of living) to come good and solidly instructed in all the articles and points that the Church believes. Once these things are firmly grasped and steadfastly presupposed as undoubtable truths, then they and reason will be two good rules by which to examine and expound all unclear texts, since the reader can be sure that no text is to be understood in such a way that it goes against them both, or against any of the points of the Catholic faith of Christ's church. And therefore if it seems to go against any of them, either the light of natural reason, along with a collating with other texts, will help him discover the truth, or else (which is the safest way) he will perceive the truth in the commentaries of the good theologians of old, to whom God gave the grace of understanding.

"Or, finally, if all that he can either find in other men's works or come up with by God's aid from his own reflection cannot suffice to convince him, and some text still seems to him contrary to some point of the Church's faith and belief, let him then, as Saint Augustine says, completely rest assured that some mistake has been made either by the translator or by the copyist, or, nowadays, by the printer; or, finally, that because of some hindrance or another he is not understanding it aright. And so let him reverently acknowledge his ignorance and go along with, and adhere to, the faith of the Church, as to an undoubtable truth, leaving that text to be better perceived when it shall please our Lord with his light to reveal and disclose it. And in this manner shall he take a sure way, by which he shall be sure of one of two things: either to perceive and understand Scripture right, or else, at the very least, never to take it wrong in such a way as might put his soul in danger."

23.

The messenger objects to the counsel of the author that the student of Scripture should rely on the commentators and on natural reason, which he calls an enemy to faith. And then the author answers those objections, proving in particular that reason is a servant to faith, and not an enemy, and must necessarily be consistent with faith and interpretation of Scripture.

"Sir," said he, "I will not deny that this way will do well. However, I fear that we would be likely to build up many errors if we were to square our timber and stones by these three rules of men's interpretations, reason, and faith—not that we find in Scripture, but that we bring with us to Scripture.

"For first, as for the commentators that you speak of, their commentaries tell us either the same tale that the text does, or else another. If they tell me the same one, I believe them only because the text says the same. And if they tell me another, then I believe them not at all, nor should I at all, unless I should believe men more than I believe God.

"And as for reason, what greater enemy can you find to faith than is reason, which contradicts faith on every point? And would you then send off to school together those two that can never agree with one another but are ever ready to fight one another and scratch each other's eyes out along the way? It also seems somewhat strange that when God has quite sufficiently left us in his holy Scripture his doctrine whereby he would have us informed of all such things as he would have us believe and do or leave not done, and has left us Scripture for no other reason than that it should remain to us as the testimony of his will (which is stated to us in writing so that we cannot not deny that we were informed of it), and there is no other reason why Scripture should be given us but to tell us his pleasure and stir us to fulfill it, we shall now not shape our faith according to Scripture, but first fashion us a faith ourselves and then shape God's Scripture according to that, and make it agree with that. This would indeed be a good, easy tactic for a lazy mason who is a bad workman: to make him a carpenter's square, and ruler, of lead, so that when he does not want to go to the trouble of hewing the stone to the square, he can bend the square to the stone, and thus still bring them together, leastways."

"As for the old commentators," said I, "they tell you the same tale that the text does, but they tell it to you more plainly, as we will more talk about later on. But surely you beguiled me just now in selling reason so short, for truly I never would have thought that you would, in regard to Scripture, like less a wise person than an irrational reader. Nor can I see why you should reckon reason for an enemy to faith, unless you reckon every man for your enemy that is your better and does not hurt you. Thus would one of your five senses be an enemy to another. Our sense of touch would detest our sense of sight, because we can see further by four miles than we can feel. How can reason—unless reason is unreasonable—more disdain to hear the truth of any point of faith than to see the proof of many natural things of which reason can no more arrive at the cause than it can in the articles of the faith? But always, for any power that reason has to perceive the cause, she will judge the thing impossible after she proves it true, unless she believes her eye to be better than her understanding.

"When you see a magnet draw iron to it, it does not grieve reason to look at this; no, reason takes pleasure in beholding something that surpasses her power to understand. For it is as plainly against the rule of reason that a heavy object should move alone in any direction other than downward, or that any physical thing should draw another with no touching, as is any article of the faith. Nor has there ever yet been a cause assigned by reason that people can perceive as probative, except only that it is a hidden property of the magnet, which is as much as to say 'I have no idea what.' And yet, as I say, reason can believe that thing well enough, and not be angry about it or fight against it. And yet all the rules that she ever learned continue to tell her that it cannot be."

"Yes," said he, "but a man's own eyes tell him that it can be. And that must needs convince him."

"Can a man, then, better trust his eyes," said I, "than his mind?"

"Yes, of course," said he. "What can he better trust than his eyes?"

"His eyes can," said I, "be deceived and think they see what they do not see, if reason gives over its hold. Unless you think the magician blows those little balls through the goblet's bottom, or cuts your belt, in front of your face, in twenty pieces and makes it whole again, or puts a knife into his eye and sees never the worse. And turns a plum into a dog's turd in a boy's mouth."

Now a crazy thing happened. At that very moment one of my servants came to ask whether they should get dinner ready!

"Wait a minute," said I, "let's get some better food first."
And at that your friend and I began to laugh.

"Well," said I, "don't be in any hurry yet, for a little
while." And so he went on his way half flustered, thinking
he had acted or spoken somewhat like a fool, as he was one
that was indeed not very sensible, and prone to do so.

And then I said to your friend, "Now you see that reason
is not so proud a dame as you take her for. She sees done in
fact by nature what she cannot perceive how, and is quite
content with that. She sees a silly fellow deceive her sight,
and her mind as well, and she takes it quite cheerfully, and is
not angry that the magician will not teach everyone his craft.
So do you think, then, that she will take such high umbrage
at God himself, her Master and Maker, doing what he
pleases, and then telling her what, and not telling her how?"

"I ask you," said I, "how do you know that our Lord was
born of a virgin?"

"Goodness," said he, "by Scripture."

"How do you know," said I, "that you should believe
Scripture?"

"Goodness," said he, "by faith."

"Why," said I, "what does faith tell you on this?"

"Faith," said he, "tells me that holy Scripture is true
things written by the secret teaching of God."

"And by what means do you know," said I, "that you
should believe God?"

"By what means?" said he. "What an absurd question.
Everyone can easily know that."

"That is true," said I. "But is there any horse or any ass
that knows that?"

"None," said he, "that I know of, unless Balaam's ass
understood anything of that [Nm 22:28–30]. For he spoke
like a good rational ass."

"If no brute animal can know that," said I, "and every
human being can, what is the reason why humans can and
other animals cannot?"

"Indeed," said he, "it is because humans have reason and the others do not."

"Ah, well, then," said I, "one must necessarily, then, have reason in order to be able to tell what one should believe. And so must reason not resist faith but walk with her, and as her handmaid so wait upon her, that as contrary as you take her to be, the reality is that faith never goes without her. But just as if a maid is allowed to get out of control, or have a few too many, or grow too proud, she will then grow profuse in speech and bandy logic with her employers and behave sometimes as if she were insane, so if reason is allowed to run wild and grow overly high-spirited and proud, she will not fail to fall into rebellion against her master's faith. But on the other hand, if she is well brought up and well guided and kept in good composure, she will never disobey faith, being in her right mind. And therefore let reason be well guided, for assuredly, faith never goes without her.

"Now, in the study of Scripture—in figuring out the meaning, in reflecting on what you read, in pondering the propositions of various commentaries, in putting together and comparing different texts that seem contradictory but are not—albeit I do not deny that grace and God's special help are the big thing here, God does nevertheless use as an instrument for that purpose our reason. God helps us to eat also, but yet not without our mouth. And just as the hand becomes the more nimble by the practicing of some feats, and the legs and feet the more swift and sure by habitual walking and running, and the whole body the more wieldy and healthy by some kind of exercise, so too there is no doubt that by study, effort, and exercise in logic, philosophy, and the other liberal arts, reason is strengthened and invigorated, and judgment—both in them and also in orators, laws, and historical writings—much matured. And although poetry is by many people taken for nothing but flowery words, it yet much helps the judgment and, among other things, makes one well equipped with one particular thing without which all learning is half lame."

"What is that?" said he.

"Indeed," said I, "a good mother wit. And therefore, in my opinion, in a mad frame of mind are these Lutherans who would now have all branches of learning, save Scripture alone, completely thrown away. These things (if one has the time for them) are, as it seems to me, to be taken and had, and with reason brought (as I said before) into the service of theology. And as holy Saint Jerome puts it [in Epistle 70], 'The Hebrews well despoil the Egyptians when Christ's learned men take from the pagan writers the riches and learning and wisdom that God gave to them and employ the same in the service of theology about the profit of God's chosen children of Israel, the church of Christ, which he has out of the hard, stony pagans made the children of Abraham.'"

24.

The messenger objects to the counsel of the author that the student of Scripture should bring along the articles of our faith as a special rule to interpret Scripture by. And the author confirms his counsel given in this regard, showing that without that rule, one could easily fall into great errors in the study of holy Scripture.

With this your friend was, as he himself put it, "somewhat satisfied" that reason was not so great an enemy to faith as she seemed. But yet he thought that she should have need rather to be well bridled than to bear much rule in the interpretation of Scripture. But as for the other point—that it is necessary for us to bring the faith with us already, as a rule to learn Scripture by, when we come to Scripture to learn by it the faith—this thing he thought in no way proper, but something, he said, much the same as if we wanted to go make the cart pull the horse.

"Well," said I, "we will soon see whether the cart pulls the horse or the horse the cart. Or whether we are even, perhaps, so blind that we cannot see well which is the cart, which is the horse."

"First," said I, "tell me, how old would you have someone be before they come to the study of Scripture?"

"By my faith," said he, "I would have the child of any Christian man start out there very young, and there continue all his life."

"In all honesty," said I, "I see nothing wrong with that, so long as you do not mean that you would have him all his life learn nothing else. And even that I could go along with, too, and quite well approve of, in some cases. But yet, if he did never in his life learn anything else, how old do you think he would be before he learned in the Bible the articles of his Creed?"

"I cannot readily tell," said he, "for I have not seen this put to the test."

"Well," said I, "since we are not sure how long in coming the learning there would be, would it not then be best that for that while he were taught his Creed before, in his own mother tongue?"

"I do not deny that," said he, "that he should learn his Creed before, because every Christian man's child should, by the law, know his faith as soon as he can. But I say that he should not therewith take it upon himself to judge and examine holy Scripture by it."

"Well," said I, "let this Christian child of ours alone for a while, and let's suppose that there was a good old idolater who had never in all his life heard anything of our Creed, or of any other god than only the man in the moon, whom he had watched and worshipped every frosty night. If this man could suddenly have the whole Bible translated into his own language and read it through, do you think that he would thereby learn all the articles of the faith?"

"I think," said he, "that he could."

"You think so?" said I. "I put the case that he believed that the whole Book was lies."

"Good heavens," said he, "by the Book itself he can learn the contrary. For the Book in telling its tale confirms its tale and teaches it to be true."

"What you say would be quite true," said I, "if it were the same thing to read a thing and to learn a thing. But, now, there could be another book written also, with lesser wonders, and fewer, and therefore less unlikely, and yet all untrue. So how, then, will he be given to know that this book telling such incredible wonders is true?"

"No," said he, "that thing he must needs believe, or else he can perceive nothing."

"Well," said I, "then there is one point of faith, one great lesson, to be learned outside of the Book, that must be learned somewhere, from either God or man, or else the whole Book will do us little service. And from whom we shall learn that, we shall see later. But now suppose that this old idolater was thoroughly convinced in his mind that the entire Book was true. Do you think, then, that he would find out therein all the articles of our faith?"

"I think," said he, "that he would."

"You think so?" said I. "So be it, then. But do you think that he will find them all out in a week?"

"No," said he, "that he cannot do."

"Well," said I, "since he at any rate will not find them all out in a day, let us leave him a little while in the searching, and we shall come back to him later and see what he will have found. And in the meantime we shall go look in again upon our good little godson, the boy, by golly, that we just now christened and taught his Creed and set to Scripture. Would this child need to know no more of his faith than his Creed before he goes to Scripture?"

"It seems to me," said he, "that it would be enough."

"Be it so, then," said I.

"What if he should by chance find some text of Scripture that seemed to him to be contrary to his Creed? If, for example, he happened upon the reading of these words—'Dii estes et filii excelsi omnes,' 'Gods are you all, and children of the high God' [Ps 82: 6]—what if he were to think that since in these words it is said that all good people are children of God, Christ our Savior was therefore not God's only-begotten Son, but the kind of son whom God, by the prophet, calls all good people?"

"He could not think that," said he. "For he would in other parts of Scripture find many passages that would well show him the contrary."

"Well said," said I, "and very true. But now, in the meantime, would you have him believe in accord with what that text seems to him to mean, against his Creed, until he has found another text in Scripture that answers it and seems to him to say more plainly the contrary?"

"No," said he, "not for one hour. For he sees that though other good persons are called God's children, and gods, they yet are not real gods, and so they are God's children not really (in the sense of naturally, by generation), but by acceptance, whereas the Creed says of our Savior that he is God's only-begotten Son, which shows him to be his son by generation."

"That is," said I, "very true, and observed good and logically, and according to the true, right faith. But now observe that you make him right away fall to the squaring of his stones like that lazy mason that you spoke of, with his rule made of lead. For now you make him examine the truth of this psalm text by an article of faith which he brought with him, and by a deducing—a process of reasoning. And so you right away find both these rules necessary to the explication of Scripture. Of which two you would in the beginning admit neither the one nor the other.

"But now go further. What if on the basis of the text 'Homines et iumenta salvabis Deus,' 'God, you will save both man and beast' [Ps 36: 6], he were to think that animals have immortal souls, as men have, and that both man and beast will in the end be saved, and so no mortal sin will be punished with everlasting pain—what if he should think these things until he came to other texts that should well prove the contrary? Would that be best? Or would it be better that besides his Creed, he had knowledge before of these articles of our faith—that only our souls are immortal, and not those of animals also, and that the pains of hell will be for sinners everlasting—and that he can thereby, with reason joined thereto, perceive that by this text, 'You will save both men and beasts,' is meant some other kind of saving and preserving, here in this world, and not that of bringing both to heaven?"

"All this he could know," said he, "by Scripture itself well enough."

"That I know well," said I. "And yet, as plainly as Christ speaks of hell in the Gospel, Origen, for all that, who was a man neither wicked nor unversed in Scripture, could not so clearly see it as not to say the contrary, and take the words of Christ in a wrong sense. And he would, perhaps, with someone who fixed only upon the words of Scripture (departing from the right sense thereof, which God and his Holy Spirit has taught his church), there bring him to such a bay that he—not just our child, but even a man well up in age and very advanced in Scripture—would in the end find himself having to betake himself to the faith of Christ's church.

"Now, suppose our child should keep reading the text of Scripture without concerning himself with the commentaries, and without any further instruction on the points of our faith than what is specified in our common Creed—which was written in the beginning, as a brief reminder by the apostles, who were not setting out in so short a thing, and clearly explaining, all that we are obliged to believe. Although he would well find in Scripture many plain, clear texts whereby the divinity of our Savior and his equality with his Father can be proved quite sufficiently, he yet would not be unlikely, on account of such other texts as seem to show him to be less than his Father, to fall into the sect and heresy of the Arians. And against those other texts, proving his equal divinity, to contrive such false glosses as they did. Whereas being previously taught, and having it confirmed by the faith of the Church, that our Savior is one God and one equal substance with his Father, he will well perceive and understand thereby that all the texts that seem to show him as less are to be understood as referring not at all to his divinity, but to his humanity only. Just as when we speak colloquially of ourselves and our own nature and say that we will die and worms eat us up, and turn us all into dust, we mean by all this our body only, and in no way intend thereby to deny the immortality of our soul.

"We could not dine today if I were to mention to you one-tenth of the things that we must needs (upon loss of heaven) believe, which neither our child, with only his Creed, and much less our old idolater, without creed, will so find out by Scripture but that both of them will be quite likely to take Scripture as backing up the wrong side unless we take with us for a rule of interpretation the articles of our faith."

25.

The author, taking the occasion of certain statements made by the messenger, affirms the preeminence, necessity, and profitability of holy Scripture, pointing out, nevertheless, that many things have been taught by God not in writing. And that many big things still remain that way—unwritten—about truths it is necessary to believe. And that the new law of Christ is the law so written in the heart that it will never not be in his church. And that the law there written by God is a right rule by which to interpret the words written in his holy Scripture. Which rule, along with reason and the old interpreters, the author shows to be the really safe way by which to wade in the great stream of holy Scripture.

"Why, then," said he, "this would be as much as to say that God did not write well his holy Scripture, if he caused it to be written in such a way that people can so easily get tripped up therein that they are as likely—or, as it seems to you, more likely—to fall into a false way than to find out the true one. And it would be better, then, that God had not given us Scripture at all, than to give us a way to walk wherein we would be more likely to sink than to save ourselves."

"Holy Scripture," said I, "is such as I have said, and yet in no way does it follow from this that God has not caused it to be written well, or that it would have been better that he had kept it from us. And albeit that this point provides a great opportunity for a long discourse—explaining and making evident that God has in that writing of holy Scripture employed such high wisdom, and shown such a wonderful restraint, that the very strange familiar fashion thereof can well make it known to the good and the wise that as it was written by men, so was it composed by God—yet, passing over the praiseworthiness, I will just say a thing or two in answer to such blameworthiness as you lay thereto. For it is almost a universal thing among people, to speak at times as though they could amend the works of God. And they are few, I think, who do not think that if they had been on God's board of advisers in the making of the world, though they dare not be so bold as to say that they could have done it better, yet if they could have been in charge of it, he would have made many things in a different fashion. And for all that, if he would yet call us all to council and change nothing till we were all agreed on everything, the world would quite likely keep going till Judgment Day as it is going already— only I don't know that we wouldn't all agree to be winged.

"But as for Scripture, to put it succinctly, God has so devised it that he has given the world an inestimable treasure there, as the case stands. And yet we perhaps would have had no need of it if the wounds of our own folly had not of our great poverty and God's great goodness required it. For at our creation he gave but two or three precepts, by his own mouth, to our first parents. And as for all else that they were to do, the reason which he had planted in their souls gave them sufficient notice thereof, the whole sum of which consisted, in effect, in the honoring of God and God's friends, with love of each to the other and to their offspring and lineage. But the precepts that he gave by mouth were three, two of them commandments (begetting and eating) and the third a prohibition (the tree of knowledge). And that one was for them continual, whereas the other two, albeit they were bound to them by precept, they and their posterity were yet not bound to at all hours and all places. It was necessary in the beginning to give them knowledge of them, inasmuch as they had no hunger to direct them to the one nor sensual, rebellious appetite to direct them to the other. But once they were apprised of them by God, then did reason interpret the rest. By it they knew that they should eat for conservation of their bodies, and procreate for propagation of their kind. And since they realized that these two things were the end and intent of those commandments, they thereby consequently knew when it was the appropriate time and place and occasion to fulfill them. But once they had, at the subtle persuasion of the devil, broken that third commandment in tasting the forbidden fruit, being then expelled out of Paradise, then, concerning their food and procreating, they had not just reason showing them what was honorable and profitable, but also sensuality, what was beastly and pleasurable. Which sensuality labored so busily to cause people to put pleasure ahead of what was wholesome and proper that for the resistance thereof, it then came to be the spiritual business and occupation of man so to maintain and train the body as not to allow it to master the soul, and so to rule and bridle sensuality as to make it subject and obedient to reason, just as God willed the woman to be subject and in obedience to the man. Wherein God would have us learn rather to let our sensual organs moan and groan than to pursue their own harm and ours too. Just as it would have been better for our father Adam and us all if he had let his wife, our mother Eve, be sad and angry both, and had, like a woman, wept too, instead of eating the apple for companionship, to please her with.

"Now did all the sin soon spring up, for the most part upon the occasions of feeding and procreating, whereof sprang covetousness, gluttony, sloth, wrath, and lechery. And many times pride and envy, as one perceiving himself to be in these things in better or worse condition than another thus began to conceive an esteem of himself with a contempt of the other, or envy and hatred toward someone. Except that pride sometimes also sprang out of the soul, and so liked itself that it envied the better, as Cain did Abel; and in order to be the more esteemed, pride longed inordinately to get by covetousness and greed many folks' livelihoods in his own hands, to make other folks serve him and honor him and depend on him out of necessity.

"And for all these evildoings sensuality was always ready to administer material; and by all the doors and windows of the body—touch, taste, smell, sight, and hearing—it never ceased to send in temptations to the soul. Nor did the devil, for his part, ever cease to diligently put them forward. Against whom did reason resist, with good counsel given to the soul; and good spirits appointed by God gave their help also; and God assisted with his aid and grace, where he found the person willing to work therewith. And in this manner continued man for a long time, not without revelation of Christ one day to come. Which faith, delivered to the father, went by mouth to the son, and so on from child to child, heard and believed among them. And whatever else was God's pleasure, that nature and reason could not clearly show them, God in his goodness gave them sure knowledge of by special messages, as he did to Noah, Lot, Abraham, and several others, of which messages some were later written and included in Scripture, but probably not all. For it is quite likely that the patriarchs in several things that they did (for instance, their several marriages and some other such things that were, by them, rightly done for the time) were explicitly commanded those things by God, for reasons well known to himself and unknown to us—things now forbidden us, and therefore unlawful for us, unless God's like ordinance or dispensation should hereafter, in general or in particular cases, be revealed to the contrary.

"But later it was the case that, the world getting worse, quite good and virtuous lineages declined and deteriorated and, by the vile consorting of evil people, fell by misconduct into such a blindness that although there were always some who perceived well their duty, yet the common people of the children of Israel were by custom of sin so blinded in their natural knowledge that they lacked in many things the right perception that reason—had it not been by evil custom corrupted—might very well have shown them.

"For the remedy whereof, God, of his endless mercy, by the law written with his own finger unto Moses on the tablets of stone [Ex 31:18], by the Ten Commandments, put back into remembrance certain dictates of natural law which their reason (overwhelmed with sensuality) had then forgotten. And to the end that they should keep his behests the better, he gave them a great heap more of laws and rituals to keep them tightly restrained in, from wildly straying abroad. And wrought great wonders that they should well see that those things were his own doing, whereby they might have the more fear of transgressing them. And there, in writing, he gave also an intimation of Christ: that God would one day send them a descendant of theirs to whom they should give hearing instead of Moses [Dt 18:15–19]. Also, before as well as after, through patriarchs and prophets, by figures and prophecies, God did not cease to foreshadow his coming, his reason for coming, his living, his dying, his resurrection, and his holy acts, in such a way that had pride and envy not prevented it, the figures and prophecies set and compared with his coming, demeanor, and doings might well have made all the Jews recognize him. And for the perceiving and good understanding of the written law, he sent always some good men whose words, right living, and sometimes also manifest miracles performed therewith, never left destitute of sufficient knowledge those who longed to learn the Law. Not to push it, or argue over it for glory, but to teach it in turn, meekly. And (as far as human frailty could allow) especially to fulfill and keep it.

"Finally, after all this, when the world was in a worse state of decline and ruin of all virtue, then came Christ our Savior to redeem us with his death and leave us his new law, whereof was prophesied long before, by the prophet Jeremiah, 'Lo, the days are coming, says the Lord, when I shall order and dispose to the house of Israel and the house of Judah a new covenant, or testament. I shall give my law in their minds. And I shall write it in their hearts. And I will be their Lord, and they shall be my people' [see Jer 31:31–33 and Heb 10:16]. This law written in people's hearts was, in accord with the words of the prophet, first brought by our Savior to the house of Israel and the house of Judah, he having been, as he himself says, sent specifically to them. 'I am not sent,' says our Lord, 'but to the lost sheep of the house of Israel' [Mt 15:24]. And also he said, 'It is not good to take the bread from the board of the children and throw it to dogs' [Mt 15:26]. But yet not only did the ready tractableness of some pagans cause them to become partakers of that bread, but also, soon after, the stubbornness and obstinate unbelief of the Jews caused Saint Paul and the apostles to say to their faces, 'The Gospel of Christ was ordained by God to be first preached to you. But since you refuse it, lo, we depart from you to the Gentiles' [Acts 13:46]. And thus the Church was gathered from, in place of them, all the world at large. All of which notwithstanding, there were at that time many converted and made good Christians from among the Jews; and many of that same people have turned to Christ since; and, in the end, the time shall come when the rest that shall then be left shall save themselves by the same faith [see Rom 11:15].

"This is called the law of Christ's faith, the law of his holy Gospel. I mean not only the words written in the books of his evangelists, but much more especially the substance of our faith itself, which our Lord said he would write in people's hearts; not only by reason of the secret operation of God and his Holy Spirit in justifying the good Christian (by the working either with the person's good will, to the perfection of faith in their soul, or with the good intent of the offerers, to the secret infusion of that virtue into the soul of an innocent infant), but also by reason of the fact that he first without writing revealed those heavenly mysteries by his blessed mouth through the ears of his apostles and disciples into their holy hearts—or rather, as it seems, it was inwardly infused into Saint Peter, his heart, by the secret inspiration of God, without either writing or any outward word.

"For which reason, when he had responded to Christ's question 'Who do you say that I am?' by saying, 'You are Christ, the Son of the living God, who have come into this world,' our Savior said to him in reply, 'You are blessed, Simon, the son of John, for neither flesh nor blood has revealed and shown this to you, but my Father who is in heaven' [Mt 16: 15–17]. And thus it appears that the faith came into Saint Peter, his heart, as to the prince of the apostles, without hearing, by secret inspiration; and into the rest by his profession and Christ's holy mouth. And by them in like manner—at first without writing, only by conversation and preaching—so was it spread abroad in the world that his faith was by the mouths of his holy messengers put into people's ears, and by his holy hand written in people's hearts, before any word of it, almost, was written in the Book. And so fitting this was, for the law of life to be written in the living minds of human beings rather than in the dead skins of animals. And I have no doubt that even had it so been that the Gospel had never been written, the substance of this faith would still never have fallen out of Christian folks' hearts, but the same Spirit that planted it, the same would have watered it, the same would have protected it, the same would have increased it.

"But it so pleased our Lord, in accord with his high wisdom, to provide that some of his disciples have written many things of his holy life, doctrine, and faith; and yet far from all, which, as Saint John says, the world could not have contained [Jn 21:25].

"These books are, by the secret counsel of the Holy Spirit, made so plain and simple that everyone can find in them some things that they can understand, and yet so lofty, on the other hand, and so hard, that there is no one so astute that they cannot find in them things far above their grasp, far too profound to penetrate. Now, to the Christian people the points of Christ's faith (the points with which our Lord would have them charged) were known, as I say; they were planted in them before; and by reason of that, they far the better understood those books. And although there might perhaps be some texts which it was not yet necessary for them to grasp, yet by the points of their faith were they put on guard, that no text might be construed contrary to their faith.

"And no evangelist was there, or any apostle, who by writing ever sent the faith to any nation unless the people there were first instructed by spoken word and God had begun his church in that place.

"And for my part, I would little doubt that both the evangelists and the apostles spoke of many great and esoteric mysteries much more openly and much more plainly by mouth among the people than ever they put them in writing, since their writings were likely enough at that time to come into the hands of heathens and pagans, such hogs and dogs as were not suitably to have those precious pearls put upon their noses, nor that holy food dashed in their teeth [Mt 7:6]. For which reason Saint Peter in his first sermon to the Jews [Acts 2:22–42] abstained from the declaration of Christ's divinity and equality with his Father, just as our

Savior himself, when the Jews who were unworthy to hear it were offended by his telling them plainly that he was the Son of God, took the doctrine back from them and covered it with the psalm verse, 'I have said you are gods, sons of the Most High, all of you,' as if to say, 'What grieves you about my having that name which God by the prophet has given to all good people?' [See Ps 82: 6 and Jn 10: 34.] In which behavior he did not deny the truth that he had said about himself, but he blinded their willfully closed eyes by hiding and putting back away the jewel that he had started to bring out and show them, the bright luster of which their bleared eyes could not endure to behold.

"And what wonder that the apostles thus did in their speech before infidels, or in their writings that might come into pagans' hands, when it appears from the Epistles of Saint Paul that amidst the Christian flock, where he taught them by mouth, he did not tell them all the truths in one telling. Not only because it would have taken too long, but also because in the beginning they might not have been able to take it well. And therefore, just as Christ said to his disciples [in Jn 16: 12], 'I have more to say to you, but you are not able to bear it yet' (which once became apparent, that time when upon the disclosing of the great mystery of the holy Sacrament, the holy flesh of his Body, the hearers said, 'Who can tolerate this offensive language?' [Jn 6: 60] and thereupon went, almost all of them, on their way), so did Saint Paul, I say, with the Corinthians, not teach them all at once. That is why he says in his first Epistle to them, 'Up till now I have given you only milk, not solid food' [1 Cor 3: 2]. And wisdom speak we (says he) among folk that are mature.

"Now, by this I do not mean that there were any points of the substance of the faith which he explained to the clergy and kept from the laypeople, or explained to one person and kept from another. I mean only that to no one, probably, did he explain everything at once. And because some came from the Jews and some came from the Gentiles, therefore as they were, so were they handled, not only by grace but also by wisdom, and not only in the points of the faith, but also in the rites and ceremonies, either of the Church or of Moses' law, of which some ceremonies were abolished—some immediately, some not—and some were taken into the church of Christ and are observed still. But in the end, when they were fit for it, they were all taught all that God would have them bound to believe. And then, I have no doubt, many things that now are very obscure in holy Scripture were by the apostles (to whom our Lord opened their minds, that they might understand Scripture) so plainly explained that they were quite clearly understood by the people.

"I do not say the whole entire Scripture. It may be that in it lies still hidden many a secret mystery, concerning the coming of Antichrist and the day, manner, and fashion of the Last Judgment, which will never be fully disclosed until the times decreed by God's high providence suitable and right for this. And from time to time, as it pleases his Majesty to have things known or done in his church, he undoubtedly so manages his revelations and in such a manner does insinuate and inspire them into the breasts of his Christian people that by the secret prompting of the Holy Spirit, they concur and come into accord as one—except heretics who rebel and refuse to be obedient to God and his church. Who are thereby cut off from the living wood of that vine, and, turning into withered branches, are kept only for the fire, first here and afterward in hell, unless they repent and call for grace, which can graft them back into the stem [see Jn 15:6 and Rom 11:22–23]. But just as it may be that there are many things not all at once revealed and understood in Scripture, but in various times and ages more and more things disclosed by God to his church, that it will please him in his high goodness and wisdom to dispense and dispose; and just as it may also be that with regard to things to be done, there may come about in his church variety, mutation, and change, so am I very sure that the Holy Spirit that God sent into his church, and Christ himself, who has promised to persevere and abide in his church to the end of the world, will never allow his Catholic Church either to agree to the making of any law that would be mortally displeasing to God or to determine or believe the contrary of any truth that God wanted believed. For then Christ, who is all truth, would have broken his promise and (which would be blasphemy and abominable to think) have turned untrue. And therefore, furthermore, just as it may be that, as I said before, some things in holy Scripture are not yet fully perceived and understood, so am I very sure that the Church does not and cannot condemnably construe it wrong, which it would do if it were to interpret it so as to make an article of misbelief and of a false, erroneous faith. Such as if it should by misinterpretation of Scripture take from it and believe that Christ is one God and equal with the Father and with the Holy Spirit, if the truth were actually otherwise. And therefore since the Church (in which Christ is actively present, and his Holy Spirit) cannot to God's displeasure and its condemnation fall into any false belief in any such substantial point of the faith, it must needs be, therefore, that Arius and all other heretics are drowned in condemnable errors. The opposite opinions of whose execrable heresies the Church was in the beginning taught by the mouth of Christ himself. And later by the mouths of his blessed apostles, who read and explained the scriptures among the people in their time, showing them in what ways the words of holy Scripture proved the truth of such articles of the faith as they taught them by mouth. And how such texts as seemed the contrary were not actually contrary. And, moreover, they explained to them the right understanding of those texts.

"And although our Savior stated and plainly proved that in Scripture were given good portents and sufficient knowledge of him, yet to the intent that we should well know that his own word and ordinance needs no other authority but himself, and is to be believed and obeyed be it written or not written, he therefore bade that some things be done, and also some things be believed, of which we have in holy Scripture no writing whatsoever. Saint Paul, in his Epistle to them, commands the people of Thessalonica to keep the traditions that he brought them either by his writing or by his mere spoken word [2 Thes 2:15]. For the words that he said among them, our Lord had told them to him for them. And thus he writes to the Corinthians that of the holy Eucharist, the Sacrament of the Altar, he had made known to them the matter and the manner by mouth, as our Lord had himself taught them to him [1 Cor 11:23]. And therefore there is no doubt that the Church was given by the apostles a fuller instruction on that matter than ever was written in all of Scripture. That was where the manner and form of the Consecration was learned. That was where many of the mystical gestures and rituals used in the Mass were learned. And if anyone has any doubt about that, let him ask himself where else we would have the beginning of the putting of the water with the wine into the chalice. For well we know that Scripture does not command it. And everyone with any sense can well know that when the Gospel speaks only of wine, no man in this world would have dared be so bold as to add anything else to it. When the Gospel speaks of only wine being turned into his precious Blood, what man would venture to mix in any water? And now the Church is so very sure of God's pleasure therein, without any scripture, that it not only dares put in water, but also dares not leave it out. And how did the Church know this thing but from God and his holy apostles, who taught it in their time? And so it went forth from age to age, continued in the Church to this day, begun by God in the beginning, without any mention made in holy Scripture.

"However, Luther says that because it is not commanded by Scripture, we may therefore choose whether we will do it or not do it. For this one point is the very foolish foundation and ground of all his great heresies: that one is not bound to believe anything unless it can be proved conclusively by Scripture. And from there he goes so far that no scripture can be conclusive proof of anything that he wants to deny. For he will not acknowledge it as conclusive no matter how obviously it is. And he will call conclusively for him that text that is conclusively against him. And sometimes, if it is too plainly against him, then he will say it is not Scripture, as is his ploy with the Epistle of Saint James. And because the old holy theologians are fully and wholly against him, he dismisses them all as worthless. And with these impressive, ingenious strategies he proclaims himself a conqueror, when, besides all the other things in which any child could see his proud, insane folly, he is shamefully put to flight in the first point, that is to say, that nothing is to be believed for a sure truth unless it shows up conclusively proved in Holy Writ.

"Granted, that point had at the first sight some semblance of plausibility. However, truth to tell, he would be a sorry scoundrel who would do nothing that his master would command him, nor believe anything that his master would tell him, unless he gave it to him in writing, as is Luther's ploy with Christ. Of whose words or acts he will believe nothing unless he finds it in Scripture, and plainly and conclusively at that. Well, he must by that stratagem condemn the church of Christ for not sanctifying Saturday, which was the Sabbath day that God instituted among the Jews, commanding that the Sabbath day be kept holy. And though the matter of the precept is a moral issue and the day a legal one, and thus it could be changed, I yet don't believe there is anyone who will think that the Church would ever have taken it upon itself to change it without an explicit directive from God. Whereof we find no mention at all in holy Scripture. By what scripture is it conclusively known that every man and woman has the power to administer the sacrament of Baptism? Let that be proved, by either commandment, counsel, permission, or example expressed in Scripture.

"There are many similar things which, as holy theologians agree, were taught to the apostles by Christ, and to the Church by the apostles, and so have come down to our day by continual succession from theirs. But I will let pass all the others and speak only of one.

"Every good Christian, I have no doubt, believes that our blessed Lady was perpetually a virgin, as well after the birth of Christ as before. For it would have been a strange thing if after that blessed birth she had been less minded toward cleanness and purity, and had cared less about her holy intention and promise of chastity, vowed and dedicated to God, than before. For surely anyone who reflects on the words of the Gospel in Saint Luke will well perceive that she had vowed virginity. For when the angel had said to her, 'Behold, you will conceive in your womb and bring forth a child, and you shall name him Jesus,' she answered him, 'How can this be? For as for man, I do not have relations with any' [Lk 1: 31–34], which, though it is spoken only for the time then present, does necessarily imply that she never would have relations with any, according to common usage. By which a nun might say, 'As for man, there is not any that has intercourse with me,' implying that there never will be. And in ordinary speech that kind of expression is much in use. A woman says of someone whom she is determined never to marry, 'We may well talk together, but we do not wed together,' meaning that they never will wed together. And that is the kind of thing our Lady meant when she said, 'How can this be, since I have relations with no man?' She meant that she never would have intercourse with a man. Otherwise her answer would have been pointless. For the angel did not say 'Behold, you *have* conceived'—which if he had said, she might well have been amazed at simply because she had not already had relations with any man. But when he said, 'You will conceive,' this could not be any marvel to her just because she had not had relations with a man already. And therefore, since she *wondered* how it could be that she would ever conceive and have a child, it must needs be that her answer meant that she never would have intercourse with a man. And therefore she was astonished, because he said it would be, and she did not know how it could be, except by the way that she had already fully resolved that it would never be. And so he then explained to her how it would come about: by the Holy Spirit coming into her, and the power of God on high overshadowing her. And then she assented and said, 'Behold here the handmaid of God; be it done to me according to your word, as you tell me.' And thus it appears conclusively that she had then a fully determined intention of virginity. And one, as it seems, that she thought not licit to change. For otherwise, when the angel delivered the message, she might have been inclined to change it even though she had previously been of another mind.

"Now, when she had, then, such a full and firm intention of perpetual virginity before the birth of her blessed child, who came, among his other heavenly teachings, to call and exhort the world from all pleasure of the flesh to purity and cleanness of body and soul, and from the desire of carnal generation to a spiritual regeneration in grace, would it not then be more of a wonder if she should then have had more regard for fleshly delight, or concern for worldly procreation, than ever she had before her celestial conception of her Maker, made man in her blessed womb? Or what man could think that God would ever afterward allow any earthly man to be conceived in that holy closet taken up and consecrated so specially to God? This revered article of our Lady's perpetual virginity the church of Christ, being taught the truth by Christ, has believed perpetually since the time of Christ. And yet there is no statement of it written in Christ's Gospel, but, rather, there are several texts so seeming to say the contrary that by the wrong understanding of them the heretic Helvidius took the occasion of his heresy, according to which our Lady after the birth of Christ had other children by Joseph. How can we then say that we could without previously learning the faith find out all the points of it in Scripture, when there are some that all people in Christendom believe, and believe themselves bound to believe, of which Scripture gives no straight-out teaching, but, rather, seems to say the contrary?

"But as I started to say, the holy apostles, being taught by their great master Christ, did teach to the Church the articles of the faith, as well as the understanding of such texts of Scripture as were pertinent and applicable to the subject. Whereby it is not unlikely that the Gospel of Saint John and the Epistles of Saint Paul were then better understood among the common people than they perhaps are now with some who take themselves for great scholars. And as the apostles at that time taught the people, so some of those who heard them did pass their teaching on, and leave their doctrine and traditions to others who came after. By reason whereof there came not only the rites and sacraments and the articles of our faith, from hand to hand, from Christ and his apostles to our day, but also the great part of the right understanding of holy Scripture, from good and godly writers of sundry times. By whose good and wholesome doctrine, set forth by their capabilities with God's good inspiration, grace, and the help of the Holy Spirit, we have also the knowledge and understanding of what the faith of Christ's church has been in every time since. And thereby we perceive that these heretics are barkers against the faith not only as it is now, but as it has been ever since Christ died.

"And therefore holy Scripture is, as I said, the highest and best learning that anyone can have, if one takes the right way in the learning.

"It is, as some good, holy saint says, so marvelously devised that a mouse could wade in it and an elephant be drowned in it. For there is no man so lowly but that if he will seek his way with the staff of his faith in his hand, and hold that fast and search the way with it, and have the old holy

Fathers also for his guides, going on with a good determination and a humble heart, using reason and rejecting no good learning, while calling upon God for wisdom, grace, and help that he may well keep his way and follow his good guides, then he will never fall into danger, but will quite safely wade through, and come to such an end of his journey as he himself would well wish. But assuredly, be he as long as Longinus, if he has a proud heart and puts his trust in his own intelligence (as does anyone, humble as he may appear, who dismisses all the old holy Fathers as worthless), that fellow will not fail to sink over the ears and drown. And of all wretches the farthest off-course will he stray who, attaching little importance to the faith of Christ's church, comes to the Scripture of God to see and test therein whether the Church believes right or not. For he doubts either whether Christ teaches his church truthfully or else whether Christ teaches it at all. In which case he doubts whether Christ in *his* words did tell the truth, when he said he would be with his church till the end of the world. And surely the thing that made Arius, Pelagius, Faustus, Manichaeus, Donatus, Helvidius, and the whole pack of the old heretics drown themselves in those condemnable heresies was nothing but overweening pride in their learning in Scripture, wherein they followed their own wits and left the common faith of the Catholic Church, putting their own specious interpretations ahead of the correct, Catholic faith of all of Christ's church, which can never err in any substantial point that God would have us bound to believe. And therefore, to end where we began, whoever will not in the study of Scripture take the points of the Catholic faith as a rule for interpretation, but, out of misgivings and mistrust, will study Scripture to find out from it whether the faith of the Church is true or not, such a one cannot fail to fall into worse and far more dangerous errors than anyone can fall into by philosophy, whose reasonings and arguments in matters of our faith have nothing like the same authority."

26.

The messenger says that it seems to him he should not believe the Church if he observes the Church saying one thing and holy Scripture another thing, because Scripture is the word of God; and the author shows that the faith of the Church is as much the word of God as is Scripture, and therefore as much to be believed. And that the faith and Scripture, rightly understood, never contradict one another. And he further shows that with regard to any question arising from holy Scripture concerning any essential point of the faith, anyone who, from all that they can hear on both sides of the question, cannot tell which view is better and more correct, has a sure and unquestionable refuge provided them by the goodness of God, to bring them out of all perplexity, in that God has commanded them in all such unclear things to believe his church.

"Truly, sir," said he, "I think it is well said, what you have said. And really, to tell the truth, I do not see what I could answer it with. And yet when I look back again upon holy Scripture and take into account that it is God's own words (which I know well you will grant), I know in my heart that I would find it hard to believe everyone in the whole world if they should say anything of which I should see that the holy Scripture says the contrary, since reason dictates that I believe God by himself far better than all of them."

"What you say there," said I, "is very true. But now I put the case that God were to tell you two things. Which of them would you believe better?"

"Neither one," said he. "I would believe them both firmly, and both the same."

"What if neither one," said I, "was likely to be true? Or both of the two seemed impossible?"

"That would," said he, "make little difference to me. For once they were known to be told by God, then no matter how unlikely or impossible they seemed, I would not and could not have any doubt that they were true, the both of them."

"That is well said," said I. "But now, if it so were that those two things seemed completely contradictory, the one to the other, what would you then think, and which would you then believe?"

"I still could not," said he, "have any doubt that they were really true, the both of them. But I would really think that I did not quite understand one of them."

"What would you then do," said I, "if he told you to believe them both?"

"Goodness," said he, "then I would ask him to tell me first what he means by them both. For though I believe that they are both true in that sense and intention in which he uses his own words, and that, thus understood, they may well be consistent and compatible with one another, yet I cannot believe both of them in that sense and understanding in which they are inconsistent and directly contrary to one another."

"That is," said I, "so well said that to my mind no one could improve upon it."

"But now I want to know," said I, "is the faith of the Church the word of God, and by God spoken to the Church, or not?"

"Yes," said he, "God speaks to his church in Scripture."

"And is nothing God's words," said I, "but Scripture? The words that God spoke to Moses, were they not God's words, all of them, before they were written? And the words of Christ to his apostles, were they not his words before they were written?"

"Yes, then," said he. "But now that he has perfected and finished the corpus of holy Scripture, everything that he would have Christian people believe, and everything that he would have the Church do, and everything that he would have the Church eschew, about all of this he has left them his mind sufficiently in holy Scripture."

"And not at all otherwise," said I, "as well? I had thought we had been at another point, in that you see the Sabbath day changed to Sunday without any word of Scripture giving any commandment of the change in the New Testament from the commandment given for Saturday in the Old [see Acts 20: 7]. And the same goes for the point that we spoke of concerning the perpetual virginity of our Lady, of which there is not one word written in Scripture. But since I perceive that the great affection and reverence that you bear to the Scripture of God—not without good reason, but without any measure—put you in the position that you take all authority and trustworthiness away from every word of God spoken outside Scripture, I would therefore ask you this question: If God in holy Scripture tells you two things that seem contradictory to one another, such as, for example, if he tells you in one place that he is less than his Father [Jn 14: 28] and in another place that he and his Father are entirely one [Jn 10: 30], which of these will you believe?"

"Good heavens," said he, "both of the two. For they can stand together well enough. For he was less as a human being, and was entirely one and equal as God."

"Very true it is," said I, "what you say. But, now, if you had been born in the days of Arius the heretic, he would not have accepted or been satisfied with this answer, but would have granted you the first part and made you go further to prove the second part. And of that text he would have made you the interpretation that his Father and he are one not in substance, but only in will. And that interpretation he would have fortified and made somewhat plausible with another word of Christ in which he beseeched his Father, saying, 'As you and I are both one, so make it that they and we may be made one' [Jn 17: 22–23], meaning by 'they' his Christian people, who will never be one with him in substance. So that as to the inequality of Christ by reason of his humanity, you must agree with him, but as to unity of Godhood, he will not agree with you, but always challenge you to prove it."

"Well," said he, "even if he did so, yet if I were prepared for that, there are plenty of texts that plainly prove it."

"That is," said I, "very true. But yet there is none that he cannot always set you another against, and as fast a gloss for yours as you will have an answer for his, in such wise that he can deceive a very wise and well-educated person, as he did in his own days and thousands upon thousands of days after. Then if it so were that in that discussion you could not make your hearers discern the truth, nor, perhaps, persuade them to believe the truth, because the false side of the argument might happen to have to the minds of many a greater semblance of truth, as it had at that time to many that then were of that sect, how would you extricate yourself from that situation?"

"Goodness," said he, "I would believe well myself the truth and go to God, and let them that would believe the false side go to the devil."

"You would," said I, "have taken there a good, sure way. But now, if you had lived in that time (albeit you are now fast and sure in the truth), you might have happened while the matter was in question, and many great scholars, well versed in Scripture, and some seeming quite holy, were set on the wrong side—you might have happened, I say, to have found the arguments on both sides so persuasive that you would not have known on which side to determine your belief. And what would you then have done?"

Said he, "You now put me to a pinch, and I shall answer you as I have heard it said that Father Mayhew, sometime almoner to King Henry VII, once answered the king at his table. It happened that there came up in the conversation the story of Joseph—how the wife of his master Potiphar (a great man with the king of Egypt) was trying to pull him to bed, and he fled away [Gn 39: 4–12].

" 'Now, Father Mayhew,' said King Henry, 'you are a tall, strong man, on the one hand, and an erudite scholar on the other—what would you have done had you been, not Joseph, but in Joseph's place?'

" 'By my word, sir,' said he, 'if it please your Grace, I cannot tell you what I *would* have done, but I can tell you well what I *should* have done.'

" 'By my word,' said the king, 'that was very well answered.' And since that answer served him well there, I shall make the same serve me here. For admittedly, if I had lived in Arius's time, what I *would* have done regarding the point that you speak of, that I don't know. But what I *should* have done, that I can well tell you—and surely hope that I would have done, too."

"What is that?" said I.

"Good heavens, I would have believed the best," said he.

"The best?" said I. "That would indeed be the best, if you knew which it was. But the case is put that the arguments based on Scripture seemed to you to impugn and refute each other in such a way that you stood in such a doubt that you could in no way discern which side said the best."

"By God," said he, "I had forgotten that."

"Well," said he, "then it would be best, and so I would have done, I think, to get down on my knees and make my special prayer to God that it might please him, in his goodness, in so great a peril not to leave me perplexed, but vouchsafe to incline my assent toward that side that he knew to be correct and wanted me to believe correct. And then I would boldly believe whichever one God put in my mind. Would this not have been the best way?"

"If it were not," said I, "the best, it might perhaps serve as a second."

"A second?" said he. "Then you take it for bad."

"No," said I, "there are two seconds, according to two ways of counting. One next to the worst, another next to the best. And your way is certainly far from the worst. But yet I dare not assent that it is the best till I understand it better. And therefore I ask you to tell me this: If, after making your special prayers, you wrote the one view on one sheet of paper and the other view on another and laid them both on the ground, and then set up a staff between them both, would you then, without bias, be willing to take the one view or the other according to how your staff should happen to fall?"

"Why not?" said he. "Or else put it upon two lots and then at random draw the one and take it. For when I have done as much as my own intellect will allow, and have heard as well all that I can from others, and yet by neither can perceive which is the better opinion, what should I do, or what could I do, further than pray for grace to guide my choice, and so, at random, boldly take the one and hold it fast, doubting not at all that God assisted my choice, if I have a firm faith in his promise? He does promise that if we ask, we shall receive—asking, as Saint James says, without any doubt [see Jn 16:24 and James 1:6–8]. And why should I not in such a complicated case, after calling for help from God, take the one view at random by lot, as the apostles did in the choosing of a new apostle to fill the position of the traitor Judas?" [See Acts 1:24–26.]

"Lots," said I, "are quite legitimate in the choosing between two such things as are both so good that we are likely to choose rightly enough whichever we take. But, now, if you were in the situation that I have heard my father jokingly say that every man is in the choosing of his wife—that you blindly put your hand into a bag full of snakes and eels together, seven snakes to one eel—you would, I think, reckon it a perilous choice to take up one at random even if you had made it your special prayer to meet with good fortune. Nor ought you in such a case to hazard it upon your prayer and trust in God without necessity."

"That is perhaps true," said he. "But in our case there is necessity. For there is no other way to escape the confusion except just to take the one or the other by prayer and firm trust in God, who has never let down those who trust in him."

"If there were," said I, "no other way, then it would to some extent be as you say. But now take another look at your case—at when you could not, upon hearing the Arians and the Catholic side argue together, perceive which side was the better, and therefore of those two tales told you by God in many texts of holy Scripture, some seeming clearly to say that Christ is not equal with his Father, some seeming as clearly to say the contrary, you could in no way find any rational argument whereby you could find yourself moved to take the one side for more plausible than the other. I now put the case that God himself were to say to you, 'I have made known the truth of this matter to such and such a man, and how my Scripture is to be understood concerning the same. Betake yourself, therefore, to him, and that thing that he will tell you, that thing believe you.' Would you say, 'No, good Lord, I will ask no one but yourself; and therefore tell me by your own mouth, or else I will take the one side completely at random and think that you would have it so'? Or would you think that God was your good Lord and had done much for you in that it pleased him so graciously for your security to bring you out of such a great perplexity, whereby you would for your own mind have remained in an unresolvable doubt in a matter of the faith, wherein it is damnable to dwell in doubt, or (which is much worse yet) have perhaps veered into an insurmountable error?"

"Truly," said he, "great cause would I have had highly to thank God."

"You would not, then," said I, "first make your prayer and then, with good hope that grace will guide your fortune, take the one side at random by lot, but you would in your prayer thank God for that provision. And then you would get you to that man as fast as you could."

"Very true," said he.

"Then if that man should tell you that Arius and his company were heretics all, and took texts of Scripture wrong, you would believe him?"

"Yes indeed," said he, "that I would."

"I put the case," said I, "that you had not doubted before, but had on your own become fully convinced that the Arians' opinion was the truth. You yet would against Arius and all his people, and against your own view also, go by the word of him whom God had told you to believe?"

"What else?" said he.

"What if you asked him," said I, "whether God has articulated that point in Scripture so sufficiently that it can be proved good and conclusively by the words of Holy Writ, and he told you yes? And suppose he thereupon brought up all the texts that you had well in remembrance already, and you brought up against them all that you could for the contrary, to the point where each of you had set out all your texts and all your interpretations that either of you could bring forward, till you both confessed that neither of you both could find anything further, he saying still that his way was the truth, and that he had by Scripture well proved it to you, and you yourself, on the other hand, for all that ever you had heard him say, perceiving in your own mind nothing else but that you had by Scripture better proved the other side. Which would you now believe? That way that, as far as you see, God says himself in holy Scripture? Or else that man whom God sent you to and told you to believe?"

"Oh, truly," said he, "I would believe him."

"Well said," said I. "But would you only believe him that the truth of the matter in question was against the Arians, or would you believe him further, in what he said about having proved it to you by Scripture?"

"I would," said he, "believe him about that also. For since God so had commanded me and had told me that he had himself instructed that man as to what senses the scriptures were to be understood in, I could not think otherwise than that this was true, even if to my own reason it appeared the opposite."

"Very well said," said I. "Now, if God had said to you that you should believe that man concerning the matter itself, and had said nothing about Scripture, then would you have still believed him about the matter? Wouldn't you even if he should have told you that he understood no Scripture at all?"

"That is true," said he.

"Now, if he should then have told you that the Arians were heretics on that point, and their opinions erroneous and false, you would have believed him?"

"What else?" said he.

"What if he had told you, moreover," said I, "that he had no idea whether or not it could be well proved by Scripture?"

"I still would," said he, "nevertheless believe to be true the thing itself that he had told me."

"What would you then think," said I, "about those texts that you did previously consider to prove quite clearly the contrary?"

"I would," said he, "then figure that they were meant some other ways than I could understand. For I could not doubt that correctly understood, they could never witness against the truth."

"In all honesty," said I, "you are speaking marvelously well."

"Do you not," said I, "take it for being one and the same whether God tells you to do a thing by his own mouth or by holy Scripture?"

"Yes," said he, "except that I take the telling by Scripture for the more sure. For there I really know that God speaks and I cannot be deceived."

"Now," said I, "this person that God tells you to go to, and to believe about everything, will it make any change in the matter whether it be a man or a woman?"

"No change at all," said he.

"What if it were a certain known company of men and women together?" said I. "Would that make any difference?"

"Never a whit," said he.

"Then," said I, "provided that it is evident to you, as I suppose it is to you and to every other Christian, that in all points of faith—both in things to be believed which are

above nature and also in things necessary to know and believe which can be perceived by the reason given us with
nature—God gives us in commandment that we shall believe
his church, then you are fully answered. For then you have
that person that you must needs go to for your final answer
and solution of all points and doubts in any way concerning
the salvation of your soul. Of which points no one can deny
that one of the most important is to take holy Scripture
always in the right sense. Or else, if we cannot attain the
right understanding, yet then at least make sure we avoid and
eschew all such misinterpretation as might bring us into any
condemnable error."

27.

*The author proves that God has commanded us with regard to
everything necessary to salvation to give firm credence and full
obedience to his church. And gives a reason why God will have us
bound to believe it.*

"That is true," said he, "if this can be shown. But where will
it be shown that God commands us in all such things to
believe the Church? For, first of all, that would seem to me a
very strange manner of commanding. For all of us who are
(as you say) commanded by God to believe the Church are
members *of* the Church, and we all, together, make up the
whole Church. So what sense would it make, then, to command us to believe the Church? This would, in effect, be no
more than to tell us all to believe us all, or each of us to
believe the others. And then if we fell into divergent opinions, why should the one side more believe the other than be
believed by the other (since both sides are members of the
Church and between them make up the Church), except
that always that side seems to be believed which best and
most clearly can back up its opinion with Scripture? For the
words of God must break the strife. He alone is to be believed; he and his only Son, about whom he himself commanded, 'Ipsum audite.' 'Listen to him,' said the Father at

the time of his baptism [see Mt 3:17 and Mt 17:5]. And therefore the person that you speak of, the one whom God sends me to, and tells me to listen to and believe, is Christ our Savior alone, and not any congregation of human beings. If we believe its words before the words of God, and instead of the Scripture of God put our trust and confidence in the doctrine and ordinance of the Church, it is perhaps to be feared that we will bring upon ourselves the reproof mentioned in the Gospel, where it is said, 'In vain do they worship me with human precepts' [Mt 15:9], and also where our Savior reproves the scribes and the Pharisees, saying to them, 'Why do you break and transgress the commandment of God for the sake of your tradition?'" [See Mt 15:3.]

"I still trust," said I, "that in the end we will agree. But a lot of work, it seems to me, it is taking to get there. But since we must, as you say (and it is true), listen to Christ our Savior and believe him, is it enough to listen to and believe him? Or are we, in addition to that, also obliged to obey him?"

"To obey him also," said he. "For otherwise he would be better not listened to."

"Well said," said I. "But are we obliged to listen to him and obey him in some things, or in all things?"

"In all things," said he, "without exception, that he commands us to do."

"Then if Christ," said I, "tells us to believe and obey his church, are we not obliged to do so?"

"Yes," said he.

"Then we may," said I, "no more doubt to be true whatever the Church tells us to believe than the things that our Savior himself tells us to believe, if he tells us to listen to his church as his Father told us to listen to him."

"That is true," said he, "if he does so. But it seems to me a strange commanding, as I said, to command each of us to believe the others."

"It does not seem," said I, "so strange a thing to Saint Paul. For he with striking earnestness beseeches Christian people to be in agreement, all in one mind, and in the faith to tell one tale, suffering no sects or schisms among them [1 Cor 1:10]. Which agreement and unanimity can never be where no one gives credence to anyone else. But among Christian people it will instantly be, if everyone gives credence to the Church."

"But yet," said he, "since they are all members of the Church, of different parties which shall believe which?"

"You take," said I, "for a great difficulty and a very complex thing something that seems to me very simple. For either first the Church has the truth and believes all one way till some one or some few begin the change—and then, though all are still members of the Church (till some on account of their obstinacy are gone out or put out), yet there is no doubt that if I will believe the Church, I must believe them that still believe that way which the whole entirety believed before—or else, if there was anything that was perhaps such that in the Church it was at some time in question, and regarded as unrevealed and unknown, if after that the whole Church comes into a unanimous accord upon the one side, either by joint determination at a general council or by a perfect persuasion and belief so received throughout Christendom that the Christian people think it a condemnable error to believe the contrary, then if any would after that take the contrary way, were it one or more, were it few or many, were they learned or unlearned, were they laypeople or of the clergy, I yet can have no doubt as to which side to believe if I will believe the Church."

"That is true," said he, "but you are not yet proving to me that God has commanded me to believe the Church."

"You somewhat interrupted me," said I, "with your other stratagem by which you would have it seem an absurdity to command us to believe the Church. I mean when you said it would seem that we were commanded nothing else but to believe each other, in which case, when divergent opinions were taken, we could not know which side should believe which. Since I have shown you the contrary of that, and have gotten that stumbling block out of the way, we shall, I think, soon see the other point: that Christ does command us to believe his church. For what his Father said with reference to him, 'Listen to him,' he said with reference to his church, when he sent it abroad to be spread forth.

"For when he had gathered his church of his apostles and his disciples, and was sending them out to preach, did he not say to them, 'Whoever listens to you listens to me'? Did he not also command that all those who would not listen to the Church should be regarded and taken as pagans and publicans?" [See Lk 10: 16 and Mt 18: 17.]

"That was," said he, "where people would not mend their ways."

"Was it not," said I, "a general command, for wherever anyone would not amend any condemnable fault?"

"Yes," said he.

"Is misbelief," said I, "not such?"

"Yes indeed," said he.

"Then," said I, "is the Church their judge upon their belief, to show them whether it is true or false?"

"So it seems," said he.

"Does their conduct," said I, "have nothing to do with faith?"

"What do you mean by that?" said he.

"This," said I. "Suppose that Luther, an ex-friar having now wedded a nun, was commanded to amend his vile conduct and put away that harlot whom he abuses in continual incest and sacrilege under the name of a wife, and he were to say that he was doing plenty rightly and that their vows could not bind them.[5] Would he not be bound to believe the Church and obey it concerning his beliefs as well as his conduct?"

"Yes indeed," said he.

[5] "Incest" according to canon law, because the marriage was between a monk and a nun.

"Then it becomes evident," said I, "that we are commanded by Christ to listen to, believe, and obey the Church in matters of faith as well as of morals. Which thing is also made quite evident by the fact that our Lord wants whoever is disobedient to be taken as a pagan or a publican. Of which two, the one offended in misbelief, the other in vile conduct. And thus it becomes evident not only that Christ is the man whom you are sent to and commanded by God to believe and obey, but also that the Church is the person whom you are by Christ commanded to listen to and believe and obey. And therefore if you will in faith or conduct or avoiding of all condemnable error (which you could fall into by a misunderstanding of Scripture) take a sure and infallible way, you must in all these things listen to, believe, and obey the Church, which is, as I say, the person whom Christ sends you to for the sure clearing up of all such doubts, the one in whose mouth speaks he himself, and the Holy Spirit of his Father in heaven.

"And surely this is much to be marked. For it is the perpetual order which our Lord has continued in the governance of good people from the beginning, that just as our nature first fell by way of pride to disobedience of God with the inordinate desire of knowledge like unto God's, so has God ever kept man in humility, bridling him with the knowledge and confession of his ignorance and binding him to the obedience of belief of certain things of which his own intellect would indeed think the contrary. And therefore we are bound to believe not only against our own reason the points that God communicates to us in Scripture, but also what God teaches his church outside Scripture, and (also against our own mind) to give diligent hearing, firm credence, and faithful obedience to the church of Christ concerning the sense and understanding of holy Scripture. Not doubting that since he has commanded that his sheep be fed, he has provided for them wholesome food and true doctrine. And that he has for that purpose to such an extent inspired the old holy theologians of his church with the light of his grace for our instruction that the doctrine in which they have concurred and which has been assented to through many ages is the really true faith and right way to heaven, its having been put in their minds by the holy hand of him 'qui facit unanimes in domo,' who makes the church of Christ all of one mind [Ps 68: 7]."

28.

The messenger again objects to this—to the claim that we should believe the Church in anything where we find the words of Scripture seeming to clearly state the contrary, or believe the interpretations of the old theologians in any essential point where they seem to us to speak contrary to the text—claiming that we can understand Scripture as well as they could. And the author responds, proving the authority of the old interpreters and the infallible authority that the Church has in that God teaches it every truth requisite to what is needed for salvation. He proves this by a deduction based partly on natural reason.

"It seems to me," said he, "that all this is fine, that we should believe the Church as Christ, as long as it says what Christ says, for that is what I think our Lord meant.

"But, now, if they tell me tales of their own, of which Christ never spoke a word and no mention is made in holy Scripture, I may then say with the prophet Jeremiah, 'Non mittebam prophetas, et ipsi currebant. Non loquebar ad eos, et ipsi prophetabant.' 'Those prophets,' said our Lord, 'ran forth of their own accord, and I did not send them, and prophesied of their own accord, when I said nothing to them' [Jer 23: 21]. And then how much more may I say this if they tell me something of which Christ or holy Scripture says the opposite? Shall I believe the Church over Christ? Would that be a good humility, to be obedient more to men than to God? I ought more, it seems to me, to believe God alone, speaking in his holy Scripture himself, than all the old Fathers if they make a gloss that goes against the text.

Nor do they themselves for their opinions say and write that they get them by inspiration, or by revelation, or by miracle. No; by wisdom, study, diligence, and comparison of one text with another. By all of which means people can now perceive the meaning of Scripture as well as they could then. And if you will perhaps say that grace helped them, which I will well grant, then I will say in reply that God's grace is not yet so far worn out that it cannot as well help us as it helped them, and so we can be for the right understanding of Scripture equal with them, and perhaps a notch above them. By what means, when we perceive that they went wrong and others after them, shall we then call it humility so to take captive and subdue our understanding, whereby God has perchance given us light to perceive their errors, that without thanking him for it, we shall so disdain his gift that we shall believe them before himself, and tell him that he himself commanded this? And therefore it seems to me that where the old theologians or the whole Church tells me the tale that God does, there he bids me believe them; but where God says one thing in Scripture and they tell me another, it seems to me that I should in no way believe them."

"Well," said I, "then in some things, you say, you will believe the Church, but not in all. In anything apart from Scripture you will not, and in the interpretation of Scripture you will not. And so, whereas you said that you believe the Church in some things, in actual fact you believe the Church in absolutely nothing. For in what will you believe it if you do not believe it in the interpretation of Scripture? For as regards the text, you believe Scripture itself and not the Church."

"It seems to me," said he, "that the text is good enough and clear enough, needing no gloss, if it be well considered and every part compared with others."

"It would be hard," said I, "to find anything that is so clear as to need no gloss at all."

"Goodness," said he, "they give a gloss to some texts that are as clear as it is that twice two make four."

"Why," said I, "that needs no gloss at all?"

"I think not," said he. "Or else the devil is in on it."

"Indeed," said I. "And yet, though you would believe someone who would tell you that twice two ganders made always four geese, you yet would take thought before you believed him that would tell you that twice two geese made always four ganders. For there you might be mistaken. And him would you not believe at all that would tell you that twice two geese would always make four horses."

"Pooh," said he, "this is a matter of jest. The twice two must always be all of the same species. Geese and horses are of different species."

"Well," said I, "then every person that is neither goose nor horse sees well that there is one gloss, nevertheless."

"But, now," said I, "the geese and the ganders are both of the same species, and yet twice two geese make not always four ganders."

"Very clever," said he. "You know well enough what I mean."

"I think I do," said I. "But I think that if you bring it out, it will make another gloss to your text, as clear as your text is; and here you are, wanting there to be for all of holy Scripture no gloss at all. And yet you do want the comparing of one text with another, and the showing of how they can fit together—as though all of that were no gloss."

"Yes," said he, "but would you have us believe the Church if it gives a gloss that will in no way match up with the text, but it appears plainly that the text, well considered, says the exact opposite?"

"To whom does that appear," said I, "so plainly, when it appears one way to you, and to the whole Church another?"

"Yet if I see it thus," said he, "then even if holy theologians and the whole entire Church should tell me the opposite, I think I am no more bound to believe them all that

Scripture means what they say it does than if they should all tell me that something is white which I see for myself is black."

"A little while ago," said I, "you were willing to believe the Church in some things. And now not only are you willing to believe it in nothing, but also whereas God would have the Church be your judge, you would now be judge over the Church. And you will by your wit be the judge as to whether the Church in the understanding of holy Scripture, which God has written to his church, does judge aright or err. As for your white and black, never will it be that you will see as black something that everyone else will see as white. But you can be sure that if everyone else sees it as white and you take it for black, your eyes are sorely deceived. For the Church will not, I think, agree to call it other than it seems to them. And it would be very surprising if you should in holy Scripture see better than the old holy theologians and Christ's whole Church.

"But first," said I, "you must take into consideration that you and I are talking not about one theologian or two, but about the consensus and unanimous agreement of the old holy Fathers. And that we are speaking not about the doctrine of one man or two in the Church, but about the common accord of the Church. Also, we are not talking about any meaning taken in any text of holy Scripture whereby arises no doubt or question concerning any essential article of our faith or rule of our conduct (for in other, incidental matters, there may perhaps be for one text ten possible meanings, all of them good enough, with no guarantee as to which is the best). No, we are talking about two meanings which are so different and contrary that if the one is true, the other must necessarily be false; and which have to do with some essential point of our faith, or rule of our conduct which is also contingent upon faith and referable thereto. Such as if someone would boldly break his vows because he thought no one was obliged to keep any. Such points, I say, let us consider to be the ones we are speaking of. And this remembered between us, we will then somewhat see what your statements do prove.

"I will not much need," said I, "to keep discussing with you by what means Scripture is understood, since you have agreed that with nature and diligence must needs go the grace of God, or else no amount of diligence or of help from nature can be of any avail. Nor do I at all disagree with you that God can and also will give his grace now to us as he gave it of old to his holy theologians, if there be no less cooperativeness and no more hindrance or impediment in ourselves than was in them. I will also grant you that we can now, by the same means that they could then, understand Scripture as well as they did then, and I will not put up much of a protest over your one notch better. Were it not for the sins that we sink in, we might perhaps understand it four, three, two times better, having their efforts therein and our own therewith. But since I am being so gracious as to grant you so many things, I trust that you will grant me this one: that if in any such point of our faith as God would have us bound to believe, they did understand Scripture one way and we another, these ways being so completely contrary to one another that if the one is true the other must necessarily be false, you will then grant, I say, that either they or we are in error."

"That must needs be," said he.

"You will also grant," said I, "that in such points as we speak of, the error would be condemnable. For we are speaking only of those points to the belief of which God will have us bound."

"I grant that," said he. "For it would be condemnable in such a case to believe wrong. And wrong should they or we believe if they or we believed a wrong article because they or we thought that Scripture affirmed it. And as condemnable would it be, and still much more, if we believed a thing of which we believed that Scripture affirms the contrary. For then we would be believing that Scripture is false."

"That is," said I, "very well said. But for further clarity let us put forth one or two examples. And what point rather than the article concerning the equality in divinity of Christ our Savior with his Father? For if the contrary belief were true, then this one would always be condemnable; plain idolatry."

"Very true," said he.

"May not," said I, "the other example be the matter that we have in hand, concerning saints' relics, images, and shrines? If our veneration of these things is—as you say many consider it—idolatry, then it is even worse for us to do therein as we do than it would be if our belief on that other point were wrong. It is then as much less good as the saints, or the images either, are less good than the holy humanity of Christ."

"That is," said he, "very true."

"Then," said I, "let's leave the first point alone (because on that we are in complete agreement) and speak of the second: the supposition that the old Fathers took the scriptures one way and we the contrary. Though it might be that we were able to understand the scriptures as well as they, yet if they so understood them that they thought this kind of veneration to be not only not forbidden but commanded by God, and pleasing to him, and we modern men, on the other hand, thought it utterly forbidden and regarded as idolatry, one side did not in fact understand the Scripture right, but was in a condemnable error."

"That no one will deny," said he.

"I do not doubt, now," said I, "that you yourself see very well how many things I could here submit for them to prove to you that they were not in such an error. First, their mental faculties, as good as our modern men's; their diligence, as great; their erudition, greater; their study, as fervent; their devotion, hotter; their number, far greater; their time, continued longer, lasting for many ages; the contrary opinions, in few, and always soon faded; they taken always for Catholic, the contrary side for heretics. Here I might submit to you the holiness of their lives, and the plenty of their grace, well evidenced thereby. And that our Lord therefore opened their eyes and allowed and caused them to see the truth. And albeit he used for this no obvious miracle or revelation perceptible to the senses—which, as you say, they make no claim or pretense of for the proof of their opinions in their interpretations of holy Scripture—yet he used the secret supernatural means by which his grace, assistant with good people who strive for it, by promptings imperceptible to themselves inclines their assent to the true side; and thus the old holy Fathers did in the point that we speak of, and in other such points, perceive the right meaning of holy Scripture at least to such an extent that they well knew it was not contrary to their creed. And here I could also submit to you that if it had been otherwise and they had therein been condemnably wrong, then—living and dying in condemnable error—they could not have been saints, as God has by many a thousand miracles, both during their lives and after their deaths, proved them to be. With this I could also submit and very rightly conclude that since those holy theologians and the Church are (as is clearly evidenced by their books) all of one faith in this point and such others, it is thereby quite evident that the Church is in the truth, and is not at all in error, in the understanding of the scriptural passages that speak of the matter in question, but those are clearly in error who do understand those texts of holy Scripture to the contrary. These things, as I say, and still many more others, I could submit. But since you did yourself put the Church and them in the same case, and so they are indeed, I will rather prove to you the accuracy of them by the accuracy of the Church than the accuracy of the Church by the accuracy of them. And that seems to me good sense. For surely, since they were but members of his church, God had his special care upon them most especially for the benefit of his church, by whose whole mystical body he sets more store than by any member thereof—saint, apostle, evangelist, or anyone else. And therefore I must ask you yet again whether the Church can have any condemnable error in the faith, by a misinterpreting of Scripture or otherwise."

"That is," said he, "somewhat hard to tell."

"Now," said I, "I am somewhat surprised that you do not remember that you yourself have already granted that these words of Christ spoken to Peter, 'I have prayed that your faith will never fail' [Lk 22:32], refer not only to the faith within Peter, personally, but also to the faith of the Church. For this was spoken to him as head of the Church."

"Yes," said he, "I remember quite well that I granted this. But I remember also that notwithstanding my granting of it, you agreed to our examining the matter again and again from other perspectives as well, wherein my concession should not bind me."

"Oh," said I, "that I had forgotten again. But let it alone, then, for the time being, and tell me this: Did not Christ intend to gather a flock and congregation of people that should serve God and be his special people?"

"Yes," said he, "that is certainly true. For Scripture plainly says this about Christ in several places, such as where the Father of heaven says to Christ in the psalm, 'Postula a me et dabo tibi gentes hereditatem tuam,' 'Ask of me and I shall give the pagan people for your inheritance' [Ps 2:8], and many other places. And otherwise, undoubtedly, his whole coming would in a sense have been frustrate and in vain."

"That people," said I, "which should be an inheritance, did he intend that it should endure only for his own days, while he lived here, or else that it should go forth and continue long after?"

"Not only that," said he, "but that it will continue as long as the world lasts, from here till Judgment Day, and afterward in heaven, eternally."

"Will this people," said I, "have among them the knowledge and understanding of what he would have them do to please God with?"

"Yes," said he.

"Will they," said I, "have this knowledge for a while, in the beginning, and then lose it, or will they have it always, as long as they continue?"

Here he began to waver a little.

"Well," said I, "can you call them his people any longer if they lose the knowledge of how to serve him and please him? If they out of laziness neglect to do their duty, as slack servants sometimes do, they yet may mend their ways and do better another time. But if they lose the knowledge of their duty, then they will never know which ways to mend. For example, a man who knows that fornication is a sin may by frailty fall into fornication; but since he knows it to be evil, though he sinned more in the doing than he would have if he had not known of the prohibition, yet the knowledge does give him admonition and the opportunity for repentance and amendment, which would necessarily be lacking if he had lost the knowledge."

Upon this, he granted that it must necessarily be that this people must necessarily have always the knowledge of how to serve and please our Lord, or else they would cease to be his people.

"Is not this people," said I, "called the Church?"

"Yes," said he.

"Then the Church," said I, "always has and always will have, by your account, the knowledge and understanding of how God can be served and pleased."

"True," said he.

"Is," said I, "that knowledge fully had without the knowledge of such things as God binds us to believe?"

"No," said he.

"What if we knew them in such a way," said I, "that we could tick them off on our fingertips, and yet we believed them not to be true. Would this knowledge serve?"

"In no way," said he, "for if you believed them to be false, even though you knew them so well that you could recite

them by rote, you could receive through them no directive
to please and serve God with them, which is the reason for
which the Church should of necessity know them."

"This is," said I, "very well said. Then since you grant
that the Church shall ever endure, and that it could not
endure without the knowledge of such things as can please
God, nor can those things be known if the knowledge is
lacking of those things that God binds us to believe, nor
the knowledge of them serve at all for our knowing and
being alerted to what pleases God unless we not only can
tell what they are but also believe them (which belief, you
grant, is called faith), from all this it consequently follows
that the Church always has and always shall have the knowledge and belief of such things as God will have it bound to
believe."

"That is true," said he, "because God has left holy Scripture to the Church, and all those things are in it, and the
Church believes it to be true. And therefore therein and
thereby does the Church have all that notification and learning of God's pleasure that you speak of, without which it
cannot endure."

"Are you there yet again?" said I. "We have several ways
proved and agreed between us that this knowledge and faith
preceded Scripture (the putting in writing), and that there
are many necessary things, both to believe and to do, that are
not in holy Scripture. And yet after all this (too long to be
repeated!), you return again to the first point (so often refuted!), that nothing is learned or known but by holy Scripture. But now, go ahead and suppose it were so; what would
you gain by that? For what if God," said I, "had left Scripture
to the Church shut up in a locked chest, that no one looked
in? Would that have served?"

"No, by golly," said he.

"What if he had left it out in the open and written in such
a way that no one could read it?"

"That would be just the same," said he.

"What if everyone," said I, "could read it, and no one could understand it?"

"As little would it serve," said he, "as the other."

"Then," said I, "since it does serve the Church as something in which to learn God's pleasure, and it could not do that, as you yourself grant, unless the Church understood it, it follows from this that the Church understands it. And thus whatever way we turn for the faith and knowledge of God's pleasure—even if it be, as you say, all known by Scripture and no part otherwise—always to this point you still bring it in the end: that the Church has the sure knowledge thereof. And then if that be so, you will not (as you a little while ago said you would) with regard to any and all texts of Scripture seeming to make an article of our faith doubtful and to call into question what we are obliged to believe, after you have read in Scripture all that can be read, and heard on both sides all that can be said, then take whichever interpretation seems to you yourself the most plausible. Nor, if you still for all that remain in doubt, will you then, after your intense prayers made to God for his grace and guidance in the choice, go take you the one view at random and stick to it, as though you were assured by your confidence in God that his grace had inclined your assent to the surer side. Rather, since I have shown you plainly, by reason, that he has given his church in all such things knowledge of the truth, you will take the sure way and put yourself out of all perplexity, if in the point itself and the scriptures that bear upon it, you take for the truth that way that the Church teaches you there, no matter how different the matter may look to you yourself or anyone else."

29.

The author proves by Scripture that God instructs the church of Christ in every truth indispensably requisite to our salvation.

"Truly," said he, "you well turn it around. But yet you made as though you wanted to prove that God had in Scripture told me that he did and always would tell his church the truth in all such matters. And now you bring it to the point that it is not holy Scripture that tells me the tale, but man's reason. And surely, as I explained to you before, I dare not well trust reason in matters of faith and of holy Scripture."

"I started," said I, "to prove it to you by Scripture, and then, at the outset, you distracted me. However, this reasoning has Scripture for its foundation and ground. And though it somewhat builds further thereon, yet not always is reason to be mistrusted where faith does not stand against it and God does not say the contrary. Unless reason has so little credibility with you that you will not now believe it if it tells you that twice two make four. I suspect you will fare by reason as someone once did by a dishonest scoundrel. He swore that he would not for twenty pounds hear that man say his Creed, for he knew him for such a liar that he thought he would never thereafter believe his Creed if he once heard it from his mouth."

"However," said I, "let us yet see whether God himself in Scripture tells you the same tale or not. God tells you in Scripture that he will be with his Church to the end of the world. I think you do not doubt that he was speaking those words to the whole Church that then existed and would ever be continued, from the apostles' days till the end of the world."

"That, in all honesty," said he, "must needs be so."

"Then this in all honesty would be enough," said I, "for our purpose, since no one is in doubt as to why he will be with his church. Unless we were to think that he would be with it for nothing, why should he be with it but to keep it and preserve it, with the assistance of his grace-imbued presence, from spiritual harms especially, and, among all the others, especially from infidelity and from idolatry—which was the specific thing from which he called into his church the Gentiles, who otherwise, with respect to moral and civic virtues, if they had not lacked the right cause and end of referring their acts to God, would have been, many of them, not far beneath many of us. Let us go further. Does he not in the fourteenth, fifteenth, and sixteenth chapters of Saint John again and again repeat that after his going he will come back to them? Does he not say that he will not leave them as orphans, as fatherless children, but will himself come back to them? Let us now add thereto the words previously quoted, that he will be with them till the world's end, and it appears clearly that he meant all of this to refer to his whole church that should be to the world's end.

"When he said to them, 'I call you friends, because all that I have heard from my Father I have made known to you' [Jn 15: 15], he spoke as to his perpetual church and not to the apostles alone—unless he also said to them alone these words, 'I command that you love one another' [Jn 15: 12], so that none should love one another later, but only they. Now, lest the things that he taught them should by the later Church be forgotten, which was more to be feared about it than about those who heard those things, he also said to them, 'These things,' he said, 'I have spoken to you, while I am still with you. But the Comforter, who is the Holy Spirit, whom my Father will send in my name, he will teach you all things, and he will put you in mind and remembrance of everything that I shall have said to you' [Jn 14: 25–26]. So that here you see that he shall again always teach the Church of new the old lessons of Christ. And he also said to them that this Comforter, this Holy Spirit, the Spirit of truth, would be sent to abide with them forever [Jn 14: 16–17], which cannot but refer to the whole Church. For the Holy Spirit was not sent into this world to dwell here with the apostles forever, for they did not dwell here that long. Now, if the Spirit of truth will dwell in the Church forever, how can the Church err in perceiving of the truth, in such things, I mean, as God will bind it to know or that will be necessary for it to know? For only to such things was our Lord referring when he said that the

Holy Spirit would teach them all things. For as Saint Paul says, the manifestation and showing of the Spirit is for utility and profit [1 Cor 12:7]. Also, of this Holy Spirit it was not promised by Christ our Savior that he would only tell his church again his words, but he said further, 'I have,' he said, 'besides all this, many things to say to you, but you are not able to bear them now. But when he shall come that is the Spirit of truth, he shall lead you into all truth' [Jn 16:12–13]. Note that our Lord said not that the Holy Spirit would *write* to his church all truth, but that he would *lead* them, by secret inspiration and inclination of their hearts, *into* all truth, which must necessarily include both information and right belief of every essential article, and of the right and true sense of holy Scripture, as far as will be requisite to conserving the Church from any condemnable error.

"Now, when the Holy Spirit will, by God's promise, be for this purpose abiding in the Church forever, and Christ himself has also said that he will not leave his church as orphans, but will come himself and be with it to the end of the world, and says also that his Father is in him and he is in his Father, and that his Father and he are both one entity— not both one person, but both one substance and, with the Holy Spirit, both one God—then it must necessarily follow that to the world's end there is residing with the Church the whole Trinity. Whose active presence being to the Church perpetual, how can it at any time fall from the true faith into false errors and heresies?"

30.

In view of the fact that the messenger had thought before that it would be hard to believe with assurance anything outside of holy Scripture even if the Church did accept that thing and command belief in it, the author points out that were it not for the authority of the Church, people could not know what scripture they should believe. And here it is proved that God will not allow the Church to be mistaken in the distinguishing of the true Scripture of God from any counterfeit.

"Now it is, I believe, proved good and clearly by Scripture, the thing that I promised to prove: namely, that the Church cannot err in any such substantial article as God will have us bound to believe. But yet, seeing that you look to nothing but Scripture alone, this I would like to know from you: whether you believe that Christ was born of a virgin."

"What else?" said he.

"Why do you believe that?" said I.

"The Gospel tells me so," said he.

"What if it did not?" said I. "Would your Creed, then, have no credibility unless it brought witnesses with it?"

"The Creed," said he, "is something by itself."

"Yet it is," said I, "not part of the Gospel, as the Our Father is. And yet I think if no gospel had ever been written, you would have believed your Creed."

"I think so too," said he.

"And for what reason," said I, "but because the Church should have told you so? But let's leave our Creed alone a while and go to the Gospel itself. Which Gospel tells you that Christ was born of a virgin?"

"The Gospel of Saint Luke," said he.

"How do you know that?" said I.

"Because I read it," said he, "in that book."

"You read," said I, "such and such a book. But how do you know that Saint Luke wrote it?"

"How do I know," said he, "about other books, except by the fact that they bear the names of their authors written upon them?"

"Do you thereby really know it?" said I. "There are many books that have false inscriptions and are not the books of them whose names are on them."

"That is true," said he. "But yet, even if people did perhaps err and get the name wrong—such as if one were to consider to have been written by Livy a historical book which was written not by him, but by some other honest and learned man—yet the books would be no less elegant or less true for that. Nor, likewise, if the Church did get wrong the real name of some evangelist and Gospel, would the Gospel be any the less true."

"That is," said I, "well said. But how are you sure that the content of the book is true?"

"Good heavens," said he, "because I am."

"That is," said I, "the reason that a young lady gives for her own knowledge of her virginity. But she could tell someone else how she knows she has it, except that she is loath to become so intimate, so as to make it known, that she could tell how she might lose it. But here is no such fear. Tell me, therefore, how do you know that the content of that book is true?"

"I think," said he, "that God tells me so."

"That is a right thing to think," said I. "But he did not tell it to you face to face."

"No," said he. "But he did tell it to others in the beginning, or else it was well known in the beginning, when he wrote it. And he was known, and believed because of his conduct and the miracles that God did for him. And after that, once it was known, the knowledge went on from person to person. And God has so brought things about with us that we believe it because the whole Church has always done so, before our days."

"Now you come," said I, "to the real point. For many things have been true that over the course of time have ceased to be believed. And many a thing has in the beginning been known for false and yet has later happened to be believed. But with the Gospels and all of holy Scripture, God provides that though perchance some of it may perish and be lost, on account of which the Church could suffer harm, but not fall into error (for the faith would stand even if the scriptures were all gone), yet never will he allow his church to make a mistake in that determination and take for holy

Scripture any book that is not. And therefore says holy Saint Augustine, 'I would not believe the Gospel were it not for the Church' [*Contra epistolam Manichaei*, 1.5]. And what he says makes good sense. For were it not for the Spirit of God keeping the truth thereof in his church, who could be sure which were the true gospels? There were many who wrote gospels. And yet the Church, by a secret prompting from God, has rejected the rest and chosen out these four as the definitely, indisputably true ones."

"That is," said he, "certainly so."

"This is," said I, "so certainly so that Luther himself is driven of necessity to grant this. He realizes that otherwise there would be no support or security in Scripture itself, if the Church could be allowed by God to make a mistake in that determination and take for holy Scripture a writing that actually was not. And therefore he concedes that this must needs be a certain, infallible ground: that God has given this gift to his church, that his church can always distinguish the word of God from the word of men."

"In all honesty," said he, "that must needs be so, or else everything would collapse."

Said I, "Then you who would believe the Church in nothing, nor give sure credence to the tradition of the Church unless it was proved by Scripture, now see it proved to you that you could not believe Scripture unless it were proved to *be* Scripture, by the judgment and tradition of the Church."

"No," said he, "but once I have learned from the Church that it is holy Scripture and the word of God, then I believe it better than I believe all the Church. I might at times through a person of little account get to know a much more substantial one. And yet when I know him, I will believe him much better than him by whom I know him, if they tell a different story and say contrary things."

"That makes good sense," said I. "But the Church does not tell you to believe the contrary of what Scripture says. What it tells you is that in such places as you would 'believe

Scripture rather than the Church,' there you do not understand Scripture. For no matter what words it speaks, it nevertheless does not mean the opposite of what the Church teaches you. And the Church cannot err in any such weighty point."

"How will I know?" said he.

"Why are we still at that point?" said I. "Have we so soon forgotten the perpetual presence of the Trinity in his church, and the prayer of Christ to keep the faith of his church from failing, and the Holy Spirit purposely sent to keep in the Church the remembrance of Christ's words and to lead it into all truth? What good would it have done to have put you in remembrance of the active presence of God with the children of Israel—his walking with them, in the cloud by day and in the pillar of fire by night, in their earthly journey— and thereby to have proved to you the much more special presence of God with his Christian church in their spiritual voyage, wherein his especial goodness well shows his tender diligence in that he vouchsafes to assist and comfort us with the continual presence of his precious Body in the Blessed Sacrament? All this would not help if the manifest explana tion that I made you and the conclusive Scripture that I quoted you cannot yet imprint in your heart a perceiving that the presence of God in his church must necessarily preserve his church from all condemnable errors in the faith and to such an extent give his church the right understanding of Scripture that it can well perceive that no part of Scripture, correctly understood, goes against any article that the Church believes as a constituent part of the Christian faith."

"Indeed," said he, "I perceive it well when I remember it, but it was not readily in remembrance."

31.

On the basis that the Church cannot err in the discernment of true Scripture, the author proves, by the argument which the King's Highness in his noble and most celebrated book pits against

*Luther, that the Church cannot err in the necessary understanding
of Scripture. And, finally, the author in this chapter briefly sum-
marizes some of the principal points already proved. And with this
the first part ends.*

"I still would," said I, "ask you one thing. Why, do you
think, will Christ not allow his church to make a mistake in
the discerning of holy Scripture from other writings, and not
allow it to take for a book of holy Scripture what is in fact
not one?"

"Lest people might," said he, "by some spurious book
thought to be holy Scripture, have great occasion given them
to conceive wrong doctrine and wrong ideas of the faith, if
God would allow his church to take a spurious, contrived
book for holy Scripture and for his own holy words."

"What you say," said I, "is very true. Now, what if in the
true Scripture he should allow his church to mistake the true
meaning with respect to a substantial matter of our faith?
Would they not be in like danger of falling by false understanding into errors like those they could fall into by false
writings?"

"Yes, that they would," said he.

"Indeed," said I, "they would be—and in much more.
For in a spurious book mistaken for Scripture, even if the
Church held it in however high a reverence on account of
some good things they found in it, and thereby should have
great occasion to believe the fraudulent errors written in
the same, yet having (as the Church always shall have) the
true faith first in heart, they would find many means to
keep out the errors. But, now, if they should falsely understand the true Scripture, there would.be no way to escape
from condemnable errors. And therefore may I say to you,
as the King's Highness most judiciously put it to Luther,
that since God will not allow his church to wrongly take
a book as Scripture, because of the danger of condemnable
errors that might ensue therefrom, and since a like danger
can ensue from the wrong construing of the meaning as

from the wrong taking of the book, it must needs follow that God will in things of our faith no more allow the Church to take a false meaning for true than to take a false book for Scripture. With this argument His Highness so clearly confuted him that he, for shame, never dared since to attack that point again, nor could come up with anything else to say but that upon his own acknowledgement, in all substantial points concerning the faith, or knowledge of virtue (what is pleasing to God), the Church has such a right understanding of Scripture that it perceives quite correctly that no text therein can be rightly understood to go against any article that the Church believes to be something that must be believed. And this point he never since dared attack or make a rejoinder to, albeit that the King's Highness with this one point alone plainly turns up and destroys the ground and foundation of all the heresies that Luther would have people believe. And therefore, of all points, Luther had the greatest reason to dispute this one earnestly; and undoubtedly he would have if he had known how."

"Assuredly," said your friend, "I am not surprised that he did not. For this point is so clear, he could not; and on it I am fully satisfied."

"Then you are," said I, "satisfied on this one also: that the faith of the Church is a right rule to carry with you to the study of Scripture, to shape you the understanding of the texts by, and by which so to take them that they are always consistent with it."

"Right," said he.

"Then you are," said I, "also fully answered in this: that whereas you said you would not believe the Church when it is telling a tale of its own, but only when it is telling you Scripture, you now see that in such things as we are talking about, that is to say, essential points of our faith, if the Church tells you something which if it were false would be condemnable, you must believe and can be sure that since the Church cannot in such things err, it is really true, every-thing that the Church in such things tells you. And that it is not the Church's own word, but the word of God, even if it is not in Scripture."

"That is quite evident," said he.

"Then you are," said I, "as fully satisfied that, whereas you recently said that it would be a disobeying of God and a putting of the Church over him if you were to believe the Church in such things as God in his holy Scripture says himself the contrary of, you now see that it can in no way be so. Since his church in such things as we are speaking of cannot err, it is impossible that the Scripture of God can be contrary to the faith of the Church."

"That is very true," said he.

"Then it is as true," said I, "that you are, moreover, fully answered on the principal point: that the scriptures cited against images and shrines and the veneration of saints do not at all make against them. And also that those things—images, I mean, and shrines and praying to saints—are things good and to be held in honor in Christ's church, since they are believed so by the Church. Which, as you grant and see the reason why you should grant, cannot (thanks to the spe-cial presence of God and instruction of the Holy Spirit) on such points be allowed to fall into error. And so we are for this matter, at last, with much work, come to an end. And therefore we will now go to dinner. And your other objec-tions that you have brought up, by which you would prove those things reprovable and make them seem idolatry, which we deferred before, those we will talk of after dinner."

"By my word," said he, "I have something else to tell you which, with all this stuff granted, will yet put us into as much uncertainty as we were in before."

"Yes?" said I. "Then we really have borne out that saying, 'The further I go, the behinder I get.' I ask you, what thing is that? For that I would really like to hear now, before we go."

"No," said he, "it would be better to dine first. My lady

will, I think, be angry with me for keeping you from it so
long. For I believe it is now very close to twelve. And she
would grow even more angry with me if I should make you
sit and muse at your meal, as you would, I well know, muse
on the matter if you knew what it was."

"If I were," said I, "like my wife, I would muse more on
it now and have no meal, for the longing to know. But
come on, then, and let us dine first, and you shall tell us
afterward."

Part Two

I.

The messenger, summarizing some of the things already proved, and for his part agreeing that the church of Christ cannot with regard to any essential point of the faith fall into any condemnable error, calls into doubt and question which is the true church of Christ, pointing out that those whom we call heretics will perhaps say that they are the Church, and we not. Of which the author states the contrary, explaining how we can know that they cannot be the Church.

After dinner we walked into the garden, and there shortly, sitting in an arbor, began to proceed with our discussion, I asking him to tell what thing that might be that made our long morning discussion frustrate and left us as uncertain as we started out.

"Sir," said he, "that I shall tell you shortly. There was principally in question whether venerating images and relics, praying to saints, and going on pilgrimages are legitimate practices or not. And I called your attention to the fact that people cited against them certain texts of holy Scripture; and I also said to you that it seemed that the texts themselves, which are the words of God, go against these practices with an authority greater than that of the glosses of men who in such ways expound the texts as to make them seem to support them. And you put forward on the other side the consensus and accord and common Catholic faith of the Church, which you said—and indeed, to tell the truth, did prove, both by reason and by Scripture—could not be erroneous; and that the Church could not err in the faith that God wants known and believed.

"You proved the matter also by miracles. When I brought up certain things that moved people to fear, partly that the miracles were not real, but especially that they were not done by God for corroboration of the faith, but were perhaps by God's sufferance done by the devil for our delusion (we getting what we deserve by our falling from the veneration of God himself to the veneration of his creatures), you proved to me yet again that the miracles were real and that it must necessarily be God who was doing them. And you proved it to me by this: that it should otherwise follow that the Church had a wrong, and condemnable, belief. Which you again proved quite solidly to be impossible.

"And when, along the way, there came occasion to speak of the contradiction there sometimes appeared to be between the texts of holy Scripture itself and the common opinion and faith of the Church, and I said that it was thought reasonable to believe Scripture, it being God's own words rather than the words of men, you there proved that the common faith of the Church was as well God's own words as was holy Scripture itself, and of as great authority; and that no student of Scripture should presume to try, examine, and judge the Catholic faith of Christ's Church by Scripture, but rather one should by the Catholic faith of Christ's Church examine and expound the texts of Scripture; and that in the study of Scripture this was the sure way, wherein, you said, great light would be given by the writings of the old holy theologians, whereby we are assured that the faith that the Church has now is the same faith and the same points that they had of old, in every age and every time. And in this part you proved yet again by reason and holy Scripture that the Church has by the teaching of God and the Holy Spirit the right understanding of Scripture in all points that are necessary to know.

"And on that basis you again deduced and proved that no text of Scripture, rightly understood, can go against the venerating of images and relics and the visiting of pilgrimage shrines; but that all these things are well proved good and pleasing to God, and the miracles done at such places done by God, since by his special, active presence he so informs and instructs his church, in so great and so substantial an article so highly involving honor or dishonor of God, that it cannot be allowed to go in for superstition and idolatry instead of faith and honor done to God.

"And this is," said he, "as far as I remember, the whole sum and effect of all that has thus far been proved between us."

"Quite so," said I. "And this is by you very well remembered, and reiterated good and succinctly."

"But now," said he, "with all this stuff granted, we have gotten nowhere."

"Why so?" said I.

"Good heavens," said he, "because someone who believed the venerating of images to be wrong and illicit might grant all of that—that the Church does not err, and that the Church has the right faith, and that the Church does not misinterpret Scripture—and when all this was granted, he might say that the Church perhaps does not believe as you say it does. For he might perhaps deny the Church to be those people that you take it to be, and say that it is those who believe what he believes—that is, that all these kinds of veneration are wrong—and who believe that those whom you take for the Church believe wrong."

"If he and his group," said I, "are the Church, he must tell where his confreres are."

"Why so?" said he. "If people should ask you and me where the Church is, we could tell them no one place, but many different countries."

"Let him," said I, "in like manner identify some groups that are known for congregations together in different countries."

"Why," said he, "in the beginning and a good while after, the church of Christ in every place hid itself, so that people could not tell in any country where it was; its members did not dare come out and show themselves."

"That was in the beginning," said I, "as long as the persecution lasted. But once the persecution ceased, it was soon known in every country where the Church was."

"Goodness," said he, "if I were to take that approach, I would perhaps say that in that situation it is still, and that the Church is that group, perhaps, that you, that call yourselves the Church, do habitually call heretics. For they now do know one another well enough, and call themselves and their confreres around the world the true church—though they dare not profess it openly, because you, that call yourselves the Church and them heretics, do persecute them as the church of the pagans did in the beginning. And therefore they do hide themselves as the Church did in the beginning. But if you would cease your persecution once and for all and let them live in peace, you would see them flock together so fast that they would soon show you the Church without even trying."

"They might," said I, "perhaps show a pack of evildoers within a while, if they were allowed to, and the kind of church that the prophet David speaks of: 'Odi ecclesiam malignantium,' 'I hate the church of malicious men' [Ps 26: 5]. But they shall never show themselves to be the church of Christ.

"The church of Christ, wherever it was in all the persecution, used to come together to the preaching and prayer, though it was secretly, in forests or private homes. They also celebrated the sacraments among themselves, such as Baptism, Confirmation, Matrimony, Holy Orders, there being priests and bishops among them; fastings, vigils kept, the Sundays hallowed, the Mass said, the Divine Office sung, and their people given Communion, as is well evidenced by the historical writings not only of the Church, but also of the pagans. And to some extent well evidenced by a letter from Pliny to Emperor Trajan. And such things must there be therein, if it be any church or congregation of Christ's. Now, these people that you speak of practice no such things among themselves; and therefore they cannot be the church of Christ."

"They preach," said he, "in private, among themselves, and all the rest they do in our churches."

"This," said I, "plainly proves that they cannot be the church of Christ. For the church of Christ ever avoided and shunned the temples in which idols and false gods were. And it was a plain renouncing of Christ's faith to do any homage thereto, even if they did it only out of fear and only with their body, thinking the contrary in their heart. For our Lord says, 'Whoever denies me before the world, I will deny him before my Father in heaven' [Mt 10:33]. And holy Scripture says, 'Spiritus sanctus effugiet fictum,' 'The Holy Spirit flees from feigning' [Ws 1:5]. But these people whom you call the Church come to the churches where the images are which they take for idols, and there they come to worship with us whom they take for idolaters. And whereas they teach among themselves that we do wrong, they come to our church, as I say, and in the sight of the world they do the same: kneel before statues as we do, set up candles as we do, pray to saints as we do—and perhaps more loudly with their mouths while they mock them in their hearts. And, moreover, many mock also the sacraments which they receive.

"And this puts me in mind also that besides all this, you cannot say, 'These whom we call heretics are the Church,' but you must tell which kind of them is the Church. For they cannot all be, since the Church is and must be all of one belief and have one and the same faith. And as it was written in the Acts of the Apostles: 'Erat multitudo credentium, anima una et cor unum,' 'The multitude of faithful, believing people were all of one mind and of one heart' [Acts 4:32]. And in the Church is the Holy Spirit, 'qui facit unanimes in domo,' 'who makes all of one mind in the house' of God [Ps 68:7]; that is, in the Church. But among heretics there are almost as many divergent minds as there are people.

"The church of Christ also is a thing that has always remained and continued. But the sects of heretics and their churches never continued, but ever dwindled and vanished quite away, so much so that of all the old heretics the books also are gone and lost, as of when there was no law made yet to burn them, so that it is easy to see that God himself destroyed those heresies, and the world clean gave them up at some time, though new heretics now, long after, take them up again. For if their opinions had anywhere continually endured, there would their books have been continually preserved, which are now quite gone, as of many years ago. And thus you can well see that the Church cannot be any such folk that in so many years have had no church nor come to any, except to those in which they say people worship idols."

"Well," said he, "perhaps they will not find it too difficult to name you a place and point out to you a group and congregation which they will say is the true church. For what if they will tell you 'Bohemia, and now in Saxony, where Luther is, and perhaps in a good part of Germany'?"

"Goodness," said I, "if they say that, then they leap like a flounder out of the frying pan into the fire. For in Saxony, first of all, and among all the Lutherans, there are as many understandings as there are heads. And all as sensible as wild geese. And as recently as they began, not only are there as many sects, almost, as men, but also the masters themselves change their minds and their opinions every day and never know where to hold them. Bohemia is also in the same situation. One faith in the town, another in the field. One in Prague, another in the next town. And even in Prague itself, one faith in one district, another in the next. So that if you locate it in Bohemia, you must tell in what town. And if you name a town, you yet must tell what district. And yet they all acknowledge that they cannot have the sacraments administered but by such priests as are made by authority derived and conveyed from the pope, who is, under Christ, vicar and the head of our church."

2.

"That none of all these can be the Church will be made quite clear also by another means. Would you say that the true church and congregation of Christ came before all the churches and congregations of heretics, or that some churches of heretics came before the church of Christ?"

"Actually," said he, "there might have been some churches of heretics before the church of Christ. For there might have been some among the Jews before the birth of Christ. And such, I suppose, were the Sadducees, who did not believe in resurrection, nor in the immortality of the soul [Mt 22: 23]."

"If we should take," said I, "that line of reasoning, we might fetch the church of Christ from really far back and begin it at Adam. For from the first good person to the last, all shall in the end be his Church Triumphant in heaven. But I am speaking of Christ's church now: that congregation that, bearing his name, and having his right faith, and being started out gathered by him himself and spread abroad by his apostles, has continued, and does and shall till his coming to the fearful Last Judgment continue, on in this world. Did this church come before all the churches and congregations of heretics, or did any of them come before it?"

"No," said he, "I think it came before them all."

"How can we," said I, "be sure of that?"

"Goodness," said he, "because always the heretics came out of it."

"That is true," said I. "For they could not be heretics except by being first in it and later coming out. And it is shown by the Gospel in which the good farmer went out to sow his seed, and when he had sown good seed, then the enemy afterward sowed his bad seed, and they grew up together [Mt 13:24–30]. It is also shown by the words of the apostle and holy evangelist Saint John, where he said of heretics, 'E nobis profecti sunt, sed non erant ex nobis.' 'They are gone,' he said, 'from us, but they were not of us' [1 Jn 2:19], meaning that before they ever professed themselves openly for heretics, yet being such in fact, since the church of Christ is a people of one faith, these folk that have another special faith by themselves, altering and contradicting the other, are not completely members of the Church even if for the time being they are in it. As it is now, any member of that body, till it be cut off for fear of corruption of the rest, hangs on it, in a sense, and has some little light or life by the Spirit of God that upholds the body of his church, being ever in a position to take occasion of amendment by some vein of that wholesome moisture of God's grace that specially spreads throughout that holy body. But those who by the profession of heresies and infidelity fall off from that body or, because of the fear of their corrupting the rest, are by excommunication cast out of the body, they completely dry up and wither away. Our Savior says it himself. 'I am,' says he, 'a real vine, and my Father is a gardener. I am the vine, and you are the branches. And every branch that bears in me no fruit, my Father takes it away. And every branch that bears fruit, he purges it to make it bring the more fruit. And as the branch can do no good being taken from the tree, just so can you do no good or serve for anything but the fire unless you abide in me' [see Jn 15:1–6]. By these words of our Savior (and many more there spoken at length), though it is shown that whoever does keep the faith, yet unless he works well with it, God will pluck him out; and that whoever, abiding in the stem by faith, does do good works, the more he does the more grace and help shall he have from God to grow the better and to do the more; yet it is also shown that all the good works that can be done will be of no use if we are out of the stem. And out of the stem of the vine are all who are not grafted in by faith, or have fallen off by public profession of heresy, or have been cut off and cast out for infidelity. For faith is the gate into God's church, just as misbelief is the gate into the devil's church. For as the Apostle says, 'Accedentem ad Deum oportet credere,' 'One cannot come to God without faith' [Heb 11:6]. And therefore whoever professes a false belief, let him be sure that he is gone out of the gate of God's church before actual excommunication, and fallen off the body of the vineyard. And if they are underground, neither professing their heresies nor actually being excommunicated and cast out, they are in the Church but not completely of it. Rather, in a sense, they are of it in such a way as a dead hand is rather a burden in the body than really any member, organ, or instrument thereof. And therefore Saint John says, as I said before, that the heretics 'are gone out from us, but they were not of us; for if they had been of us, they would have remained with us.' Not meaning by this what some would have it seem: that a good person is not a member of the Church, or in God's favor, during all the time that he is good, if he happens to become bad afterward. No, he means that in going their way, away from us, they showed that they were in fact wicked while they were with us; and so, though they were with us, they yet were not of us. For even if heretics and infidels are among faithful and right-believing people, they yet are not of them. And thus it is shown, as you said before, that the church of Christ is prior to all the churches of heretics, and that all congregations of heretics have come out of the church of Christ."

"That is very true," said he.

"Well," said I, "if that is true, as indeed it is, then no sect in Bohemia can be the right church. For the church which we call the Church, that believes as we believe, was there before them all. And never yet has any church of heretics had a church to use that was not built by our church. So it is evident that none of them all can be Christ's church, but Christ's church must necessarily be that church which existed before all of them, and from which they all have sprung and since severed themselves, which is the church that they all do not deny to believe against them the points which we believe and they reject."

3.

The messenger submits that the true church is perhaps not the people that we take for it, but a hidden, unrecognized class of those only who are predestined by God to be saved. To which the author responds, explaining why this cannot be so.

"Perhaps," said he, "it could be said that there is no need to identify any place where the true church and true Christian congregation is, but that since every place is of neutral significance in that regard, it may be that all the good individuals and chosen people of God that are predestined to be saved—whatever region they may be in, and however scattered they may be, here one and there one, here two and there two—that these are the true church of Christ. And are in this world unknown as yet, while the Church does but wander in the pilgrimage of this short life."

"Goodness," said I, "this stuff goes from bad to worse. And actually, this point is their last resort. For first they see plainly that they must necessarily grant that the true church can neither be wrong regarding the right faith nor mistake holy Scripture or misunderstand it to the introduction of infidelity and false belief. And this ground all the heretics themselves find so sure and firm that they well realize that unless they want to openly and utterly deny Christ altogether, it cannot be undermined. And since they manifestly see this, and as clearly see also that the Church (which is in fact the true church) condemns all their ways—from which condemnation, since the Church cannot err in the discerning of the truth, it must necessarily follow that they themselves mistake the whole entire matter and are completely in a wrong way—therefore they are driven to deny that the Church is the people who are known as the Church. And to go seek another, they know neither what nor where, and build up in the air a church all so spiritual that they leave therein at length neither God nor good human being.

"And, first, where they say that there are none in it but those who are predestined to be saved, if the question were of the Church Triumphant, in heaven, then they would be right. But we are speaking of Christ's Church Militant, here on earth, and therefore their frame goes as far wide of the place they should set it on as heaven and earth stand asunder. For first I want to know, if the Church is none but those predestined to be saved, whether all that are predestinates are members of it."

"Why not?" said he.

"Then," said I, "those that are predestined to be saved— can they or can they not at various times be sinners in their days?"

"What if they can?" said he.

"Can they not," said I, "also at various times in their days be in a wrong belief and a false heresy, and afterward turn around, repent, and reform, and so be saved at last, since God has predestined them to be?"

"What then?" said he.

"Good heavens," said I, "then it will follow that someone could be a member of the true church and so still continue, and never be thrown out, while being a stark heretic."

"Yet," said he, "he is, all that while, a living member of the Church by reason of God's predestination, since, even if he is not certain of this, it yet is in fact a certainty that he is and always will be a member of the true church."

"It is," said I, "certain in fact and well known to God that he so will be. But it is just as certain that for the time being he is not, unless everything that ever shall be is already present in fact, since it is present to God's knowledge. In which case Saint Paul was as good when he was a persecutor as when he was an apostle, and as truly a member of Christ's church before he was born as he is now in heaven."

"Well," said he, "though perhaps not all those that are living and predestined to be saved are in it, it still could be that there are none in it but predestinates."

"But it could be," said I, "that, since people are changeable, someone who is a predestinate may be at many times in his life evil. And that someone who will in the end fall into sin and baseness, and thus finally cast himself away, will at some time of his life be good, and therefore, for that time, in God's favor. For God blames or hates no one for what that person shall will, but only for that malicious will that he has or has had already. And thus shall there by this reasoning be good people outside of Christ's church and wicked people within it; right-believing people outside of it and heretics inside it; and both the one and the other without reason or good cause why."

4.

The messenger submits that even if the Church is not the number of only the folk predestined to Paradise, it yet could perhaps be the number of good and right-believing folk here and there, unrecognized as such, who could perhaps be those whom we condemn as heretics for holding opinion against images. Of which the author proves the contrary.

"Well," said he, "it still could be that the true church of Christ is all those who believe aright and live well wherever they are, even if the world does not know who they are, and even if few of them know each other. For God, as Saint Paul says, knows who are his [see 2 Tm 2: 19]. And Christ says that against his church the gates of hell shall not prevail; but the gates of hell do prevail against sinners. And therefore it is clearly shown that there can be no sinners in his church, and that there are no members of his church except good folk. And to them our Lord is present, and he keeps them from errors and gives them right understanding of his holy scriptures. And where they are makes no difference, and how few they are all together does not matter. For our Savior says,

'Wherever two or three are gathered together in my name, there am I also, among them' [Mt 18:20]. And so his true church is here and there, made up of only good people, to the world unknown and to himself well known. And even if they are comparatively few, yet they make up, all around the world, a good many among them. As God said when the children of Israel were fallen into idolatry and worshipping the idol Baal to such an extent that it seemed all were in that position and no one knew who was otherwise, yet our Lord said, as appears in the nineteenth chapter of the first Book of Kings, 'I shall reserve for myself seven thousand that have not bent their knees before Baal.' So that where the synagogue and church were then, this was unknown to man, but it was well known to God. And they were not his church who seemed to be, but a group ungathered, that no one was aware of or would have guessed. And so it may perhaps now be that the true church of Christ is not, and for many days has not been, the people that seem to be the Church, but some good people scattered here and there, unknown, till God gather them together and make them known; and perhaps they are those who believe against images, and whom we now call heretics."

"This is," said I, "an argument that Luther himself makes. By which he would bring the true church of Christ out of knowledge, and would put it in question whether the saints that the Church honors were good persons or not. And would have it seem maybe not; that they were perhaps not good. And that the really good people and saints were some others whom the world (on account of their open lewd conduct) regarded as evil. But whereas he says that the church or synagogue of the right belief was then unknown, that is not true. For it was well known in Jerusalem and Judaea, though it had been unknown who the faithful were in Samaria. And Scripture also does not say that these seven thousand whom he would leave still in Israel that had not bent their knees before Baal were undercover and unknown, but he says only that such a number of such folk he would leave. But now, for our purpose, since you will have the true church a secret, unknown, not company and congregation, but scattered number of only good individuals, do you want these good individuals who by your reckoning make up the true church to have the same faith as, and none other than, the one had by us who are now considered the Church, or else a different faith and belief?"

"What if they have the same?" said he.

"Goodness," said I, "then your newly built church will not at all help your case. For they will as firmly confirm veneration of images, praying to saints, and going on pilgrimages as we do. And as thoroughly condemn as heresy your opinion to the contrary."

"That is very true," said he. "But it may be that the faith and belief of that true church will be that all this stuff is erroneous and as plain idolatry as was the worshipping of Baal."

"On which supposition," said I, "Christ did not keep himself seven thousand from the worship of Baal in all the regions that bear the name of Christendom, except these modern folk of Saxony and Bohemia that you yourself grant to be the heretics, as sects having come out of the Church. And it would be more than amazing if all of the church of Christ should be completely among infidels and heretics, and no part of it at all in the great unchangeable Christian countries which have kept their faith in one constant fashion transmitted from the beginning. For this I am sure of: that in all those regions, as I say, if anyone has any such belief against images and saints, he yet comes to the church among his neighbors, and there bends his knees to Baal (if the images be Baal) as his neighbors do. But come, let us go on a little further.

"Suppose there were some such secret good folk as you speak of, who had the right belief and were the right church, and they were so scattered asunder that they were unknown to the world. Has not God set an order in his church that some shall preach to the rest for exhortation to good living and information as to what good living consists in, such as in faith and good works?"

"Yes," said he.

"Did not Christ also command," said I, "that sacraments be administered in his church by the priests of the same?"

"Yes," said he.

"Now," said I, "suppose some infidels, such as Turks or Saracens, having heard the name of Christ, did long to know his Scripture and his faith. Hearing that there are many people, whole nations of them, that profess themselves for Christians, but that they are all blatant idolaters and in a misbelief and clearly deceived and beguiled (and this especially by the clergy that teach them), but that there are, however, still a few good, right-believing folk who are not deceived, who among them do constitute the actual true church—but who they are, or where they are, or how to ask for them, or if one stumbles upon them, how will one recognize them, these things no one can tell them—how will these infidels come to the faith, and from whom will they hear it? For having been warned beforehand that there are many sects of heretics and only one true church, they would never be so mad as to learn from those who they might think were wrong. And how would they now come to the ones who were right, when the true church is unknown?"

"They might," said he, "come upon Scripture."

"They would," said I, "there be like the eunuch who could not understand without a teacher [see Acts 8: 27–39]. And then if they came upon a wrong teacher of a wrong church, everything would be distorted. And also they would not trust the scriptures, or reckon that they had the right books of scripture, among false sects, but would look to receive the true scripture from the right and true church. And thus it here becomes evident that on this supposition, God left no established way for his Gospel and faith to be taught.

"But let's let go of these infidels and speak of ourselves, who, on the supposition that this way is right, are as wrong as they in fact are. Where, then, are the preachers of this true church, who should preach and teach us better? For it is no church if it has no preachers."

"It has," said he, "some that preach sometimes, but you will not tolerate them. You punish them and burn them."

"No," said I, "they are smarter than that. They will not be burned because of us, for they will rather swear on the Bible that they never said such and such, or else that they will say it no more. And this makes it evident that there is no such secret, unknown church of Christ that, having such opinions, is the true church. For the true church has always had some who have firmly stood by their faith and their preaching, and who would never recant it with God's word, even if the refusal meant their death. And this church that we are members of, that takes your church for heretics, has had in it many such martyrs, who believed as we do, against your opinions, as is evidenced by the historical accounts and by many of their books; whereas of your secret church I have never yet in all my life found, or heard of, any member who would not have forsworn your faith to save his life.

"Also, where are your priests and your bishops? For a church must have those, to be the church of Christ; but your church cannot have any, you being unknown to one another. And although some such churches have the false opinion that every man is a priest, and every woman too, yet this heresy, false as it is, will not serve this unknown church. For the holders of that opinion do claim that no one may, for all that, take it upon himself to preach or relate to people as a priest till he is chosen by the congregation. And where can that happen in this imaginary church, of which no member knows another? And while our Lord did say, 'Wherever two or three are gathered together in my name, there am I with them,' he was saying not that every two or three, whatever they were, would make up his church, but that wherever there come together in his name two or three who *are* of his church, there is he with them. And so does that one scriptural, Gospel text plainly show, as is well set out and explained by the holy theologian and glorious martyr Saint Cyprian, in his epistle against Novatian.

"Also, when our Savior said that whoever will not correct himself upon having his fault explained to him in front of two or three witnesses should have a complaint lodged against him to the Church, did he mean a secret church that no one would know where to find? [See Mt 18: 15–17.] And when the Apostle writes to the Corinthians that sooner than enter pleas and wrangle in the courts before the infidels, they should set up to be judges in their temporal affairs members of the Church who are not highly thought of, of what church is he speaking—one that no one knows where to look for? [See 1 Cor 6: 4.] This unknown church, which they are driven to seek who are loath to know the Church, will never serve. No, the church of Christ is a church well known. And it was his pleasure to have it known and not hidden. And it is built upon so high a hill of that holy stone, I mean upon Christ himself, that it cannot be hidden. 'Non potest abscondi civitas supra montem posita,' 'The city cannot be hidden that is set on a hill' [Mt 5: 14]. And he would have his faith divulged and spread abroad openly, not always furtively whispered. And thus he bound his preachers to stand by it and not retract his word for any pain. For he said that he did not light that candle to put it and hide it under a bushel basket, for no one would do that, but he had kindled a fire which he would not have lie and smolder as coals do in quench, but he would have it burn and give light [Lk 11: 33 and 12: 49]. And therefore it would be foolish to say that Christ, who would have his church spread throughout the world and everywhere gathered in community, would have it turned into a secret, unknown, individualistic thing severed asunder and scattered about in corners, unknown to all the world and to themselves too.

"Now, where they say that there are no members of the Church except only those that are good folk—this would make the Church completely unknown, no matter how many the people or how large the place. For who can know of that multitude which individuals are actually good and which are bad, since the bad may suddenly, unbeknownst to the world, be converted, and the good as suddenly go bad.

"Now, they proffer for the proof of that opinion words of Christ which Luther also quotes for the same purpose in the book that he wrote against Ambrosius Catharinus; that is to say, the words where our Lord said to Saint Peter that against his church the gates of hell would not prevail [Mt 16: 18], by which words Luther does (as he thinks, and says himself) in a wondrously brilliant way prove that no one can belong to the Church except those who do not sin. For this argument he makes: Christ says that the gates of hell will not prevail against the Church; but 'the gates of hell' is nothing but the devil, and he prevails against all folk that sin; ergo, no folk that sin are the Church. And about this impressive argument it is a wonder to see what boast the mad man makes: that he has clearly proved that the Church is not these people whom we take for the Church, because they are sinners. This argument has so many fallacies and flaws in it, and so much incongruity and absurdity following upon it, that it is more than amazing that a child with one week's study in sophistry could without embarrassment find it in his heart to put it forth as any serious argument. For, in the first place, if someone denies to him that 'the gates of hell' does in that passage mean the devil, then he can never prove it, and then his argument is completely wiped away. And, indeed, several old commentators and Doctors of the Church in that text take 'the gates of hell' to mean the great tyrants and heretics through whose persecutions and heresies—two gates, as it were—many a person has gone into hell, and say that our Savior promises in that text that neither of those two gates, that is to say, neither pagan tyrant nor baptized heretic, will prevail against the Church. For even if they have destroyed and will destroy many members of the Church, they yet will not be able to destroy the Church, but the Church will stand and be by God preserved despite all their teeth. And thus you see how soon Luther's special arguments were overthrown with truth.

"And even if one wanted to grant him that 'the gates of hell' did here signify the devil, we nevertheless would not need to grant him that the devil, since he is called by God by the name of 'the gates' (which is not done for nothing), does prevail against everyone who sins. For he that sins and rises back out of sin—and thus comes within the gates, and yet the gates cannot hold him, but he breaks out of the gates— the gates do not prevail against him, but he prevails against the gates. And thus is again refuted Luther's brilliant argument which he bases upon the text.

"It also is obvious that this is a really insane argument. For where he says that against the church of Christ the gates of hell do not prevail, but that they do prevail against our church, that is to say, all the Christian people whom we call the Church, under obedience to the pope, ergo, they are not the church—this argument proves that there is on earth no church at all. For what church on earth can he find or imagine that does not sin, and especially if this thing were true that he himself says among his other heresies, where he adamantly holds that all the good works of good people are sins, and that people sin in what they do that is good? And thus he would have the Church be only a secret, unknown class of folk that do not sin, and yet he professes that there are none such. And so, as he attempts to do away with the true church that is well known, making as though he would discover a better one, he leaves in the end no church at all. And to such a foolish and false end must they necessarily bring it, all who will make it a number of only such as are good people and do not sin. For if a person should be in it always when they are out of sin, and out of it when they are in sin, then one could perhaps be in it in the morning and out of it at noon, and in again at night. So that who was in it, or when, or where it was, who could tell? And that uncertainty would necessarily give rise to all those clashes and inconsistencies with Scripture that we mentioned before.

"The Church therefore must necessarily be the common, known multitude of Christian people, good and bad together, as long as the Church is here on earth. For this net of Christ's has, for the time being, good fishes and bad [Mt 13:47–50]. And this field of Christ's bears, for the time being, good grain and weeds, till it shall on Judgment Day be purified, and all the bad thrown out, and the good alone remaining [Mt 13:24–30]. And then when the Apostle wrote to the Corinthians about that man who had lain with his mother-in-law [1 Cor 5:1–5], he commanded that he should be separated out from the Church; which he never was, after the deed was done, till the excommunication was pronounced; up to then he was still, for all his sinning, in the Church, although he was wicked and was out of God's favor. Christ himself said to his apostles, 'Now you are clean, but not all' [Jn 13:10], and yet they all were in his church, even though one of them was, as our Savior himself put it, a devil. 'Did I not,' he said [Jn 6:70], 'choose twelve of you, and one of you is a devil?' And if no one belonged to the Church but good people as long as they were good, then Saint Peter would once have been not part of the Church after Christ had appointed him its chief.

"But our Lord, in this his mystical body of his church, carries his members, some sick, some whole, and all sickly. Nor are they for every sin clean cast off from the body, but only if they are, for fear of their causing infection, cut off, or else by their own will they depart and separate themselves, as do these heretics who either reject the Church willfully themselves or else for their obstinacy are put out. For till their stubborn hearts do show them incurable, the body yet bears them about, sick and wicked and stone-cold as they are, to see whether the warmth of the grace going through this whole mystical body of Christ's church might yet beget and keep some life in them. But when the time shall come that this church shall wholly change her place and have heaven for her dwelling instead of earth, after the final judgment has been pronounced and given, when God shall with his spouse, this church of Christ, enter into the delightful wedding chamber to the bed of eternal rest, then shall all these scaly and scabby pieces scale clean off and the whole body of Christ's holy church be left pure, clean, and glorious, without blemish, wrinkle, or spot. She is (and will be, I think, for the duration, as long as she is here) as scabby as ever was Job, and yet her loving Spouse does not leave her, but continually attempts by many kinds of medicine—some bitter, some sweet, some easy to take, some hard, some pleasant, some painful—to cure her."

5.

The author states and proves that this common, known multitude
in Christian nations, not cut off or fallen off by means of heresies,
is the true church of Christ—good people and bad together.

"And finally—to put out of question which is Christ's true church, since it is agreed between us and granted throughout Christendom, and is a really true conclusion, that by the Church we know Scripture—which church is it by which you know Scripture? Is it not this company and congregation of all these nations that, without any dividing into factions and cutting off from the rest, profess the name and faith of Christ? By this church we know Scripture; and this one is the true church; and this one has begun with Christ, and has had him for its head, and Saint Peter, his vicar after him, the head under him, and ever since, the successors of him continually, and has had his holy faith and his blessed sacraments and his holy scriptures delivered, kept, and conserved in it by God and his Holy Spirit. And even if some nations fall away, yet just as however many boughs may fall from a tree, even if more fall than are left on it, they still create no doubt as to which is the original tree even if each of them is planted again in another place and grows bigger than the trunk it first came from—just so, when we see and well know that all the companies and sects of heretics and schismatics, however big they become, came out of this church that I spoke of, we know evermore that the heretics are they that are cut off, and that the Church is the trunk that they all came out from. And since only the church of Christ is the vine that Christ spoke of in the Gospel, that he takes for his mystical body, and since every branch cut off from the tree loses its vital nourishment, we must needs well know that all these branches of heretics fallen from the Church, the vine of Christ's mystical body, no matter how fresh and green they may seem, are yet actually but witherlings that shall shrivel and dry up and be able to serve for nothing but the fire."

6.

The messenger submits that since the Church is this known multi-tude of good people and bad together, of whom no one knows which are the one class and which are the other, it could perhaps be that the good class in the Church is those who believe the venerating of images to be idolatry, and the bad class those who believe the contrary. Which objection the author answers and refutes.

When I was finished speaking, he said, "Sir, you have, in all honesty, fully satisfied me concerning the sure, undoubted knowledge of the true church here on earth. But yet it seems to me that one little question remains concerning our main issue."

"What is that?" said I.

"Indeed, sir," said he, "it is this: that though the true faith is in the Church, and the Church cannot err therein; nor can the Church interpret any text of Scripture in such a way as to make a mistake about the faith; nor is there any scripture that, rightly understood, does or can make a stand against the faith of the Church; and also the Church is none

DIALOGUE CONCERNING HERESIES, PART TWO

other than, as you say, and as I see it is indeed, this whole common congregation of Christian people, good and bad, not separating themselves for perverseness, nor being put out for their obstinate faults—it nevertheless is quite obvious that though the right faith is in the Church, it is not in every member of the Church. And that though the Church cannot err in such things, yet some members of the Church can. Now, it seems to some people that it could well happen, perhaps, that the good, right-believing, not-mistaken folk are those who believe it to be idolatry to venerate images or pray to saints. And, on the other hand, that those who believe the contrary are that part of the Church that is the wicked, wrong-believing, grievously mistaken people."

"That would be a very strange construction," said I. "Just now, you were wanting us to think that in the Church there are none other than good people. Will you now agree that there are in it *some* good people?"

"Yes," said he, "that has to be the case."

"Well," said I, "those who do evil, are they good people?"

"No," said he.

"Do those act rightly," said I, "who do idolatry in deed, though it be against their hearts?"

"No," said he.

"But all," said I, "come to church and venerate images, and all pray to saints. So if that is idolatry, then the church of Christ is all evil. For thus do they that are of the contrary side, for fear of being recognized as such. Also, if someone is acting rightly or preaching rightly, is he a good person if he denies it for fear?"

"No," said he.

"But, now," said I, "all that are of that stripe, if they happen to take some risks and get caught, they will first perjure themselves and afterward abjure their opinion, so that if their opinion were good, they themselves would yet be bad."

"But yet," said he, "if their opinions be good, then they

are not as evil in hiding their understandings out of fear as are those who act and preach against their right opinions and persecute them for saying the truth. Just as some who flagged and fled from martyrdom were not as evil as those who persecuted them."

"That would be quite right," said I, "if these people's opinions were right. But yet, even if they were right, these people would still be bad."

"And the others worse," said he.

"That is well said," said I, "but they and the others are the whole Church. And if yours are bad, as you grant and must necessarily grant that they are, then if the others were bad too, there would be in the Church no good people. But you yourself do not deny that in the Church it must necessarily be that there are some good people. And there can be none that are not on either your side or the other. Ergo, since those on yours are bad, those that are good must necessarily be the others. But none of those on this other side could be good people if they were idolaters and persecuted your side for saying the truth, and forced them to deny the truth. Ergo, this other side is not idolaters, and the opinion of your side, for which they persecute your side, is not right. And thus it is evident, it seems to me, that the good people in the Church are against you, and the bad with you."

7.

The author does some defending of the truth against the heresies holding against images, and, summarizing somewhat briefly what has been proved, thus finishes and ends the proof of his side of the argument.

"And I have not even mentioned yet all the good people, well known for good people, and holy people, and now saints in heaven, who have condemned your side and written against you. And your side therefore is in turn so strongly against saints because it sees its heresies impugned and condemned by their holy writings. Nor, besides this, have I said anything about the general councils condemning your side by good, solid authority confirmed and corroborated by the whole body of Christendom, led thereto, both long ago and ever since, through the secret operation of the Holy Spirit, who could never allow (as you yourself agree) the church of Christ to continue so wholly and so long in such condemnable idolatry as this would be if it were superstition and not a part of authentic faith and true, devout religion. Wherefore—since I have proved to you that the Church cannot err in so great a point, nor against the right faith mistake the meaning of holy Scripture; and also that these people who believe in the licitness of image veneration are the true church of Christ; and that both the good and the bad members of the Church do engage in it, the good ones honestly and the bad dishonestly; and that all the good ones of old have approved of and made use of this way and condemned the contrary view, which has even been declared false and heretical by whole general councils of Christendom, corroborated by the faith and custom of all the people, as well as having been brought into such consensus by God's Holy Spirit, who governs his church—I need never go further or comment on your texts or arguments to the contrary. For this side thus proved good, it must necessarily follow that the other side is without merit, unless you have anything further to say against this. Which if you do have, never hesitate to bring it up. For I do not want to be so hasty as to leave any corner of the matter not ransacked for any questionable thing we can possibly find there."

"In all honesty, sir," said he, "I am in this matter right up against the wall, and do not see how to go further."

"Now I assure you," said I, "that if I myself could think of any further objection, I would not fail to bring it up. But in all honesty I think that we have gone as far into this matter as we can both get. And, I am sure, as far as ever did Luther, or anyone else I know of who has said or written anything on that side."

8.

*The author commences the answer to the objections previously
made by the messenger against venerating images, praying to
saints, and going on pilgrimages. And first he answers, in this
chapter, the objections made against praying to saints.*

"Now, therefore, as I say, I need not go further. But yet I will
say something about the things which, as you say, do move
many to take the venerating of images for idolatry. And it
being so taken, and their opinion being so highly regarded,
they consider it a basis for thinking that the miracles done in
front of the statues, or through invocations of saints, are
illusions from the devil.

"We will start with the saints themselves, and along the
way we will speak of their relics, statues, and pilgrimage
sites, as occasion arises in our discussion. And first of all, in
all seriousness, saving that the books and other writings of
holy theologians condemn the heresies of these men—their
displeasure and anger at which sets them on fire to study
how to diminish the reputation of them that thus stand in
their light—if it weren't for that, I would much wonder what
motivates these heretics to impugn the venerating of saints
and forbid us to pray to them. And albeit I now see the cause
of their malice, I still cannot be much less amazed by the
madness of these men who show their bad will so openly
that they have neither a rational argument nor a good pretext
to cloak or cover it with.

"First they call into question whether saints can hear us.
And if they do, yet whether they can help us. And, finally, if
they could, yet they would have us think it foolish to want
them to, since God can do it better and will himself do it
sooner than all of them will.

"Now, where they doubt whether saints hear us, I wonder
where that doubt comes from, unless they think them dead as
well in soul as in body. For if their holy souls live, no one with
any sense will think them to be worse, and of less love and
charity toward people who need their help, now, when they

are in heaven, than they were while here on earth. For in all that while, no matter how good they were, yet the best was worse than the worst is now. As our Savior said about Saint John the Baptist, that there was no woman's son greater than he, and yet the least that was already in heaven was his better [Mt 11:11]. We see that the nearer that folk draw thitherward, the more well disposed they are toward people here. And thus Saint Stephen, when he saw heaven open for him, he began to pray for them that maliciously killed him [Acts 7:60]. And do we think, then, that being in heaven he will not vouchsafe to pray for them that devoutly honor him, but has less love and charity being there than he had when going there? If the rich man who lay in hell [Lk 16:19–21] did yet have—not just for fear that his own punishment would increase if his brothers came to condemnation as a result of his bad example in sin, but also out of natural love and fleshly favor toward his kin (which fleshly affection, unaccompanied by grace or virtue, can perhaps coexist with the state of damnation)—if he had a care and concern for his five brothers, is it likely that saints, then, being so full of blessed charity in heaven, will care nothing for their brothers in Christ whom they see here in this wretched world?

"Now, if there be no doubt (as I trust there is none) that their holy souls are alive, they want us to do right. And as little doubt that they are alive if God is their God as he is indeed. And he being the God not of the dead but of the living, as our Savior says in the Gospel [Mk 12:27]—for all live still, and ever shall, that he has taken to himself and once given life to—there remains, then, nothing further to see but whether they can do us any good or whether they cannot, either because they cannot hear us or because they cannot help us.

"And first, I really wonder if they think the saints cannot help us. For while they were here they could, as appears in the Acts of the Apostles. And since feebleness and lack of power are here part of our misery, and strength and abundance of power are one big part of well-being, a lot they would have gained in this respect if they were now less able than they were before to do good to those they very much wanted helped! For whether they are able there to do it themselves or only by their intercession made to God, this makes no difference to our argument, so long as by means of them, the one way or the other, we receive help as a result of our devotion toward them and prayer made to them."

"I think," said he, "that they can indeed do much more than they could before, both by power and by prayer. But it is somewhat hard to think that they should hear us and see us, and especially in so many places at once. For though they are not delimited in space (since they lack bodily dimension and measurability), yet they, and angels also, are so specifically located, where they are at any given time, that they are not in several places at once—as saints are, in sundry and very far asunder countries, called upon at once."

"You wonder," said I, "if saints hear us, and you find it hard to believe that they do. And I—when we see that the things we pray for, we obtain—wonder much more how anyone can have any doubt as to whether the prayers are heard or not. When the saints were in this world at liberty, and could travel all over the world, do we think that in heaven they stand tied to a post?

"But the wonder is how they can see and hear in sundry places at once. Well, suppose we two could do no more than feel, and neither see nor hear. We would find it just as amazing—or, if we could not be amazed by this, since we could not hear about it, we still would be far from any conceiving in our minds—that it is possible for a person to see or hear further than they can feel. For we who know this by experience, and do actually see and hear, still cannot see the cause or in any way cease to wonder by what logic and means it can be that I could see two churches or two towns, a mile apart from each other, and both of them as far from me as from each other, and measure such great distances with so small a measure as the little pupil of my eye. And how one person can hear at once the voices of many people, or how the words of any one person can come at once into the ears of many people who are standing far apart, is just as hard to comprehend. And when all the explanations are given—that beams are sent out from our eyes to the things that we behold, or that the forms of the things seen are brought by magnification from the thing to our eye, or that the air is struck by the breath of the speaker and equally rolls forth in circles to the ears of the hearers—when all the explanations are heard, we still will rather delight in investigating these matters than be able to find anything in them that is able to make us understand them.

"Now, when we can with our fleshly eye and ear, in this dense body, see and hear things far distant from us, and occurring in different places far distant from one another, do we really find it that hard to believe that blessed angels and holy souls, being wholly spiritual substances, free of all burdensome flesh and bones, can in doing the same as far surpass and exceed us and our natural powers as the soul itself, during life, exceeds our mortal body? And are we going to be unable to believe that they hear us, even though we find that they help us, unless we can perceive by what means they do it—such as whether they see and hear us by their coming here to us, or by our voice going from here to them, or whether it's that God sees and hears everything and communicates it to them, or whether they behold it in him as one beholds in a book the thing that one reads, or whether God by some other way does reveal it to them as one does in speaking—unless we can know the means, we else will not believe the matter? As intelligent would be someone who, because he cannot perceive by what means he can see, would refuse to believe that he can see."

"Yet I see," said he, "no reason or need for us to pray to them, since God can as well both hear us and help us as can any saint in heaven, and will as gladly."

"What need do you have," said I, "to pray any physician to cure your fever, or to pray and pay any surgeon to heal your sore leg, since God can both hear you and heal you as well as the best, and loves you more and can do it sooner, and can supply his salves more cheaply, and give you more for your words than they for your money?"

"But this is his pleasure," said he, "that I shall be healed by the means of them as his instruments, although actually he does it all himself, since the things they do it with are given their healing properties by him."

"So has it," said I, "likewise pleased God that we shall ask help of his holy saints, and pray to them for healing. And this is not a making them equal to God himself, even if they do it by his will and power, or he does it at their intercession. Though God will (as stands to reason) be chief and have no match, he yet does not forbid that one human being pray another for help. And though the Father has given all judgment to his Son [Jn 5: 22], the Son yet does delight to have his holy saints be sharers in that honor, and on Judgment Day to have them sit with him [Mt 19: 28]. Was Elisha made equal to God because the widow prayed him to revive her dead son? [See 2 Kgs 4: 28–35.] Were the apostles equal to Christ because they were prayed to for help after his death, and even during his life? [See Mt 10: 1 and Acts 5: 12–16.] And many things did they do at folks' prayer. And sometimes they were prayed to for something and they tried to do it, but could not, and the parties in question had to go from them to their Master for it [Mk 9: 14–29]. And yet it was all right with him that they were prayed to. And for proof of this, he allowed them at people's devout urging and prayer to do many miracles. And sometimes they were prayed to be intercessors to their Master. Such as when they came to Christ and said, 'Dimitte illam, quia clamat post nos,' 'Get this woman taken care of, for she keeps calling out after us' [Mt 15: 23]. And do you then think that, he being all right with this and giving people occasion to pray to them while they were with him on earth, he will be angry if we do them as much homage when they are with him in heaven? No; I think, on the contrary, that since it is his pleasure to have his saints held in honor and prayed to so that they can be for us intercessors to his high Majesty, whereto, before we presume to approach, it becomes us and well behooves us to make friends of such as he has in favor, he will disdain ever to look on us if we are such presumptuous and impudent boors that upon boldness of familiarity with him, we disdain to make his especially beloved friends our intercessors. And when Saint Paul exhorts us to pray for one another [see 1 Tm 2: 1 and James 5: 16], and we are glad to think it a right thing to do to pray every poor man to pray for us, should we think it a bad thing to do to pray holy saints in heaven to do the same?"

"Why," said he, "by that reasoning I might pray not only to saints, but also to every other dead person."

"So you may," said I, "with good reason, if you see no other likelihood than that they died a good person. And so we find, as I recall, in Saint Gregory's *Dialogues*, that someone received help by prayer made to a holy man, recently deceased, who was himself still in purgatory. It pleased our Lord thus to let the world know that he was in his special favor although he was still in the pain of his purgation. For our Lord loved him nevertheless, though he did not lift for him the order of his merciful justice. And therefore let no man take his trouble or sickness as a token of God's hatred, unless he feels himself resenting it and being impatient and disgruntled with it. For then it is a token of wrath and vengeance, and is to the sufferer as fruitless as it is painful. And in effect nothing else but the beginning of his hell, right here. But on the other hand, if he takes it patiently, it purges; if gladly, it greatly merits; and glad may he be who is with meekness glad of God's punishment. Saint Augustine (as is recorded by Possidius), lying terribly sick himself with an intermittent fever, cured someone else with his prayer, and yet himself died of his sickness. Wherein there was to him

248

more mercy and favor shown than if he had been cured too. For now instead of health he had heaven, where he would never be sick again."

"Indeed," said he, "but I have always heard it said that we should not pray to any dead person except conditionally, saying, 'If you are a saint, then pray for me.'"

"Why so," said I, "any more than in praying to a live person, where I am not bound to say, 'If you are a good person, pray for me'? But since I may reasonably think the living to be good when I do not know them to be the contrary, so may I consider those who are dead."

"Why," said he, "then of what use is canonizing? If this be true, I will never aspire to be canonized, as long as I live."

"You'd better not," said I, "nor seven years after, either. For it would be but a nuisance for you."

"But why are they canonized, then?" said he.

"Those," said I, "who are not canonized, you may for the most part both pray for them and pray to them. As you may for and to those who are still alive. But someone who is canonized, you may pray to him to pray for you, but you may not pray for him. For as I think it is Saint Augustine who says, anyone who prays for a martyr is insulting the martyr. And with regard to everyone, you can hope rightly and be seldom certain, but of the canonized you can consider yourself sure."

9.

The messenger yet again objects to the use of relics, and expresses a great deal of doubt regarding canonization. To which the author responds.

"How can I," said he, "be sure of them? Can the taking up of a man's bones, and setting his carcass in a showy shrine, and then kissing his bald scalp, make a man a saint? And there are even some unenshrined, because no one knows where they lie. And some about whom people question whether they ever had any body at all. But indeed, to make

DIALOGUE CONCERNING HERESIES, PART TWO

up for that, there are also some that have two bodies, one to lend to some good fellow that is missing his. For as I said before, some one body lies whole in two places far apart, or else the monks of one of them are beguiled. For both the places plainly affirm that it lies there. And at each place they show the shrine. And in the shrine they show a body, which they say is *the* body, and boldly stand by this, that it is it, citing old writings, and miracles also, as the proof. Now we must admit either that the miracles at the one place or the other are false (or done by the devil) or else that the same saint actually had two bodies. Which, to my mind, would be as great a miracle as the greatest of them all. And therefore it is likely that somewhere there is being venerated as a relic of some holy saint a bone that was, perhaps, as Chaucer says, a bone of some holy Jew's sheep. Our Savior also seems, in the Gospel, to rebuke and reprove the Pharisees for refurbishing the sepulchres of holy prophets and making shrines of their graves [Mt 23:29–31]. Whereby it is evident that he would not have the dead bodies venerated and set in gorgeous golden shrines.

"And even, besides this, you will find many more venerated, I think, than enshrined, and many enshrined that you do not find canonized, even if you look them up in all the record books in Rome. And when they are enshrined and canonized too, yet since the Church in the canonization process uses a means that can cause them to make a mistake, since they go by the testimonies of human beings (both as to the candidates' lives and as to their miracles), which human beings may perhaps be lying, then why may it not be that the Church is deceived in the canonization process? And that they could, for lack of true knowledge, believing untruthful people, at times canonize as saints folk that are quite far from being such? I dare not say as much as Saint Augustine does. For he does not forbear to say straight-out that many bodies are venerated for saints here on earth whose souls are buried in hell."

"You have," said I, "said many things very stoutly. But yet, let us first consider what all of them together add up to. For, supposing that it were all true, it amounts to nothing further than that we could be mistaken about some whom we take for saints. It proves neither that there are no saints, which I well know no one with any sense will say, nor that if there are any, they should not be venerated or prayed to. Unless you would say that if we could possibly be mistaken about some, we therefore should venerate none. In which case you should, by that reasoning, never accept the help of any physician, since you might happen to get a quack because you have no knowledge of medicine yourself. For by people's testimonies you could be as well deceived there as here.

"Now supposing, first of all, that of saints and of relics, some were true and some were false, yet the veneration that you think we should give to them all should be on the basis that (this standing, along with them, unknown and undiscerned) you considered all those relics authentic and all those people God's beloved servants. For if you knew which of them were true and which false, you then would venerate the true and tread the false underfoot."

"No doubt about that," said he.

"Then," said I, "if we were in some cases beguiled, I see no great danger coming to us thereby. For suppose there came into your area a great many of the King's friends, and you for his sake showed them great hospitality. And suppose there came among them, unbeknownst to you, some spies who were mortal enemies of his, wearing his badge and seeming to you to be close friends of his; and reported to be such. Would he blame you for the good welcome you gave his enemies? Or would he thank you for the good welcome you gave his friends?"

"He would, I think," said he, "thank me for my good treatment of them both, since both seemed good to me and both received their hospitality from me only for the reason that they seemed to be his friends, and for his sake."

"What you say," said I, "makes good sense. But now I put the case that you had an inkling, or even an explicit warning, that some of those that seemed his best friends were enemies of his, but which ones they were, no one could tell you. What would you do now? Give them all hospitality and treat them all with honor? Or, informing them that you hear it said straight-out that some of them are no good, therefore tell them all to take a hike or they'll be sorry?"

"No," said he, "there is no doubt that I would expect to be thanked if I should cherish his enemies as his friends, rather than spitefully treat his friends as his enemies."

"Very well," said I. "And this would be true even if you had warning that some of them were his enemies. But what thanks would you then deserve if you should shake off both where you had no such warning at all, but would say that you dared not give any of them hospitality because you thought that perhaps it might be that some were worse than they were taken for? For that is the kind of situation you are in here. You do not know that any person venerated as a saint is not one; you only *think* that you are not *sure* whether all of them are or some are not."

"Yes," said he, "Saint Augustine, as I told you, gives me warning that many are not."

"You are," said I, "wrong about that, as I shall explain to you later. But in the meantime, take good note of this and let it stand as a sure ground: that your entire objection, if it were valid, would avail not against the venerating of saints or of saints' relics, but against the venerating of such as are not saints or saints' relics. And that being proved, and this thing that is now in question having been at the beginning admitted and agreed between us to be something not at all able to affect our main issue, let us go further into this and investigate whether we find any such cause of doubt in any, or have good reason to reckon ourselves sure that all are saints indeed whom the church of Christ holds in honor and veneration as saints.

"First, as for the quote that you ascribe to Saint Augustine, I have often heard it cited in like manner for the same purpose. But certainly those who so take Saint Augustine are terribly mistaken. I dare be so bold as to say that Saint Augustine never wrote any such thing, but that it is a statement, run in many mouths, started by a misunderstanding and believed without examination. For certainly the statements that they take advantage of, which he makes in the first part of *De Civitate Dei* and repeats in his book about the concern and care that people should have for those who are dead—those statements, I say, go far wide of any such mark. For there he speaks only of costly burying, and of the making of sumptuous sepulchres, and of doing the dead bodies of rich men worldly honor in the carrying forth and interring of the body, as is clearly and evidently shown by the subject that he is writing about.

"And certainly, since our Lord never would among his Chosen People give the glory of his name to another [Is 42: 8], and never put up with idolatry among the Jews, but always either right away punished and purged it or so severed the flock of idolaters that it might well appear where his faithful flock remained (as it did when, Samaria having fallen into idolatry, the right synagogue of the Jews remained in Jerusalem and in Judea), it is highly unlikely that, his Holy Spirit having been sent into his Church here to remain in and instruct it, and he himself also being with it and giving it his special assistance to the end of the world, he would allow his church either to be unknown or in such a way to err and be deceived as to give honor to the devil instead of himself, or to his enemies instead of his friends. And therefore, when the Church by diligent investigation finds a person's life to have been holy; and in addition it is well witnessed that God, by his miracles, testifies to the person's blessedness and the favor in which the person stands with him in heaven, declaring, by the relief and benefit which he gives to many people for that person's sake, that he will have that person honored and held as a saint in his church here on earth; and—either by a canonization announced to the people by those in charge of his church (after the exercise of such diligence) or perhaps, without canonization coming of it, simply by the widespread reputation for holiness and by the many miracles seen—this thing becomes such a firm and common conviction throughout the whole people of Christendom that the person is accepted and taken for an undoubted saint, be the bones transported or not, the body found or not, then even though by natural possibility it could be that people were deceived about such things, as you have said, yet we can and well ought in this situation to boldly trust that the grace and aid of God and his Holy Spirit assisting his church has governed the judgment of his ministers and inclined the minds of his people to such a consensus. And that he has not allowed them to err in a thing so vitally affecting his honor and worship. For either it is being bestowed rightly, where he wills that it should be, upon himself or his holy saints for his sake, or it is being deflected from there and by an erroneous mistaking of truth—truth necessary, fitting, and proper for the Church to perceive for God's honor (the kind of truth God sent the Holy Spirit to teach his church)—the same honor is being bestowed upon people that he in no way wants to have it, but whom he sets apart for eternal reprobation. For the body's being enshrined or not does not make the saint a matter of doubt. No one has any doubt about our Lady, or about Saint John the Evangelist, although their bodies have not been found. And if they were, I think there is no good Christian who would not be happy to see them enshrined and held in honor.

"For whereas you would take away the reverence from all relics because some are dubious, in that of some saints the head is, as you say, and of some the whole body, displayed in two different places, it may happen, for all this, that of one head there may be several parts, and each part, in people's common speech, is called the head. For in Amiens is 'Saint John the Baptist's head,' as people call it in talking, even those who have been there and seen it. But then if they are asked further questions about it, they mention that the lower jaw is missing. This may well happen also, and does so happen in fact, with some saint of whom in two different countries there are different shrines, and it is reckoned and reported that in each of them is laid the whole body, and the pilgrims at neither place look into the coffin of that shrine to see whether it is all or part. In some place, perhaps, lay the body, and by some circumstance the body was removed from there long ago, and yet the shrine is still shown with some of the relics remaining therein. It also may well happen that there were two good, holy persons in different countries who both had the same name. And perhaps in some place there may be some authentic relics that are unidentified or misidentified. For in olden times, when people would hide holy saints' relics during invasions from infidels, at the finding again the names had perhaps worn off, and some relics might remain unidentified, and some perhaps be lost or wrongly identified. As I myself saw at Barking Abbey, near London, about thirty years ago, as I recall. An old statue was being placed in a new tabernacle, and the back of the statue being all painted over and, as of a long time before, laden with beaten gold, it happened to crack in one place, and out there fell a cleverly made little door, at which fell out also many relics that had lain, unbeknownst, in that statue, God knows how long. And likely would have lain for as long again if God had not by that happenstance brought them to light. The bishop of London then came there to see that there was no deception involved. And I, among others, was present there when he looked at it all and examined it. And in all honesty, the appearance of it was to me a marvel to behold. I have forgotten much of it, but I remember there was a little piece of wood, roughly in the shape of a cross, with thread wrapped around it. It had no inscription, and what it was we could not tell, but it seemed as newly cut as if it had been done within one day before. And several relics had old inscriptions on them, and some had none, but among others there were a number of narrow kerchiefs which were identified there as our Lady's, and of her own making. Rough they were not, and they were not large, but they served, as it seemed, to be put in a plain and simple manner upon her head. But they surely seemed to me as clean pieces of needlework as ever I saw in my life, and they were, moreover, as white for all their long lying as if they had been washed and laid up within the hour. And how long that statue had stood in that old tabernacle, no one could tell, but there was in that whole church none, as they thought, that had longer remained undamaged. And they guessed that four or five hundred years ago, that statue was hidden when the abbey was burned by infidels, and those relics hidden therein. And later the statue was found, and set up many years after, when those who had hidden it were gone. And so the relics remained in there unbeknownst until now, when God gave that happenstance that opened it. And thus, as I say, it can perhaps happen that some names are forgotten or maybe mistaken, and yet God is well content that the relics be held in reverence, since he specially favors their persons and needs not at all their names to know them by. As he shall one day so fully restore again many a glorious body that they shall not lose the least hair of their head that can serve to beautify them, of whom the names, perhaps, the whole world has long ago forgotten. And the name is not so very requisite but that we can mistake it without peril, so long as we nevertheless have in reverence the relics of holy people; but as for pigs' bones being taken for holy relics, or damned wretches being venerated as saints, albeit that if that did happen, it would not hurt at all the souls of those who made such mistakes, any more than if we during Mass venerate a host which perchance some bad priest, through negligence or malice, has left unconsecrated, yet it is never to be thought, though such a thing could happen on the spur of the moment, that God will ever allow such a thing to last and endure in his church.

"For although his church uses one means that could, as you say, beguile it, which is the record and witness of human beings, it yet has in such things, as Saint Thomas and other holy theologians write, another means as well which never can beguile it. And that is the assistance of God and the Holy Spirit. For else the Church might be most easily beguiled in the receiving of true Scripture, wherein, externally, the Church takes but the testimonies of human beings, from mouth to mouth and hand to hand, without other examination. But that secret means that inclines its credence toward the accord of everyone's believing in the same thing—the means which is the secret prompting of God—this is the sure means that never can in any essential point fail here in Christ's church. For if it could, everyone would be in a very unsettled state. And that point once taken away, Scripture and all walks with it. And in this mind, as it seems, was very surely and steadfastly confirmed the holy apostle Saint Paul, who in his first Epistle to the Corinthians writes in this vein: 'Obsecro vos fratres, per nomen Domini nostri Iesu Christi, ut idipsum dicatis omnes, et non sint in vobis scismata, sed sitis integrum corpus eadem mente et eadem sententia,' 'I beseech you, my brothers, by the name of our Lord Jesus Christ, that you say all one thing, and let there be no schisms or different sects among you, but be you one whole, entire body, of one mind and one judgment' [1 Cor 1: 10]. It is true that, in teaching them the right way, he went so far as to forbid that an angel from heaven be believed if any would come and preach another gospel [Gal 1: 8]. But yet in this text I am especially struck by the fact that he calls upon them only for agreement, bidding them all only to agree on the same thing. He makes no mention of agreement on the best thing, or on the truth, but only exhorts them to avoid all discord and division and by common consent to agree all as one, meaning by that, as it seems to me, that if the church of Christ, meaning well, does all agree on any one thing concerning God's honor or the human soul, it cannot be but that this thing must needs be true. For God's Holy Spirit, who animates his church and gives it life, will never allow it to all give consent and agree together to any condemnable error. And therefore he would never allow the Church so fully to agree to the venerating of saints and reverencing of relics if it were a thing such as some would have it seem; that is to say, a condemnable, inauthentic, made-up thing.

"Wherein as much as you allege to diminish their credibility—that it might seem, as you say rightly enough, that some of them were faked—still I have never known it to be proved that any of the ones accepted and approved by the Church have ever yet to this day been disproved, either here in Christ's church or among the Jews in their synagogue before Christ's day; and even they held saints (such as patriarchs and prophets) in honor, and their bodies and relics in reverence. Now, if of such people as seemed to be good, we had never found any to be hypocrites, then even though it could be that some were such, we yet would not, I think, believe that any of them actually were, if we never had known this examined and proved to be so. And why, then, shall we have doubts and misgivings about saints or relics? Of the ones accepted by the Church as authentic, we have never, that I know of, since God made the world, examined any of either group and proved them inauthentic—neither, as I say, in the church of Christ nor in the synagogue of the Jews, which two groups alone were God's chosen people. And yet the Jews, as well as we, both held saints, as I said, in honor and held their relics in great reverence, as is evidenced by the Gospel as well as the Old Testament.

"Jacob, that holy patriarch, on his deathbed commanded his children to carry his body to the burial out of that country of Egypt, and so they did [Gn 49: 29 and 50: 5–14]. And Joseph also directed his relatives that when they should later depart from Egypt, they should carry his bones with them [Gn 50: 25]. The dead bones of the prophet Elisha, as the Bible mentions, raised a dead body to life [2 Kgs 13: 21]. And do you think, then, that those bones were not there honored as holy relics?

"And in the Gospel, Christ our Savior reproves the Jews not for adorning the sepulchres of the ancient prophets—he was well content with the honoring of them—but for condemning themselves in adopting the mentality of the prophets' slayers, intending to kill Christ as their forefathers did his holy prophets. For as for the dead bodies of the holy prophets, that God would have them held in honor and reverence he made clear by the fact that he raised a dead body by having it come in contact with the dead bones of the prophet Elisha, as I said to you before.

"Did not our Lord, in the finding of that holy relic his Holy Cross, reveal it by miracle, and make his own cross known from the crosses of the two thieves, by the raising of a dead man with the touch thereof? Wherein is to be noted, by the way, that there was between his and theirs no noticeable difference. They were nailed as he was; otherwise there would have been no doubt upon the first glance as to which of them was his. Was not the body of Saint Stephen found by miracle, and the head of Saint John the Baptist also? Yes, for certain; and many another holy martyr more, who else would have lain unknown. Whereby it became quite evident that God would have not their souls only, but also their bodies, and, in a manner, the very soles of their shoes, prized for their sakes, and themselves for his sake. Was not that woman healed by the touch of our Lord's garments? [See Lk 8: 44–46.] Have there not, both among the Jews and among Christian people also, been many who got miraculously cured just by touching the clothes of holy saints? And do we then question whether God would have us venerate them, when he so well and above nature rewards us for the veneration we do them?"

10.

The messenger makes many objections to the making of pilgrim-
ages, the using of relics, and the venerating of saints, on the basis of
the many superstitious behaviors exhibited therein, and the illicit
requests made of the saints, and the harm resulting therefrom.

"Sir," said he, "you have to my mind very well covered the
matter of its not being blasphemous to pray to saints or to
venerate them and hold their relics in some reverence. But,
sir, all this is far from being the main sore point. For even if
saints can hear us, and heal us too, and are willing and eager
to do so, and also God is pleased that they, and their relics
and statues too, be held in honor, yet neither he nor they can
be pleased with the manner of the veneration. First, taking
away his own veneration, in that we give them the same
veneration, in every respect, that we give to God. And secondly, taking away their veneration from them also, in that
we then give to their statues the same that we give to themselves, taking their statues for themselves, and so make not
only themselves but also their statues God's peers and equals.
With this, as I have said before, neither God nor good saint
can, nor ought any good person, be happy and pleased."

"Indeed," said I, "if that is the case there, then what you
say is quite right."

"What do we say, then," said he, "about the harm that
comes of the going on pilgrimages—the gadding about in
idleness, with all the carousing, reveling, and debauchery,
gluttony, wantonness, vandalism, and lechery? Do you believe that God and his holy saints would not rather have
them sit still at home than thus come approach them, with
such pious rituals?"

"Yes, certainly," said I.

"What do we say, then," said he, "about something I have
not yet spoken of, in which we do them little reverence:
when we send every saint to his or her office and assign them
a profession, whatever we please? Saint Eligius we make a
horse doctor, and we must rather let our horse run unshod

and ruin his hooves than shoe him on his feast day, which we must, in that respect, more religiously keep high and holy than Easter Sunday. And because one smith is too few at a forge, we appoint Saint Hippolytus to help him. And on Saint Stephen's feast day we must let all our horses' blood with a knife, because Saint Stephen was killed with stones. Saint Apollonia we make a tooth puller, and to her we may speak of nothing but toothaches. Saint Zita women set to finding their keys. Saint Roch we set to curing the plague, because he had a sore. And with him is joined Saint Sebastian, because he was martyred with arrows [a symbol of the plague]. Some are of help only for the eyes. And some for a diseased breast. Saint Germanus only for children. And yet he will not so much as look at them unless the mothers bring with them a loaf of white bread and a pot of good ale. And yet he is smarter than Saint Wilgefortis, for she, the good soul, is, so they say, served and content with oats. The reason for which I cannot perceive, unless it be because she is supposed to provide a horse for a bad husband to ride to the devil upon. For that is the thing she is so besought for, they say. As a matter of fact, women have therefore changed her name, and instead of Saint Wilgefortis they call her Saint Disencumber, because they believe that for a peck of oats she will not fail to disencumber them of their husbands. It would take a long time to relate to you the different customs of many a fine shrine, but I will tell you one or two.

"The one Pontano speaks of in his dialogues, how Saint Martin is venerated, I have forgotten the town, but the custom I cannot forget, it is so bizarre. On his feast day his statue is carried around in a procession through all the streets. And if it is a nice day, then they usually, as he comes by, toss rose water and all kinds of pleasant-smelling things at his statue. But if it happens to rain, they pour out chamber pots upon his head, at every door and every window. Is this not a sweet service and a devout devotion? And this, as I say, Pontano writes, and tells where it is.

"But this that I shall now tell you, I dare as boldly assure you of as if I had seen it myself. At St. Valery's, here in Picardy, there is a beautiful abbey, where Saint Valery was a monk. And about a furlong or two away, up in a forest, there is a chapel in which the saint is especially gone to for relief from kidney stones, by people coming not only from those areas, but even from outside of England. Now, there was a young gentleman who had married a merchant's widow. And, having a little spending money that was burning a hole in his pocket, in the first year of his marriage he took his wife with him and went overseas for no other purpose than to see Belgium and France and ride out one summer in those countries. And having someone in his entourage who related along the way many strange things about that shrine, he thought he would go somewhat out of his way either to see if it was true or to laugh at this servant if he found it to be false, as he really thought he would indeed. But when they came into the chapel, they found it all true. And on seeing it, they found it more ridiculous than he had made it sound. For just as at other shrines you see waxen legs or arms or other such parts, so in that chapel, of all their offerings that hung on the walls, there were none other than men's privates and women's privates, made of wax. And then there were, besides these, two round rings of silver, one much larger than the other, through which every man did put his, at the end of the altar. Not every man through both, but some through the one and some through the other. For they were not both of a bigness, but the one was larger than the other. Then there was also a monk, standing at the altar, who blessed a number of gold threads from Venice. And he handed them to the pilgrims, teaching them how they themselves or their loved ones should use those threads to ward off kidney stones: they should tie them around their privates and say I cannot tell you what prayers. And when the monk had explained the procedure, the gentleman had a servant who was a married man and yet a merry fellow, and he, thanking the monk for the thread, asked him to teach him how he should tie it around his wife's privates. Which, unless the monk had some special skill in making knots, he thought would be problematic, since her privates were somewhat short. Needless to say, every man laughed then, except the monk, who flung up his rings and threads in great anger and went his way. Was this not—Wait! By God, I had almost forgotten one thing that should not for anything be left out. As this gentleman and his wife were kneeling in the chapel, a good, sober woman came up to him there, saying that there was one special procedure used at that shrine, most effective against kidney stones, that she did not know whether he had yet been informed of. If it was done, she dared bet her life that he would never in his life have a kidney stone. And it was this: she needed to know the length of his thing, so that she could make in that length a wax candle which would burn up in the chapel, and certain prayers would be said there during that time. And this was against kidney stones the very best defense. When he had heard her (and he was one that seriously feared kidney stones), he went and asked his wife her advice. But she, like a good, faithful Christian woman, did not go in for any such superstitions. The rest she could put up with well enough, but as soon as she heard of this burning up of the candle, she knit her brows and, earnestly blessing herself, said, 'Watch out, in the name of God, what you do. Burn up, she says? Goodness, God forbid. It would shrivel up your thing, on pain of my life. I beg you to beware of such witchcraft.'

"Is this kind of service and veneration acceptable and pleasing to God and his saints? Now, when people venerate saints in such a way that they make them equal to God, and statues in such a way that they take them for the saints themselves; and then again, on the other hand, honor them with such superstitious practices that the pagan gods were worshipped with no worse; and finally, which is the worst thing of all, pray to them for illicit things, such as when thieves pray to the thief who hung at the right side of Christ to give them good luck in their robbing, and have found him a name also, calling him Dismas, I believe, and his companion Gismas, to rhyme with it—do you not think that this stuff going on among the people is such as would be likely rather so to provoke God and his saints to displeasure that the devil would therefore have license and liberty to work his wonders, in mockery of our superstitious idolatry, than so to please and gratify our Lord that he would perform miracles for the corroboration of that manner of venerating which we can well see all reason, religion, and virtue denouncing?"

II.

The author answers all the objections raised by the messenger in chapter ten, and some of those discussed by the messenger more at length in previous chapters.

"Your whole account, in effect," said I, "contains three things. One, that the people venerate the saints, and their statues also, with like honor as they give to God himself. Another, that they take the statues for the things themselves. (Which points do suggest idolatry.) The third is the superstitious fashion of the veneration, together with the desire for illicit things. And on the basis that the veneration that the people give to the saints and the statues is such, you conclude that it is something displeasing to God and to all saints, and that from this it is quite evident that the miracles also are not the work of God but delusion worked by the devil.

"The first point, which you have now brought up twice, is immediately, quickly, and briefly answered, for it is not true. For although people kneel before saints and statues and incense them also, it yet is not true that they venerate them in every respect the same as they do God."

"What respect is missing?" said he.

"Good heavens, the chief one of all," said I. "Which is that they venerate God with the view that he is God, which view in veneration is the only thing that makes it latria—not any certain gesture or bodily observance. Not even if we were to grovel on the ground to Christ, having therewith the view that he was the best human being we could imagine, and thinking him not God. For if the lowly manner of bodily observance were the thing that would make latria, then we would be running a great risk of idolatry in the courtesies we show to princes, prelates, and popes, to whom we make as deep genuflections as to God Almighty, and sometimes kiss their hands (and sometimes our own before we presume to touch theirs), and in the case of the pope, his feet. And as for incensing, the poor priests in every choir are as well incensed as the Blessed Sacrament. So that if latria, that is, the honor due exclusively to God, consisted in such things, then we would be big idolaters in the reverence we do not only to saints and their images, but also to fellow human beings, one to another among ourselves. But although duty dictates that God should have with our body the most humble and lowly reverence that we can possibly devise, that bodily reverence is yet not latria unless we so do it that in our mind we regard and acknowledge him as God, and with that regard and intent do him that reverence. And I think that no Christian so does it to any image, or saint either. And thus is dismissed the danger of idolatry, the first point you spoke of.

"Now, as regards the second one—that the people take the statues for the saints themselves—I trust there is no man so mad, nor woman either, but that they know living people from dead stones, and wood from flesh and bone. And when they prefer, as you mentioned, our Lady at one shrine to our Lady at another, or one cross to another, or make their invocations and vows some to the one and some to the other, I think it is easy to see that they mean nothing other than that more miracles are done by our Lord and our Lady, or by our Lord *for* our Lady, at the one than at the other. And that they intend in their pilgrimage to visit some of them one place and some another as their piety happens to lead them, or partly, sometimes, according to how convenient the location is for them. But the attraction for them is not the place, but the fact that it pleases our Lord by manifest miracles to induce people to call upon him or his Blessed Mother, or some other holy saint of his, in those places more particularly than in some others.

"The thing itself also shows that they do not take the statues for our Lady herself. For if they did, how could they possibly in any way think any more of the one shrine than of the other? For they cannot think any more of our Lady than of our Lady. Moreover, if they thought that the statue at Walsingham was our Lady herself, then they would have to think that our Lady herself was that statue. And then if in like manner they thought that the statue at Ipswich was our Lady herself, and (as they therefore would have to think) that our Lady herself was that statue at Ipswich, then they would have to think, moreover, that all three of those were the same thing. In which case any two of them would be the same thing. And so they would by that reasoning have to believe that the statue at Ipswich is the very same statue that is at Walsingham. Which, if you ask any of those whom you take for the most simple-minded, other than a born fool, I dare bet you she will deny. Besides this, take the most simple-minded fool you can choose, and she will tell you that our Lady herself is in heaven. She will also call a statue a statue, and she will tell you a difference between a sculpture of a horse and an actual horse. And then it is quite evident that whatever her words are about her pilgrimage, if by a common manner of speaking she calls the statue of our Lady 'our Lady,' as people say 'Go to the King's Head for wine,' meaning not his actual head but the sign, so she sees in that statue nothing but our Lady's statue, no matter what she calls it. And if you want clear proof that she takes neither our Lady for that statue nor that statue for our Lady (as both she must take if she takes either one), talk with her about our Lady and she will tell you that our Lady was greeted by Gabriel, and that our Lady fled into Egypt with Joseph, and yet she will not in the telling say that Our Lady of Walsingham or of Ipswich was greeted by Gabriel or fled into Egypt. And if you ask her whether it was Our Lady of Ipswich or Our Lady of Walsingham that stood by the cross during Christ's Passion, she will, I guarantee you, answer that it was neither one. And if you ask her further, 'Which lady, then?' she will name you no statue, but the Our Lady who is in heaven. And this I have tested often, and you can when you want, and will find it true, except if it is someone who is so truly a fool that God will give her leave to believe what she pleases. And surely, on this point, I personally think that all those heretics who make as though they found so much danger of idolatry among the people because of confusion about statues are just inventing that fear to have some cloak with which to cover their heresy wherein they bark against the saints themselves. And when they are caught, then they say they mean only that misplaced faith that women have in statues.

"Now, as regards the third point, about the superstitious manner of venerating and the illicit petitions made to saints—for both of which things one example will serve, the one about women offering oats to Saint Wilgefortis to have her disencumber them of their husbands—to some extent it is indeed as you say, and yet not everything is reprehensible that you seem to find so. For instance, to pray to Saint Apollonia for help with our teeth is not witchcraft, considering that she had her teeth pulled out for Christ's sake. Nor is there any superstition in such other similar things. And perhaps since Saint Eligius was a farrier, it is no great fault to pray to him for the help of our horse."

"Well, then," said he, "since Saint Crispin and Saint Crispinian were shoemakers, it would likewise be a good thing to do to pray them sit down and mend our shoes. And pray to Saint Dorothy for some flowers, because she always carries a basketful."

"No," said I, "those things are not at all the same. For the one has to do with something we do not at all need, and the other with something we can do for ourselves, or easily find someone who will. But as for your horse, that is something for which, as well as for our own bodies, a quite good doctor may find his abilities insufficient, and which is to many a man a greater loss than he can well recover. And although God commanded that we should chiefly seek heaven, and promises that if we do so, all other things that we need shall be given us [Mt 6:33], and wants us to live not at all in anxiety and trouble of mind for any fear of lack, realizing that our Father in heaven provides food for the very birds of the air, which he values not nearly as much as he does us [Mt 6:25–26], yet he did not will the complete opposite, but that we should with our bodies work for it, having our hearts all the while in heaven. And he willed also that we should ask it of him, without whose help our work will get us nowhere. And therefore our daily food is one of the petitions of the Our Father, the prayer that the Lord himself taught his disciples [Mt 6:11]. And that horse he does not value so little but that, rather than it should perish, he reckoned it no violation of the Sabbath day to pull it out of a pit [see Lk 14:5]. And therefore, indeed, it seems to me that the devotion goes somewhat too far if the smiths will not, regardless of the need, shoe a horse on Saint Eligius' feast day, when it is plenty permissible to pray for the help of a poor man's horse. But as for your teeth, I think if they were really aching, you would yourself think it a thing worthwhile, and not too simple-minded, to ask help of Saint Apollonia, and of God too."

"Yes indeed," said he, "and of the devil too, rather than languish. I would do as the Lombard did for the gout. When he had long called upon God and our Lady and all the holy company of heaven, and was still feeling not a bit better, he began at last to call as steadfastly to the devil for help. And when his very dismayed and astonished wife and family rebuked him for calling on the devil, he, well knowing that what he was doing was wicked, and that if the devil helped him it would be for no good, cried back as loudly as he could, 'Ogni aiuto e bono!'—'Everything is good that helps!'

" 'And so, I think, would I," said he, "call on the devil too, rather than live in pain."

"No," said I, "whatever you may say, I cannot think you would put your faith in the devil as that Lombard did. You would, rather, conduct yourself like that other one who, when the friar interrogated him in confession as to whether he had any involvement with witchcraft or necromancy, or put any faith in the devil, answered him, 'Credere en le diable? My sir, no. Io graund fatigue a credere in Dio'—'Put faith in the devil? No, no, sir. Myself, I have enough trouble putting faith in God.' And so would you, I think, be far from all putting of faith in the devil. You have so much trouble believing in God himself that you are loath, I think, to deal much with his saints!"

When we had laughed a while at our merry tales, I said, "In all honesty, as I was about to say to you, it actually is somewhat as you say. For it is bad, and bad that it is tolerated, that superstitious fashion of veneration. And as for what you related about Saint Martin, if it is true, it has no excuse, except that it has no relevance to our issue. For that is not an honoring, but an insulting and a dishonoring of a saint. Regarding the offering of bread and ale to Saint Germanus, I see nothing much amiss there. Where you have seen this custom observed, I cannot tell. But I have myself seen it oftentimes, and yet I do not recall ever seeing any priest or lay church worker fare the better for it, or take one sip, but it is all given to children or poor folk who pray for the sick child. And I would think it would be no impropriety in such fashion to offer up a whole ox and distribute it among poor people. But now, as for our merry matters regarding St. Valery, since the place is in France we shall leave the matter to the University of Paris to defend. And we will come home here to St. Paul's, and put forward one example of both (that is to say, the superstitious fashion and illicit petitions): if women there offer oats to Saint Wilgefortis in trust that she will disencumber them of their husbands. However, neither can the priests tell till they find them there that the foolish women bring oats there, nor is it, I think, so often done, or is so much brought at once, that the church can make much profit from it beyond the feeding of the canons' horses."

"No," said he, "all the oats of a whole year's offerings will not feed three geese and a gander a week together."

"Well," said I, "then the priests do not countenance this thing out of any great greediness; and also, what the silly women pray for, they cannot hear. And anyway, if they pray only to be disencumbered, I see no great harm or illicitness there. For this they can be by more ways than one. They can be disencumbered if their husbands change their encumbering conditions. Or if they themselves perhaps change their encumbering tongues—the cause, perhaps, of all their encumbrance. And, finally, if they cannot be disencumbered except by death, it yet could be by their own, and thus their husbands would be safe enough."

"No, no," said he, "you find them not such fools, I guarantee you. They make their pacts in their bitter prayers with as much confidence as if they were in writing; and they will not throw away their oats for nothing."

"Well," said I, "to all these things there is one obvious, easy answer, and that is that they do not affect the gist of our argument, which consists in this: whether the thing that we are speaking of (such as praying to saints, going on pilgrimages, or venerating relics and images) can be done rightly. Not whether it can be done wrongly. For if something can be done rightly, then even if many did misuse it, that still would not at all diminish the goodness of the thing itself. For if we should on account of the misuse of a good thing, and on account of the evils that result sometimes from the abuse thereof, not amend the misuse but utterly do away with the whole observance, we should then make extraordinary changes in the world. In some countries they commonly go out hunting on Good Friday, in the morning, as a common custom. Will you abolish that bad custom, or will you throw away Good Friday? There are cathedral churches into which the country folk come in procession at Whitsuntide, the women following the cross with many an unwomanly song—women who are such chaste wives as outside of the procession you could not pay to speak one such foul, obscene word as they there sing for God's sake in whole obscene songs, as loudly as their throats can cry. Will you amend that indecent behavior, or will you do away with Whitsuntide? You speak of indecencies carried on at shrines. Are there, do you think, none observed on holy days? And why do you not then advise us to completely do away with them, Sundays and all? Some get drunk during Lent, on wine-dipped buns and biscuits, and yet would not, I think, want Lent done away with. And Christmas? If we consider how commonly people abuse it, we may think that they take it as a time of license for all manner of indecency. And yet Christmas is not to be thrown away among Christians, but rather Christians are to be admonished to amend their customs and conduct themselves at Christmastime in a more Christian manner.

"And look at Christ's own coming and giving us our faith and his holy Gospel and sacraments. Are there not ten the worse off for it for every one the better? Are not all the pagans, all the Jews, all the Turks, all the Saracens, all the heretics, all the evil-living people in Christendom the worse off (through their own fault) for the coming of Christ? I believe they are. And yet no one with any sense would wish that Christ had not come here. Nor would it have been at all right that God should have left ungiven the opportunity for merit and reward, that good folk would with his help gain through his coming, on account of the harm that wretches would take therefrom by their own sloth and malice. Nor, likewise, would it be at all right that all venerating of saints and reverencing of holy relics and honoring of saints' images—by which good, devout folk do gain much merit—we should abolish and prohibit because some folk do abuse it.

"Now, as for the bad petitions, even if those who make them are, as I trust they are not, a great many people, those who make bad requests of saints are yet not as many as those who ask the same of God himself. For whatsoever they will ask of any bona fide saint, they will ask of God also. And commonly among the wild Irish (and among some in Wales too, they say), when they go out robbing they bless themselves and pray to God that he send them good fortune, that they may meet with a good purse and do harm and take none. Shall we therefore find fault with everyone's prayers because thieves pray for success in robbery? This makes, as I say, no sense even in a case in which those abusing a good thing are a great many people. And whereas the worst thing you allege in our argument is that, as you put it, 'the people' commit idolatry in that, you say, they take the statues for the saints themselves, or the cross for Christ himself—which, as I said, I think none of them do, since many a cross has on it no figure of Christ, and they do not believe that the cross which they see was ever in Jerusalem, nor that it is the Holy Cross itself, and much less, then, do they think that the figure that hangs on it is the body of Christ himself—the fact is that even if some were so mad as so to think, it nevertheless would not be, as you call it, 'the people.' For a few dotty dames make not the people. And, moreover, if it were, as you would have it seem, a whole people indeed, a good thing still should not be done away with because of its misuse by bad folk."

12.

The author confirms the validity of our belief in and practice of the veneration of images by showing the agreement of the old holy theologians of the Church in approving of the same, which is quite evident in the writings of these men whom God has by many miracles attested to be saints. The messenger again expresses doubt as to whether or not we can be sure that the miracles reportedly done by them were real, or that they themselves are saints. Whereupon the author proves that of all the miracles reportedly done by any saints, we can be the most sure of theirs, and consequently, on account of their miracles, the most sure of them, that they are definitely saints. And in this chapter he also proves that the miracles and accord of those holy theologians do prove that this church in which they have written, and in which miracles have been done, must necessarily be the real, true church. Whereupon, finally, is proved once again the truth concerning the principal question; and with this the second part ends.

"And we are very assured that the thing is good, and our practice of it good, and our belief in it right, not only by the reasonings and authority by which I have proved it to you more than once already, but also by the fact that all the old theologians of Christ's church who are saints—Saint Jerome, Saint Augustine, Saint Basil, Saint John Chrysostom, Saint Gregory [the Great], and all such others, as we clearly read in their books—did as we do regarding that, and believed as we do about it. And since we see what they believed, we need not doubt what is best that we believe. For if any religious sector believed better than another, we can be sure that of the best were they that believed and lived so rightly that God has approved them as saints and by miracles openly declared that their faith and way of living were to his liking. Whereas, on the other hand, of such sectors as believed otherwise—as were these manifold sects of obstinate heretics—we see not one saint among them, nor one miracle done for them."

"I do not really know," said he, "whether this argument you make would firmly convince the other side or not. For someone could perhaps answer you that there is many a glorious saint in heaven from whom we see no miracles on earth, and whom we may not even have heard of."

"That may well be," said I, "and I believe it to be quite true."

"May it not also be," said he, "that although it would be hard not to think that out of so many miracles some must be authentic, yet since also some could be faked, could it not be that those were faked which reportedly were done by those that you mentioned? Those, I mean, who in the olden times wrote on your side. I mean those whom you call the old theologians of the Church whom the Church takes for saints."

"This," said I, "is worse than any claim that we have discussed up to now. Before, the worst was that we should not pray to any saints. And now you maintain either that we do not have any or, at the least, that we do not know who any of them are."

"Oh yes," said he, "you can have saints, and know them to be saints, including many a one since the apostles' time, even if those whose literary output you would authorize by their being canonized are not saints."

"Then you fall," said I, "back into that position of thinking that it may be that the Church may take for saints and venerate as saints people who are not saints."

"Surely," said he, "the proof that you have presented to me against that, though it is somewhat plausible, yet seems to me not very strong, nor apt or sufficient to force a person to give assent to it. For though the active presence of God and his Holy Spirit makes it impossible for his whole Church to agree and consent together in any condemnable error, he still might well allow it to err in regard to the knowledge and veneration of a saint, and to mistake for a saint someone who was a damnable wretch. For in this there would be no more danger to the human soul, or more honor taken from God, than when the people venerate an unconsecrated host, mistaking it, through the fault of a bad priest, for the sacred Body of our Lord himself. And this you do not doubt does sometimes happen."

"Do not forget now, by the way," said I, "that you still agree that God will not allow his whole church to agree in any condemnable error and fall into a false faith. And along with that, remember that though it would not be a condemnable error to take for a saint someone who is not one, or for a relic a bone that is not one, it yet would be a condemnable error to venerate any if we should be venerating none at all. And therefore, since the Church believes that we should venerate them, that kind of belief cannot be any kind of error, but must needs be correct, and that kind of veneration cannot be any kind of idolatry, but must needs be good and acceptable to God. And so, our main contention still standing fast and sure, we shall look a little further and see what your statements will add up and amount to.

"You do not deny," said I, "that there are some saints and some miracles."

"No," said he.

"To what purpose," said I, "were miracles specially wrought by God? Was it not for the intention of making known his messengers and the trueness of his message? Such as when he sent Moses to Pharaoh—were not the miracles done by God to make Pharaoh perceive thereby the trueness of his words?"

"Yes," said he.

"When Christ," said I, "sent his disciples to preach, the power that he gave them to do miracles—was it not for the proof of the doctrine that they taught, as is well attested in the Gospel?"

"Yes," said he.

"If this be thus," said I, "as indeed it is, then of all miracles you have the most reason to believe in those that are told and reported as done for the theologians of Christ's church, since miracles were particularly devised by God for a knowledge of his true messengers and a proof of their message. So that, whereas according to you we are not utterly wrong about saints and miracles, but yet we could be wrong about theologians whom we take for saints, and about their miracles, it now seems, on the contrary, that we are more sure of them and theirs than we are of all the others."

"This is well said," said he. "But yet it always runs through people's minds that miracles can be faked."

"That is fine," said I, "so long as it also runs through people's minds that not all of them are faked. And then, if you think any are true, this argument still stands: that since miracles were specially given by God for recognition of his theologians and elucidation of his doctrine, those miracles are specially to be taken for true that are reported to have been done by his theologians. For they serve as confirmation of his holy doctrine. And, because you say that miracles can be faked, what we said about Moses and about Christ's disciples now reminds me of something. There were also in olden times false theologians and false, faked miracles, were there not?"

"Yes, of course," said he.

"By whom were those miracles faked?" said I.

"Goodness," said he, "there were some faked by people, as there are now; and some by the devil—as perhaps there are now too."

"Well," said I, "so be it, both of the two, if you like. But in olden times were not both of the two found out and vanquished by the true theologians sent by God, and by the true miracles wrought for them by God? Such as when the serpent of Moses devoured all the serpents made by the witchcraft of the Egyptian magicians [Ex 7: 9–12]. And when the prophet Daniel did by the footprints of the false priests find out the means whereby the food was eaten that they pretended was being eaten by the idol Bel [Dn 14: 10–21]. And when the prophet Elijah vanquished by miracle the false prophets of Baal [1 Kgs 18: 19–40]. And the holy apostles and disciples of Christ did, at their word, break all into pieces the false idols, right before the eyes of the pagan people. So that always God has prepared his true theologians to destroy by plain miracle the false miracles whereby people were and could be deceived.

"Is this not the case?" said I.

276

"Yes," said he.

"Well, then," said I, "if our old holy theologians were false, and their doctrine untrue, and their miracles faked, it is not enough now to say so. If any of those who say so are sent by God to do this denouncing, then they must prove that they are so sent. And that not in words only, but let some of them come forth and at their word break our images, as Christ's theologians did the pagans'. And to prove our miracles fake, let them do some real miracles themselves."

"As for miracles," said he, "they are not an article in anyone's creed. And there is no sect of heretics so simple-minded that they could not, if they set their minds to it, soon match you with miracles. They could fake fifteen in a forenoon. And then, as we said just now, it would be thought that even if some were untrue, yet not all were lies."

"It would be easy indeed," said I, "if those they reported them to were mad and would not do any investigating."

"But I know that even if they did," said he, "a few individuals of average intelligence could still invent and fake something in such a fashion that it would be believed, and hard to pry out the truth about."

"Granted," said I. "And yet it would not have a long hold among good Christian people, but God would either bring its falsehood to light or soon cast it out of credence. What effort did Philostratus put into writing a book full of lies whereby he wished to have Apollonius of Tyana appear to be, with respect to miracles, an equal to Christ? And when he had it all done, he never found one old woman who was dotty enough to believe him.

"But pray tell me," said I, "are there not of heresies many sects?"

"Yes," said he.

"Are there," said I, "any more true churches of Christ than one?"

"No more," said he.

"Is it not the one," said I, "that is truthful?"

"Yes," said he.

"Are not, then," said I, "all the heretical sects untruthful?"

"Yes," said he.

"Who would be likely," said I, "to fake and lie: the company that is the truthful party, or some of them that are untruthful?"

"It is," said he, "more likely that all of the untruthful ones would lie than that the company that is the truthful party would."

"Then false and faked miracles," said I, "are they lies or not?"

"What else?" said he.

"Then," said I, "by your argument it seems that they would much more likely occur in the midst of every sect of heretics than in the Church."

"So it seems," said he.

"How does it happen, then," said I, "if miracles are faked goods, that among all the untruthful sects of heretics, where such untruthful stuff should by all reason be the most rife, none at all is spoken of, but miracles are told of only in the church of Christ, which alone is, as you agree, the truthful party?"

"There are," said he, "perhaps some done, either miracles or marvels, but they dare not speak of them for fear of persecution."

"If they were," said I, "false marvels only done by the devil, it would not help your case. For then you must grant that real miracles of God are done only in Christ's church. And if there had been real miracles of God done for any sect that we call heretics, that sect would have been not a sect of heretics, but the true church. (Or else God would have by miracles testified to the trueness of a false faith, and that is impossible.) And from there it would follow that unless there are of Christ two churches of two contrary faiths, and both true, which is impossible, else not some but *all* the miracles done, reported, and wrought in the one church

278

either have been faked or have been done by the devil; from which it would follow that our church was not the true church, but a false sect of heretics, which is, as I have already proved to you in several ways, definitely impossible.

"But, now, for the further vindication of our party therein, and for the further proof that ours is the trustworthy church, and that only the theologians and the doctrine of our church are corroborated by miracles, never have there been any done for the theologians of any sect of heretics. For had any true miracles been done by God for any such sect (in which case it would be not a false sect, but the true church), all the persecution there could have been could never have silenced the talk thereof, as is well evidenced by the miracles done in our church in all those times that it was persecuted, both by Jews and by pagans. Now, since there are so many false sects and but one true church, and miracles are not spoken of in any but one, it is a good indication that the sum and substance of them is true. For else they would as likely be spoken of in more, since of the false and lying sects there are so many. And then too, miracles being true and being done in only one of all those many companies each calling itself the Church, it is a valid conclusion that the same one in which alone they are done is the only real, true church of Christ, to which is given the special assistance of his Holy Spirit and marvelous majesty.

"And certainly, of all the miracles that God has ever wrought for his church, I do not readily see in my mind one more marvelous than this one: that, as many sects of heretics as have sprung and parted out of Christ's church, and each of them striving to be taken for the true church, yet our Lord has never to this day allowed the devil to do for them any wonder that might have the semblance and appearance of a miracle, nor, as untruthful as they themselves are, has he thus far allowed them to do so much as fake a miracle for their side. This is to my mind not only a great wonder, but also, considering their conceded untruthfulness, very clear evidence that they could never have been kept from it but by the special providence of God and his tender protectiveness over his chosen church, by which it has to this day pleased him that miracles (among other things) have been one good and sure mark of distinction between his church and all those erroneous sects that have sprung out of it and are not his church, but want to seem to be. For as for pagans, Turks, and Saracens, who by open profession are of other flocks and do not bear the name of Christ or look for him, he sometimes does allow the devil to delude them with wonders and marvels. But the Jews who are still longing for him, their miracles, as far as I can hear, are gone, to the intent that they may know that he has left them and given them up, he who was wont to work all those wonders for them. Now, as for heretics, who falsely feign themselves to be his own flock, and presume to bear and profess his name, he keeps them from the honor of any miracle-doing, to the end that the lack thereof among all their sects, and the doing of miracles in his only church, may be, among many other things, one good distinction and sure sign whereby all these false sects of them may be discerned and known from his real, true church; that is to say, from the whole congregation of true Christian people in this world who without intermixture of obstinate heresies profess the right, Catholic faith.

"Now, not only is it true that miracles are wrought only in the Church and thereby do show which is the true church, but also they do show that those holy theologians for whom God has done them were good men and of the right belief. For if it were the way that you a little while ago would have had it seem—that it might perhaps be the case that the holy theologians of our faith (the ones whom we take for saints) are in fact not saints or even saved souls, but perhaps those are saved souls and saints in heaven (though it is unknown here on earth) who did teach here the doctrines that we now call heresies—then it would be an amazing change, that whereas God among the Jews provided that in every age there were some good men who by their good conduct and his astonishing miracles were so conspicuous and well known to the people that folk had them always like bright, living stars whose doctrine they could confidently believe and whose example they could safely follow, he would now in his special church of Christ not only do nothing like that, but also do the complete contrary. For on the supposition that he has taken that way that you say—to let, ever since the apostles' days, all the accurate interpreters of his and their holy writings, all the theologians of the real, true faith, lie unknown to the world, and then, on the other hand, promote with miracles or allow to be promoted with marvels, in such a way that his church should take and accept for saints, such evil persons or hypocrites as construed Scripture wrong and ever since his apostles' days have taught treacherous errors and led his flock out of the right way and onto a bypath leading to hell with wicked heresies and idolatry—then God has *not* sent the Holy Spirit, nor still remained in the Church himself, to teach it the truth, as he said he would. Rather, he will then have helped beguile it himself, which would be impossible for God to do, and worse than blasphemous for anyone to think. For this would not be like the sufferance of an unconsecrated host, the example you gave. The people's invincible ignorance with their devout affection can without harm to their souls be suffered in something that happens so seldom and lasts for so short a while. But if God were to leave all the good interpreters unknown and allow his church to be deceived with miracles and marvels done by those who taught heresies and promoted idolatry, then he himself, as I say, would be not only allowing his honor and right faith and religion to be perpetually lost, but also himself helping to destroy it. Which could only be thought possible by someone worse than Judas and more mad than any man in Bedlam.

"And therefore it can in no way be that the Church can be mistaken in that it takes for saints these holy theologians of the Church. And, they so being, can it in any way be that the doctrine wherein they concur and agree can be false or untrue? And since the things we are speaking of—I mean the praying to saints, the venerating of images, the reverencing of relics, and the going on pilgrimages—are a part of that doctrine, as is clearly evident from their books, we can quite safely conclude that none of these things is condemnable or displeasing to God, but, rather, they all are things highly to his satisfaction and liking. And since we further perceive that their books are written in different regions and sundry ages, we thereby well perceive that these things are part and parcel of the rites, customs, and belief of Christ's church, not only now and recently, but continually from the beginning to this day. And since it is plainly proved to you that the Church can in no way be allowed by God to fall thereby into any condemnable error, it is finally most definitely concluded that none of these things is one. And consequently proved that no text of Scripture seeming to indicate the contrary can rightly be so taken or understood. And that the Church cannot to the prejudice of the faith misunderstand Scripture. And that the substantial points of the faith, therefore learned from the Church, constitute one of the safest rules that can be found for the right interpretation of holy Scripture. And that no sect of heretics can be the church of Christ; but that our church is the true church. And it is also clearly proved that in substance the miracles done in it daily are neither faked by people nor done by the devil, but produced only by the mighty hand of God. And such objections as you brought up against any of the aforesaid points are, as far as I can see, sufficiently answered, unless you have any further objection to make in their regard. Which if you do have, you will get no thanks for sparing me."

To which he said—and swore, as well—that he so fully felt himself answered and satisfied with all this that he thought himself able to satisfy and convince with it anyone he should happen to meet with who would hold the contrary. Whereupon for that day we parted, till another time, in which we planned to go through the rest of the things that he had brought up in the beginning.

Part Three

I.

The messenger, having in the meanwhile been at the university, presents to the author an objection which he learned there against one point proved in part one: namely, that in the essential points of the faith, equal credence is to be given to the Church and to Scripture. Which objection the author answers and refutes.

One morning about two weeks later, your friend came back. He came once again from the university, where he was, as you know, studying before he came to you. And there he had now, he said, visited some of his old acquaintances, and as the opportunity arose in conversation, had relayed to some of them real fresh-learned men a good part of our former disputation and discussion, held between us before his departure. Which, he said, they took great pleasure in and very much wished they could have been present at. But, to be sure, he said that some of them seemed to take very sorely to heart the harsh handling of the man whom you write of, and the burning of that New Testament, and the forbidding of the reading of Luther's books, which were, some of them thought, not nearly as bad as they were made out to be. And finally, regarding the burning of heretics, there were some who thought the clergy to be therein far outside the right order of charity.

"I am," said I, "very glad that it has been your fortune to be there. Not so much for anything you have told them of the conversation we have had already, concerning praying to saints, venerating images and relics, and going on pilgrimages (where, I think, you told them nothing new, for I do not doubt that they could have told you more on the matters themselves than you have heard or could hear from me), as because I think that among them (they being, as you say, so

284

well-educated) either you have heard something whereby you are already convinced on the one side of some of these issues that we shall be speaking of, whereby our involvement with them can be the shorter, or else you are the more strongly instructed for the other side, whereby our discussion shall be the fuller and the matters the more clearly covered, for the more ample satisfaction of whoever you yourself or your employer will hereafter happen to find in any doubt about these things that we shall now bring up and discuss."

"Indeed," said he, "they have somewhat shared with me their views there on some of these issues, as you will hear when we happen to come to them."

"I will gladly hear that," said I, "and shape you such answers as my poor wit will serve me. However, I ask you to be frank with me about one thing. Were they satisfied, did they consider themselves convinced, about those things that were at last, after much ado, settled between us?"

"In all honesty," said he, "to tell the truth, all were except one, and he was about all things except one. And, to your great praise and high commendation, they said so about these matters."

"No," said I, "let their praise pass, lest you make me too proud. But I ask you to tell me, not which one disliked one thing, but what one thing it was, and why he disliked it."

"Certainly," said he. "For all that I could bring to bear upon him, he never could agree that the faith of the Church, outside of Scripture, is as sure, and as binding on us with regard to the belief thereof, as the words of holy Scripture."

"Why," said I, "if you remembered well what we said, you had enough with which to prove that to him."

"Indeed," said he, "so I had, and so I did, and in such wise that several ways I brought him into an impasse that he did not know how to escape. But then he said to me that he would not do with me as I had done with you. It was not, he said, at all wise for a man to use against his adversary always the shield. For thus must all the peril be his, and his adversary remain safe; whereas, on the other hand, if he uses the sword also, and strikes occasionally and drives the other to his defense, he may thus happen to put him in half the peril. And likewise he said that even if I proved my side so clearly to him that he could not express dissent, yet if I would in turn answer him for a while, he might perhaps bring me to the same point on the other side, and then the matter would stand still unsettled. For of two contraries, if both the sides are proved, then they both remain unproved. 'And therefore,' said he, 'I ask you to answer me this a little: When you believe the Church, why do you believe the Church? Do you not believe it because it tells the truth?'

" 'Yes, of course,' said I, 'what else?'

" 'And how do you know,' said he, 'that the Church tells the truth? Do you know that in any other way than by Scripture?'

" 'No indeed,' said I, 'but then again, by plain Scripture I know it very well. For Scripture tells me that God has fully taught and teaches his church and bids me believe his church.'

" 'Well, look at that!' said he. 'For all your long discourse, see where you are brought to now. You were, in every which way, claiming before—and you seemed to prove it, too, the whole time that you were doing the arguing and I was doing the responding—that the Church is, in all essential points of our faith, as much to be believed as is Scripture, and that we would not be believing in Scripture were it not for the authority of the Church, as you say Saint Augustine says. And now, when I am doing the arguing and you the responding, I have driven you to the wall with a few words, and proved to you that the Church is not to be believed—and that even you yourself do not believe it—but for the authority of Scripture.' And after he had said all that, the rest of those present expressed great approval, and I was then stumped, and said I would reflect on it further. But he laughed and said he would lend me this one and not be too hasty with me; he would let me put off repayment till I had spoken with you again."

When your friend had finished, I said, "Indeed, he dealt with you like a courteous creditor. And since he has given you such a long time before due date, you will not need, I trust, to die in his debt. And to tell the truth, you do not owe him much. For you can bring him back his own money, and tell him it is no good. But I have noticed that it is, as he says, a great advantage for him to be on the offensive. For he has such skill in arguing that he will soon bring the answerer to a perilous point if he happens upon one who will answer him in as accommodating a way as he would like him to. But on the other hand, if he had happened upon one who would have answered him as contrarily as the boy answered one Caius, a poet at Cambridge, then he would by his going on the offensive have gained nothing at all. For Caius, for his amusement playing with the boy, who was a little smart-aleck, said that he would prove the boy an ass. When the boy denied it, Caius said, 'Well, thou wilt grant me this, first: that everything that hath two ears is an ass.'

" 'No indeed, Master, I will not,' said the boy.

" 'Thou wilt not?' said Caius. 'Ah, wily boy, there thou wentest beyond me. For if thou wouldst have granted me that, I would have proved thee an ass forthwith.'

" 'Indeed, Master,' said the boy, 'you well could, and so could every fool.'

" 'Well,' said Caius, 'I will go now another way to work with thee. Thou wilt grant me that every ass hath two ears.'

" 'No indeed, I will not, Master,' said the boy.

" 'Why so, boy?' said he.

" 'Indeed, Master,' said he, 'because some ass may happen to have not even one, for they may be cut off, the both of them.'

" 'Well,' said Caius, 'I give thee up as a hopeless case. Thou art too contrary a boy for me.'

"And so if you had not granted what he wanted, he would have won nothing at your hand."

"Why," said your friend, "what thing have I granted him that I shouldn't have?"

"Actually," said I, "no more than all that you ever granted. For first, when he asked you whether the reason why you believe the Church is not because what the Church is telling you is true, though your answer which you gave there was not the cause of your being refuted, nor the thing whereby you were confounded, you yet did not answer well there when you granted that."

"Well," said he, "for what reason should I believe the Church, or anyone else, if not because they are telling me the truth?"

"Sometimes," said I, "it happens thus, but sometimes it happens otherwise. For if a known liar tells you a story you already know to be true, you will believe him because he is telling you the truth. But, now, if a man known to be truthful tells you something you do not already know to be true, you do not believe him because the thing is true, but you believe the thing to be true because you believe the man to be truthful. And thus you do not believe the Church because what the Church is telling you is true, but you believe the thing to be true because the Church tells it.

"But yet that answer of his was not, as I say, the thing that did you in. For, now, if you had answered him in such a way as I have indicated to you, though you might have made him blink a little with that, he yet could and probably would have gone further with you, and have asked you how you know that you should believe the Church. And what answer would you then have made to that?"

"Goodness," said he, "then I could have said that I believe the Church because in such essential points of faith the Church cannot err."

"That would have been very well said," said I. "But he would have asked how you know that."

"Then," said he, "I would have had to say the same thing that I did: that I know by clear and obvious Scripture that the Church in such things cannot say anything but the truth. And then I would have presented him with the passages that you quoted to me for the same argument before."

"If you had spoken thus," said I, "you would have answered him truthfully, but yet not to your best advantage."

"Why so?" said he.

"Because," said I, "your next answer would have been to say, as is true, that you believe that the Church in such things cannot err because you believe that God has taught and told those selfsame things to the Church."

"Then he would have gone on to ask me," said your friend, "what thing makes me believe that God has taught and told the Church those things."

"So he would have," said I, "and so might he well."

"Then we would have come," said your friend, "back to the same point, where he would have confounded me as he did before."

"No," said I, "not if you gave a good answer to that."

"Why," said he, "what other answer could I give but to grant him frankly that I believe that thing for no other reason but only because Scripture says it to me?"

"Could you not?" said I. "What if never a scripture had been written in this world? Would there never have been any church or congregation of faith-filled and right-believing people?"

"That I don't know," said he.

"Don't you?" said I. "Between Adam and Noah, among those who never themselves heard God speak, were there never any folk who believed in God and had a correct faith?"

"Yes," said he, "I suppose there were some, but it would seem there were very few. For there were few saved in Noah's ship."

"The world had at that time," said I, "gotten worse and

worse, as it is getting now. But it is not unlikely that there were many right-believing people in the meantime."

"That is," said he, "likely enough."

"Now, as for the days," said I, "of Noah himself, though there were few saved alive, that yet does not prove that the people were all wrong-believing and without faith. For it fared with them as it now fares with us, that there were many who believed the truth and had a faith, but they followed the flesh and sank for their sin. For there appears in the story of Genesis nothing further than that the world was washed with the water of the great flood because of the filthiness of their fleshly behavior [see Gn 6: 4—8: 22]. And although from the first Epistle of Saint Peter it might seem to have been because of some lack of belief on their part [1 Pt 3: 19–20], it yet may be that this extended no further than to the lack of fear in the credence of God's warning, and the excessive hope and bold expectation of God's further favor and sufferance. Whereof they repented afterward, too late for this present life; and yet many, through God's mercy, not too late for the ultimate salvation of their souls (as appears in the commentary of the good and great scholar Nicolas de Lyra on that same text), which in no way could have been so had they lacked faith. Which faith what scripture had they to teach them? Or, for that matter, all the people who had any faith from Adam's time to then? Also, were there no faith-filled folk at all from Noah to Moses—and not him, either, till he had the Law delivered to him in writing? Did Abraham never believe any more than those things that we find in Scripture to have been expressly told him by God? Were his father and all his other relatives infidels? Were there no other people, in all that long time, who had a right faith?"

"Yes," said your friend, "I really think there were."

"There were," said I. "Of that you can be sure. And why did anyone then believe the church—that is to say, the number and congregation of good and right-believing folk, from whose mouths and tradition they heard the true belief—

against the wrong, erroneous belief that was in all the rest of the world, among infidels and idolaters? Why did anyone do this but because they believed that God had taught those things to good people before, and that it was and would be still the good lesson of God? And then what thing made them believe that God had taught them so? It was not Scripture that made them believe that, whereas according to you, nothing can tell us that belief but Scripture.

"I ask you to tell me, what scripture has taught the Church to know which books are actually Scripture, and to reject the many others that were written about the same matters, and that were written in such a way and in the names of such men that (saving for the Spirit of God given to his church) anyone with any common sense would have been likely enough either to have taken both sets for holy Scripture or to have rejected them both as not being holy Scripture? And surely in the accepting of the one and the rejecting of the other, there would have been, at the very least, such diverse opinions that the whole Church would never have taken all of the one set and rejected all of the other had not that agreement been inspired by that Holy Spirit 'qui facit unanimes in domo,' 'which makes the Church all of one mind and accord' [Ps 68: 7]. And therefore—even if against those who will believe nothing but Scripture, we prove the authority of the Church by Scripture, and in such a way prove it to them by Scripture that they will be forced either to grant further that they are obliged to believe the Church about things not specified in Scripture, and as fully as they believe Scripture itself, or else they will be denying Scripture too—we still should have believed God's church even if Scripture had never been written, as those good, faith-filled folk did who believed rightly before Scripture was written. And now, Scripture itself does not make us believe Scripture, but the *Church* makes us *know* Scripture. And God without scripture has taught his church the knowledge of his authentic scripture from all counterfeit scripture. For it is not, as I say, Scripture that makes us believe the word of God written in Scripture (for one could, as perhaps many do, read all of it and believe of it not a whit), but it is the Spirit of God that with our own tractableness and good endeavor works in his church, and in every good member thereof, the credence and belief whereby we believe as well the Church concerning God's words taught us by the Church, and by God engraved in people's hearts, without scripture, as his holy words written in his holy Scripture. And thus you perceive that where you granted, to that man who challenged you on this, that we believe the Church by no other way but by Scripture, there you did not answer him well. For we do, besides on the basis of Scripture, believe the Church because God himself, by secret inspiration of his Holy Spirit, does (if we are willing to learn) teach us to believe his church. And also, if we will walk with him, he leads us into the belief thereof by the selfsame means by which he teaches us and leads us into the belief of his holy Scripture. For just as when we hear Scripture or read it, if we are not rebellious but exert ourselves to believe, and we take captive and subdue our understanding to serve and follow faith, praying for his gracious aid and help, he then works with us and inwardly does incline our hearts toward assent to what we read, and, after a little sparking of our faith, increases the credence in our incredulity, so does he in his goodness likewise incline and move the mind of every equally tractable and well-willing body to the giving of firm, steadfast credence to the faith that the Church teaches them in such things as are not in Scripture, and to the believing that God has taught his church those points by his holy word not in writing. And now, if you had answered him thus, I definitely believe that you would have completely disarmed him and broken his flashy sword in two. Which to my mind, I assure you, however flashily it may glitter in one's eyes when being flourished, yet whoever fights with it will find to be neither sharp nor sure if it falls on a good shield and not on an unarmed man."

"By my word," said your friend, "it now seems so to me too. And though the brightness blinded my eyes at that time, I yet trust he will win no renown by it when we meet again."

2.

In passing, there is discussed to some extent the superstitious fear and scrupulosity that that person who was forced to abjure did, so it is said, start out with, the strain of which drove him to the delight in such liberty as brought him to the contempt for the good devotional things commonly used in Christ's church. And in this chapter is discussed to some extent the good middle ground, between scrupulous superstition and reckless carelessness, that should be taken in the singing or saying of the Divine Office.

"But to be sure, sir, concerning the abjuration of that man whom we spoke of, they are extremely convinced that he was done very wrong. Not in that the opinions he was accused of espousing are Catholic ones (for about that, you have said enough), but in that he was unjustly charged with having preached them, when he had not done so. And thus are they very credibly informed, by both spoken word and written testimony of people who were present thereat. And therefore I sorely long and would be very glad to hear how those charges were proved."

"Now, I am," said I, "for my part, very sorry, so help me God, to lose time in that, a thing virtually fruitless—saving that it may perhaps serve as a fruitful lesson. No man should hereafter be so quick to believe such things as he shall happen to hear spoken against the Church, in the support of any man convicted of heresy, when he sees as much said against the condemnation of this man, in which, so to say, they can have no more of a hold than if they were to say that the crow is white. And actually, to tell the truth, there cannot to my mind be a more apt metaphor to apply to their statements. For just as someone who would say the crow is white must, if they want to be believed, go tell that tale to a blind person, and might perchance be by that person as much believed as someone who will say the contrary, till they are either by more people or by more honest people put later out of credence, so must these folk who thus speak and write of him seek, as they do indeed, such hearers as are blind in the matter and know nothing about it, whom they persuade with false representations to conceive a bad opinion of the judges, in order to incline their hearts first, for pity, to a favoring of the man, and afterward to a favoring of the things he was forced to abjure. I have myself seen a letter written in London, and sent from there, by a priest who is reputedly a trustworthy one, but actually, as I later saw proved, a plain pestilent heretic. In which letter he wrote that the man we are now talking about had no more abjured any heresy than had he himself or the man he was writing to. And yet his writing was as false as God is true. With it he labored covertly to make the man believe that the opinions were not heresies. And that the man who allegedly had abjured them had not actually done so, but had well avowed them and steadfastly stuck by them. Lo, thus do those who are of that sect propagate their contentions with lies. And it stands to reason that they do so. For since their sects are false, lies are for them most fitting. And yet it is crazy of them to boast of him. For he forthwith forsook them, and always before his judges he admitted, from the outset, that the contentions were plain, false heresies, and their holders, moreover, heretics. Saying for himself that he never preached them. And so they had no cause to be proud of this man who in public hearing, as soon as the first word was spoken, repudiated and condemned them. But they, perhaps thinking that for all his denying with his mouth, he still actually favored them and their heresies in his mind, therefore pardoned those words which they thought spoken only out of weakness, for fear and faint heart. And therefore they would still be glad, among people who did not know about the matter, to maintain and uphold his authority in anticipation of more favorable circumstances. And assuredly, this that I am about to tell you, I have heard reported. I cannot guarantee that it is true, but I have, as I say, heard it reported, quite credibly, that the man we are speaking of, the one who abjured, used to say among some in that sect, 'Let us preach and promote our way. And if we are accused, let us say that we did not say that; and anyway some of them we will always win in the meantime.' And although I cannot, as I say, guarantee you that he said that, I yet assure you that, to my mind, his manner in his legal case, before his judges, was as consistent as could be with that intent and purpose. For certainly the gist of his defense was nothing else but an obstinate, shameless denial of charges good and plainly proved."

"By my word," said your friend, "that really surprises me. For he was called a good man, and a very devout one."

"I will not," said I, "as I told you in the beginning, attempt to impugn his conduct, since the question stands not but in his teaching. And yet I can be frank with you and tell you what I have heard. He was (as it was said), after he turned from the study of law, in which he was an advocate and to some degree well-educated, to the study of Scripture—he was, as I say, very fearful and scrupulous, and began at once to fall into such a scrupulous holiness that he considered himself obliged to keep and observe the biddings of Christ so strictly, so very literally, that because our Lord tells us that when we want to pray, we should go into our room and shut the door [Mt 6: 6], he thought it therefore a sin to say his breviary anywhere else, and would always make sure to be in his room, with the door shut, when he said his Matins. Which thing I indeed once heard him deny in the presence of a dignitary. But I heard another man, who was more credible than two of him (and if I said more than ten, I think I would not be lying), and who was one of his most tried-and-true friends, respond to that by acknowledging it as true, right to his face. However, I do not tell you this thing for any great flaw in the man. For it was more foolish and painful than evil and sinful. But people definitely do say that in the end, with the weariness from that superstitious fear and servile dread, he went as far in the opposite direction. And under pretext of love and liberty got so drunk of the new must of base lightness of mind and vain gladness of heart, which he took for spiritual consolation, that whatsoever he himself wished to take for good, he immediately thought it approved by God. And so framed himself a faith, framed himself a conscience, framed himself a devotion, wherever he liked; and wherever he liked, he set himself at liberty."

"And if that is so," said your friend, "then look, you see what comes of this saying of the Office."

"Of saying the Office?" said I. "This is much like what happened at Beverley lately, when, many of the people being at a bear-baiting, the church suddenly fell down during Vespers and crushed some of those who were then in it. A good fellow who later heard the tale told said, 'Look, now you can see what comes of being at Vespers when you should be at the bear-baiting.' However, what caused the harm there was not the being at Vespers, but the fact that the church was badly built. And likewise it never did that man or anyone else any harm, it does nothing but good, to say the Divine Office. The occasion of harm is in the superstitious fashion that their own foolishness joins thereto, such as, some think they do not say it unless they say every psalm twice."

"Honestly," said your friend, "then if I were as he is, I would mumble it up apace or else not say it at all."

"That would be as bad," said I, "on the other side. There is between the two extremes a happy medium that could serve."

"Yes," said he, "but you know what the wife said that complained to her crony about her husband's cantankerousness? She said her husband was so ornery that there was no pleasing him. 'For if his bread,' said she, 'is doughy, he gets angry.' 'Goodness, no wonder,' said her crony. 'Goodness indeed,' said she, 'and you know what, my friend? If I bake it

all to hard coals, he is still not happy either, by Saint James.'
'No,' said her crony, 'you should bake it to a point in between.' 'A point in between?' said she. 'Goodness, I cannot
happen upon it.' And likewise in a set of Matins it is very
difficult to discover that point in between. And then to say it
too abruptly is lack of devotion, and to say it too intently is
somewhat superstitious. And therefore, as I see it, the best
way to say it would be not at all."

"Yes," said I, "but then again, God is as cantankerous a
husband as the one you spoke of, who will not be happy with
his bread burnt to coals, or doughy, either."

"But, by our Lady," said he, "be he happy or not, I think
he gets very doughy bread now and then. For Matins, I tell
you, is in some places sung faster than I can say it."

"Perhaps," said I, "it needs to be. For if they should sing
Matins no faster than you say it, they would, I think, sing it
very few times in a year."

"That is true," said he, "but some who say it make me
really wonder whether the bees in their hives make a habit of
saying Matins along with them. For just such another buzz-
ing they make."

"Certainly," said I, "that is as true as it is bad. For just as it
is a vice and something of an offense to be in the service of
God superstitious instead of religious, overly fearful and
scrupulous instead of devout and diligent, so is it a much
greater offense to be reckless and negligent in it. For accursed is he, as holy Scripture says, who does the work of
God negligently [Jer 48: 10]. The peril thereof is evidenced
by Eutychus, the young stripling (spoken of by Saint Luke,
in the Acts of the Apostles) who, falling asleep while the
apostles and the disciples were occupied in reading, preaching, and prayer, fell out of a high window down to the
ground, and there would have died, God knows in what
condition, if the merits of Saint Paul had not revived him
[Acts 20: 9–12]. And now, if those are accursed by God who
do his work negligently, how much more accursed are those

who throw their work away and leave it completely undone—such work, I say, as they are obliged to do?

"But we are spending more time than necessary on this
matter. For it is not very relevant to our present concern,
except that if it is true that the man whom we are talking
about fell first into such superstition, then it is more likely
than not that the devil did throw him into it for no other
intent but that he might afterward, for the very weariness
thereof, bring him into a contempt for all the things that he
was grown weary of, and set him in a delight in liberty.
Whereby, with relying on his own wit, he might reckon
everything good or bad according to how he himself chose
to regard it. Which was the ready way to bring him to these
heresies into which he was now fallen."

3.

*The author shows that people ought not lightly entertain suspi-
cions about any judgment given in the court. And that much less
should anyone venture to criticize a common law. And he shows
also the reason why the law admits less weighty testimony in
heinous criminal cases than in less weighty cases, having to do with
deals or contracts.*

"Fallen?" said your friend. "What? Wait a minute—we are
now gone over the stile before we have come at it. It is still in
question between us whether or not it was justly judged that
he was fallen into them. For I think it no sin to doubt that
until I hear how the case was proved."

"Indeed," said I, "that is, as you say, the matter we have to
talk about first. And yet if you never heard anything further
about it than that he was judged guilty, then even if you had
always in your own mind accounted the man very virtuous
and of right belief, yet since he cannot be good unless a
greater number of men than he is are bad whom you ought
no more to think ill of than him, and specifically his judges,
who are chosen and appointed for being unbiased, and who
without likelihood of standing anything to gain or lose are

assigned to consider, examine, and by their judgment settle the case of another person, whereas the parties themselves may reasonably be more mistrusted—both the accuser, who may be speaking out of malice, and particularly the party accused, who is quite likely to lie to defend himself against a charge that would put him in peril if he was found guilty of it—you therefore ought not to mistrust the judgment unless you knew firsthand that the case was in fact judged wrongly, or you had full and certain information thereof from very good, respectable folk who were present and impartial."

"To be sure," said he, "many think that if any such information can serve, they have had enough thereof, both oral and written, from men of wisdom, learning, and honesty who were present throughout the handling of the matter."

"Well," said I, "we shall leave their wisdom and learning alone. But as for their honesty, this will somewhat show itself upon the truthfulness or untruthfulness of their reports. Wherein, first, I ask you, could they say that he was not convicted by as many witnesses, and as good and credible ones, as the law requires?"

"So many," said he, "and such as the law requires? Would to God that we could as easily find good, honest men as we can find so many such. For the law does, as I hear it said, require but two, and, moreover, in a heresy case does not much care how bad they are; they could even be heretics themselves. And is this not an astonishing situation, that whereas in a matter of a little money no law allows the admitting of any witness who is not honest and credible, the law made by the Church should in so great a matter—one so seriously threatening the utter destruction of a person in body and goods, with a death the most painful that can be imagined—allow the admitting of a convicted felon, and give faith and credence to an infidel, someone they have time and again proved false to God in his faith?

"Nor do I think but very flimsy the excuse that I have previously heard offered for the Church on this point: that such shabby witnesses are admitted in heresy cases because the crime is so great and so odious that therefore it deserves to be handled with the more rigor and the less lenity. That is something I will well agree makes good sense in the punishment of the crime, when it is proved. But, before God, not in hatred and persecution of the person before the crime is proved.

"But, now, in that they accept the testimonies of such no-account, dishonest fellows for a proof, they prosecute the person and not the crime. Whereas it seems to me that, on the contrary, the more heinous, odious, and abominable the crime is, the more slow we should be to believe it, and the more certain and complete proof should we have before we judge anyone to have been so evil as to commit it."

"There is," said I, "no doubt that the world is so bad that there are many so wicked that they will be ready enough to bear false witness. And yet God forbid that it is as bad as you say—that those could be found sooner than good, honest people. And also, supposing that the witnesses were dishonest and would lie, yet when they are astutely and separately examined, they can seldom have so well prepared their story ahead of time that their untruthfulness will not in some part of it show up. And finally, the law does not bind the judge so strictly to the statements of the witnesses as not to leave many things to be pondered and weighed by his wisdom. For it is with a judge as it is with a physician, for whom have been written many good books able to give good light and instruction, and yet if anyone were to bind him so strictly to his book that he should use not at all the discretion of his brain, he would at times give really bad service.

"And yet it is, as Aristotle says, well done indeed to make the laws so sufficient that as few things as possible shall remain uncovered and be left to the discretion of the judge, since the common laws are commonly made by a number of people that is much larger than that of the particular judges, and by many who are as wise as judges. And besides that, the laws are for the judges a sure and substantial shield with which to defend and keep themselves from the hatred and verbal abuse that otherwise would follow upon their verdict on the one side or the other, be their judgment no matter how just. For people are always so partial to themselves that our hearts always think the judgment wrong that causes us distress. For be it right as can be, we reckon as wrong everything we feel harmed by.

"But yet, of all things, precisely the law should best content us, because it is the farthest removed from all cause of suspicion. For, given that a judge deals with a present matter, and with persons whom he sees and knows—for which reasons it can happen that favoritism, hatred, hope, fear, pity, cruelty, bribery, entreaty, or some other motivation inclines him to misconduct himself in the matter—the *laws* always are made only for the punishment of things that are yet to come, and who it is that will fall into peril, the makers cannot tell. Perhaps their foes, perhaps their friends, and (since people's behavior is mutable) perhaps themselves; for which reason the makers of the law made by the people for criminal cases have to be impartial. And therefore I am the more astonished, since that fault you find now is not in the judges but in the law itself, wherein you think it wrongly provided that on account of the hatred for a heinous crime, the perhaps innocent person should be put in peril of a painful death by the taking of more unreliable testimony than would be taken as sufficient in a case of far less consequence. You would, indeed, to some extent have had a point if the hatred of the crime were the whole cause. But there you go far wide of the mark. For the chief reason why in heinous criminal cases, such as theft, murder, treason, and heresy, the law admits as witnesses people that it will not accept in a case about some financial or other kind of contract made between two parties, is that otherwise all such heinous crimes would go unpunished, and as a result the world would swarm full of such injurious people, for lack of evidence and examination in the matter. For those who go about such a heinous deed as, once coming to knowledge, would bring them to a shameful death—these people do not ordinarily take along with them a notary or an honest witness to make an instrument thereof, as many do and everyone can do in a contract or pact. No, they usually do it by stealth, as covertly as they can. By reason whereof, reason proposes and necessity mandates (unless you would have everything go bad) the acceptance of such witnesses as they are wont to take into their confidence, who are, as you well know, none but such as they are themselves. And sometimes, which may seem stranger, we are even content, and it stands to reason that we be, with the witness of the parties themselves. For instance, suppose that ten thieves robbed four men at once, in a forest. Even if all that they made off with was the funds shared by all four, and even if all ten, when they were arrested, should deny it good and steadfastly, yet if I were their judge (since all witness serves but only to induce a credence or credulity in the judges' minds), I would not hesitate (unless some other circumstance stood in the way) to believe the four plaintiffs in their own suit against all ten defendants. And although in a case concerning a contract made between two parties, a judge might perhaps be induced in his own mind, without any doubt running contrary to this, to give credence on such a point to the one party against the other because of the well-known truthfulness and integrity of the one, and in the other party the contrary, yet the law does—throughout the world, almost—prohibit him so to proceed in a civil case, lest there should be brought into custom that form of judgment in which, because of the profit ensuing to that party, there would be occasion to corrupt the judge, and also inasmuch as that manner of proceeding is completely unnecessary in civil cases, since the parties can, if they wish, for the surety of their bargains, have them put in writing or backed up by good witness. Which if they do not care to do, either for foolishness, laziness, or trust, it makes good sense that it rather result in loss for them than, for the redressing of their oversight, bring into place that form and fashion of judgment that could be the cause of other people's wrongful trouble. Whereas in heinous criminal cases, not only is there not always such cause of corruption, specially favoring condemnation of the side on which alone falls the deficiency and peril that you speak of, but also there is, as you see, this inevitable necessity, for lack of possibility of other evidence and witness—until you provide that thieves and murderers will agree to take with them honest witnesses that may bear witness against them."

4.

The author makes known upon what ground and cause the man was convicted. And also several other things not brought up then, at the trial, which make it quite evident that he was greatly guilty. And thus, in passing, he shows why in a heresy trial it would not be reasonable to allow, after the slated witnesses have given their testimony and the charge has been well proved, any new witnesses to be received for the accused party.

"However, though this holds good for such matters in general, yet for this one matter that we now speak of, we stand in a far different situation. For this man was convicted not by the words of one or two, but by the oaths of one or two over twenty, not such men as we now speak of—Lollards and heretics—but respectable men, and of almost all classes: folk in religious orders, farmers, and noblemen."

"Indeed," said he, "to tell the truth, I did hear it said that there were many witnesses. But I also heard that he offered to bring in twice as many—and of such as were just as much present as they, and stood as near as they, and understood as well as they, and slept no more at his preaching than a parson does at his celebration of Mass—who would testify fully for him."

"Whether he said that or not," said I, "that I cannot tell you, but this I know well. He himself was well versed in the law, and never could say that he was denied any favor that the law would grant. And many a witness was there to whom he made no objection, and who he could not deny had been at his sermons and heard him. So then, when he was so clearly proved guilty by so many who were so respectable and so far above any suspicion of corruption, it perhaps would not have been a good idea to bring in, after those slated witnesses, new witnesses concerning the principal charge. For should that be done, then either the new witnesses would attest the same thing that the others did before, or else they would attest the opposite, or, finally, say something that could neither make nor break him. Now, if they did the first, that is to say, depose as the first group did, then we would be no further than we were before, and that time would have been wasted and the proceedings delayed in vain. If they did the third, deposing, perchance, that they themselves were not present, or were asleep, or did not really understand what he said, or did not well remember it, we would still be at the same standstill.

"Posit, now, that second possibility (which would, so to say, be the only thing that might seem to give him a leg to stand on): that the new witnesses would testify that they at that same time were present and stood near him, paid close attention to him, and well remembered that he did not say such and such; yes, and perhaps that he said the opposite. This case is possible, but certainly it is so seldom likely that it is not worth changing a law for. But, now, if that should so happen, here would be a great confusion. And how could any verdict be given if the second group were to be believed as much as the first?"

"That," said he, "is immaterial. For if the truth thereby appears to be on his side, either clearly or possibly, then the judges can acquit and clear the defendant. And it would be better that the guilty be acquitted than that the innocent be punished."

"It would be a strange thing," said I, "if the law should in such a case as this, after the slated witnesses have given their testimony and the charge has thereby been well proved, then examine other witnesses afresh upon the principal point. This would in my mind be perilous, not only because of the threat of subornation and dishonest instruction of witnesses (a thing easily done on the basis of the sight of what has already been deposed), but also because if the affirmative be proved (especially in this heresy case, it being by so many sufficiently proved that this man taught and preached such things in his public sermons), if others who were present at the same sermons would now depose the contrary, it could be that the first group heard something which the second group did not notice, as many times does happen. And also it is more likely that one person will forget something that they did hear than that another will remember something that they did not hear. And if some did perhaps add that he said the opposite of those things that were testified against him, then it can at best be no better taken than that he in one and the same sermon said, taught, and preached both of the two: that is to say, the truth and the heresies. In which case he would well deserve the sentence of having to acknowledge his guilt and be corrected for it."

"Definitely," said he, "and yet it always seems to me that it ought to be heard, all that anyone wants to say, and that it should all be taken in the best way for the one accused, and especially in regard to heresy purportedly being preached where so many are present."

"To be sure," said I, "what would be the best way, God knows; for I cannot tell. But this I know well: that the whole world, virtually, is in agreement in understanding that with regard to all such heinous crimes, reason dictates the complete opposite and goes quite against your way of thinking. And whereas you think your way of thinking worthy to take special place in the proving and examining of heresies, it certainly seems to me that of all crimes, heresy is the one in regard to which it could least be allowed. For well you know that heresies are false beliefs and factious ways full of feverish activity. And such as give themselves thereto are staunch and studious about the furtherance of their seditious sect. And since thcy are fallen from God and his true faith, they have no great care about truth, nor have too many scruples about lending an oath till they need in a like case to be paid back. So that if their 'nay' can stand against other good people's 'yea,' and where the heresy is proved to have been preached, people can there be heard and believed in deposing the contrary, the false preacher can be brazen enough to say whatever he pleases. For he will never fail to have his witnesses ready."

"Yes," said he, "but this way would not serve him. For people might take exception to his witnesses if they are heretics."

"No," said I, "not if they *are* so, but if they are *proved* so. And that they never will be, if your way is accepted. For each of their witnesses will always serve another."

"Indeed," said he, "it seems somewhat perilous, as you say, if people should, against the affirmative proved, side with the contrary witnesses, for the negative, in any crime that is seditious and has folk of evil conscience fervently falling into it every day. But yet I really wonder about one thing. For I have heard it credibly reported that there were two men—both of them beneficed, both of them very astute, both of them very virtuous—who as well heard him preach as did those who had deposed against him. And these two affirmed and offered to depose that he did not preach the things he was accused of having preached. And certainly had I been one of his judges, I would have believed those two over twenty others, unless testimonies are assessed only by count and not by weight."

"Assuredly," said I, "my thinking and yours are not far apart. For since all witness serves to induce the judge's mind to conceive a credence and an opinion, or, rather, a certain persuasion on the one side, I myself could not but believe some two better than some twenty. And would not fail to weigh all the testimonies rather than take them by tally.

"However," said I, "of those two that you speak of, the one was indeed such as you say; but as for the other, he was not even then considered very bright and shining, and since that time he has proved glaringly bad. But even if the one was, as he was indeed, a very good man, yet for the man's exoneration he was no very good witness. Neither would the other have been, even if he had been as good a man as he. Nor would forty more men, as good as the better of these two, speaking as these two did."

"Why," said he, "they did not speak well for him?"

"Yes," said I, "for as far as they went, but they did not go far enough."

"Ah," said he, "their words were probably taken too narrowly."

"They were," said I, "taken as broadly as they were spoken. What these witnesses said was that he did not preach such and such heresies in a place where they heard him in London. But then the accusations made against him, and the testimonies made concerning them, were about those heresies preached at various places outside of London; and thus their words went as wide of his defense as if someone arraigned for a felony done at Salisbury on Shrove Tuesday were to bring to the bar good witnesses who would depose and swear for him that he did no such thing at Shrewsbury on Holy Thursday, for they were with him there all that day themselves. But in the end, he was declared guilty by more than twenty, and declared not guilty by nary a one. And therefore if his judges did him wrong, there was never a man who was done right. And, moreover, there were in addition to the witnesses some letters written in his own hand to one of his judges, which letters I have since seen, that sounded in my ears, too, like heresies as bad as those he was accused of. Which letters were never brought before the court until, after the testimonies were circulated and read, he showed up obstinate, steadfastly persisting in the denial and proudly refusing to submit himself to his abjuration. For then the judge to whom they were written said that since he refused to be reconciled to the Church, he would keep no confidence of his. And thereupon he brought in those letters and filed them among the court records.

"This man had also been, before that, accused to the greatest prelate in this realm—who, for his tender favor borne to the university, did not proceed very far in the suit against him. Rather, accepting his denial (which he made together with a solemn oath that he from that time forth would be no propagator of heresies, but would in his preachings and scriptural expositions impugn them), he dismissed him very kindly, and of his goodness and generosity even gave him money for his legal expenses. And yet none of these facts were mentioned in the charges against him. Which if they had been, would perhaps have put him in jeopardy.

"I myself was also, since his abjuration, present (as it happened) with a distinguished prelate at such a time as a certain man who was a heretic of long standing had been in examination and had there admitted that he had held, taught, and in several countries spread around almost all the heresies that any vile heretic holds."

"Can you not tell his name?" said he.

"Which of them?" said I. "For he had more names than half a page can hold."

"Where did he live?" said your friend.

"Everywhere and nowhere," said I. "For he walked about, as an apostle of the devil, from shire to shire and town to town throughout the realm, and had in every diocese a different name. By reason of which he did a lot of harm for many years before he could be found out. This heretic in the end acknowledged all his other heresies to be evil, and offered to recant them, but as for his denunciations of images, relics, and pilgrimages, those things, he said, were not heresies but very good and valid positions, for he heard them preached, he said, by 'the great theologian,' naming the man we have been speaking of, and he told where; acknowledging also that he liked his sermons so much that he did not hesitate to walk twenty miles to hear him. And there was even, since that, another heretic who admitted for his own part the like. So that you can see that good Christian folk were scandalized by his preaching, and heretics liked his preaching, and grounded their heresies upon his preaching. So mind you what manner of preaching it was likely to be.

"I told you also, just now, that one of those two that you took for such good and astute men was afterward found to be worse than many would have thought. Yes, sir, so it was, indeed, that he was accused of having bought many books by Luther, Lambert, and Zwingli, and others of that ilk, and it was well attested, and by himself also admitted, that he had bought of those books very many, which he finally brought forth from where he had laid them up no less suspiciously than secretly, and so secretly that all the town should have long looked for them before they should have found them.

"He had also gotten a priest of his, and a lay servant of his besides, to buy many of the same suit, and two and three copies of some, which were sent out by them to several young scholars, such as they found properly witted, suitably educated, and newfangledly minded. And thus he endeavored to corrupt the realm. He previously had had another parish priest—who also fulfilled his pastoral responsibilities as this other one did—who was later proved a very pernicious heretic."

"But what," said he, "was done to this ringleader?"

"Actually," said I, "he was done a great favor (and, according to some, a great wrong, too) in that he was not judged publicly. At any rate, because he was held in high esteem, there was out of pity much regard given to the preservation of his good name. And virtually nothing was exacted of him but his amendment, with the acknowledging of his guilt. For it is a fact that that man was of such a poor spirit in Christ that, despite any oath that could be administered to him, it was a long time before his pride, and its fear of shame, would allow him to tell the truth. After which—once it was acknowledged in his handwriting—then, as far as I have heard, he was given in adjudication, without any other abjuration, the private taking of a solemn oath that he should do no such thing anymore, upon pain of a backsliding into heresy; and so, with a certain private penance, he was dismissed.

"But the thing that I tell you my tale for is this. This man—besides the fact that virtually all the books which he had bought from this Lutheran sect were diligently read over and studied, and marked up with such manner of notes in the margins, the words written in his own hand, where the worst things were, that he left no reader of them in any doubt as to what fervent affection he bore to them—he had, I say, besides all this, several letters (I do not know to whom, but they were written in his own hand) in which were plenty of pestilent heresies. And a sermon also, worse than them all, written in his own hand also, ready to be preached, as it seemed, if the world would so change that the circumstances would allow it. And when he was, during his examination, sorely pressed upon to tell for what intent he had prepared such a sermon and laid it up so secretly, he at last, being destitute of any explanation that might bear any semblance of a good reason, said, 'Well, I see well that I must tell everything. I am loath to hurt anyone.' And thereupon he told how it was for the most part written by the man who abjured; the specific man whom we are talking about. So that now, putting all these things together—the confession of this man, his close friend and companion in such matters, his old accusations of similar matters, the confessions of the heretics who based their heresies in the same matters upon the authority of his sermon, and in addition to all this, the more than twenty witnesses plainly proving the case against him—I would love to know who was done right if he was done wrong, even if he had been treated a great deal more severely than he was."

5.

The author proves that the ecclesiastical judges did the man a marvelous favor, and one almost more than licit, in admitting him to such an abjuration as they did, instead of leaving him to the secular authorities.

"Why," said he, "what more fiendish severity could they have shown him, for a first offense, than to force him to recant and to carry the fagot?"

"Well," said I, "someone might rather carry two cold ones around his neck than have one carry him hot, on a fire at his feet."

"Seriously," said he, "they could not have done that to him for a first offense."

"No," said I, "not if he willingly returned to the Church, acknowledging his guilt, and was ready to abjure all heresies, and penitently submitted himself to penance. But otherwise, if the person should prove obstinate and impenitent, the Church neither is bound nor ought to receive them, but may utterly forsake them and leave them to the secular authorities. But, now, he was so obstinate that he for a long time would not abjure. And his judges, in their exceptional kindness, gladly gave him several days, and allowed some of his best friends, the ones whom he most trusted, to visit him. And yet scarcely could all this make him submit himself to making his abjuration. And finally, to save his life, they were forced to devise a form of abjuration the like of which I had never seen. Nor would I ever, in so clear a case, were I the judge, allow the like hereafter."

"What kind of abjuration was that?" said he.

"Indeed," said I, "his abjuration was such that in it he did abjure and forswear all heresies, acknowledging himself lawfully convicted. But whereas they usually admit in their own abjuration that they have held such heresies and are guilty of them, that he would in no way do. As clearly as his guilt was proved, and by as many, he yet, even if it should mean his death, would not admit that he was guilty, but always kept maintaining, under oath, that they all slandered him."

"It could be," said he, "that he had forgotten that he had thus preached."

"That would," said I, "be really amazing. For I am certain, since he had preached thus in so many places, that he had done it not by any spur-of-the-moment accident, but by a deliberate intent which, unless he went insane, it would not be very possible for him, in so great a matter, to forget. And besides this, it was also deposed that in a place where he preached, he was immediately after the sermon confronted about it. A reputable layman called him to task, telling him that he had preached terribly and explaining to him wherein. To which he answered not that he had not said that, or that he had not meant that, or that they had misunderstood and wrongly interpreted his words, but that he would be preaching there again soon after, and would prove his preaching correct by quoting the old holy theologians of the Church. And this happened to him not long before his being accused. Was it now possible, do you believe, that he could have forgotten this?"

"It was," said he, "possible enough that the whole thing was false, and that they all did lie. For so might they possibly do, being but men, and even if they had been more than they were. And then, he perhaps knowing that they did so, why should he falsely admit to guilt because of the falsehood of other folk?"

"That is," said I, "true if he so knew it. But how could that be so, against so many witnesses sworn and deposing the matter upon their oaths, their being, though they were but men, yet men of intelligence and integrity, and some well-educated also, and men who bore him no dislike for anything other than his bad preaching, men almost all of whom could have had no other connection with him, folk who never had any other issue with him, and many of whom had little or no acquaintance the one with the other, so that there was no fear of their conspiring together in one tale?"

"Yet," said he, "it is possible that they could all be lying."

"And," said I, "what about the fact that he had been reported in other places before, as he was indeed not only to that most distinguished prelate that I mentioned to you, but, besides him, to two other bishops too?"

"Well," said he, "and yet they that thus reported him could happen to be lying too."

"And," said I, "what about the fact that his own secret acquaintance admitted that he wrote the first draft of that ungodly sermon that I told you about?"

"Did you hear that firsthand?" said he.

"Firsthand," said I, "no, but those I heard it from were men of such respectability, and integrity as well, that I do not think anyone would doubt their story."

"As well regarded as they may be," said he, "and as trustworthy, too, I could doubt their story well enough on a particular occasion—for, perhaps, their lack of impartiality, since they were not under oath. And what if I did not disbelieve them all? It yet could be that they told the truth and that other man lied, attributing the first draft of that sermon to this man to exonerate himself."

"The attributing of it to him," said I, "could not exonerate himself. For he admitted that he himself liked it and approved of it, and therefore copied it out, and even added many more things to it."

"Well," said he, "and yet all of this could be."

"And," said I, "what about the heretics who grounded their opinions upon his sermons?"

"Could it not be," said he, "that they lied?"

"And," said I, "what about those who had reported him to other prelates before?"

"By God," said he, "just as I told you before, it could well enough be that they lied."

"And then," said I, "what about all those twenty who deposed against him now?"

"Good heavens," said he, "as I told you just now, it could be that they did just the same."

"This is," said I, "a strange thing to me."

"Why," said he, "should this be strange to you? It seems to me it should be strange to no one, but rather, quite obvious to everyone, that it could be so. For I ask you, *could* it not be so? Is it not possible that they could all lie, even if they were as many more?"

"Possible?" said I. "To that I say not no, but that it would be possible even if they were a thousand times as many."

"Well," said he, "since it could be so, then suppose for the sake of argument that it was so. Did he not then do right in continuing to say so? And if he had died for that, would he not have died for the truth? For, knowing within himself that all of them were slandering him, he was not obliged to join them in slandering him and confess against himself an untruth, but would have been in serious sin had he done so. What do you say to this?"

"I say," said I, "to this that all the force and effect of your conclusion hinges upon the case which you propose, that all those who ever said or testified anything against him lied, the whole lot of them. Which case you think must needs be granted, because it is possible. And then, that case once granted, you deduce your conclusion very confidently. And in all honesty, you thereby so bring me to my wit's end that I do not quite know which way to answer you, admitting your case. However, it seems to me that your case, though it is possible, is rather to be granted at a university, in a debate, than at a court, in a trial. And I ask you to let me, for proof of this, put to you another hypothetical case, which in all honesty I am half ashamed to put to you, except that you drive me to seek a stratagem. And yet my case will not in my opinion be much unlike yours.

"Suppose Wilkins has laid a wager with Simkins that along a certain path specified by them, traveled enough by both humans and horses, there has recently walked a horse or two, and that he will prove it so clearly that the contrary cannot be true. Simkins says, and lays his wager on, the contrary, and then the both of them choose us for judges. We come, all four of us, onto the path, and Wilkins shows us on the ground, partly in the dirt and partly, perhaps, in the snow, the prints of horse feet and of human feet also, over a long distance, ten consecutive miles, if you will, till they come to a lake, where there has gone away by ship no one can tell who or to where—it makes no difference to our brilliant scenario. But, now, suppose Wilkins says he has won his wager, 'for look, here you see the prints of the horse feet all along the path, shod and all, with the very nails in them, so that it can be no other way but that horses have walked here.' And suppose Simkins, after all this, says that he has won the wager, since it is not proved that any horses have walked there; for it could be that they were geldings or mares. Here we would get involved in a great question of the law: whether the gray mare may be the better horse or not, or whether one has an intelligent-looking face or not who looks as much like a fool as a ewe looks like a sheep. And if in this question the parties took exception to our judgment, we could take it further and ask the advice of learned men and judges."

"We could," said he, "by way of suit, to be sure of the matter, make it an arbitration case. Or, unless it would constitute a violation of the praemunire statute, we could have it tried in the Roman Rota."

"Very well," said I. "So I well see that by your wit and mine together, one means or another we would find for a conclusive end to it, if the doubt were in that point. But, now, suppose Simkins did not stop there, but said this: 'Look, *here* you see that *people* have walked along this road. So how, then, can you be sure that any horse came here? For I put the case that these people who came here had in their hands long steel poles with horseshoes fastened to them, and always as they went along, they pricked them down hard in the ground.'"

"Pooh," said he, "this would be a brilliant invention."

"Truth to tell," said I, "to me it would not seem very plausible. But, now, what if Simkins is contentious and says the wager is his unless it be proved that it cannot be otherwise than that horses have recently walked there, and then says to us, 'Look, sirs—as you see, it could be otherwise, since people could make with their hands all the horseshoe prints on the ground'? If we then said that this never was the case, he would ask us how we can be sure of that, when we cannot deny that it could be the case, and then he would keep pressing us with this question 'Could it not be so?'"

"It could," said he, "by possibility be so."

"Then," said I, "once we have granted him that it could be so, then he will immediately postulate that it is so. And then, once we have granted him his scenario because of its possibility, then he will in short order conclude that the other one is not as definitely proved as it must be for Wilkins to win the wager. What should we say to him now? To whom should we give the wager?"

"In all honesty," said he, "I have no idea what to say to him. And the matter is so mad that as for the wager, what I would give Wilkins I have no idea, but as for Simkins, unless he better challenged the proof, if the wager were but a butterfly I would never award him one wing."

"Assuredly," said I, "and you shall rule that case for me. For if you give him nothing, he gets as little from me. But, now, what if he were to get angry that his excellent invention is not taken more seriously, or his intelligence held in higher regard, and would then help along his side of the argument with an oath, and swear on a Bible that he himself saw when the people made those prints on the ground with horseshoes held in their hands? What would you then say?"

"Goodness," said he, "then I would say—and swear, too
—that in addition to losing his wager, he had like a false,
foolish knave lost his integrity, and his soul, too."

"Precisely," said I, "and for anything I see thus far, I would
dare be bold enough to swear with you. And then, leaving
Wilkins alone with Simkins, letting them dispute their
sophism themselves, let us come back home to our own case.
In which, when there were so many such clear and obvious
testimonies against the man of whom we have been speaking
all this time, although it is possible that all of them could be
false, yet no impartial judge could think this was the case
unless it was proved to be, and by other means than the mere
oath of the accused party, who is swearing alone against
them all."

"Yet," said he, "for all that, if he in fact knows that he did
not do it, he does only right to stand by the truth."

"What you say is quite true," said I. "And Simkins, too—
if he saw the people make the horseshoe prints on the road,
then no matter how unlikely it seemed to us, he yet would
have done plenty right to say it, and swear it too, and steadfastly stick by it. And yet you remember, by golly, that had he
so sworn, you and I both said just now that we would quite
confidently have believed he was lying. And might we not
well believe the same in our case too?"

"Yes," said he, "I should think so indeed. And therefore
the judges did him nothing but right in considering him
guilty and therefore compelling him to abjure. But yet they
showed him in this no such favor as you speak of, in that they
admitted him to his abjuration without his having to admit
to being guilty. For had they forced him to do that, they
would to my mind have clearly and obviously done him
wrong, since it could be that what he said and swore to was
the truth. And then they would have been forcing him to go
against his conscience and speak untruthfully of himself.
And they would have been doing this not only completely
against right, but also without necessity, considering that

they could, as in the end they did, find another way to get him to abjure. And therefore they did take the best way, both for him and for themselves too, but since they did therein nothing other than what they were duty-bound to do, it is quite evident that he received therein no such favor as you would make it seem that they showed him."

"Well," said I, "since you yourself agree that he would have been done no wrong even if no favor had been shown him, your message is still answered as far as his abjuration is concerned. And now if I should prove to you that his judges did show him such favor, I am afraid that I should somewhat seem to be accusing them of having done, if not wrong, yet very close to wrong, in that it appears, if not that the favor shown was against the law, yet at the very least that the law was for that favor stretched so far that the leather could scarcely hold. However, they choose for me. For since I have said it, I will tell you why, and so much the more boldly between the two of us, since I do not perceive in you any such manner of mentality toward them that you would blow abroad any guiltiness of unlawful favor found in them."

"Ah, well said," he replied, laughing. "You think I would more readily talk about their harshness than any instance of their favor."

"Well taken of you," said I. "I see well that a man cannot have a good opinion of you without your conscience construing it to the contrary. But, now, for the matter, I trust we are both agreed that even if it were the case that the man was in fact not guilty, yet the testimonies against him were so many, so good, so clear and convincing, and so much more than sufficient, that neither his judges nor ourselves either, nor, I think, even his own father either, if he had heard them, could have thought him anything other than very greatly guilty."

"Surely," said he, "that is true."

"Now," said I, "that being true, that they could regard him in no other way even though he still swore the contrary, must it not necessarily be that because he denied under oath those things which they could not but believe true, they necessarily had to believe him to be lying and perjuring himself the whole while?"

"That does follow," said he.

"Now," said I, "when someone is accused and convicted of heresy, what thing will the law have the Church receive him to?"

"What thing?" said he. "Indeed, to mercy!"

"No," said I, "mercy is the thing, as it seems, that it receives him by, not the thing that it receives him to."

"Then it is," said he, "to penance."

"That seems well said," said I. "For the Church by mercy receives him to penance."

"But now," said I, "does the Church publicly receive to penance any person appearing and proving still impenitent?"

"No," said he.

"Does not one appear still impenitent," said I, "who still appears perjured and still standing in perjury? And given that the first part of penance is confession and humble acknowledging of the guilt, can the Church consider penitent someone who still refuses to confess his guilt, who is still speaking falsely, lying, perjuring himself?"

"The Church," said he, "cannot know with certainty whether he is swearing truthfully or falsely, and therefore they cannot with certainty judge him to have committed perjury. For it may be, by possibility, that all the witnesses lied."

"It may be too," said I, "by possibility, if we go this way to work, that all the men who ever have said they came from Rome were lying, and that all the apostolic briefs and bulls that ever were believed to have been brought from there were faked, for all that anyone can tell who has never been there himself. For some one man could be lying, and some one bull or brief could be fake, and so could some others, this one and that one, and so forth—all the rest. For like possibility is there in every one as in any one. And perhaps as for your own self, you have never even talked with twenty who have told you they have been in Rome."

"No, no," said he, "not, I think, even with ten."

"And how many bulls," said I, "and briefs, have you seen that came from there?"

"By our Lady," said he, "bulls, very few, and briefs, none at all, for I never ask to see them."

"Then," said I, "you could by your own reasoning as well doubt whether there is any Rome or not as whether that man lied and committed perjury or not. But over this point I will not long wrangle with you. For surely, the case standing in such a state that his judges could not otherwise think of him but that he was guilty of things which he was still denying under oath, then even though they could have thought along with this that they could possibly be mistaken in that view, yet as long as they could not think or have any other view but that he (though what he swore could possibly be true) had in fact lied under oath and was in actual fact persevering in perjury—the matter now standing, I say, in such a state—then, since anyone who with such plain-appearing perjury persists in denying his guilt and falsely defending himself cannot be considered repentant of his guilt, and since no impenitent person ought to be admitted to penance, I will not say that his judges did wrong, but it certainly seems to me that I can rightly say that they showed him great favor in that they received him to penance without his admitting to being guilty. And I really think it was an unduly favoring fashion of abjuration, and one so strange that the like has very seldom been seen, if ever it was seen before. And that they allowed it in the hope that God shall send him more grace in time to come; and so I beseech him to do. For I assure you that I, for my part, can never conceive a good hope of his amendment as long as I see still abiding in his heart that pride that cannot, for fear of shame, allow him to admit his guilt."

6.

The author shows, with regard to this person who abjured for his own worldly reputation and for the more fruit from his preaching (should he be allowed to preach in time to come), that it would be much better for him if he openly and voluntarily confessed the truth. And that now, by stubbornly persisting in the denial, he both shames himself and would, if he preached, bring the word of God into discredit.

"It is," said he, "perhaps better thus. For then he would discredit himself, and the word of God also, if he should hereafter preach again."

"No indeed," said I, "then he would, rather, *deliver* himself, and the word of God also, from discredit. For then everyone would see the devil cast clean out of his heart, and hope that he would from then on be a very good man. Whereas now, thinking him to be persevering in a proud perjury, we can think nothing else but that he must needs be very wicked still, even if we should hereafter hear him preach no matter how correctly. And this would be a serious discredit to the word of God, that people should see someone whom they hear preach correctly be so proud a hypocrite, and on top of that, so foolish too, that for a false hope of preserving his own reputation, he tries as hard as he can to make the world believe that twenty honest men committed perjury against him. About which there being no one insane enough to believe him, he loses (if he preaches in this plight) his whole entire objective and wins nothing but the opposite: that is, double shame, for his proud perjury and his malicious mind, instead of the praise that he hopes and preaches for."

7.

The messenger poses a question: If someone is sworn by a judge to tell the truth about himself concerning a crime that he is suspected of having committed, whether he may not legitimately swear on his oath to an untruth when he thinks that that truth cannot be proved against him. To which the author responds that he is bound upon

pain of perjury to tell and confess the truth. And the much more of
a sin and folly it was, then, for this man, who thus abjured, to
perjure himself about something that he well knew would be
proved; and a shameless folly to stubbornly stand by his perjury
when he saw the case so clearly proved in fact. And with this he
finishes the discussion of that abjuration.

"In all honesty," said he, "I am beginning to be of your mind
on this matter. For the charge being so clearly and obviously
proved, it was and is both sin and folly to persist in the
denying. But there comes to my mind something about
which, although it is a little off from our subject matter, I
would be glad to hear what you think."

"What thing is that?" said I.

"Indeed," said he, "I have heard some very learned men
say that if someone is accused of a crime that he is in fact
guilty of, but this is not known and cannot be proved, then
under an oath administered to him he may and ought to
swear not guilty, because about secret and unknown things
no man can be his judge. For only God is judge of the human
heart. And if someone should confess it where he need not,
before judges who are not competent—that is to say, publicly
confess before human beings his secret transgression, of
which God alone is judge—then he would be committing
detraction against himself, which would be a serious sin. For
holy Scripture says, 'Curam habe de bono nominem,' 'Have
a care for your good name' [Sir 41: 12], and 'Melior est nomen
bonum quam divitiae multae,' 'Better is a good name than a
lot of riches' [Prv 22: 1]. And it also says, 'Maledictus homo
qui negligit famam suam,' 'Accursed is anyone who does not
care what people say about him' [see Prv 13: 3 and 19: 16].
And I have therefore heard some very learned men say that in
this case a man may boldly deny the allegation upon his oath,
no matter how true it is, so long as his guilt is so hidden as not
to be capable of being proved by any witness."

"Indeed," said I, "it is a large and long matter to speak of
perjury. But as for this point, I hold it in my mind to be one

of little question. For I hold this once and for all, as a sure and infallible conclusion: that a person can never legitimately commit perjury. It is, of course, true that a person's oath is open to interpretation and is not always bound absolutely to the words. If, for instance, a judge, in a court, were to put me under a general oath to give truthful answers to such things as should be asked of me, and then, after my oath was given, he were to ask me certain questions about matters belonging not at all to his jurisdiction, I would not by my oath be bound to answer him, since no such thing was in my oath intended. And likewise if a priest who had heard someone's confession was called before a judge and sworn as a witness regarding that person, he could boldly swear he knew nothing about the matter. Not by virtue of the common explanation—that the confession was made to him not as to himself as such but as to God's minister—but by virtue of the fact that he is by law exempted from telling any such thing, no less than if what he was ordered to answer under oath was this: 'What do you know about this matter outside of confession?' For otherwise, if there was a tyrant who wanted to compel him to swear explicitly to what he knew from the person's confession, that confessor would to my mind have no choice but to tell him bluntly, 'Sir, I will not swear to that for you, nor on such a subject give you any answer, even if I have to die for this. It is not because of anything I know that would implicate this person in this matter if I went ahead and told you his whole entire confession, but because of the evil that would come of such a precedent. For if I should now get an innocent person acquitted by swearing truthfully that I heard no such thing in his confession, I would in some other court case have to either commit perjury or, by refusing to respond under oath, make the person the more suspect in that I refuse to swear to as much for that one as I did for another. And therefore I will not make any answer in this case, because of the peril it may lead to in another.'

"With this answer, or some similar one, he must plainly

refuse to swear, regardless of what punishment he may have to endure for it. And, likewise, if any judge wanted to put any person under oath to tell him the truth about any crime which was so unknown that the judge himself had never heard anything about it, but simply wanted for his own pleasure to know by means of the person's oath whether there was perhaps any such thing or not, the party may refuse to swear or to give him any answer about that. But, on the other hand, if he has been denounced to or found out by him, by way of either common knowledge or other information giving rise to such conjectures and likelihoods that the law gives the judge authority to administer to the party an oath for the further investigation of the matter, there he is plainly bound, upon pain of eternal damnation, to tell and disclose the plain truth, without any covering up or craftiness, and to have more regard to his soul than to his shame. For as for those texts which you adduced, they are far from relevant here. For they mean nothing other than that one should in one's conduct avoid not only sin but also any occasion whereby people might have reasonable cause to bad-mouth oneself wrongly. And this was never meant to refer to the shame that someone suffers from his own confession of a sin that he did in fact commit. For by that he does not lose his good name, but rather *gets* his good name, among good folk. As for what bad people may say, there is no telling. But certainly, as I say, if someone had been all evil, evil as a devil, and after repenting of his sin would for a part of his penance willingly undertake the suffering of public shame, there is not one good Christian who would after all of that not like him not only no less, but a great deal the better. And if all such public confession is sin, there was much sin practiced among good folk many a day in Christ's church when it was much better than it is now.

"Look at Achan, who had committed sacrilege; this is written of in Joshua [7: 10–26]. He was exhorted by Joshua to confess his guilt publicly and give glory to God, who had had him found out through drawings of lots. And he did so, and meekly suffered for his sin as well the shame, and the curiosity of the world, as the pain and bitterness of death. And therefore I have no more doubt about that thief now being a glorious saint in heaven than I do about the thief that Christ promised Paradise to, hanging on the cross [Lk 23: 39–43]. And surely if people's old offenses were still their infamy after their amendment, then Saint Peter would be little beholden to Saint Matthew and others of his companions who have disgraced him in their Gospels, telling how shamefully, after all his crowings, he both forsook his Master and forswore him [Mt 26: 33–35, 69–74]. If a good man goes bad, the better he was the more sin there is in it, and the more shame also. And does it not then stand to reason, conversely, that if a bad man turns good, the worse he was the better it is for him, and the more honor there is also? Our Lord says himself that over one sinner coming back to grace there is more joy in heaven than over a whole hundred good folk that never sinned [Lk 15: 7]. And do we then consider someone shamed by the knowledge of his sin here among sinful people, when his humble confession and meek amendment wins him so much honor in heaven? Trust me: really and truly, when someone has done evil, if he is duly sworn, it is an honorable shame and a joyful sorrow for him to confess the truth. And good folk, though they abhor the sin, yet love and commend the person as one who was bad and is good. And the shame that he conceives in his heart before the world, it gets him great honor before God, and the momentary glowing heat in his cheeks speedily burns up and wastes the never-wasting fire of hell, standing him in further stead by taking care of a great part of his purgatory. And therefore, on the point that we are speaking of, without long discussion I tell you plainly my mind: that no one can be excused from the risking of endless damnation who would, in reliance on any expert's opinion, hide or cover up his guilt by any trickery, after he has been administered a lawful oath to tell the plain truth about it. And whoever will say the contrary, he must needs opine plainly against the law and say that no judge can lawfully administer an oath to the party. For to what purpose would the oath be if the party could lawfully perjure himself? And also, if the judge cannot lawfully administer to him the oath, then he may refuse to swear, but he may not first swear to tell the truth and then speak falsely. That is something that every person must upon pain of damnation eschew, even if he should foolishly take an oath when he could lawfully have refused to."

"Honestly," said he, "it seems to me you take the sure way."

"Well," said I, "if this be so in the case of someone who is sworn where the allegation, as he thinks, cannot be well proved, then how far wrong went that man whom we were speaking of, to perjure himself in a case concerning preaching that he well knew was so public that it would be plainly proved what sin there was in it? And what sin, and folly as well, was there in his still sticking to his perjury when he saw the allegation already proved so clearly, and by so many who were so good, so honest, and so impartial, that he could now gain nothing by the denial but bad opinion, and almost a despair of his amendment, in all who ever heard him?"

"In all honesty," said he, "all of this is very true, and therefore we shall leave him alone till God sends him a better frame of mind."

8.

The author explains why Tyndale's translation of the New Testament was burned, giving examples of words changed badly and for a bad purpose.

"But now, I ask you, let me know your mind concerning the burning of the English translation of the New Testament which Tyndale did, and (as people say) quite well, which makes people really wonder about that burning."

"It is," said I, "to me a great wonder that any good Christian having the least bit of sense in his head would at all wonder or complain about the burning of that book, if he knows the content. Whoever calls it the New Testament is calling it by a wrong name, unless they want to call it 'Tyndale's Testament,' or 'Luther's Testament.' For Tyndale had, in accord with Luther's counsel, so corrupted it and changed it from the good and wholesome doctrine of Christ to the diabolical heresies of their own that it was a completely contrary thing."

"That would be a wonder," said your friend, "that it should be so completely contrary. For to some who read it, it seemed very much like it."

"It is," said I, "nevertheless contrary, and all the more dangerous. For just as to a genuine silver coin a falsified copper coin is nevertheless contrary although it is quick-silvered over, and it is so much the more false in how much it is counterfeited the more like to the truth, so was the translation so much the more contrary in how much it was craftily contrived to seem the same, and so much the more dangerous in how much harder it was for uneducated folk to tell the difference."

"Why," said your friend, "what errors were there in it?"

"To tell you all of them," said I, "would very nearly be to read you the whole entire book, in which there were found and noted as wrongly and treacherously translated a total of over a thousand texts."

"I would," said he, "really like to hear such a one."

"Whoever," said I, "should study for that should study where to find water in the sea. But I will show you by way of example two or three that are such that every one of the three is more than thrice three in one."

"That would be," said he, "very strange, unless you mean more in weight. For in number, one can be but one."

"Assuredly," said I, "they are as weighty as any can lightly be. But I mean that each one of them is more than thrice three in number."

"That," said he, "is something of a riddle."

"This riddle," said I, "will soon be solved. For he has mistranslated three words of great weight, and every one of them is, as I would guess, more than thrice three times repeated and reiterated in the book."

"Ah, that may well be," said he, "but that was not well done. But I ask you, what words are they?"

"One is," said I, "this word 'priests.' Another, 'church.' The third, 'charity.' For as for priests, wherever he speaks of the priests of Christ's church, he never calls them 'priests,' but always 'seniors'; the Church he calls always the 'congregation'; and charity he calls always 'love.' Now, these words in our English tongue do not express the things that are meant by those others; and also it appears (the circumstances well considered) that he had a pernicious intent in making those changes. For first, as for priests and priesthood, although in times of old it was commonly the custom to choose quite elderly men to be priests, and therefore in the Greek tongue priests were called 'presbyters,' or as we might say, 'elders,' yet neither were all priests elderly when they were chosen (as appears in what Saint Paul writes to Timothy, 'Nemo iuventutem tuam contemnat,' 'Let no one scorn your youth' [1 Tm 4: 12]) nor is every elderly man a priest. And this word 'senior' signifies nothing at all in our English tongue, but is a French word used in English more than half in mockery, when one man wants to call another 'my lord' in scorn. And if he means to take the Latin word 'senior,' that word in the Latin tongue never signified a priest, but only an older man. If he would in English call priests by that name of older men, then he would be signifying their age rather than their office. And, moreover, the name does in English clearly signify the aldermen of the cities, and not at all the priests of the Church. And thus can we perceive that, rather than call a priest by the name of a priest, he wanted to find a new word, he neither knew nor cared what.

"Now, where he calls the Church always 'the congregation,' what reason did he have for that? For everyone well sees that though the Church is indeed a congregation, yet it is not every congregation that is the Church, but only a congregation of Christian people—which congregation of Christian people has in England always been called and known by the name of 'the Church.' Which name what good reason or pretext could he find to turn into the name of 'congregation,' which term is common to a company of Christians and a company of Turks?

"Like wisdom was there in the change of this word 'charity' into 'love.' For though charity is always love, yet love is not, as you well know, always charity."

"The more pity, by my faith," said your friend, "that ever love was sin. And yet it would not be so much so taken if the world were no more suspicious than they say that good Saint Francis was, who, one time when he saw a young man kiss a girl in the way of good company, knelt down and held up his hands toward heaven, earnestly thanking God that charity was not yet gone out of this wretched world."

"He had," said I, "a good attitude, and did like a good man, who puts the best face upon everything."

"So say I too," said he. "But how far are folk fallen from that good attitude now. People nowadays have grown so full of mistrust that many a man would actually believe his wife was bad if he should but find her in bed with a poor friar."

"You really are a rogue," said I. "But yet, seriously, how do you like the changing of these words?"

"To be sure," said he, "not at all. And that it was not right or wise to do it, I am sure no good, wise person will deny. But yet whether Hutchins [aka Tyndale] had in the translating of them any malicious intention or not, there I will, till I see further, play Saint Francis' part and judge the man no worse than the matter requires."

"First," said I, "would you have the book still go out and be read with that wording?"

"No, in all honesty," said he, "that I would not, if he uses it so very often."

"With that statement," said I, "you hit the nail on the head. For certainly if he changed the common, familiar word into a better one, I would well accept it. If he changed it into something as good, I would tolerate it. If into a somewhat less good one, as long as he did it seldom, I would overlook it. But, now, when he changes the familiar, usual names of such big things into names so far inferior, and these he repeats not seldom but so often, and so continually inculcates that in practically the whole book his vile change he never changes, upon this behavior no one could put any face but that the man had wicked intent—except such a good, silly soul as would believe all was well when he found his wife where you said just now. If he called charity sometimes by the mere name of love, I would not object to that. But, now, since 'charity' signifies in Englishmen's ears not every common love, but a good, virtuous, well-ordered love, anyone who will studiously flee from that name of good love and always speak of 'love' and always leave out 'good,' I would definitely say that that person is up to no good."

"In all honesty," said he, "that is not unlikely."

"Then," said I, "when you see more you will say it is much more than likely. For now it is to be considered that at the time of this translation, Hutchins was with Luther in Wittenberg, and he put in the margins certain glosses worded for the promoting of the ungodly sect."

"By Saint John," said your friend, "if that is true, that Hutchins was at that time with Luther, it is a clear indication that he worked somewhat according to his counsel and was willing to help advance his theses here. But whether Luther's theses are so mad as they are made out to be, that we shall see hereafter."

"Very true," said I. "But as for the collusion between Luther and him, that is something well known and openly admitted by people coming from there who have been arrested for and convicted of heresy here, some of whom were sent here to sow that seed around here, and to send word there from time to time as to how well it sprouted.

"But, now, the reason why he changed the name of charity, and of the Church, and of priesthood, is not very difficult to perceive. For since Luther and his cohorts have among their other condemnable heresies this one that all our salvation depends on faith alone, and that toward our salvation good works count for nothing, it therefore seems that he is purposely endeavoring to diminish the sacred sentiments that people associate with 'charity,' and is for that reason changing that name of holy, virtuous affection into the mere name of 'love,' a name common to the virtuous love that man bears to God and to the lewd love there is between a lowlife and his ladylove. And because Luther utterly denies the true Catholic Church on earth, and says that the church of Christ is but an unknown congregation of some folk, two here and three there, no one knows where, having the right faith (by which he means only his own newly forged faith), therefore Hutchins in the New Testament cannot abide the word 'church,' but turns it into the word 'congregation,' intending for it to seem to English people either that Christ in the Gospel never spoke of the Church or else that the Church was only a congregation such as could give them occasion to say that a congregation of some such heretics was the church that God spoke of.

"Now, regarding the reason why he changed the word 'priest' to 'senior,' you must understand that Luther and his adherents hold this heresy that all ordination is nothing. And that a priest is nothing else but a man chosen among the people to preach; and that by that election to that office he is a priest immediately, without any more ado, and again not a priest whensoever the people choose another in place of him; and that a priest's office is nothing but to preach. For as for saying Mass, and hearing confessions and granting absolution therein, all this he says that every man, woman, and child can do as well as any priest.

"Now Hutchins, therefore, as a way to propagate this opinion, does, in accord with his master's heresy, do away with the name of priest in his translation, as though priesthood was nothing. Wherever Scripture speaks of the priests that were among the Jews, there he does in his translation call them still by the name of priests. But wherever Scripture speaks of the priests of Christ's church, there he does away with the word 'priest' in his translation, because he wants to make it seem that Scripture never did speak of any priests different from laymen among Christian people. And he says straight-out in his book on obedience that priesthood and all 'holy orders' among Christian people are but made-up inventions, and that priests are nothing but officers chosen to preach, and that all the consecration whereby they are consecrated is worth nothing. And that is why, in all of his translation, wherever he speaks of them, the word 'priest'—which to us, in our own tongue, has always signified an anointed parson, consecrated to God by ordination—he has changed to the word 'senior,' which is not a word in our language, but either is used half in mockery, when we speak French in sport ('Dieu vous garde, senior'), or, at the most, betokens nothing but 'elder.' So that it is easy to see what he meant in the changing of these words."

"In all honesty," said your friend, "it truly appears that he did not mean well."

"Surely," said I, "you would well say so if you saw all the places which I shall get you to see when you like, and you shall soon judge them for yourself. For it would take too long to relate them all now. And I have related to you these few not because they are the chief ones, but because they came first to mind. For else I could in short order relate to you many more things as far out of tune as these are. For he commonly changes the word 'grace' to this word 'favor,' whereas not every favor is grace in English, for in some favor there is little grace. 'Confession' he translates into 'acknowledging.' 'Penance' into 'repentance.' 'A contrite heart' he changes to 'a troubled heart.' And there are many more things like those, and many texts dishonestly translated for the support of heresy, some of which I shall show you when we look in the book. Which things we shall not discuss now, since they are not worthy of being brought into debate. But I tell you this much for this reason only: that you may perceive that he has thus conducted himself in his translating with the intention of thereby propagating Luther's heresies and his own. For first he would make the people believe that we should believe nothing but plain Scripture, in which point he teaches a plain pestilent heresy. And then he would with his false translation make the people believe further that such articles of our faith as he is striving to destroy, and which are well proved by holy Scripture, are in holy Scripture not at all spoken of; and that the preachers have for all these fifteen hundred years been purposely misquoting the Gospel and englishing the Bible wrongly to lead the people out of the right way."

9.

The author points out another great indication that the translation was dangerously devious and done for a bad purpose.

"But to the intent that you shall doubt even less what good fruit was intended by this translation, and easily judge for yourself whether or not it well deserved to be burned, you shall understand that there has since that time come out another book, written in English and published, it says, in Germany—a foolish book railing against the clergy and in large part written in rhyme, but the gist of it is all against the Mass and the holy sacraments. In this book the author rails against all those who caused Tyndale's translation of the New Testament to be burned, saying that they burned it because it destroyed the Mass. Whereby you can see that he considered that translation very good for their purpose of destroying the Mass."

"By the Mass in honor of our Lady," said your friend, "that book is a poor support for the other one. For it reveals a reason for which it well deserved to be burned, and the author with it, if it was written to destroy the Mass. But who wrote that second book?"

"Actually," said I, "this does not appear in the book. For the book is published anonymously. It was in the beginning believed to have been written by Tyndale, but whether it in fact was or not, we are still not very sure. However, Tyndale has since that time put out in his own name another book, entitled *Mammona,* which book truly is a *Mammona iniquitatis,* a veritable treasury and wellspring of wickedness. And since then he has also put out an even worse one, entitled *The Obedience of a Christian Man*—a book able to make any Christian man who would believe it leave off all good, Christian virtues and lose the merit of his Christianity. In the preface of his first book, the one called *Mammona,* he says that one Brother Jerome wrote that other book we are talking about. He says that this Brother Jerome, giving up his order (the Friars Observant), came to him where he was, telling him that he was going to take off his habit and leave religious life and try to serve God; and that afterward he left him and went to Roye (who is, as I think you know, another apostate), by whose counsel, Tyndale says, Brother Jerome wrote the book—in which, Tyndale says, he dislikes his rhymes and his excessive railing. And he also says that he fears that Brother Jerome will not really make good on all that he promises in that book."

"What?" said your friend. "Is that all the fear that he finds in himself, and all the fault that he finds with the friar and his book?"

"Yes, seriously," said I, "every whit."

"Then he finds," said your friend, "no fault with his apostasy?"

"No more," said I, "than I told you."

"Nor does he find," said your friend, "any fault in that the friar's book says that Tyndale's New Testament was burned because it destroyed the Mass?"

"Not a whit," said I, "more than you hear."

"And he fears," said your friend, "nothing else but that the friar might fail to perform something that his book promises?"

"That is all," said I. "Now, what he promises in it, this I honestly do not remember. But it does seem that whatever it is, Tyndale wanted it well performed."

"He had," said your friend, "much more reason, it seems to me, to fear that people would figure that his translation must be highly defective since he makes no response to those statements in the friar's book where he says that the New Testament that was burned did destroy the Mass."

"What you say," said I, "is to my mind very true; and he most likely would have made a response had he not agreed with what the friar said. But definitely, as for the translation, I shall show you so many texts in such ways corrupted that you shall not, I feel sure, greatly doubt what he meant in his doing of it." And with that I showed your friend a copy with the places already noted, which copy I had had lent to me, with permission, for that express purpose. In which he saw so many corruptions, and of such a kind, that although we somewhat discussed some of them along the way, he yet finally said whoa and sincerely acknowledged that the book in such a way translated was very bad and not at all fit to be read.

10.

The author states that Tyndale's translation was too bad to be corrected.

But yet he said that the errors could be corrected by some good men, and then the book printed again, if nothing stood in the way but that.

"Surely," said I, "if we really think about it, the errors are, as you see, so many and so spread through the whole book that just as it would be as soon done to weave a new piece of fabric as to sew up every hole in a net, so would it be almost as little trouble, or not as much, to translate the whole book all over again as to make in his translation as many changes as there would have to be before it was made good. Besides which I believe there is no sensible man who would take the loaf of bread which he well knew was by his enemy's hand once poisoned, even if he saw his friend afterward scrape it no matter how clean."

11.

The messenger finds fault with the clergy, in that he says they have made a synodal decree that no Bible in English will be allowed. And in this chapter the messenger, while he is at it, much criticizes the conduct of the clergy. About which the author speaks his mind a little, putting off for the moment his response to the objection made against the decree.

"Sir," said your friend, "I will not much wrangle with you over that point. But surely the thing that in this matter makes the clergy most suspect, and wherein, as it seems, it would be very hard to defend them, is this: that they do not condemn only Tyndale's translation (which there is good cause to condemn), but, moreover, they condemn all others, and, as though a layman were not a Christian man, they will allow no layman to have any at all. On the contrary, when they find any in his keeping, they charge him with heresy for it. And thereupon they burn up the book, and sometimes the good man along with it, alleging for the defense of their doings a law of their own making: a decree, passed by a provincial synod, whereby they have forbidden any man to have any, upon pain of heresy. And this law really is provincial, for it holds only here. For in all other countries of Christendom the people have Scripture translated into their own languages, and the clergy there find no such fault with that. Which means that either our people is the worst of all peoples or else our clergy is the worst of all clergies. And, by my word, for all that I can see here or perceive by means of people who have been elsewhere, our laypeople are as good and upright as any anywhere. And if any are otherwise, the occasion and example come from the clergy, among whom we see much more vice than among ourselves.

"Whereas they should be setting us examples of virtue and the light of learning, now their examples, what they are we see. And as for learning, neither will they teach us except only seldom (and that will be only such things as please them: some interpretations of their own making) nor will they allow us to learn by ourselves, but by their ordinance they pull Christ's Gospel out of Christian people's hands. I really cannot see why unless it is lest we should see the truth. The Jews, both the educated and the uneducated, are not prevented from reading their law. And yet in the Old Testament there are things that to uneducated folk are far more foreign and perilous than anything in the New. So why, then, should our laypeople be forbidden the Gospel unless they consider us inferior to Jews? I can, in all honesty, see no excuse they could find for this. For Scripture is to good folk the nourisher of virtue, and to them that are bad it is the means of amendment. And therefore as long as the clergy do withdraw it from us, if our souls are in good health they are taking away our food, and if our souls are sick they are taking away the medicine. And therefore, as I said, the fault is not in the condemning of Tyndale's translation, but in that they have by an express law forbidden us to have any at all."

"Your words," said I, "are somewhat pointed and sharp. But surely they prick somewhat more the men than the matter. For, since you in fact are talking about two things—the one, the synodal decree by which, you think, the clergy of this realm have evilly prohibited all translations of Scripture into our tongue, and the other, the moral depravity of the clergy in general—on the first point, which indeed is relevant to our subject matter, I can and will with a few words answer you. But as for the other, the one which has to do with the men, where you accuse the clergy of being in their personal lives very immoral (just as men much worse than you say that we are), and you even, as though their own faults were too few, blame them for ours too (of which you call them the cause), on this point I will not have any academic discussion with you, or enter into any debate, or willingly concern myself with the matter. For as I told you in the beginning, since we are talking only of people's learning, I will not concern myself with people's behavior, nor in the treating of this matter either praise or dispraise the conduct of any individuals, except some of those who are for their heresies and evil doctrine thrown out of Christ's church and through all Christendom condemned and made infamous already by their own obstinate malice. But yet, where you speak of other countries, making an argument that our clergy is worse than all the others, I know well that the whole world is so wretched that the clergy and laity everywhere are all bad enough—God make us all better. But yet, going by what I have seen myself, and have heard from credible folk, just as you say about our laity that we are as good and as upright as any anywhere else, so I confidently dare say that the clergy of England, and especially that sector with which you find the most fault—that is to say, that sector which we commonly call the secular clergy—is in terms of learning and upright living well able to match (and, were it not that comparisons are odious, I would go further and say 'able to far outmatch'), number for number, the clergy of any Christian nation.

"I well know that there are in it many who are very vile and wicked. And surely wherever there is a multitude, it is not, short of a miracle, very possible for it to be otherwise. But now, if the bishops would ever take into the priesthood better and fewer laymen (for of us they are made), the whole matter would be more than half amended.

"Now, where you say that you see more vice in them than in ourselves, the truth is that *everything* in them is greater, because they are more obliged to be better. But otherwise the wrong things that they do are the selfsame sins that we ourselves commit. Vices which, as you say, we see more in them than in ourselves, the reason being, I suppose, that we *look* more at theirs than at our own, and behave the way that Aesop says in a fable: Every man carries over his shoulder a double wallet, and in the bag that hangs at his breast he puts other folks' faults, and this one he picks up and peers into often. In the other he stores up all his own, and it he swings at his back. This one he himself never cares to look into, but others who come after him cast an eye into it now and then. Would to God we were all of the mind that every man thought no man so bad as himself. For that would be the way to amend both them and us. Now they blame us and we blame them, and both parties are blameworthy, and each is readier to find the other's faults than to correct their own. For in reproach of others we are so studious that nothing, either good or bad, passes unreproved. If they are friendly, we call them frivolous. If they are solitary, we call them strange. If they are serious, we call them solemn. If they are merry, we call them mad. If they are companionable, we call them corrupt. If they are holy, we call them hypocrites If they keep few servants, we call them misers. If they keep many, we call them pompous. If a bad priest does a bad deed, then we say, 'See, look what example the clergy gives us,' as though that priest were the clergy. But then we forget to look what good men are in it, and what good counsel they give us, and what good example they show us.

"We behave as do the ravens and the carrion crows, that never concern themselves with any live flesh, but where they can find a dead dog in a ditch, thereto they flee and thereon they feed with gusto. Thus where we see a good man, and hear or see a good thing, there we take little heed. But as soon as we see a bad deed, thereon we gape, thereof we talk and feed ourselves all day with the filthy delight of bad conversation. Let a good man preach, a short account of it will serve us, and we will not much regard either his exhortation or his good example. But let a lewd friar be caught with a wench, we will scoff at and rant about the whole order for all the year after, and say, 'Look what example they give us.' And yet when we are done speaking, we will follow the same, and then say that we learned it from them, forgetting that we do not care to hear about and follow the examples of some others whose words and deeds would give us light to do better if we cared as much to learn the better as to follow the worse."

"Indeed," said he, "speaking of light, they say that if a woman is beautiful, then she is young, and if a priest is good, then he is old. And yet I have seen a priest give light to the people who was but very young."

"Goodness," said I, "God forbid that it be otherwise. You can see that often if you want to."

"Truly," said he, "it is a pity that we see such light so seldom, this wretched world being in such darkness as it is. For I never saw it but once. Nor, as it seemed, did more than a few of the other people, either. For, seriously, they stared at it as fixedly as though they had never seen it before."

"How did that happen?" said I.

"Indeed," said he, "it happened that a young priest very devoutly, in a procession, carried a candle before the cross for lying with a wench, and carried it lit the whole long way. From which the people took such spiritual pleasure and in-ward solace that they immediately started laughing. And one merry merchant said to the priests that followed him, 'Sic luceat lux vestra coram hominibus!' ('Thus let your light shine before the people!' [Mt 5: 16]).

"Really," said I, "it would be a pity if a bad priest were not punished. But yet it is as much of a pity that we take such a wretched pleasure in the hearing of their sins, and in the sight of their shame. It is good for them to look at their faults, but for us it would be better to look less at theirs and more at our own. But certainly many of us take such delight in hearing of their distress that it seems we are glad when one of them does any such thing as may give us occasion to see them punished or held in derision. Which wretched appetite and sinful passion is even worse, and much more deserving of being cursed by God, than the vile mentality of Ham, who got cursed by his father, Noah, because he made a spectacle of him by showing forth in scorn the private parts of his father, who by a chance occurrence lay asleep uncovered—which parts Shem and Japheth, the blessed children, reverently covered, walking backward to him so as not to see him [Gn 9: 21–23].

"And surely we have little cause to laugh at their lewdness. For undoubtedly, if the clergy be wicked, we must needs be worse, as I once heard preached by Father Colet, the good dean of St. Paul's. For he said that it cannot be otherwise than that we must always be a notch below them. For certainly, he said, it can be no lie what is said by our Savior himself, who says of them that they are the salt of the earth, and that if the salt ever gives out, the world must needs grow unsavory [Mt 5: 13]. And he says that they are the light of the world [Mt 5: 14]. And then if the light, says he, is darkened, how dark will then be the darkness—that is to say, all the rest of the world, of which he called only the clergy the light. However, although there are, among both us and them, many who are very bad (whose faults are the fault of neither the laity nor the clergy, but of those wicked persons themselves), yet I trust that neither their group nor ours has gotten to the point where there are not many good people in ours, and as for theirs, I don't know if I may say many more, but certainly I think many better."

"I am afraid," said your friend, "that those many are very few in relation to the multitude."

"I cannot," said I, "look into their hearts to see who is good and who is bad, nor would I have the leisure, if they were all known, to go around and do a head count to see which class is the larger. And therefore, for the time being, I trust in God that the better class is the bigger. However, if there were actually very few in it, I would still truly think that the world fares the better on account of those few, and is in their virtue and prayer, by God's great mercy, sustained and supported, since we find in Scripture more than one text showing plainly the profit that a whole sinful city, or sometimes a whole region, takes by the prayer of a few godly people. And there is no doubt that, just as someone in the priesthood who is bad is far the worse because he is in it, so someone in it who is good is very far the better for his priesthood, and his prayer to God (for himself and all others) far the more efficacious."

12.

The author mentions one special blessing that we have with regard to a priest: that no matter how bad he may be, his badness cannot take from us the profit of his Mass. Whereupon the messenger raises a question: whether it would be better to have fewer and better priests, with fewer Masses, or more and worse in order to have the more Masses. To which the author responds.

"And no matter how bad a priest may be, even if he in some ways does a lot of harm to both himself and others, we yet have by a privilege and immunity of his priesthood this advantage (besides the administering to us of the sacraments, the goodness whereof his badness cannot diminish): that even if he is as immoral as can be, and, moreover, so impenitent and so far from all purpose of amendment that his prayers are before the face of God rejected and abhorred, yet that sacred sacrifice and sweet oblation of Christ's holy Body offered up by his office can in no way be polluted by the filth of his sin, but highly helps uphold this wretched world from the vengeance of the wrath of God, and is to God as acceptable, and to us as efficacious, because of the thing itself, as though it were offered by a better man, although perhaps neither will his prayers joined with it much profit others nor the oblation himself, God being the more greatly vexed with him for presuming to touch it while being so bad."

"Indeed," said your friend, "if this is the case, then I wonder why you said just now that it would be good to make fewer priests, that they might be taken only from the better, and the worse rejected. For if their Masses are so good for us no matter how bad they themselves are, then it would seem better for us to make still more even if they were still worse, so that we could have more Masses."

"That argument," said I, "will not hold. For though God of his goodness, however bad the priest may be, well accepts the oblation of Christ's holy Body for the sake of other folk, he yet is highly displeased with that priest's presumption. And we never ought to seek our own well-being with our neighbor's harm. And also we should, as a duty to God, rather forgo the profit that we ourselves might attain by a Mass than see his Majesty disreverenced by the bold presumption of such an odious minister as he has forbidden to come around him. The same as if you sent to a prince a present which was very pleasing to him, but the messenger was someone he much disliked, to the point of having had him banned from the court. If you were not aware of this, your gift could not lose its credit—though his malapert boldness might perhaps be punished, and would well deserve to be. But on the other hand, if you knew the messenger to be one that the prince would not want coming to him, you would keep your present at home and forgo the credit rather than knowingly send it by such a messenger; or else, even if your present was very great, your credit would be very little. And certainly, likewise, whoever so certainly knew a priest to be bad, immoral, and mortally displeasing to God would get, I think, little credit if he made him say Mass. And therefore the prelates shall do well to see to it, as much as they can, that God shall rather be more seldom presented with the pleasing present of the Mass than be more often offended with a displeasing messenger. And indeed, if all the bishops were of my mind (I know some who are), you would not of priests have the plenty that you have.

There was a time when there were very few in a big city, and in a monastery of five hundred in one house, there would scarcely be four monks who dared be priests. Then was all ordination held in high honor. We find that then the rank of deacons was a great thing, and of such dignity that sometimes when one of them went on a pilgrimage, he did not want it known that he was ordained, because he did not want folk to do him reverence along the way. But as for nowadays, if he be a deacon and priest too, he shall need to fear no such pride, but rather rebuke and insult. And although this has come about because of the lack of virtue among them and the lessening of piety among us, yet much of all this mess is the result of there being so great a number of priests and their being such a familiar sight among us. Which thing must needs diminish on our part reverence and regard for them, which we never have but for things rare and scarce. We would not value gold if it were as common as chalk or clay. And of what is there now such a plenty as of priests?"

"Honestly," said he, "there is a greater plenty of priests than of good men, and there are too many as long as they are not better chosen."

"Doubtless," said I, "there should in the choosing be more careful attention paid not only to how learned they are, but much more especially to how they live. For without virtue, the more learned they are, the worse they are, except that learning is a good provision toward the day when God sends them the grace to mend their ways. Which otherwise it would perhaps then be too late to look for, especially if the proverb you spoke of were true, that if a priest is good, then he is old. But this is a real certainty, that it is not very possible for there not to be many very bad men in that band, it being such a great multitude. There was, as I say, a time when few men dared presume to undertake the high office of a priest, even when they were chosen for it and called to it. Now every rascal runs and boldly puts himself forward as qualified. And whereas that dignity passes all princes, and the lowborn desire it for worldly advantage, yet men of this class come to it with such a mad mind that they almost consider God much beholden to them, that they deign to take it. But if I were pope—"

"By my soul," said he, "I wish you were, and my lady your wife popess, too."

"Well," said I, "then she would arrange for the nuns. And as for me, concerning the choice of priests, I really could not arrange better provisions than are by the laws of the Church provided already, if they were as well kept as they are well made. But as for the number, I would surely see a way for us not to have such a rabble that every common man must have a priest in his house to wait upon his wife, which practically no man lacks now, with the result that priesthood is scorned as an office as vile as that of the man's horsekeeper."

"That is," said he, "true indeed. And as even worse, for they keep hawks and dogs, and it certainly seems to me a more respectable service to wait on a horse than on a dog."

"And yet I suppose," said I, "that if the laws of the Church which Luther and Tyndale would have all broken were all well observed and kept, this stuff would not be thus, but the number of priests would be much diminished and the remainder much the better. For it is provided by the laws of the Church, to the intent that no priest should to the disgrace of the priesthood be driven to live in such a vile way or worse, that no one should be admitted to priesthood until he has an entitlement, either from his own patrimony or otherwise, to a sufficient annual income. And to this day they are not otherwise accepted."

"Well," said he, "then why do so many of them go around begging?"

"Goodness," said I, "because they foil the law, and themselves also. For they never have the grant of a benefice that can serve them in sight for that purpose, but they secretly waive it before they get it, or else they could not get it. And thus the bishop is blinded by the sight of the document, and the priest goes a-begging despite all his grant of a good living, and the law is circumvented, and the order is brought into disgrace by the begging and lewd conduct of the priest, who is forced either to roam helter-skelter and live on stipends or worse, or else to serve in a secular man's house, which would not be necessary if this breach was stopped. For you would have few enough priests if the law were actually observed that none were made except men who without collusion were assured of a living already."

"Then it might happen," said he, "that you might have too few to fill the positions and benefices that are provided for them, unless the prelates would provide that ordination was not so commonly conferred, but would always receive men into holy orders as positions and benefices become vacant, to give to them, and no faster."

"Certainly," said I, "for all that I can see at the moment, that would not be much amiss. For thus they would need no such entitlements at all, nor need either run helter-skelter or live in laymen's houses, by reason of which there now and then comes about no little corruption in the priests' morals, from the society of laypeople and company of women in their houses."

"No, by our Lady," said he, "I will not agree with you there. For I think they cannot easily meet with much worse company than themselves, and that they rather corrupt us than we them."

13.

The messenger submits that it would be good that priests have wives. To which the author responds.

"But I would think it would in great part amend this matter if they could have wives of their own."

"Indeed," said I, "so say Luther and Tyndale also, except that they go somewhat further. For Tyndale (whose books are practically nothing else but the worst heresies culled

from Luther's works, and Luther's worst statements translated by Tyndale and put out in Tyndale's own name) does,
in his insane book on obedience (in which he rails at length
against all popes, against all kings, against all prelates, all
priests, all religious, all the laws, all the saints, against the
sacraments of Christ's church, against all virtuous works,
against all liturgical services, and ultimately against virtually
everything that is good)—in that book, I say, Tyndale holds
that priests must have wives. And this he cleverly bases on
the words of Saint Paul where he writes to Timothy,
'Oportet episcopum esse irreprehensibilem, unius uxoris
virum'—that a bishop must be an irreproachable man and
'the husband of one wife' [1 Tm 3: 2–4]. And that it must be
considered whether he has well brought up his children and
well governed his household. From these statements Tyndale, following Luther's lead, concludes it to be an obvious
thing that priests must necessarily have wives, and that Saint
Paul would have it that there should in no way be any other
priests but married folk. Is it not now a wonder with what
spectacles Luther and Tyndale have espied this thing now in
these words of Saint Paul? In which, of so many great, astute
Fathers and holy saints as have often read and deeply pondered those words before, there was never a one who had
either the intelligence or the grace to perceive that great
special commandment these fifteen hundred years, until
now that God has at last by revelation disclosed this high,
secret mystery to these two magnificent creatures Luther
and Tyndale, lest that holy friar should have missed out on
his marriage to that holy nun, and Tyndale on some good
marriage that I think he is on his way to. Tyndale does not
in his book give any answer to that point, but rants and
raves on and on without discussion, simply saying that
Scripture is clearly on his side there. And always he passes
over, as though he never heard it, what all the holy theologians there ever were in Christ's church have said: that the
scripture which he alleges to be very plainly for him is very

plainly against him, as it is indeed. For Saint Paul in that text, seeing that as yet, at that time, outside of ordaining young men (which he thought not generally appropriate), they else could ordain to the priesthood no men except such as either were or had been married, the Apostle therefore, having with regard to the choice of priests a special regard for celibacy, and wanting to go as near to 'no wife' as could be, did ordain, as God had instructed him, that whosoever should be admitted to priesthood should be the husband of one wife. Meaning someone who then had, or before had had, no more than one, and who never had had two. He meant not what mad Luther and Tyndale would now make the world so mad as to believe—that a priest must necessarily have one, or that he may never lack one, or that he may have one after another, or the mere forbidding of two at once—but only that no one should be admitted to priesthood but only such a man as never had had nor would have but only one. Which is what always was and has been understood by those statements. And always—not only where Saint Paul taught, but also everywhere in Christendom where the other apostles planted the faith—it has been so observed. Which is an obvious proof, concerning the prohibition of any more wives than one, and the forbidding of the bigamy of wedding one wife after another, that this was the express ordinance of God, and not of Saint Paul, whose letters wherein he writes anything about this matter had perhaps not come into the hands of the other apostles when they yet took the same order from the same Spirit who taught it to him. For this is certain: that ever and everywhere in Christendom, the bigamy of having two wives in succession has been a hindrance and impediment to the receiving of Holy Orders, and has for a long time been a hindrance even if the first wife had been wedded and buried before the man's baptism. And now these two sagacious men, against the old holy Fathers and astute theologians, and against the continual custom of Christ's church begun so many hundreds of years ago, and continued by the Spirit of God, have espied at last that Saint Paul says and means that a priest *may* marry twice and have one wife after another, and that he *must* do so. For according to Tyndale, a priest must always have one wife at the least. And surely if we depart from the correct understanding of Saint Paul's words and believe Tyndale, that it is there meant and commanded, because of this word 'oportet,' that a priest must have one, then Tyndale can on the basis of this text tell us that a priest is at liberty to have twenty at one time—or two, if he wants—since Saint Paul says no more than that the bishop must be the husband of one wife. Which words Tyndale can tell us are borne out if he is the husband of ten wives. For the husband of ten wives would be the husband of one as the father of ten children is the father of one, if the wives were as congruous as the children are—as Luther and Tyndale will undoubtedly soon make them, by Scripture, if their own interpretation can be taken as authority against the understanding that God has given to all good Christian people these fifteen hundred years. Now, as I say, upon Tyndale's taking, Saint Paul would not mean that a priest should have but one wife (since that 'but' is not in Saint Paul's words), but he would mean that a priest *must* have at least one—as though Saint Paul would prefer that the priest had twenty, save for the overburdening. And it even seems that Tyndale does in fact take it this way—that a priest could have several wives at once—especially in light of the great explanation that he gives here. For on this basis—that Saint Paul, since there were at that time few to choose from, for ordination to the priesthood, other than married men, decided therefore that in the choice of the bishop there should be taken into account how the candidate had governed his own household, because anyone who had misdirected his wife and children would be unfit for a large curacy—Tyndale says that there should never be ordained to the priesthood any man other than one who has a wife and children and who has shown by his governance of them that he is fit to exercise authority. (As though we never saw any never-married man govern a household better than many who have gotten married!) And if the having and good ruling of a wife is as important a proof of a man's fitness to be a priest as Tyndale takes it to be, then—since Saint Paul, according to Tyndale's interpretation, cannot be shown to forbid the having of several together—it would be best, according to Tyndale's logic, particularly to ordain to the priesthood a man who has had many wives and all at once, and many children by each of them, if he has guided them all well. For it is more proof of being a wise governor to rule well five wives than one, and forty children than four.

"But, now, so that every child may see the wisdom of Tyndale (and of his master Luther) in the interpreting of holy Scripture, of which he speaks so much and understands so little, I ask you to consider similar statements of Saint Paul about a very similar matter. Saint Paul, just as he writes to Timothy that a bishop must be the husband of one wife, also writes to him that for a widow to be formally selected and taken in to be provided for out of the goods of the Church, she must be no younger than sixty, and have been 'the wife of one husband' [1 Tm 5:9]. Now, put together these two texts, about the bishop and the widow, and consider the words 'one wife' in the one and 'one husband' in the other. If we shall take as Tyndale does that 'one' directive about the bishop—that Saint Paul means not that he has, or has had, only one wife, but that he must needs have a wife—then we must likewise give to Saint Paul's directive about the widow the interpretation that Saint Paul means not a widow who has never had more than one husband, but a widow who has had one husband. As though Saint Paul was fearing or forbidding nothing except that Timothy might take in such a widow as had never had any husband at all! Isn't this an intelligent construing? Now, if Tyndale will agree (as he necessarily must, unless he is crazy) that Saint Paul, in giving the command that the widow should be one who had had one husband, meant by this such a one as never had had more than one, then he must necessarily grant—and so, too, must his master Luther—that Saint Paul in like manner, where he said that a bishop must be a good man and the husband of one wife, meant that he must never have, or have had, any more than one. And not that he must necessarily have one, or that he must have at least one, and could have many more than one, either successively or all together, if he wanted. And in this matter Tyndale has no escape hatch. For since this word 'one,' in 'one wife' and 'one husband,' was not put in by Saint Paul for nothing, it must necessarily signify either that there should be no more than one or that there should be at least one. If he should mean that a bishop should have at least one wife, and that the widow should have had at least one husband, then he would rather that they had more than so few; and everyone can see how foolish that interpretation is. Now, if Tyndale will say that by this word 'one' Saint Paul meant that there should be but one wife at a time, and one husband at a time, in that case Saint Paul did so speak of the bishop as though he had said, 'A bishop must be a good man and have but one wife at a time.' In which words Tyndale will have lost his argument. For then it was only a prohibition of any more than one, and not a commandment, but a mere permission for one. And, moreover, it would not have much relevance, since in Saint Paul's day a layman had but one wife at a time. And the foolishness of this interpretation appears in the words spoken by Saint Paul about the selection of the widow, wherein Tyndale would by this approach make Saint Paul be saying this: 'Select and take in only such a widow as has had but one husband at a time,' as though in his day it was the custom that wives could have two husbands at once."

"Actually," said your friend, "I think Saint Paul did not mean that. For in that case wives in his time would have been little better than grass widows are now. For they are still as exclusive as a barber's chair, and never take but one at a time."

"Actually," said I, "the foolishness of such folk, who seek for God's Scripture such new construings against the true sense that God has for these fifteen hundred years taught his whole Church, is made quite apparent by the fact that there never yet has been a pope who was so covetous that he dared give a dispensation in this regard, seeing the agreement of Christ's church so full and unanimous there, and the intention of Saint Paul so clearly being to make allowance for only one, to the utter exclusion of any more than one, that whoever would construe him otherwise must needs fall into such obvious idiocies as Tyndale and Luther do. And thus you see how soundly Tyndale and his master interpret this scripture, and with what authority they confirm this noble new doctrine of theirs, by which they would condemn all in Christendom as breakers of the law of God as long as they do not allow any priest to take a wife—or, rather, as long as they allow him to be without a wife. For wives they must needs have, by Tyndale's account, whether they want to or not."

"By my word," said your friend, "if Tyndale and Luther have no other foothold than that text of Saint Paul, they are likely to take a fall. But I think they say more than that."

"As a matter of fact," said I, "Tyndale does indeed have another argument. He says that celibacy is an exceedingly rare gift, and that unchastity is exceedingly perilous for that state of life. And thereupon he concludes that priests must needs have wives. But, now, what if someone were to deny to him, though celibacy is a great gift, that it is a rare gift. For though it is rare and exceptional with respect to the rest of the people (those who do not have it), it yet is not actually exceptional, for many people have it. And Christ says that not everyone receives it, but he does not say that no one receives it, nor that few receive it. And he highly commends those who for his sake do accept it [Mt 19: 12]. What impropriety is there, then, in his taking into his special service men of that sort that he most specially commends? Or if we granted to Tyndale that few men can live celibate—which is obviously untrue, since many have done this and are doing this—but, now, if we did, I say, grant him that thing, then although he might perhaps conclude from that that there should not be so many men ordained to the priesthood and bound to celibacy as could not live celibate, he yet could not conclude what he now concludes: that no priest should be allowed to live celibate, but that every priest must necessarily have a wife. For this is his argument: Few men can live celibate; ergo, every priest must take a wife. If we should impugn the form of this argument, Tyndale would rail and say we were engaging in sophistry, and sensible men would say we were idly occupied in that we were striving to show this fallacy that so clearly shows itself. And therefore we shall leave his brilliant argument alone, since it suffices us that everyone with any sense can well see that from his irrational argument one of two things must necessarily follow: either Christ, in commending perpetual celibacy, did commend a thing not commendable, or else, if every priest must needs have a wife, then it is not permissible to make a priest of the sort that is by God's own mouth commended."

"Certainly," said your friend, "it seems to me that they go too far there, in saying that priests must necessarily have wives. But it seems to me that this they could rightly say, and I too: that it is not a right thing to do to bind them with a law that they shall not have them; that it can be a right thing to do to let those who want wives have them, as they do in Wales. And I hear it said that in Germany this makes their lives a lot easier. For just as here the good wife keeps her husband from her maids, so there the parson's wife keeps her husband from all the wives in the parish."

"As for Wales," said I, "you are wrongly informed; for they do not have wives. But it is true that there are some places where incontinence is little looked into, whereof much harm grows in the country. And as for Germany, the part of it where that is practiced (which is only where Luther's sect is accepted), whoever well considers what profit has come to them by such ungodly ways will, I think, have no great fancy to follow them."

"Well," said he, "leaving Wales and Germany aside, yet priests did have wives in the olden times, when they were better than they are now. And they still do in Greece, where they are better than they are here."

"As for the priests of Greece, I will not criticize them," said I, "for I do not know them. But something was not right there, that God has allowed that whole empire to fall into the hands of heathens. And, too, those there are not as free as you think they are. For though a married man taken there into the clergy is not and cannot be separated from his wife, but is there allowed to minister in the office of a priest notwithstanding his marriage, yet if a man is unmarried at the time that he enters the priesthood, he then professes perpetual continence and never marries afterward, as I have learned from people who have come from there.

"Now, where you speak of olden times, surely you will understand that those who married were not so many as you would perhaps think."

"Maybe," said he, "no more would there be now. Some of them would have no wives even if that law were let go. For as a good fellow once said to his friends who wondered why he did not marry, and who thought he was abnormal if he did not care for the company of a woman—he said to them that he would rather lose a finger than lack a woman; but would rather lack the whole hand than have a wife. So if the priests were at liberty, some of the worst sort would still, I think, rather have women than wives. But others who wanted to be more respectable would, I suppose, get married. And some, perhaps, would even live in perpetual continence, as few do now."

"God forbid," said I.

"Well," said he, "those who would do so would not be forced to. But, if I am to be bold and say what I think, it certainly seems to me a very cruel thing that the Church should make a law binding a man to celibacy against his wishes, celibacy being something to which God would never bind any man."

"The Church," said I, "binds no man to celibacy."

"That is true," said he, "unless a priest is a man."

"You mistake the matter," said I, "as I shall show you later."

"There would," said he, "be many harms avoided, and much good coming of it, if those who wanted to could have wives."

"What good or harm would come of it," said I, "would be shown by experience, which we might be the more confident about putting real trust in were it not that we now find it bad in Saxony, where we see this tried out anew. And as for what you said about the olden times when the priests were better, we definitely—as I would, if you had not stopped me, have gone on to say before—can well tell from writers of olden times that of those good men, very few were married And virtually none got married after taking that office. And of those who had wives before, many willingly (with the consent of their wives) gave up carnal relations with them. And (since the good or harm coming of the matter is best shown by experience), besides the evidence that we have now in Saxony, where this change is begun with an infinite heap of heresies, it is easy to see that the good Fathers who advised in favor of the making of that law, with the thing almost accepted as general custom before, and with the concurrence of virtually all of Christendom, which ratified and accepted it after, had a good experience thereof and found this the best way before the law was made. And therefore I will not dispute with you about it. But where you charge with unreasonableness those who made it, because they, as you see it, bind men to celibacy against their will, there would be something in what you say if the Church compelled any man to be a priest. But, now, when every man is at liberty not to be a priest unless he wants to, how can any man say that the Church lays a bond of celibacy around any man's neck against his will? The Church does in fact do nothing further than provide that, since men will of their own wills live some celibate and some not, the ministers of the sacraments shall be taken only from that set that will be willing to profess celibacy. Whoever finds fault with that is casting aspersions on not only the clergy but also the laity, who are and have been all this time sharers in the authority of the making and conservation of this law. The provision of which no man can criticize unless he is either in that heresy of thinking that the cleanness of celibacy is not more pleasing to God than the carnal use of matrimony, or else in that of thinking it is wrong to provide that the priests who shall serve God in his holy sacraments should be taken from the purest and most pleasing sort. For whom the very pagans had such respect that their priests dared not presume to offer sacrifice to their idols until after a certain time of physical cleanness, of abstaining from their wives. And some of them were bound to the keeping of perpetual celibacy, by the loss of that part of their body wherewith they could have done the contrary."

"Yes indeed," said he, "that was a good, sure way."

"It was," said I, "sure indeed, but not as good as this one. For therein would be lost the merit that good men obtain by resisting the devil and restraining their fleshly impulses. But, as I wanted and was about to say, in the old law given to Moses, the priests of the temple, for the time of their ministration, gave up their own houses and the company of their wives. And therefore they served the temple by turns, as shows up clearly in the beginning of Saint Luke's Gospel. So that celibacy was thought, both by God and by people, something appropriate and suitable for priests, among those who most extolled carnal generation. And then how much more specially now for the priests of Christ, who was born of a virgin, lived and died a virgin himself, and exhorted all his to the same? Since some are content to follow his counsel on that point, and some to live otherwise, what way would, I say, be more appropriate than to take into Christ's temple, to serve around the Blessed Sacrament, only such as are of that set that are pleased and minded to live in the clean manner called for by Christ's holy counsel?"

"True, if they wanted to," said he.

"They are," said I, "saying that they want to when they come there being already aware of the law. And to the intent that fewer should break it, I therefore would, as I said, have more care taken in the choosing. And since it is hard to have that many be that good, I would have fewer men ordained. But to say that the Church binds men to celibacy against their will because they will not take them into the priesthood unless they first profess celibacy—this is as far from rational as if you were to say that they bind men to celibacy against their will because they will make none of them monks except those who will promise to live celibate. Which promise everyone well knows they make by their own decisions, even though the Church will make no men monks or priests except those who will do that. And as for whether this arrangement in the Church is better than the contrary would be, men both good and sensible had experience of them both before the law was made, and this one has been well approved of throughout Christendom for a long time since. Before I would assent to a change, I would want to see a better author of it than such a heretic as Luther or Tyndale, and a better example than the seditious and schismatic priests of Saxony."

"Certainly," said he, "you have well exonerated the Church with respect to that law. But whatever the reason may be, upon my honor, bad they are, and as far worse than us as they are obliged to be better; and we are even the worse for them."

"There are," said I, "many quite good ones among them; and otherwise there would be something wrong with us. And there are also many bad ones, and some the worse for us. Now, which group is the better or the worse, that I will not debate. But this I will say: that it would be best that they thought themselves the worse, and we, ourselves; and that each man thought himself the worst.

"I wish we were all in the same position with our own faults as my father says we are in with our wives. For when he hears folk blame wives and say that so many of them are shrews, he says that they falsely accuse them. For he states categorically that there is but one shrewish wife in the world, but he says, indeed, that every man believes that he has her, and that that one is his own. So would I fantasize that every man would believe that there was but one bad man in the whole entire world, and that that one was himself. And that he would consequently go about the amending of that one; and thus would all become well. Which thing we would accomplish in short order if we would ever once turn around that wallet I told you about, and cast behind us the bag with other folks' faults, and cast the bag that bears our own faults—cast it for once in front of us, at our breast. It would be quite a goad, for us to look at our own faults for a while. And I boldly dare say that both they and we would much the better amend if we were as ready to pray for each other as we are to look for things to reproach and rebuke in each other."

"Really and truly," said he, "I believe that is true, and I pray to God that we can do that."

14.

The author answers the question raised before, in chapter eleven, concerning the synodal decree, and shows that the clergy are far from being guilty of the wrongdoing imputed to them on that score. He also makes it known that the clergy have not forbidden that the Bible be written and read in English.

"But now, back to the matter we had in hand. You said you would answer my objection regarding the law whereby the clergy of this realm have forbidden all the people to have any of Scripture translated into our tongue—which is, as I said, to my mind, a law it was wrong to make."

"Indeed," said I, "that is easy to answer. Put the blame on those who made it."

"Indeed," said he, "that I do. For who made that decree but they?"

"Certainly," said I, "nobody else; nor they either."

"No?" said he. "What? Everyone knows it!"

"Actually," said I, "many people talk about it, but no one knows it. For there is in fact no such decree. There is, it is true, a decree that speaks of this matter, but not at all in such fashion. For you shall understand that the great archheretic Wycliffe, whereas the whole Bible was long before his time translated into the English language by virtuous and well-educated men, and read quite reverently, with devotion and sobriety, by good, godly people, took it upon himself, for a malicious purpose, to translate it anew. In which translation he purposely corrupted the holy text, maliciously planting in it such words as might in the readers' ears serve as support for such heresies as he was trying to sow, which he promoted not only with his own translation of the Bible, but also with certain introductions and glosses which he added to it. And these things he presented in such a way (which was no great achievement), with arguments which would sound reasonable and plausible to uneducated laypeople, that he corrupted in his time many folk in this realm. And by means of other evil books which he wrote in Latin, and which were later taken into Bohemia and taught there by John Huss and others, he was the occasion of the utter subversion of that whole realm, in terms of both faith and morals, with the loss also of many a thousand lives. And just as he started up again the old heresies of those ancient heretics whom and whose errors the church of Christ had condemned and subdued in many different eras before, so does Luther again begin to set up his. For virtually all that he has, he gets from him. Except that, lest he should seem to say nothing on his own, he added in some things himself that are of such a nature that never was there a heretic before his day who was either wicked enough to be so sinful, or foolish enough to dare be so shameless, as to write, say, or, I believe, even think the like."

"I really would like," said he, "to hear some of them, for the man is taken for being too sane to think as crazily as people make him out to."

"Well," said I, "that we shall soon see, when we come to it. But as for our present subject, after it was perceived what harm the people were being done by the translation, introductions, and glosses of Wycliffe, and also the commentaries of some others who after his death helped propagate his sect, then for that reason—and because it is dangerous to translate the texts of Scripture from one language into another, as holy Saint Jerome attests, since in translation it is hard always to keep the same meaning intact—it was, I say, for these reasons, at a council held at Oxford, stipulated on pain of severe punishment that from then on, no one should translate into the English tongue or any other language anything written by him, whether book, tract, or treatise, nor should anyone read, in public or in private, any such book, tract, or treatise that was written in the time of the said John Wycliffe or since, or that would be written any time after, until that translation was approved by the bishop of the diocese, or, if necessity should dictate, by a provincial council. And this is a law that so many have been speaking of for so long, and that so few have in all this time cared to find out whether or not they are telling the truth about. For I trust that in this law you see nothing unreasonable. For it does not forbid the reading of the translations that were already well done long ago, before the time of Wycliffe; and it condemns his not because it was new, but because it was bad; and it does not prohibit the making of new ones, but only stipulates that they shall not be read if they are wrongly written, until they are by good examination corrected—unless they are such translations as Wycliffe made, and Tyndale, where the malicious mind of the translator manipulated things in such a way that it would be labor lost to try to correct them."

"I really would like, in all seriousness," said he, "to see that decree. I will even be sitting on pins and needles till I do. For not only I myself, but also all others that I have ever heard speak of it till now, have taken it far differently. But surely I will see it myself before I go to bed."

"You shall be relieved sooner than that," said I. "For I cannot bear to see you sit that long on pins and needles. And therefore you shall see it right now."

And with that I brought him the edition of the synodal decree with Lyndwood's commentaries, and turned for him to the section titled 'De Magistris.' When he had read it for himself, he said he much wondered how it happened that, the matter being so clear, people are so far misled as to report it so far wrong.

"This comes," said I, "partly of malice, partly of sloth and negligence, in that folk are more willing to believe and keep telling something that may contribute to a discrediting of the clergy than to investigate and be sure whether or not what they are saying is true."

15.

The messenger makes against the clergy the claim that, even if they have not made a law of this, they yet will in fact let no one get hold of an English Bible, but, rather, they routinely burn them where they find them, and sometimes burn the person too. And for an example he brings up one Richard Hunne, claiming that the chancellor of the London diocese murdered him in prison and afterward hanged him (making it look as though he had hanged himself), and, after that, convicted him of heresy on the basis of his having had an English Bible, and so burned the Bible and him together. To which the author responds.

"I submit," said he, "that this opinion has, rather, come about in another way, that is to say, by reason of the fact that the clergy, although the law does not support them in this, do yet in fact take all translations out of every layman's hands. And sometimes with those who are burned for heresy, or convicted of it, they burn the English Bible regardless, be the translation old or new, bad or good."

"Indeed," said I, "if this were so, then in my opinion it would not be a right thing to do. But I believe you are mistaken. Granted, what you have seen, I cannot say. But I myself have seen, and can show you, Bibles beautiful and old, written in English, which have been known to and seen by the bishop of the diocese, and left in laymen's hands, and women's too; to such as he knew to be good Catholic folk who would use them with piety and sobriety.

"It is true that all those found in the hands of heretics, they routinely take away. But, as far as I could ever discover, they do not have any burned except only those found to contain errors. Many of which are set forth with pernicious prologues or interpretations insidiously made by Wycliffe and other heretics. For no good man would, I believe, be so mad as to burn up a Bible when they found no error in it nor any law that disallowed its being looked at and read."

"Fine," said he, "but I have heard good men say that right here in London, not many years ago, in the days of the bishop that last died, they burned up as beautiful Bibles in English as anyone has laid eyes on, and, moreover, as free of error, for all that anyone could tell, as is any Bible in Latin. And they even, besides this, burned up the dead body of the man himself, whom they themselves had previously hanged in the bishop's prison, making as though the man had hanged himself. And for the burning of his body they had no basis except only that they had found in his house English Bibles. With which they never found any other fault but that they were in English."

"Who told you this tale?" said I.

"As a matter of fact," said he, "several honorable men who saw it, and in particular, one who saw the man hanging in the bishop's prison before he was cut down. And he told me that it was proved good and clearly that the chancellor and the guards had killed the man first and then hanged him afterward. And that they had charged him with heresy only out of hatred, because he had filed a praemunire suit against several persons, over a suit (about a funerary offering) taken in the court of the Archbishop of Canterbury. And then they proved the heresy charge by nothing else but the possession of a good English Bible. And on the basis of the heresy charge thus proved against him, whom they had hanged so that he could not defend himself, they burned up God's holy Scripture, and with it the body of a good man. For I have heard him called a very honorable person, and one of substance."

"Definitely," said I, "of substance. He was, I think, easily worth a thousand marks. And about his worldly dealings among the people, I have heard nothing negative. But certainly as regards his beliefs about Christ, it seems to me that I may venture to say that he was not honorable. And as regards truth in words, whoever it was that told you this tale was not actually as honorable as I think you take him for."

"Why," said he, "do you know the matter well?"

"Indeed," said I, "so well do I know it, from top to toe, that I suppose there are not very many men who know it much better. For not only have I several times been present myself at certain investigations of it, but I have also, many different times, talked separately with almost all those, except for the dead man himself, who knew the most about the matter. Which matter was many times in various places investigated.

"But in particular, at Baynard's Castle it was investigated at great length one day, and everyone that could be found who could tell anything about the matter, or who had said they could, had been sent for well in advance and was already there well ahead of time. And this investigation was held before several great lords, ecclesiastical and temporal, and others on the King's honorable council, sent there by His Highness by the very reason of the blessed zeal and princely desire he bore to the search for the truth. Whereto his godly mind was much inclined by the fact that he had been informed by a very honorable man that there was someone who had told a friend of his that he could go take by the sleeve the one who had killed Hunne—for Richard Hunne was the name of the man you speak of.[6] I was also myself present at the trial held at St. Paul's—the one in consequence of which his books and his body were burned. And from all these things I very well know that the man from whom you have heard about this case has told you tales that are far from the truth."

"Actually," said your friend, "he told me one thing that you mention now: that there was someone who said he could go take by the sleeve the one who killed Richard Hunne. And that he in fact did so before the lords, and even came up there to the chancellor and said, 'My lords, this is he.' But when he was asked how he knew it, he testified that it was by an occult art so unlawful that it could not be used for a proof. For it was, they say, by necromancy. And so the bishops who

[6] The tailor Richard Hunne was a Londoner who refused to pay a priest the mortuary fee demanded after the burial of his child in 1511 and was later imprisoned in Lollards' Tower at Lambeth after heretical books were found in his residence; while in prison, he seems to have committed suicide (there may have been foul play) in 1514 after charging that clergy in his case had violated the Statute of Praemunire (CW 6.2, 317). See John Fines' article in *The Oxford Dictionary of National Biography,* vol. 28 (Oxford: Oxford Univ. Press, 2004), for a detailed explanation of the case and its continued relevance in the 1520s because of debates over clerical abuses and the alleged anticlericalism of the London populace (830). As More scholar Louis Martz argues in the insightful *Thomas More: The Search for the Inner Man* (New Haven: Yale Univ. Press, 1990), More's treatment of the Hunne case in the *Dialogue* uses satire to ridicule "the flimsy grounds of gossip that can lead to anticlerical uproar" (105–106, n21). More also addresses the complaints against clergy at length in his *Supplication of Souls* (CW 7, 12–30, 139–41, 147–49).

were there would have had that man burned too, for witch-craft. And he also told me that there was someone else who had seen many men who had hanged themselves. This was a man who had long been in office under several of the King's almoners, to whom the goods of such men as kill themselves are assigned, by the law and his office, as deodands to be given in alms. This man, according to what I have heard, made known to the lords, on the basis of such experience as he had, good and clear indications by which they well perceived that Hunne never did hang himself. I have heard also that a churchman, one who was quite fond of the chancellor and was a supporter of that side, yet could not deny before all the lords that he had told a layman, a friend of his, that Hunne would never have been accused of heresy if he had never filed the praemunire suit. And by Saint Mary, that was a danger-ous statement. However, it was not really as relevant to the case as the other two things were."

"Yes, actually," said I, "all three had the same relevance, when they were all heard. But to tell the truth, many other things were alleged there that upon the hearing seemed much more suspicious than these. Which yet when they were answered always lost more than half their strength. But as for these three matters, I assure you that they proved mere trifles, and such that if you had heard them, you would have laughed at them for seven years after."

"I beg you," said he, "let me hear how they proved to be such."

"I am loath," said I, "to let you, and lose your time in such trifles. However, since you are so sorely longing for it, then rather than you should lose your child over them, you shall have them, all three, in as short a time as I can manage.

"First you must understand that in order that the coming together of the lords from Greenwich to Baynard's Castle for the inquiry into the matter should not be frustrate, there was such diligence exercised beforehand that everyone who would be giving testimony in the inquiry was already present before the lords arrived. And where they began was with the first point that you spoke of, it being the specific thing that the King's Highness had sent them there to examine. Wherefore, after making the speech about the reason for their coming, the greatest temporal lord there present said to a certain servant of his own, who was standing there beside him, 'Sir, you told me that someone told you that he could go take by the sleeve the one who killed Hunne. Have you brought him here?'

" 'Sir, if it please your lordship, it was this man who told me that,' he said, pointing to someone whom he had caused to come there. Then my lord asked that man, 'What do you say, sir? Can you do what you said you could?'

" 'Actually, my lord,' said he, 'if it please your lordship, I did not say as much as that. This gentleman did somewhat misunderstand me. But I did indeed tell him that I had a neighbor who told me that he could do it.'

" 'Where is that neighbor?' said my lord.

" 'This man, sir,' he said, bringing forward someone who had also been summoned to be there. Then he was asked whether he had said that he could do it.

" 'Actually, no, my lord,' said he, 'I did not say that I could do it myself, but I said that someone told me that he could do it.'

" 'Well,' said my lord, 'who told you that?'

" 'Actually, my lord,' said he, 'my neighbor here.' Then that man was asked, 'Sir, do you know someone that can tell who killed Richard Hunne?'

" 'Actually,' said he, 'if it please your lordship, I did not say that I for sure knew someone that could tell who had killed him, but I did indeed say that I knew someone who I truly thought could tell who killed him.'

" 'Well,' said the lords, 'at last, even if with a lot of to-do, we are getting somewhere. But what makes you think that he can tell?'

" 'No, actually, my lord,' said he, 'it is a woman. I wish she were here with your lordships now.'

" 'Well,' said my lord, 'woman or man, it is all the same. *She* shall be gotten hold of, wherever she is.'

" 'By my faith, my lords,' said he, 'if she were with you, she would tell you wonders. For, by God, I have known her to tell many astonishing things before this.'

" 'Why,' said the lords, 'what have you heard told by her?'

" 'Indeed, my lords,' said he, 'if something had been stolen, she would have told who had it. And therefore I think she could as well tell who killed Hunne as who stole a horse.'

" 'Certainly,' said the lords, 'so think all of us too, I trust. But how could she tell it? By the devil?'

" 'No, by my word, I think,' said he, 'for I could never see her use any worse way than looking in one's hand.'

"At that the lords laughed and asked, 'What is she?'

" 'Actually, my lords,' said he, 'a Gypsy, and she was lodged here at Lambeth, but now she is gone overseas. However, I believe she is not in her own country yet, for they say it is a great distance from here, and she left just a little over a month ago.' "

"Really, now," said your friend, "a lot of use this proceeding turned out to be. Here a big post was well whittled to a pudding prick. But I ask you, to what point came the second matter, the one about the man who had been in office under so many of the King's almoners that he knew from his own experience, and proved, that Richard Hunne had not hanged himself?"

"As a matter of fact," said I, "he was called in next. And then he was asked how he knew it. But I wish to God you could have seen his face. The man had likely gone somewhat too far in what he had said. He was very terror-stricken; he looked as though his eyes were about to fall out of his head and into the lords' laps. But he answered the question, and said that he saw that very clearly, for he saw him both before he was taken down and after.

" 'So what?' said the lords. 'So did many others, who yet from what they saw could not tell this.'

" 'No, my lords,' said he, 'but I have another kind of sight into such things than other men have.'

" 'What kind of sight?' said they.

" 'Actually,' said he, 'it is not unknown that I have worked for a great while under several of the King's almoners, and have seen and scrutinized many who have hanged themselves, and thereby if I see someone hanging, I can tell immediately whether he hanged himself or not.'

" 'By what indication can you tell?' said the lords.

" 'Actually,' said he, 'I cannot tell the indications, but I perceive it well enough by my own sight.'

"But when they heard him speak of his own sight, and therewith saw what sight he had, looking as though his eyes were about to fall in their laps, few of them could keep from laughing, and they said, 'We certainly see well that you have a sight all your own.' And then one lord said merrily, 'Perhaps just as some man is by experience so knowledgeable about jewels that he can perceive by his own eye whether a stone is genuine or counterfeit even though he cannot quite make another man perceive the indications, so this good fellow, though he cannot tell us the signs, yet has such an experience in hanging that he himself perceives upon the sight whether the man hanged himself or not.'

" 'Yes, actually, my lord,' said he, 'it is just as your lordship says. For I know it well enough myself, I have seen so many by reason of my office.'

" 'Why,' said another lord merrily, 'your office has no more experience in hanging than has a hangman. And yet he cannot tell.'

" 'No, sir,' said he, 'if it please your lordship, he does not deal with those that hang themselves, as I do.'

" 'Well,' said one of the lords, 'how many of those have you dealt with in your days?'

" 'With many, my lord,' said he, 'for I have been officer under two almoners, and therefore I have seen many.'

" 'How many?' said one of the lords.

" 'I cannot tell,' said he, 'how many, but I well know I have seen many.'

" 'Have you seen,' said one, 'a hundred?'

" 'No,' said he, 'not a hundred.'

" 'Have you seen ninety?' At that point he reflected a little, like someone standing in doubt and not wanting to lie, and at last he said that he thought no, not quite ninety. Then he was asked whether he had seen twenty. And to that, without any hesitation, he answered, 'No, not twenty.' At that point the lords really laughed, at seeing that he was so sure that he had not seen twenty, and was in doubt as to whether he had seen ninety. Then he was asked whether he had seen fifteen. And to that he quickly said no. And likewise with ten. At last they came to five, and from five to four. And there he began to reflect again. Then they came to three, and then, for embarrassment, he was constrained to say that he had seen that many and more. But when he was asked when, whom, and in what place, necessity drove him at last to the truth, whereby it came out that he never had seen but one in all his life. And that was an Irish fellow called Crookshank, whom he had seen hanging in an old barn. And when all his expertise was boiled down to this, he was told to take a hike. And someone said to him that because he was not yet expert enough in the craft of hanging, it was a pity that he had no more experience thereof by one more."

"Indeed," said your friend, "this was a mad fellow. Did the third story come to as silly a point?"

"You shall hear," said I. "The layman who had reported it as having come from the mouth of the churchman was a quite distinguished man, and had a great reputation for honesty and integrity. And of course the churchman was also a man of distinction, and he was well known for both intelligent and virtuous. And therefore the lords highly doubted, knowing them both for such as they were, that they would be likely to find either the one or the other either making a dishonest statement or dishonestly denying the truth.

"And first the layman, before the lords, in the hearing of the churchman standing by, said, 'My lords all, so help me God and all things holy, this expert theologian here said to me, by his own mouth, that if Hunne had not filed the praemunire suit, he would never have been accused of heresy.'

"'What do you say, expert theologian?' said the lords. 'Was that true? And if not, then why did you say that?'

"'Assuredly, my lords,' said he, 'I did not at all say that. Indeed, what I actually said was that if Hunne had not been accused of heresy, he would never have filed the praemunire suit.'"

"'See, my lords?' said the other. 'I am glad you find me a truthful man. Will you command of me any more service?'

"'No, by my word,' said one of the lords, 'not in this proceeding. As far as I am concerned, you may go when you wish. For I have discerned, good man, that as long as the words are all the same, it makes no difference to you what order they are in, but it is one and the same to you, a horse mill and a mill horse, "Drink before you go" and "Go before you drink."'

"'No, my lords,' said he, 'I will not drink, God bless you.' And therewith he made his obeisances and went his way, leaving some of the lords laughing, to see the good, plain old honest man, how, as contrary as their two tales were, yet when he heard them both again, he noted no difference between them but took them both for the same, because the words were the same."

"By my word," said your friend, "these three things turned out to be very funny, and I would not for anything have missed hearing them. For here one can see that misunderstanding makes for misreporting. And that a tale that flits through many mouths catches many new feathers, which when they are pulled off again leave it plucked as bare as a coot, and sometimes as bare as a bird's ass. But I truly think, for all this, that there was great evidence given against the chancellor, for he was eventually indicted with Hunne's death and was for a great while in prison, and in the end never dared stand trial by twelve men for his acquittal, but was forced to get via friendship a pardon. But I beg you, for my mind's sake, to tell me what you yourself thought about this."

"In truth," said I, "there were several suspicious things charged against him, and they were all very solidly responded to in his favor. However, about the telling of a tale, it does often happen that when everything has been heard that can be said on the subject, the hearers will nevertheless think some one way and some another. And thus, although I cannot think but that those jurors, who were very honest men, gave the verdict that they themselves, in their own consciences, thought to be the right one, yet in my own mind, for anything that I ever heard about it in my life, so help me God, I never could think that it was."

"If he had not been guilty," said your friend, "he would never have appealed for his pardon."

"Yes," said I, "I have heard very wise men say, before this, that they would never refuse either God's pardon or the King's. It would not be wise, in a case containing many reports that make one look suspect, be they no matter how false, to rely upon twelve men's mouths where one can find a safer route. But I really think that if he had been guilty, he would never have gotten his pardon. For although there never was, I believe, brought into this world a prince of more benign nature, nor of more merciful mind, than is our sovereign lord that now reigns (and I hope will long reign) over us, and thus never a one who could have found it in his heart to more freely forgive and forget offenses done to and committed against himself, yet His Highness has such a fervent passion for right and justice in other people's concerns, and such a tender zeal for the protection of his subjects—of whose lives he in his high wisdom considers many imperiled by the giving of pardon to a few willful murderers—that never was there, I believe, a king that ever wore the crown in this realm who has in this many years given to such folk so few. And therefore I feel sure that in the case of such a deliberate, premeditated, heinous, cruel deed as this would have been if it had been true, all the friends that could have been found for the chancellor could never have gotten his pardon to come about in such a manner had it not been that, on the basis of the reports of all the circumstances, the highly judicious King, who (this is the truth, no flattery) pierces as deep into the bottom of a dubious matter as anyone I have ever seen in my life, had well perceived his innocence. And since I truly believe that if he had been guilty he never could have gotten for such a heinous murder any pardon from the King's Highness, I dare be much more confident of his innocence now. For you shall understand that he never appealed for a pardon. Rather, after a long examination of the matter, the chancellor, as well as the other man indicted with the deed and arraigned upon the indictment in the King's court, pled not guilty. And thereupon the King's Grace, being quite sufficiently informed of the truth, and, because of his blessed disposition, not wanting any false charge sustained in his name, ordered his attorney to acknowledge their pleas to be true, without any further trouble. Which thing in so faith-filled a prince is a clear declaration that the charge made against the chancellor was untrue.

"And as for myself, in all honesty, as I told you before, I have never in my life heard (and I have, I believe, heard everything that could well be said) anything about it that inclined me, after both the sides were heard, to think that he was guilty. And especially considering, besides all this, that Hunne was (as those who well knew him say he was indeed), even if a fair dealer among his neighbors, yet a man arrogant and set on the glory of a victory, which he hoped to have in the praemunire suit—about which, it is said, he did a lot of boasting among his close friends, saying that he expected to be spoken of long after his day, and have his affair called, in the annals, 'Hunne's Case.' When he realized that it would go contrary to his plan, and that in the civil court he would not win his spurs, and, moreover, in the ecclesiastical court he saw so many of his secret sores unwrapped and exposed that he began to fall into fear of worldly shame, it is to me much more likely that for weariness of his life he rid himself of it—which kind of turn of mind we see not seldom happen—especially since the devil might perhaps have joined to it a remarkable hope of that which did happen afterward, that the suspicion of his death would be laid to the charge and peril of the chancellor. This is, I say, much more likely to me than that thing of which I never heard the like before: that the bishop's chancellor would kill in the Lollards' Tower a man suspected so strongly—and convicted—of heresy, whereby he could get himself in trouble, when if he hated the man (for he would not kill him, you well know, if he loved him), he could easily bring him to shame and perhaps to a shameful death also."

"In all honesty," said your friend, "if I knew that it was true that he was actually a heretic and in danger of being so proved, I would well think that in malice and despair he hanged himself."

"God," said I, "knows the truth about everything. But what I have heard, I will tell you. I myself was present at St. Paul's when the bishop, in the presence of the mayor and the aldermen of the city, condemned him as a heretic after his death. And then there were read publicly the depositions, by which it was well proved that he was found guilty of misbelief regarding the holy Sacrament of the Altar, and of several other heresies as well. And on that basis was the judgment given that his body should be burned; and so it was.

"Now this is," said I, "to me a full proof. For I assure you, the bishop was a very sensible, virtuous, and astute man."

"By our Lady," said he, "the proof is the better by so much."

"I shall tell you," said I, "another thing, when you hear which, you shall perhaps believe it still the better."

"That I would be eager to know," said he. "For as far as I can hear, no one held him suspect of any such thing before."

"Indeed," said I, "that I cannot tell. But it so happened that, as I remember, six or seven years after Hunne was thus hanged, and his body burned, for his having been a heretic, there was someone in Essex, a carpenter who used to make pumps, who had set out (with others such as he was himself) to commit grand larceny; and as a result he was brought to the court. Where, by the commandment of the King's Grace, an eminent statesman of this realm and I myself had him in examination. Wherein, among other things, he acknowledged that he had long held several heresies, which he said that his brother, who was a parish clerk, had taught both his father and him. And I assure you, those heresies were of a height. Then he told us what other cunning masters of that school he had heard give lectures, and specifically in a place in London which he named for us, where he said that such heretics were wont to meet for their Bible studies in a private room at midnight. And when we asked him the names of those that were wont to haunt those midnight lectures, he related several, and among others he named Richard Hunne. Which we somewhat wondered at in our minds, but we said nothing about that, but let him relate on, all such as he could call to mind. And when he stopped and could remember no more, then we asked, about those he had named, who they were and where they lived. And he told us about some of them that were convicted, and some that had fled, and some that were even at that time living still in the town. And along the way, when we asked him what man was that 'Hunne' that he spoke of, he described to us his appearance and his house. 'And where is he now?' said we. 'Goodness,' said he, 'I went to Tournai, and when I came back from there, then I heard it said that he was hanged in the Lollards' Tower, and his body burned, for his having been a heretic.' And thus we there learned long after that Hunne had frequented heretics' lectures by night long before; which we relayed to the King's

Highness, as the man had testified. And His Highness, though he was sorry that any man should be so wicked, yet did highly rejoice that God in his goodness was bringing such hidden evildoings more and more to light. So afterward we (by order of the King) had in examination that man's brother, who, indeed, would not confess anything, either about the felonies or about the heresies. But yet his brother did stand by what he had said, and avowed it to his face, with such indications and observations as made it quite obvious that he was telling the truth. And it certainly would be astonishing if he had falsely fabricated such heinous things against his own brother, his own father, and himself, being not at all compelled to do so, nor put either in pain or in fear of it. Now, the father was dead, and we could not come by anyone else whom we could have further examined with regard to that night school, saving that he—the man who, as I told you, attested this matter—told us also, at that first time, about one man in London, taken for good and honorable, who was, he said, also a pupil of his brother's in those heresies; which man, because of his good reputation, we decided not to deal with till we had gotten hold of the other brother. As soon as we had that brother in custody, and he was committed to the Marshalsea Prison, this other man—who was, as I told you, reported to us as a heretic and a pupil of his—came to me to intercede and petition for him, claiming to be doing this out of charity. And seeing that we thought we could not fail to get hold of him when we wanted to, we therefore refrained from examining him till we should have examined the other man, the one he was interceding for. But we had no idea then in what way we would lose him. For it in fact so happened, unfortunately, that after calling on me to help him whose pupil in heresy he was reported to be, he was in his own house suddenly struck and slain. And that wretched end had he. What conscience he died with, God knows, for I can tell you nothing further."

"But, by Saint John," said your friend, "from that whole story it seems to me very clear that Hunne himself was not free of guilt in that affair."

"Certainly," said I, "it seemed that way, as far as I could tell, to as many as ever heard about it, and would have even more clearly seemed that way had they been present at the examinations and seen in what manner the man came out with it."

"But yet," said your friend, "as for his English Bible, even if Hunne was himself a heretic, the Book could still be good enough. And there is no good reason why a good book should be burned with a bad man."

"You well call me home," said I, "and well refresh my memory. For that was the thing whereby you took occasion to talk of Hunne. We talked so long about him that at last I had forgotten why and how we entered into that discussion. And yet those books have no little relevance to the matter that we had in hand; I mean, toward the perceiving of what persuasion Hunne was of. For it is a fact that at the time that he was denounced as a heretic, there lay open his English Bible (and some other English books of his), so that everyone could see the verses annotated in his own handwriting—such wordings, annotated in such a way, that no one with any sense, who was good, would have any great doubt after seeing them what wicked intentions the men had, both the one who thus annotated them and the one who thus wrote them. I do not remember now the particulars of the matter, nor the exact words as they were written. But this I remember well: that besides other things framed for the fostering of several other heresies, there were in the prologue of that Bible such statements regarding the Blessed Sacrament as good Christians were very horrified to hear, and which gave the readers undoubted occasion to think that the Book was a copy of the edition put out by Wycliffe, and by him translated into our tongue. And whether the Book was even burned, or was secretly kept, I cannot say with certainty. But truly, if the clergy were of my mind, it should be somewhere preserved, for the perpetual proof of the matter, there having gone around so much suspicious rumor about it. Which, as I believe, would all be well answered, to the full satisfaction of the mind of anyone both sensible and good, once they had inspected, read, and carefully considered that Book."

16.

The messenger relates some reasons he has heard given by some of the clergy as to why Scripture in English should not be allowed. And the author explains why he thinks it would be a good thing to have the Bible in English. And with this, part three ends.

"Sir," said your friend, "I still, for all this, cannot see any reason why the clergy should keep the Bible out of the hands of laymen who know no language but their native one."

"I had thought," said I, "that I had plainly proved to you that they do not keep it from them. For I have explained to you that they keep from them none except such translations as are either not yet approved as good or else already condemned as bad, as Wycliffe's was, and Tyndale's. For as for the other, older ones that were there before Wycliffe's day, they remain lawful and are in some folks' hands had and read."

"What you say is true," said he. "But yet, as women say, somehow it always happened that the cat winked when one of her eyes was out. Surely so is it not for nothing that the English Bible is in the hands of so few, when so many would so love to have it."

"That is very true," said I. "For I think that, even if the favorers of a sect of heretics are so fervent in the propagating of their sect that they do not hesitate to put their money together and make a purse among them for the printing of a perniciously written or perniciously translated book (of which, even if it happens to get forbidden and burned, some copies will be sold before they are caught sight of, and each

377

of the favorers will lose only his share), yet I think probably no printer will be too hot on putting any Bible into print at his own expense (whereof the loss would lie wholly on his own neck) and then hanging upon a perilous trial of whether the first copy of his translation was made before Wycliffe's day or since. For if it was made since, it would have to have been approved previous to the printing. And surely how it has happened that in all this time God has either not permitted or not provided that any good, virtuous man has had the inclination to do a faithful translation of it, and thereupon either the clergy or at least some bishop or other to approve it, this I cannot tell at all. But be that as it may, I have heard, and am hearing, so much said on the matter, and so much doubt expressed about it, that perhaps it would hinder and deter any one bishop from allowing it without the assent of the rest. And while many things are adduced against it, there yet is, to my mind, not one thing that more puts good men of the clergy in doubt about allowing it than this: that they sometimes see many of the worse sort more fervent in the calling for it than those whom we find far better. Which makes them fear that such men desire it for no good, and that if it were had in everyone's hands, there would arise great peril, and that seditious people would do more harm therewith than good, honorable folk would take fruit thereby. Which fear I assure you does not at all frighten me. No matter who would of their malice or foolishness take harm from that thing that is of itself ordained to do everyone good, I would never for the avoidance of their being harmed take from others the profit which they could take and do not at all deserve to lose. For otherwise, if the abuse of a good thing should cause the taking away thereof from others who would use it well, Christ should himself never have been born, nor brought his faith into the world; nor should God have ever made it, either, if he should, in order to prevent the loss of those who would be damned wretches, have kept away the occasion of reward from those who would, with the help of his grace, exert themselves to earn it."

"I am sure," said your friend, "you do not doubt that I am fully and wholly of your mind regarding this contention that the Bible should be in our English tongue. But yet, that the clergy is of the contrary mind and would not have it so, that is clearly shown in their not allowing it to be so. And, moreover, I hear in every place, almost, where I find any educated member of the clergy, that their minds are all set on keeping Scripture from us. And they search out for that stance every rotten reason that they can find, and solemnly set them forth for all to see, though five of those reasons are not worth a fig.

"For they begin as far back as our first father, Adam, and explain to us that his wife and he fell out of Paradise through desire of knowledge and learning. Now if this would serve, it must drive every person, priest and otherwise, from the knowledge and study of Scripture, lest that learning drive them all out of Paradise.

"Then they say that God taught his disciples many things in private, because the people should not hear them. And therefore, according to them, the people should not now be allowed to read it all.

"And they even go on to say that it is hard to translate Scripture out of one tongue into another, and especially, they say, into ours. Which they call a tongue vulgar and barbarous.

"But of all the things, most especially they say that Scripture is the food of the soul, and that the common people are like infants that must be fed only with milk and pap. And if we have any tougher food, it must be chewed before by the nurse and put that way into the baby's mouth. But it seems to me that though they make us all infants, they shall find many a shrewd brain among us, that can tell chalk from cheese well enough. And, if they would once take us our meat in our own hand, we are not so poorly toothed but that within a while they shall see us chew it ourselves as well as they. For let them call us little babies if they wish; yet, by God, they shall for all that well find with some of us that an old knave is no child."

"Surely," said I, "such things as you speak of are the kind of thing that, as I to some extent said before, puts good folk in fear about allowing Scripture in our English tongue. Not for the reading and receiving, but for the presumptuous chewing of it. The fear is that people will much concern themselves with such parts of it as they are least qualified to. For undoubtedly, as you said about our mother Eve, an inordinate appetite for knowledge is something that will drive anyone out of Paradise. And inordinate is the appetite when uneducated people, if they read it in their language, start busying themselves in scrutinizing and discussing the great, secret mysteries of Scripture, which though they hear, they are not able to understand. This thing is plainly forbidden us who are not equipped for or appointed to it. And thus holy Saint Gregory Nazianzen, that great, august Doctor of the Church, strongly attacks and criticizes all such bold, officious dabblers in Scripture, and explains that it is shown in Exodus, by Moses ascending up upon the mountain, where he spoke with God, and the people staying below, that the people are forbidden to presume to deal with the high mysteries of holy Scripture, but ought to be content to stay below and not deal with anything higher than is appropriate for them, but rather, receiving from the height of the mountain, by way of Moses, what is delivered to them—that is to say, the laws and precepts that they must keep, and the points they must believe—look carefully at all of that, and often, and get plenty involved with it. Not to debate it, but to fulfill it. And as for the high, secret mysteries of God, and hard texts of his holy Scripture, let us know that we are so unable to ascend that high up on that mountain that it shall become us to say to the preachers appointed thereto what the people said to Moses: 'You hear God, and let us hear you' [Ex 20: 19]. And it is a fact that the blessed, holy theologian Saint

Jerome greatly complains about and castigates that loathsome familiarity whereby the ordinary laypeople, men and women, were in his day so bold in the tackling, debating, and expounding of holy Scripture. And states straight-out that those who will consider themselves to understand it by themselves, without a teacher, will have experience prove otherwise. For this is something that takes a good amount of help, and a long time, and a whole mind given greatly to it. And certainly since, as the holy apostle Saint Paul says in several of his Epistles, God has by his Holy Spirit so instituted and established his church that he will have some be expounders and some hearers, some teachers and some learners [see 1 Cor 12:28–30 and Eph 4:11], we do plainly pervert and turn upside down the right order of Christ's church when the one group encroaches upon the other's office. Plato, the great philosopher, expressly forbids those not admitted to this office, or qualified for it, to much involve and busy themselves in discussions and debates about the temporal laws of the city, which should not be discussed except by folk fit for this, and in an appropriate place. For otherwise those who cannot attain a very good understanding of them begin to dislike, criticize, and scorn them. Whereof follows the breaking of the laws, and disorder of the people. For till a law be changed by authority, it ought rather to be observed than scorned. Or else the example of one law boldly broken and totally disregarded sets a precedent for the rest to be treated the same. And commonly the best laws will least please many of the common people, who mostly desire (if it would mean that they could be listened to and followed) to live all at liberty, under no law at all.

"Now if Plato, so wise a man, saw such to be good in temporal laws—things of men's making—how much less appropriate is it for every man to boldly occupy himself with the exposition of holy Scripture, which is so devised and composed by the high wisdom of God that it far exceeds, in many texts, the capacity and reach of the human mind. It was also stipulated by the Emperor [Justinian], in the civil law, that the common people should never be so bold as to engage in disputations upon the faith or holy Scripture, and that no such things should be held among them or before them. And so, as I said before, the particular fear in this matter is that we would be too occupied in chewing Scripture ourselves, which you say we would be able enough to do. Which undoubtedly the most intelligent and the best educated, and those who have for many years given their whole minds to it, are yet unable to do. And then far more unable must needs be whoever will boldly upon the first reading, because he knows the words, therefore take it upon himself to teach others the meaning, jeopardizing his own soul and the souls of others, too, by bringing people into mad ways, sects, and heresies that have long ago been introduced by heretics and condemned by the Church. And thus in these matters, if the common people could be free to chew it, as you put it, and to hold disputations about it, then would you have the more blind the more bold, the more ignorant the more energetic, the less intelligent the more inquisitive, the more foolish the more talkative about great uncertainties and high questions of holy Scripture and of God's great and secret mysteries—and this not soberly, out of any good sentiment, but presumptuously and irreverently, while feeding and feasting. And there, when the wine was in and the wit out, would they take it upon themselves, with foolish words and blasphemy, to handle holy Scripture in a more casual manner than they would a Robin Hood ballad. And some would, as I said, solemnly take it upon themselves, as if they were established experts, to interpret the text as they pleased, and therewith fall themselves and drag others down with them into seditious sects and heresies, whereby God's Scripture should lose its honor and reverence and be, by means of such an irreverent and unbecoming demeanor, absolutely and completely abused among many people, to the contrary of that holy purpose that God ordained it for. Whereas if we would concern ourselves with it no further than to read it good and devoutly, and in what is clear and obvious (such as God's commandments and his holy counsels) exert ourselves to follow it, with help of his grace asked for that purpose; and in his great, marvelous miracles, reflect on his divinity; and in his lowly birth, his godly life, and his bitter Passion, exercise ourselves in such meditations, prayer, and virtues as the subject matter shall supply us occasion, acknowledging our own ignorance where we find a difficulty; and, relying there on the faith of the Church, wrestle with no such text as might bring us into a state of doubt and uncertainty about any of those articles on which every good Christian is clear—by this manner of reading, no man or woman can take harm in holy Scripture. Now, then, the things, on the other hand, that uneducated people can never by themselves get a good grasp of—such as in the psalms and the prophets and several parts of the Gospel, where the words are spoken sometimes as in the person of the prophet himself, sometimes as in the person of God, sometimes of some others (angels, devils, or human beings), and sometimes of Christ our Savior (not always in the same fashion, but sometimes as God, sometimes as human being, sometimes as head of this Mystical Body, his Church Militant here on earth, sometimes as head of his Church Triumphant in heaven, sometimes as in the person of his sensorially perceptible parts of his own body, other times in the person of some particular part of his Mystical Body), and these things, with many others, oftentimes alternated, and, extemporaneously, sundry things on different matters differently mixed together—all these things which it is not possible for uneducated people to grasp, it would be more than madness for them to occupy themselves with. They should, instead, leave all these things to those whose whole study is spent thereon, and to the preachers appointed thereto, who can explain such things to them at suitable times and places with reverence and authority, the sermon so tempered as to be meet and suitable always for the present audience. Whereto it appears that our Savior himself, and his apostles after him, always had a special consideration. And therefore, as I say, I really can in no way agree with you that it would be appropriate for uneducated people to busy themselves with the chewing of holy Scripture rather than have it chewed for them. For that is the province of the preachers, and of those who after long study are admitted to teaching and expounding it. And to this effect go all the statements, as far as I perceive, of all holy theologians who have written anything on this subject.

"But never did they mean, as I see it, the forbidding of the Bible's being read in any vernacular tongue. And never yet have I heard presented any valid reason why it would not be appropriate to have the Bible translated into English. All of those arguments that have been made, no matter how brilliant and glorious they may seem at first sight, yet when well examined could actually, for all that I can see, be as well adduced against the holy writers who wrote the Scripture in the Hebrew tongue, and against the blessed evangelists who wrote the Scripture in Greek, and, likewise, against all those who translated it out of each of those languages into Latin, as against those who would translate it good and faithfully out of Latin into our English tongue. For as for our tongue being called barbarous, that is but a bugbear. For so is, as everyone with any education knows, every foreign tongue to people of another. And if they would call it barren of words, there is no doubt that it has plenty enough to express our minds on anything whereof one person has carried on a conversation with another. Now, as regards the difficulty which a translator finds in expressing good and vividly what the author says—which is hard always to do so faithfully as not to sometimes diminish either the meaning or the grace that it carries in the former tongue—that point has lain in the full view of those who have translated Scripture already, either out of Greek into Latin or out of Hebrew into either of them, as is evident (to those who are learned) from the many translations which we read already.

, "Now, as regards the harm that can be caused by such blind broncos as will, when they read the Bible in English, be more busy than will become them, those who touch on that point harp on the right string and are right on key about the great harm that would likely come to some folk. However, the cause of that harm would still be not the English translation, but their own ignorance and foolishness; which, in my opinion, is still not a sufficient cause to exclude the translation and deprive other folk of the benefit thereof. What should be done is, rather, to make provision against such abuse and let a good thing go forward. No one with any sense would do away with all weapons just because murderers misuse them. Nor, as I say, did any such concern prevent Scripture from being written first in a vernacular tongue. For Scripture, as I said before, was not written but in a vernacular tongue such as the whole people understood; and not in esoteric symbols, but in such common letters as almost everyone could read. For neither was the Hebrew nor the Greek tongue, nor the Latin either, any other speech than such as all the people spoke. And therefore if we should claim that to translate the Scripture into our tongue would be wrong because it is ordinary and common to every Englishman, then it was just as wrong to translate it into Greek or into Latin, or to write the New Testament first in Greek or the Old Testament in Hebrew, since both of those tongues were as truly plebeian as ours. And, moreover, by that argument not only should Scripture be kept out of our tongue, but in addition to that, the reading of it should be forbidden both to all such laypeople and to all such priests, too, who can get no more than the grammar, and very scantily that. All which company, even if they can understand the words, are yet as far from perceiving the meaning in hard and puzzling texts as would our women be if Scripture was translated into our own language.

"However, in truth, seldom has it been seen that any sect of heretics has started out being made up of such unlearned folk as knew nothing more than the language in which they read Scripture. Rather, these sects have always ordinarily sprung from the pride of such folk as had, along with the knowledge of the language, also some high persuasion within themselves of their own erudition. Whose authority some other folk have soon after—partly through malice, partly through gullibility, and in great part through pleasure and delight in newfangledness—subscribed to, thus increasing the faction. But the head has always ordinarily been either some proud learned man or at least some proud dabbler in some learning besides the language. So that if we should, for fear of heretics that might happen to come about thereby, keep Scripture out of any language, or out of the hands of uneducated people, then we should for like fear be forced to keep it out of all languages, and out of the hands of educated people too, and not know whom we could trust with it. To which there is, it seems to me, no answer but that if any good thing shall go forward, some risk must needs be taken. And some folk will not fail to be bad. Against which things provision must be made that as much good may grow from it, and as little harm come of it, as can be managed, and not to keep the whole benefit from any whole population because of harm that could come to some party by their own folly and fault. As if a sorry surgeon were to cut off the leg at the knee to keep the toe from the gout, or cut off a man's head at the shoulders to keep him from toothache. There is no scriptural text so hard that a good, virtuous man, or woman either, will not find in it something that will excite and increase their devotion. Not to mention that every sermon will be the more satisfying and fruitful to them when they have in their minds the scriptural text that they will there hear expounded. For even if it is, as it is indeed, great wisdom for a preacher to use discretion in his preaching and to take into account the characteristics and capacities of his audience, this yet in no way rules out that the whole audience can without harm have read, and have ready in mind, the scripture that he will in his sermon elucidate and expound. For there is no doubt that God and his Holy Spirit has so judiciously tempered their speech through the whole corpus of Scripture that everyone can take good from it, and no one harm, except those who will in the study of it rely proudly on the folly of their own wit. For although Christ did speak to the people in parables and expound them in private to his especial disciples (and sometimes would forbear to tell some things to them also, because they were not as yet able to bear them), and the apostles in like manner did sometimes refrain from saying to some people things that they did not hesitate to say straight-out to others, yet all of this in no way stands in the way of the translation of Scripture into our own tongue, any more than into Latin. And that fact—that Christ and his apostles used such discretion in their utterances of such unknown, unheard-of mysteries either to Jews, pagans, or newly baptized folk—is also no cause to keep the corpus of Scripture out of the hands of any Christian people so many years steadfastly confirmed in faith, unless we would say that all the expositions which Christ made himself upon his own parables to his trusted servants and disciples, away from the people, should now at this day be in like manner kept from the commoners, and no one allowed to read or hear them but those who in his church represent the state and office of his apostles. Which I well know that no sensible person will say, considering that those things which were then ordinarily most kept from the people are now the most necessary for the people to know. As is quite apparent in virtually all such things as our Savior at the time taught his apostles apart. Of which the profit that one good, devout, uneducated layperson might take by the reading, I would not withhold on account of the harm that a hundred heretics would fall into by their own willful misuse, any more than our Savior hesitated for the well-being of such as would with his grace be of his little chosen flock to come into this world and be 'lapis offensionis et petra scandali,' the stumbling block and the stone bringing falling and ruin to all the willful wretches in the rest of the world [1 Pt 2:7–8].

"Finally, it seems to me that the synodal decree of which we were speaking just now has settled this question already. For when the clergy therein agreed that the English Bibles should remain which were translated before Wycliffe's day, they consequently did agree that there was nothing wrong with having the Bible in English. And from the fact that they forbade that any new translation be read till it was approved by the bishops, it is quite obvious that their intent was that the bishop should approve it if he found it free of error, and also (as stands to reason) correct it where it was erroneous, unless the man who did the translation was a heretic or the errors were such and so many as would make it easier to do it all over than correct it. As was the case, on both counts, with the translation by Tyndale.

"Now, if it so be that it would perhaps be thought not a thing suitably to be ventured to put everyone in a flash flood at once and rashly dash out holy Scripture into the teeth of every worthless lout, it yet seems to me that there might be implemented here a control system such that neither would good, virtuous lay folk lack it nor rude and rash brains abuse it. For it could be, with conscientious effort, translated good and accurately by some good Catholic and well-educated man—or by several, dividing the work among them and afterward bringing together their separate sections. And after that the work could be accepted and approved by the ordinaries, and by their authorization so put into print as all the copies should come, the whole set of them, into the hands of the bishop. Which he can according to his discretion and wisdom deliver to such as he sees to be respectable, sensible, and virtuous, with a good admonition and fatherly counsel to use it reverently, with humble heart and lowly mind, rather seeking therein occasion of devotion than of debate.

And providing, to the extent possible, that the Bible is after the decease of the party brought back and reverently returned to the ordinary. So that as nearly as can be managed, it will be had only from the hands of the ordinary, and by people he sees and regards as such as shall be likely to use it to God's honor and the merit of their own souls. If any of them is later proved to have abused it, then the use of it will be forbidden that person, either forever or until they have gotten more sense."

"By our Lady," said your friend, "I do not disapprove of this way. But who should set the price of the Book?"

"Really," said I, "that I reckon a thing of little importance. For it would not be a great matter either for anyone, almost, to give a coin or two above the average price for a book of such great profit, or for the bishop to give them all out for free, by which he could serve his diocese at a cost of ten pounds, I think, or twenty marks. Which sum, I dare say, there is no bishop who would not be glad to spend on something that could give his whole diocese so special a pleasure with such a spiritual profit."

"By my word," said he, "I yet think that the people would grumble about getting it in this way, delivered to them at the bishop's hand, and would rather pay the printer for it than get it from the bishop for free."

"It might happen that way with some," said I. "But yet in my opinion there would be in that attitude more willfulness than wisdom or any good disposition, in such as would not be willing so to receive them. And therefore I would think, in all honesty, that it would fall out thus with few. But, before God, the greater worry would be that those might grumble and be sorely aggrieved who requested it and happened to be denied it. Which I suppose would not often happen to any honorable householder who requested it in order to have it be, by his discretion, reverently read in his house. But if it were not put in the hands of every ignorant lad, so that he could ineptly read a little when he liked and then toss the Book at his heels, or hold with others like himself a theological debate and a pub parliament upon, I trust that no one with any sense will find fault with that. You were speaking not long ago of the Jews, among whom the whole people have, you say, the Scripture in their hands. And you thought it unreasonable that we should reckon Christian people less worthy than they to do that. Wherein I am, as you see, of your own opinion. But yet I wish to God we had the same reverence for God's Scripture that they have. For I assure you, I have heard it said—by very respectable folk who have been in their houses—that a man could not pay a Jew to sit down on his Bible of the Old Testament; that, rather, he takes it in hand with great reverence when he wants to read it, and reverently lays it up again when he is done. Whereas we, God forgive us, think little of sitting down on our Bible with the Old Testament and the New too. Which offhanded handling, as it proceeds from little reverence, so does more and more engender in the mind a heedlessness and disregard of God's holy words. We find also that among the Jews, though their whole entire Bible was written in their native tongue, and those books of it in which their laws were written were ordinarily in every man's hands, as things that God would have commonly known, repeated, and kept in remembrance, yet there were also certain parts of it which the common people of the Jews of olden times, both out of reverence and because of the difficulty, did refrain from dealing with. But now that there is torn asunder the Temple veil which among the Jews cut the people off from the sight of the mysteries [Mt 27: 51], and now that God has sent his Holy Spirit to be actively present with his whole church and teach all necessary truth, though it may therefore be the better sanctioned that no part of holy Scripture be kept out of the hands of honorable lay people, I would yet wish that no part of it should come into the hands of people who, to their own harm and perhaps their neighbors' too, would handle it too casually and be too bold and busy with it. And also, although holy Scripture is, as you said a while ago, a medicine for the sick and food for the healthy, yet since there is many a sorely soul-sick body that takes himself for healthy, and there is in holy Scripture a whole feast of so many different foods that, given the dispositions and states of sundry stomachs, one person may be harmed by the selfsame thing that will do another good, and sick folk often have such a distorted sense of taste that they like most the food that is the most unwholesome for them, it therefore would not, as it seems to me, be unreasonable that the ordinary—whom God has in the diocese appointed as chief physician, to discern between the healthy and the sick, and between disease and disease—should according to his wisdom and discretion furnish to everybody their part, what he should perceive to be good and wholesome for them. And thus, just as he would not fail to find many to whom he could commit it in its entirety, so too, to tell the truth, I could see nothing wrong therein if he should commit the Gospel of Matthew, Mark, or Luke to some man to whom he should yet forbid the Gospel of Saint John, and allow some to read the Acts of the Apostles whom he would not allow to get into Revelation. There would be many, I think, who would get a lot of profit from Saint Paul's Epistle to the Ephesians, in which he gives good counsel to every kind of people, and who yet would find little fruit for their understanding in his Epistle to the Romans, which contains such high difficulties as very few learned men can very well get at. And it would be likewise with several other parts of the Bible, in the Old Testament as well as the New, so that, as I say, though the bishop might to one layman grant and commit with good advice and instruction the whole Bible to read, he still might well, with good reason, prohibit to another the reading of some part, and forbid a busybody to deal with any part at all, beyond what he hears set out and explained to him in sermons; and likewise take the Bible back away from such folk as prove to be by their blind presumption abusing the occasion of their profit, to their own hurt and harm. And thus may the bishop order the Scripture in our hands with as good reason as the father does by his discretion decree which of his children may because of their maturity keep a knife to cut their meat, and which ones will because of their carelessness have the knife taken away from them, lest they cut off their fingers. And thus am I confident, without prejudice to other men's judgment, in telling you my mind in this matter: how Scripture could, without great peril and not without great profit, be brought into our language and taken to laypeople, men and women both. I even mean thereby nothing short of this: that the whole Bible could, to my mind, be allowed to be spread around in English. But if there were too great a fear that perhaps all might thereby be let, then I would rather see put into effect such a control system as I speak of, or some such other as wiser men can better devise. However, from what I read recently in the letter that the King's Highness translated into English (a letter of his own, which His Grace wrote, in Latin, in response to the letter from Luther), it seems to me that His Majesty is of his blessed zeal so minded to present this matter to the prelates of the clergy (among whom I have perceived some of the greatest and best to be of their own minds already strongly leaning in this direction) that before long, we laypeople shall in this matter, unless the fault be found in ourselves, be quite fully satisfied and content."

"In all honesty," said he, "that will to my mind be very rightly done. And now I am, for my mind, on this whole matter, fully content and satisfied."

"Well," said I, "then we will go to dinner, and the rest we will finish after." And therewith we went to eat.

Part Four

The author explains why it would not be a good thing to do to allow Luther's books, or those of any other heretic, to go out and be read among the people, even if there were some good things in them among the bad.

After dinner, when we had rested a little, your friend and I drew ourselves aside into the garden. And there, sitting down in an arbor, he promptly began to proceed with the matter, saying that he had well perceived that not only in his part of the country, but also at the university where he had been, there were those who had no bad opinion of Luther, but thought that the clergy had banned his books out of malice and ill will, to the end that folk should not really see and completely perceive what he says, or at least what thing he means by his words. Which will be made apparent, they think, not by a line extracted from the middle of a page, but by a careful consideration of the whole text. Without which one could impute a wrong blameworthiness, they say, to the best writers who ever wrote in this world. But they think that the clergy will not have his books read because in them laymen can read the priests' wrongdoings—which was, they say, the very cause of the condemnation. For otherwise, they say, whether he had written rightly or wrongly, his books would still have been kept in people's hands and read. For there are in it, they think, even if some parts are bad, many things yet rightly said, of which it is not reasonable that people should lose the profit because of the bad. And people also think it reasonable that everything be heard that can be said regarding the truth to be known concerning the matters of our salvation, to the intent that when everything is heard and understood, people can for their own safety the better choose and hold the right way.

"Indeed," said I, "if it were now doubtful and unclear whether the church of Christ is in the right rule of doctrine or not, then it would be really necessary to give a good hearing to everyone who could and would argue anything on either side, for it or against it, to the end that if we were now in a wrong way, we might leave it and walk in some better one. But now, on the other hand, if it so be, as indeed it is, that Christ's church has the true doctrine already, and the selfsame that Saint Paul would not give an angel from heaven any hearing against, what sense would it now make for us to show ourselves so distrustful and wavering about it that in order to find out whether our faith was false or true, we would give audience not to an angel from heaven, but to a foolish friar, to an apostate, to an overt incestuous lecher, a plain agent of the devil, and a manifest messenger of hell? In regard to which words, if you would perhaps think that I am being too harsh in calling him by such odious names, you must take into account that in his ranting books he does not refrain from calling by as bad names, both untruthfully and gratuitously, those whom it is his duty to highly reverence, whereas I do, between us two, call him but what he himself has shown him, in his writing, in his conduct, and in his mad marriage. And, moreover, I neither do it nor would want to were it not that the matter itself does by reason require it. As I see it, it is necessary to tell how wicked he is, because the worse the man is, the more mad it is for sensible people to give his false fables a hearing against God's undoubtable truth, taught to his church by his Holy Spirit and confirmed by such a multitude of miracles, by so much blood of holy martyrs, by the virtuous conduct of so many blessed confessors, by the purity and cleanness of so many chaste widows and undefiled virgins, by the wholesome doctrine of so many holy theologians, and finally by the unanimous accord and agreement of all Christian people these fifteen hundred years. And therefore not any regard to his ranting against the clergy is, as some would have it seem, the cause of the condemnation of him and the suppression of his books. For the good men of the clergy are not that sorely distressed by those who criticize the wrongdoings of the bad, nor are the bad themselves so tender-eared that for the mere talking about their wrongdoings they would banish the books that were good in other things besides. For else the books of many old holy Fathers could not have lasted so long, wherein the vices of those in the clergy who are bad are very vehemently rebuked. No, the real reason why the reading of his books is not allowed is that his heresies are so many, and so abominable, and the 'proofs' wherewith he professes to make them worthy of acceptance are so far from reason and truth, and so far against the right understanding of holy Scripture—of which, under the pretext of a great zeal and love for it, he labors to destroy the credibility and good use—and, finally, he takes so far everything against good custom and virtue, inciting the world to wrong opinions about God and to boldness in sin and wretchedness, that from the reading can come no good, but much harm. For if it were basically good, and, due to error or oversight, there were some weeds mixed in with the wheat, and those weeds could be separated out and the rest remain intact, people would have been all right with that, as they are in such other cases. But, now, his is not besprinkled with a few spots, but with more than half venom is poisoned all the wine—which is in itself right rotten. And this is done on purpose and out of malice, not without an evil spirit accompanying his words in such a way that the contagion thereof is likely to infect a feeble soul, just as the stench of a plague sore infects a whole body. Nor is the truth to be learned from every man's mouth. For just as Christ was not pleased that the devil should call him God's Son even though it was true, so is he not pleased that a devil's scion, such as Luther or Tyndale is, should teach his flock the truth, for infecting them with their false, diabolical heresies besides. For just as the holy Scripture of God, because of the good Spirit who authored it, is of its own nature apt to purge and amend the reader although some who read it will of their indomitable malice turn it to their harm, so do such writings as Luther's are, in the writing of which the devil gives counsel (and along with it, an emanation from his presence), although the goodness of some will enable them to triumph over the malice thereof—walking unharmed with God's help, as the psalmist says, upon the serpent and the cockatrice, and treading upon the lion and the dragon [Ps 91:13]—still, such works are in themselves always very unwholesome to have anything to do with; they are fit and apt to corrupt and infect the reader. For the proof of which we need no other example than this that we have in hand, if we consider what good the reading of his books has done in Saxony. And this we find more than too much proved here among us: that out of ten who engage in reading his books, you will scarcely find two who will not not only cast off prayer and fasting and all such godly virtues as holy Scripture commends and the Church commands and virtuous people have always held in high esteem, but also fall into outright contempt and hatred thereof. So that what fruit would grow of the reading, you may soon guess."

2.

The author shows many of Luther's heresies to be so abominable, and some of them also so silly, that just the mere mention of them is enough, without any further discussion of them, to cause any good person to be horrified by them and ashamed even to appear so foolish as to hold them. And the author gives several examples, some of which are newly set forth in the English books of Tyndale, who in some respects is even worse than his master Luther is himself.

"And in all honesty I would think that any good man, unless some reasonable necessity should compel him to do this, would otherwise, if he but once heard his opinions related, be very loath to lose his time in the reading of his idiotic 'proofs,' or even of the very titles and names of them."

"If they are indeed such," said your friend, "and not mistaken or misrepresented."

"It seems to me," said I, "that the fruit which you see spring from them should suffice to make you perceive them for wicked. And certainly the state of life of a friar who weds a nun when his state of life is that of a friar should make it easy to know that his teaching is not very good."

"Certainly," said he, "I cannot deny that these are bad signs."

"I will," said I, "do more for you. For I will find a way for you to see his own books, and there to perceive for yourself that people are not slandering him."

"I ask you," said he, "to let me hear some of his opinions by spoken word for now, and as for the seeing of them in his own books, I shall think about that later."

"He first began," said I, "with indulgences and with the pope's power, categorically denying either of them to be of any effect at all. And soon after, to show what good spirit moved him, he denied all of the seven sacraments except Baptism, Penance, and the Sacrament of the Altar, saying straight-out that all the rest are but fabricated things and of no effect.

"Now, these that he leaves in as good, it is good to see how he handles them. For in Penance he says that there is no need for either contrition or satisfaction. Also he says that no priest is needed for the hearing of confession, but that every man—and every woman, too—is as competent to hear confessions and give absolution, and do everything that a confessor is supposed to do, as is a priest."

"Goodness, sir," said your friend, "this way would be advantageous in one respect. For the greatest difficulty I find with confession is when I see many confessors at a Penance service, and yet upon the sight I can scarcely like one of them well enough that I would tell any such tales to him once in seven years, if I had a choice. But, now, if I could in accordance with Luther's way make my confession to a beautiful woman, I would not hesitate to go to confession weekly."

"You would," said I, "perhaps tell her a tale that you would not tell every man. But yet if some men told to a beautiful woman some tales that they tell in confession to a foul friar, they would, I think, occasionally wish they had kept their counsel in their own breast."

"Goodness," said he, "that can happen also in the confession that is made to a priest."

"It would indeed be possible," said I. "And Tyndale, in his book on obedience, or rather disobedience, says that the curates do go and relate to the bishops the confessions of those of their parishioners who are rich, and that the bishops thereupon do summon them and charge them with their secret sins, and either put them to public, shameful penance or compel them to pay at the bishop's pleasure. Now I dare say with confidence, and I suppose all the honest men in this realm will say and swear the same, that this is a very foolish falsehood concocted in his own mind; something that he never in his life saw any instance of. We see in some rather the contrary fault: that not only the rich, but also the poor openly keep whores and openly live in adultery, without making any payment or doing any penance or having anything, practically, ever said to them. But with that, Tyndale finds no fault in the bishops. For he says straight-out that the bishop has no authority to punish any such thing at all. But he does not forbear, on the other hand, to slander the bishops and the curates too, making up the story that the one group does reveal folks' confessions to the other. And when he has thus slandered them, then forthwith, as though he had proved his story true, he takes the same false, fabricated lie for a basis on which to build a case for the destruction of the holy sacrament of Penance. For on the basis of that lie and others like it, he says plainly that confession to the priest is the worst thing that ever was invented. Now, if that were true (it actually being as false as he that said it), then how did it happen—which question Luther and he are asked often, and they always make as if they did not hear it—how did it happen, I say, that of so many virtuous, intelligent, and knowledgeable Fathers as have been in Christ's church in so many hundreds of years, never a one had the intelligence or the grace to see this big thing, but all of them teach confession, till now that there has come Tyndale, who in this point goes even further than his master Luther? For Luther says he would by all means have confession stand, but he would have it made at liberty, as well to women as to men. But Tyndale will have none at all, because he wants to slander both the bishops and the curates, claiming that they would between them disclose our confessions."

"Honestly," said your friend, "that is a thing that I never heard to have happened."

"Nor he either," said I. "That I dare say with assurance. And yet I well know that, as you said just now, it would be quite possible that priests would reveal folks' confessions, and with many of them nothing in this world would be more likely, either, if God and his Holy Spirit were not, as is the case, present and working with his holy sacrament. But certainly, while there are many things that quite clearly prove the sacrament of confession to be a thing instituted and devised by God, yet if all the rest were lacking, this one thing would to me be a plain persuasion and a full proof, which thing I find in the noble book that the King's Highness wrote against Luther: namely, that in so common a custom of confession oftener than once in the year, where no man refrains from telling such of his secrets as upon the disclosing or the close keeping thereof commonly depends his reputation, and oftentimes his life also; and so many of that sort that hear them are unsophisticated, and in all other things so unthinking and loose-lipped, and some, moreover, so bad in all their behavior that for money they little scruple to steal, rob, and murder too—and could many times with the disclosing of some such things get so much as some of them would kill a man for less than—yet we never find any man taking harm by his confession, or any cause given of complaint, through any such secrets revealed and told by the confessor."

"In all honesty," said he, "this is very true and a big thing in my opinion. But undoubtedly if confession ever came to women's ears, there would be a drastic change. For it would be hard for God and the devil, too, to bridle their tongues."

"Yes, yes," said I, "a woman can keep a confidence well enough. For even if she tells a confidante, she still tells it only in confidence, and that confidante to her confidante in no other way, and so when all the confidantes in the town know it, it is still just in confidence. And therefore I mention it not for any harm that would come by them, but for the novelty thereof."

"Now, seriously," said your friend, "this was a most amusing mad invention of Luther's; and Luther is just about as mad as Tyndale. For it would be almost as good to have no confession at all as to set women to hearing it."

"Indeed," said I, "had that been advisable and not against God's will, this would probably have been discovered by some good men before these days, in this long time of so many hundreds of years. However, he does come close enough to taking it all away. And several of his pupils besides Tyndale do now utterly reject it. And he himself leaves little substance and little fruit in it. For he would have us not be too concerned about any full confession of all mortal sins, nor be very conscientious about calling to mind our sins, nor about pondering the circumstances or weight and gravity of them, nor about taking any grief for them. Now, these things taken away, and the sacrament of Penance left such as he would have it, consider for yourself what fruit a person is likely to find in it. A man who takes a confessor, he cares not whom, and then confesses he cares not what, disposing him to repentance he cares not how, good works in satisfaction counting for nothing—what kind of amendment will this man come to? And especially if, besides all this, he can take for his confessor a beautiful woman such as a young man would have a lust to open his mind to. Is it not perfectly obvious that this foolish fellow so plays with this holy sacrament of Penance that he is going about its utter destruction? And yet this is one of the three that he leaves in, taking four away expressly."

"Certainly," said your friend, "so he does this one too, as it seems to me."

"Indeed," said I, "and he handles the sacrament of Baptism not much better. For he extols Baptism but to the suppression of Penance and of all good living. For therein he teaches that the sacrament itself does not have any effect at all, but only the faith does.

"Item: He teaches that faith alone suffices for our salvation with our baptism, without good works. He says also that it is sacrilege to attempt to please God with any works and not with faith alone.

"Item: That no one can do any good work.

"Item: That the good and righteous always sin in doing well.

"Item: That no sin can damn any Christian, but only lack of belief. For he says that our faith swallows up all our sins, however great they may be.

"Item: He teaches that no one has free will, or can do anything with it, even if the help of grace is joined to it, but that everything we do, good and bad, we do nothing at all there in ourselves, but only allow God to do everything in us, good and bad, as wax is wrought into a statue or a candle by human hands, without doing anything itself thereto.

"Item: He says that God is as truly the author and cause of the bad will of Judas in the betraying of Christ as of the good will of Christ in the suffering of his Passion.

"As for Matrimony, he says straight-out that it is no sacrament; and so says Tyndale, too.

"Item: That if a man is not able to do his duty to his wife, he is obliged to secretly, without scandalizing anyone, provide another to do it for him."

"Really," said your friend, "it was courteous of him to be so considerate. He is a true gentleman, I guarantee you. No wonder his wife is so fertile, if he makes her such provision."

"Assuredly," said I, "this brilliant idea he does have; and he, and his disciple after him, say on such subjects a lot of other beastly things, of such a sort as respectable ears could scarcely abide to hear.

"About the sacrament of Holy Orders, he says that priesthood and all holy orders are but a fabricated invention.

"Item: That every Christian man and every Christian woman is a priest.

"Item: That every man can consecrate bread into the Body of Christ."

"This really is a shameful statement," said your friend.

"Hold on," said I, "and you will hear worse yet. For he goes on to say that every woman and child can consecrate bread into the Body of our Lord."

"Surely, then," said he, "the man is just plain insane."

"He goes," said I, "further yet, saying that the canon of the Mass is bogus.

"Item: That the host in the Mass is no oblation or sacrifice.

"Item: That the Mass with its canon in the form that is and always has been used in Christ's church is a sacrilege and an abomination.

"And though much of this concerns his damnable heresies regarding the Blessed Sacrament, he still has many more wicked teachings about it. Among others, he teaches that it is heresy to believe that there is not, in the Blessed Sacrament, real bread and real wine joined with the Body and Blood of our Lord.

"Item: Zwingli and Oecolampadius, pupils of Luther, have built further upon this ungodly ground of their master, and teach that the Blessed Sacrament is not the real body or blood of our Lord at all.[7] And Luther himself, although he now writes against them on this, yet (as is shown by many things) intended and planned to put forth, in the course of time, the same heresy himself, till he changed his mind for the envy that he bore toward them when he saw that they themselves would each be head of a sect (for that he could not stand for any man to be but himself). But before, as I say, he did maintain it himself. And therefore he made a way toward it by these other heresies that I have related to you, and by several others more.

"For he teaches also that the Mass avails no one, alive or dead, except only the priest himself.

"Item: He teaches that people should go to Mass as well after supper as before breakfast, and in their regular clothes, as they go all day, without candlelight or any other honorific ritual used therein.

"Item: He says it would be best that people never be given Communion but once in their life. And that never till they lie a-dying, just as they are but once christened and that at their beginning.

"Item: He teaches that every man and woman should take the holy Sacrament, and not refrain from touching it and handling it as much as they please.

"Item: He says that the Blessed Sacrament is ordained by God to be received, but not to be worshipped."

"In faith," said your friend, "these things are far out of line."

"You see now," said I, "how he handles all the blessed sacraments. But, now, he has other wild heresies on the

[7] Johannes Oecolampadius (real name Huszgen) was a priest and scholar who served at first as cathedral preacher at Augsburg and entered the Bridgettine monastery in 1520 to avoid taking sides in the disputes centered on Luther; in 1522, however, he joined forces with the Reformers and went on to marry in 1528. He played a part in the dissemination of Reformation principles and argued controversially for increased participation by the laity in Church government (*Oxford Dictionary of the Christian Church*, 1182).

loose. For he teaches, against Scripture and all reason, that no Christian is or can be bound by any law made by human beings, nor is obliged to observe or keep any.

"Item: He teaches that there is no purgatory.

"Item: That all people's souls lie still and sleep till Judgment Day.

"Item: That no one should pray to saints, or attach importance to any sacred relics or shrines, or do any reverence to any images."

"By my word," said your friend, "I had forgotten—when I was at the university this last time, during the conversation that I had with my friends there on that subject, one of them made to me the objection that the veneration of images has been condemned before, by a great council in Greece."

"There was indeed," said I, "a council once convened in Greece, by an emperor who then was a heretic there; it was afterward, in the eighth synod, by the general council, condemned and nullified.[8] So this has no more bearing on the matter than if in Saxony and Switzerland and other such places, such people as have turned away from the faith would now gather themselves together and hold, as they would call it, a general council, wherein they could determine what they wished. All of that would not put in question the right belief of the Catholic Church, which is always that known people still persevering as one body with Christ our Savior in their previously firmly confirmed faith, from which faithful body these other, withering branches are blown away by the devil. And therefore, just as a council of Lutherans assembling themselves in Saxony could make no authority against the true faith of the Church, so also unable to prove its point was that council in Greece, which made no interruption of the right belief in, and godly custom of, veneration done to saints and images, which nevertheless, for all that, continued on in all of the Catholic church of Christ, and has ever since."

[8] The council was the Second Ecumenical Council of Nicaea, held in 787.

"Indeed," said he, "that is true."

"But yet," said he, "there was in our discussion someone versed in the law—we were, in fact, in his room. And he said that if he wanted, he could show a bona fide law, included in the decrees of the Church, which if laid in the view of those who would take upon themselves the defense of any veneration to be done to images, would make them all stare openmouthed. Then not only I, but all the rest also, wanted very badly to see that law. Which for a while he seemed rather reluctant to bring out, as if it was something being kept as a secret mystery.

"But finally he brought out a book of the decrees, and from it he did, honest to goodness, read to us a clear text (as it seemed to me and all those present) in which Saint Gregory [Pope Gregory III] is writing to a certain bishop who has broken down the statues in his church, and there Saint Gregory, although he berates him for breaking them, yet for all that commends him for not allowing them to be venerated."

"Did you," said I, "read that law yourself?"

"Honest to goodness," said he, "I stood close by and looked at the book while he read it."

"Did he," said I, "or you either, read the next law following in the book?"

"No, actually," said he, "for it seemed to me this was enough."

"So it was, actually," said I, "and too much, too, without more. But if you had read either the next law following or the gloss upon the selfsame law that you read, you would then have seen that the law which he showed you lends little support to his argument."

"By my word," said he, "as for the gloss, neither I nor any other man who was there ever cared to look at it, since the text was clear and easy to understand. And as for the law next following, we did not afterward look at it, for we thought we would find it contrary. And if we did, then we still would not have known which we should believe."

"Oh, yes," said I, "you would not have had much doubt about that if you had read the law that follows, for it is a synodal law, made during the sixth synod,[9] in which it is stated quite plainly that images are to be venerated among Christians, and which well clarifies in what way we venerate them and ought to: namely, no image is to be venerated as God is; nor is the hope of our health to be placed in the image; nor are we to expect that it is the image that shall judge our souls in time to come; but rather, we venerate the image, and reverence it, and well ought to, for the remembrance of the thing that the image represents. And, moreover, though we do the image honor and reverence, yet as for divine honor and homage done only to God—that kind of veneration called latria—this we neither do nor may do either to an image or to any creature in the whole entire world, either in heaven or on earth. And this you would have seen if you had read, as I say, either the law next following or the gloss on that law that you read."

"Fine," said he, "but in the law itself that we did read, good Saint Gregory clearly says the contrary. For he there commends the bishop because he would not allow the images to be venerated at all."

"That phrase 'at all,'" said I, "you more add in yourself than find in the book. For the book in fact says no more than that they should not be given the kind of veneration denoted by this Latin word *adorare*. By which word he understood the divine veneration called latria."

"How do we know," said he, "that he understood it in that way? For I do not much believe the gloss."

"You can," said I, "tell this from the law that follows. Wherein, albeit there is used the same word, *adorare*, there yet is explained how we may 'adorare'—that is to say, how we may 'worship'—images."

"Well," said he, "if that law says 'quod possumus adorare'

---

[9] A synod at Rome, held in 731.

406

[they may be adored] and Saint Gregory says 'quod non licet adorare' [they may not licitly be adored], are not the two plainly contradictory?"

"Yes," said I, "if in both cases that word 'adorare' was used in the same sense. But when the synod used that word for such veneration as we may give to a creature, and Saint Gregory uses it only for such veneration as may not be given except only to the Creator, then they are not at all contradictory."

"But yet," said he, "how can I be sure that Saint Gregory took it in that way? For it is obvious from the law, as you yourself say, that the word can be taken otherwise. For the very law itself takes it otherwise, and therefore perhaps so did he, and thereby forbade that any kind of reverence be done to images."

"That," said I, "would be very unlikely—that Saint Gregory was of one mind and the whole synod of the contrary. But, now, since you make the matter out to be so clear from the words of Saint Gregory incorporated in the decrees, and will not believe the gloss, which shows clearly that he meant only to forbid us to do such reverence to images as is due only to God, will you be willing here to believe Saint Gregory himself if he tells you himself that he meant nothing else?"

"Yes, before God," said he, "I should think so indeed."

"Then," said I, "we shall agree well enough." And with that I took down off a shelf, from among my books, the "register" of Saint Gregory's epistles, and therein turned to the very words which are by Gratian taken out of his second letter to Serenus, Bishop of Marseilles, and incorporated in the decrees. And then I had him read, word for word, the statements as they are couched in the decree. And by the comparison of the one with the other, I made him see that Gratian had taken but a part of the letter, and that from other statements in the letter itself it is evident that Saint Gregory was calling for a withholding of no other veneration from images except only divine veneration and observance due to God. This shows up clearly in several other things in the letter, such as where he says that it is not licit to worship anything wrought by hand, since it is written, 'Dominum Deum tuum adorabis et illi soli servies,' 'You shall adore your Lord God and him alone shall you serve.' Now, in this scriptural text is meant no other veneration or service than divine honor and the service called latria, as is well known to the learned. And whoever will affirm the contrary, and say that in Scripture is forbidden every kind of veneration of images, must affirm also that it is forbidden by Scripture to give any kind of veneration and any kind of service to any kind of creature. For Scripture says there, 'You shall venerate and serve God alone,' and so we should, according to that interpretation, neither venerate nor serve father or mother, teacher or prince or king. And in the same place Saint Gregory says that we do venerate only the Holy Trinity, which shows that he is speaking only of divine veneration, called latria, which is done with a mind that regards the object of the veneration as being truly God. For otherwise, if by those words he forbade the giving of any kind of veneration to any being except the Trinity, then he forbade the giving of any veneration to any saint, including our blessed Lady. And everyone well knows how reverently he himself venerated our Lady and all saints, as well from many books and letters of his as from the litany which, as his letters well show, he ordained to be used with great devotion in honor of God, our Lady, and all holy saints. And moreover, by the great honor that he did to saints in churches expressly dedicated to them, and also great honor and reverence shown to their holy relics, as appears in his own books and letters. And, finally, if there had been lost that letter of his out of which the decree is taken, the wording of the decree itself would yet have sufficed well enough. For therein it is stated that images are the books of laypeople, wherein they read the life of Christ. And so if it is, as it is indeed, a good and virtuous thing to kiss devoutly a book in which Christ's life and death are expressed by writing, then why should it be a bad thing to kiss reverently the images by which Christ's life and Passion are represented by sculpture or painting?"

"In all honesty," said he, "I am well satisfied on this matter, and so would be those who then were with me, if they had seen all that I see now."

"They can," said I, "easily see as much whenever they care to look for it. But now, to return to the subject, neither the bishop of Marseilles, who broke the statues that they speak of, nor the council in Greece either, schismatic as it was, ever went as far as do Luther and Tyndale and their company, who not only scorn images as worthless but also leave no saint unblasphemed, not even Christ's own mother. For Luther cannot abide the common anthem of our Lady, the most devout Salve Regina, because we therein call that blessed virgin our advocate.

"Item: He says that every other woman now living, if she has the same faith, can as rightly be prayed to as our Lady, and profit us as much with her prayer.

"Item: He teaches that people should give no veneration to the holy cross that Christ died on. He says that if he had it whole, or all the pieces of it, he would throw it in such a place as no sun should ever shine on it, to the end that it should never be found to be venerated more.

"Item: Of all feasts, he says that he hates the feast of the Holy Cross and the feast of Corpus Christi.

"He teaches also that no man or woman is obliged to keep and observe any vow they have made to God of virginity or widowhood or other chastity outside of marriage, but that they may marry as they please, their vow notwithstanding."

"And how does he prove that?" said your friend.

"Indeed," said I, "by the breaking of his own, when he married the nun. And now he rails against all celibacy, and says that if a priest lives celibate, he is like the priests of the idol Cybele.

"It would take a long time to write out for you all the abominable heresies of this new sect. But I have related some of them so that you can thereby consider whether he that teaches such things is not going about the utter destruction of the whole faith, religion, and virtue of Christendom. And that he is not in any of these points being slandered, I will find a way for you to see in his own books. There you will see how madly he endeavors to prove them."

"*Prove* them?" said your friend. "Most of these theses are too abominable to be discussed. And to make him hated by all good folk, it is enough to hear them related. But I really wonder how he fell into such a heap of heresies."

3.

The author shows by what occasion Luther first got into the devising of these heresies. And that the occasion was one that makes it quite evident that he was driven thereto by malice and just kept going from bad to worse, not knowing where to stop; and that he refuses to submit to the judgment of anyone on earth concerning the truth or falsehood of his opinions, except only himself.

"Now, that is," said I, "something worth considering—how this wicked friar began to put together these evil theses. You must understand that there was an indulgence service held in Saxony, for which service, in accord with the custom there, Luther was the preacher; and he preached to the people, encouraging them to participate in it, and supporting its legitimacy, all that he possibly could, not without great advantage to himself. Then, soon after, it so happened that the giving of the service, with the advantage thereof, was taken from him and assigned to someone else. For anger over which he fell into such a fury that forthwith he began to write against all grantings of indulgences. However, because the thesis was new and foreign, he began first by way of doubts and questions only, submitting himself and his writings to the judgment of the Pope, and requesting to be informed of the truth. Whereupon, when he was answered in writing by the master of the papal palace, he then grew more enraged and started ranting against him, and wrote also another book, against the power of the pope, affirming that his power over the Church was never instituted by God, but was established only by the joint agreement of Christian people, for the avoiding of schisms. But yet he said that all Christians were obliged to submit to it and obey the pope, and that the Bohemians were damnable heretics for doing the contrary. But soon after, when he was in such a way answered, by good and knowledgeable men, that he perceived himself unable to defend what he had affirmed, then he fell from reasoning into ranting, and utterly denied what he had before affirmed. And then began to write that the pope had no power at all, from either God or man. And that the Bohemians, whom in his previous writings he had called damnable heretics, were good Christians, and all their opinions good and Catholic. Then when he was summoned by the Pope to appear before him, he appealed to the next general council that should be convened under the influence of the Holy Spirit. So that whatever general council was afterward convoked, he could scoff at and rant about it, and say it was not the one that he appealed to, since it was not convoked under the influence of the Holy Spirit."

"He took," said your friend, "a good, wily way."

"As wily as it was," said I, "he yet would not stick to it, but fled from it to another. For now you shall understand that he even, soon after that, in the book by which he not answers but rails against that book wherein our sovereign lord the King, like a most faith-filled, virtuous, and most erudite prince, clearly and effectively disproved and confuted that most venomous and pestilent book of Luther's, entitled *The Babylonian Captivity,* in which he strives to destroy the holy sacraments of Christ's church—in that book, I say, Luther, who had previously appealed to the next general council, utterly denies the authority of all general councils and regards them all as of no account."

"By my word," said your friend, "the man was either very careless before or very no-account after, when he changes so often and writes always the longer the more contrary not to his adversary only, but also to himself. But I ask you, how does he defend his inconsistency?"

"Indeed," said I, "he says that he sees further than he saw before. In response to which the King's Grace tells him that it is unlikely that he should see better through a pair of bad spectacles, of ire and envy."

"Very true," said your friend, "by my word. But yet I hear it said that he offered to abide by the judgment of learned men on all his theses, and would have done so had his offer been accepted in time."

"Actually," said I, "he did once promise to abide by the judgment of the University of Paris, and thereupon were held public debates, and the exact words recorded by notaries sworn for both the parties. But when his opinions were afterward, in Paris, by the university, condemned, then he refused to abide by their judgment, and reverted to his old expedient of ranting.

"He also appeared at Worms, before the Emperor and the princes of the empire, with a safe-conduct. And there he admitted and acknowledged the said pestilent book written against the sacraments, as well as many others of a similar sort, to be his own, and offered to abide by them. Which he could confidently do, being given by the safe-conduct good security about himself, that he could suffer no harm. Then he was invited to engage in debates on his tenets, provided that he would agree upon some persons, virtuous and well-educated, who would be the judges of those debates, and that he would be willing to abide by their judgment upon the same. Whereupon he agreed to engage in debates, but he would in no way agree to make any living men judges of them, nor abide by the judgment of any man on earth."

Luther hilariously gives himself away

4.

The author shows how Luther, in the book that he himself wrote about his own deeds in the city of Worms in Germany, so madly forgets himself that he unwittingly discloses certain foolish things about himself that one will really laugh at and be very surprised to see.

"And that these things are true is well apparent to all the world in the book that he himself wrote about his demeanor and deeds in the city called Worms, in Germany. Whoever reads that book will get a big kick out of both seeing in it the insane vainglory of that foolish friar and also, together with that, seeing him yet get so far carried away from himself with foolishness that in a line or two he lets out all that he was attempting to hide in all the rest of the book. For you shall understand that although he wrote that book himself, he yet wrote it in such a way as to have it seem to be of some other man's authorship and not his own, to the intent that such worshipful words as he speaks about himself might in the ears of the reader make him seem some honorable person. Which words otherwise spoken by his own mouth, he well knows that all the world would wonder at. Now, in this book (besides the fact that he leaves out some things there said and spoken, where the words recorded could bring him no honor, and relates some things advantageous to his side, presenting the other side scantily and in bare-bones fashion, and even with some parts pared off, to make it seem the more tenuous), one thing he observes diligently: that, whereas when speaking of the Emperor he never calls him anything but simply and solely 'Charles,' he never speaks of himself without setting forth his name in big capital letters and with solemn titles—'The Man of God Luther.' And whereas about those who spoke against his errors, he writes that they burst out in virulent and venomous words, when he comes to his own answer he writes thusly: 'But then Father Martin, for his incredible humanity and kindness, answered in this benign way.' And sometimes with these words: 'The most benign Father most mildly made answer.' And, finally, he finishes and ends his book with, as it were, the Gloria Patri to the whole psalm: 'This holy, devout man, therefore, born precisely to teach and preserve the Gospel of God, may our Lord long preserve for his church with his holy word also. Amen.' Now, who was there ever gone so suspicious that they ever would have suspected that he who wrote such glorious words about Luther should be Luther himself? For where should one find so verily a vainglorious fool that would not within himself be ashamed of himself to think such things of himself? But, now"—you who read this—"I ask that you for God's sake see how utterly this itch and tickling of vanity and vainglory had cast him clean out of his mind and memory. For whereas all the rest of the book was contrived and manipulated in such a way as to have it seem written by someone else and not himself, suddenly the foolish fellow betrayed himself unawares. For in one place, forgetting himself, he speaks thusly: 'When this was spoken, then the Emperor's advocate, in a chiding manner, said that I had not answered to the purpose, and that those things which had been condemned and determined in general councils of old should not now, of new, be brought back into question by me, and therefore I should give a plain answer whether I would revoke my errors or not. Then to this I responded in this way: "Given that it is so. . . ."' Look, here you can see the incredible humility and lowly mind of this most benign Father, who under the guise of an unknown herald blows out himself his own boast. Then you can see, moreover, the marvelous, profound prudence of this man who did not have the sense to watch out that he not himself divulge his own so foolish device in the vain vaunting of his own false boast and praise, when even if the statements had been true, yet even an actual born fool would have been ashamed to write them."

"By my word," said your friend, "this device was madly

conceived by Luther, and madly handled, and madly forgotten about, for him to show himself so foolish, unless pride, as the proverb goes, must needs have a shame."

5.

The author shows the perpetual inconstancy of Luther, and his inconsistency and contradiction with himself.

"Now, as for his consistency," said I, "it shows up in what I have related before of his continual changing in his heresies from day to day, from worse to worse, which course he kept regarding not only the matters mentioned above, but also almost all the rest. For concerning purgatory, he wrote at first that although this could not be proved by conclusive Scripture (as he maintained), there yet was no doubt that there is a purgatory, and that thing, he said, was to be firmly believed by all Christians. And then he wrote that he marveled at the madness of such perfidious and foolish heretics as were born in the past one hundred years and are not ashamed to deny the existence of purgatory, which the whole church of Christ has believed in for these fifteen hundred years. Now, what consistency is there in this friar who wrote this about heretics who deny purgatory, and within a while after denies it himself, saying, in the sermon that he wrote about the rich man and Lazarus, that all people's souls lie still and sleep till Judgment Day?"

"Goodness," said your friend, "then some people will have a sleep of a fair length. They will, I think, when they awake forget some of their dreams."

"By my faith," said I, "anyone who believes Luther, that their soul will sleep that long, will, when they die, sleep in wretched rest."

"I very much wonder," said your friend, "what evil ailed him, for him to come up with this insane idiocy."

"Into this opinion," said I, "or rather, into the feigning of this opinion (for I truly think that he himself does not think as he writes), he fell because of the ill will and hatred that he bore to priesthood. Due to the malice of that ungodly attitude of his, he would be content that everyone lie in the fire of purgatory till Judgment Day rather than that any priest be given one penny to pray for any soul."

"This is," said your friend, "very likely."

"Like consistency," said I, "has he shown regarding the matter of religious vows. For in his book *The Babylonian Captivity* he writes that neither human being nor angel is able to dispense with the vow made by a human being to God. And soon after, he wrote that no vow could bind anyone, but that everyone may boldly break theirs, of their own volition. But it is quite obvious that he wrote the first out of anger and malice toward the Pope, and then changed to the second out of a lecherous lust toward the nun that he intended to marry."

6.

The author shows how Luther has been forced, for the defense of his indefensible errors, to renounce and forsake the whole procedure of examining and proving which he initially promised to adhere to. And how, like a man shameful and shameless, he now has no proof in the world but his own word, and calls that the word of God.

"His inconsistent mind and really diabolical intent specially showed itself also by this, that I shall now relate to you. In the beginning the man had the mentality that commonly such fools have: he considered all the world wild geese except himself, and all the intelligence and learning to reside in his own head. And then, thinking that he would find no match, but that he would as he pleased be able to prove the moon made of green cheese, he professed in his books that he would for the proof or disproof of his opinions submit to natural reason, to the authority of the old holy Fathers, to the laws and canons of Christ's church, and to the holy Scripture of God, with the interpretations of the old holy theologians. But soon after, when he perceived himself mistaken in his opinion, and saw himself conclusively confuted and confounded by Scripture, natural reason, the laws and determinations of the Church, and the unanimous agreement of the holy Fathers, interpreters of Scripture, then he began to sing another song. For then, as for reason, he refused to submit to it, saying that the matters of our faith are things beyond reason, and that reason hinders us in our faith, and is to faith an enemy. And as for the laws of the Church, he, with other blasphemous heretics, publicly burned them at Wittenberg, singing in derision a dirge around the fire for the law's soul. And then he would submit to nothing but Scripture alone—and not to that, either, unless it was very clear and obvious. But, now, if it was in question whether Scripture was clearly for him or against him, there he would submit to no one's judgment but his own. For as for the whole faith of Christ's church, continued for so many hundreds of years, he set it utterly at naught, calling it men's inventions. And as for the scriptural interpretations given by Saint Jerome, Saint Augustine, Saint Ambrose, and all the old holy Fathers of so many years past, he would hold them in no esteem at all, but (with blasphemous words) did not forbear to write, 'I do not care about Augustine, I do not care about a hundred Cyprians, I do not care about a thousand Jeromes, I do not care about anything but Scripture alone; and it is clearly on my side.' As though none of these ancient, holy, intelligent men had understood any scripture till he came. And now he was, by this irrational mode of proceeding, driven to another diabolical scheme, against saints. For to the intent that their authority should not, through the devotion and reverence that all good people bore them, diminish his credibility, he was forced to strive to bring people into that heresy whereby they would pray to no saints, but would have their statues pulled down, all their shrines done away with, all their relics thrown out, all their honor and people's devotion toward them withdrawn. It went so far that he could not abide even the honoring of our blessed

Lady, or of the Holy Cross, or of Christ's blessed Body, as his
abominable books plainly declare."

7.

*The author tells what things caused people to fall into Luther's
foolish and absurd sect. And he mentions also what harm the
followers of that sect have done in Germany, Lombardy, and
Rome.*

"It is," said your friend, "a wonder to me that the people,
being before brought up in the right belief, could find it in
their hearts to give him a hearing about any such heresies as
these are."

"You must understand and can perceive," said I, "that he
did not set forth all of them at once. Instead—just as Tyndale
has begun here in England with something that looked good
on the surface, though he had corrupted it and meant badly
indeed, putting forth first the New Testament manipulated
in such a way that unlearned folk were likely to take harm
and conceive sundry heresies in their hearts before they
could perceive his dishonesty, and then after that, by way of
two other books, openly showing himself to fall short of
Luther in nothing except that he has not yet married a
nun—so also did Luther put forth in the beginning nothing
more than the thesis about indulgences, as I told you; and
there he did not affirm anything against the determination of
the Church, but submitted himself thereto. Now, with this
demeanor there was no one offended. But yet he did, at that
time, intend a further mischief, which he little by little pur-
sued and brought to pass. And one particular thing with
which he spiced all the poison was the liberty that he so
highly commended to the people, bringing them into the
belief that having faith, they needed nothing else. For as for
fasting, prayer, and other such things, he taught them to
abandon and disdain them as vain and unfruitful rituals, and
also taught them that, being faith-filled Christians, they are
so near of kin to Christ that they are in a full freedom and

liberty discharged of all governors and any kind of law, spiritual or temporal, except the Gospel only. And although he says that of a special perfection it would be a good thing to do to submit to and bear the rule and authority of popes, princes, and other governors (which rule and authority he calls but tyranny), he yet says that the people are so free, on account of faith, that they are no more obliged to do that than they are to submit to injustice. And this doctrine Tyndale also teaches, as the specific theme of his holy book on disobedience. Now, in Germany this doctrine sounded so good to the common, rustic people that it blinded them in the looking at the rest and could not permit them to reflect and see to what end the same would ultimately come. The temporal lords were glad also to hear this stuff against the clergy, and the people as glad to hear it against the clergy and against the lords too, and against all their governors of every good town and city. And finally it escalated to the point where at last it began to break out and turn into open force and violence. For, intending to begin with the weakest, there gathered themselves together for the propagating of these wicked heresies a rowdy company of that unhappy sect, and first rebelled against an abbot, and afterward against a bishop. The temporal lords made a game and a sport of all this, and looked the other way, longing for the lands of the clergy till they had acted almost like the dog Aesop tells of, who, to snatch at the shadow of the cheese in the water, let fall and lost the cheese that he carried in his mouth. For so it was that shortly after those rustic Lutherans became so bold and began to grow so strong, they also set upon the temporal lords. Who, had they not set hand thereto the sooner, would have while looking for other men's lands been likely shortly to lose their own. But they so acquitted themselves that they slew nearly seventy thousand Lutherans in one summer and subdued the rest in that part of Germany into a right miserable servitude. However, in the meanwhile many criminal deeds they did.

"And furthermore, in several other parts of Germany and Switzerland this ungodly sect, through the negligence of the governors in big cities, has grown to the point where finally the common people have compelled the rulers to follow them, whom if they had taken heed in time, they could have ruled and led.

"And now it is too piteous a sight, to see the pitiless indignities done there, in many places, to God and all good people, with the astonishing change from all appearance and semblance of Christendom into a truly tyrannous persecution, not only of all good Christian people, alive and dead, but even of Christ himself. For there shall you see now the splendid monasteries destroyed, the places burned up, the religious put out and sent to seek their means of subsistence—or, in many cities, the places still standing, with more insult done to God than if they were burned up to ashes. For the religious—monks, friars, and nuns—are clean drawn and driven out, except those who would agree to forsake their vows of chastity and get married, and the places dedicated to cleanness and chastity left only to these apostates and prostitutes, for them to live there in lechery.

"Now, the parish churches, in many places not only are they defaced, all the furnishings taken out, the holy images pulled down and either broken or burned, but also the Blessed Sacrament is thrown out, and the abominable beasts (which horrifies me to think about) do not find it horrifying to contemptuously defecate in the pyxes, and, in many places, to use continually the churches as public conveniences. And in such a contemptuous way that when a stranger from some other place, where Christ is worshipped, visits these cities, some of those unhappy, wretched citizens do not fail, for courtesy and kindness, as it were, to accompany them in walking about to show them the sights and attractions of the town, and then bring them to practically no place except the churches, to show them in derision what uses the churches serve for.

"Also of this sect were the great majority of those ungodly people who recently entered into Rome with the Duke of Bourbon. They not only robbed and plundered the city (their own friends, as well as the opposite side), but, like veritable beasts, also violated the wives in the sight of their husbands, and slew the children in the sight of the parents. And, to extort the bringing out of more money, when the men had already brought out absolutely all they had in order to save themselves from death or further pain, and were negotiating pacts and promises of peace without further disturbance, then the wretched tyrants and cruel tormentors, as though all of that counted for nothing, did not desist from putting them from time to time to intolerable tortures. And old, ancient, honorable men those savage heretics did not hesitate to hang up by the private parts, and from many they pulled them off and flung them in the street. And some would be brought out naked, each with his hands bound behind him and a cord tied fast to his member. Then there would be set in front of them, in their way, others of those tyrants with their barbarous pikes, the points toward the breasts of these poor naked men And then one or two of those wretches would stand behind those barbarous pikes and pull the poor souls by the member toward them. Now, then, their whole cruel sport, what made them laugh, was to see the helpless naked men either, in shrinking from the pikes, tear off their members, or else, for pain of the pulling, run their naked bodies in deep upon the pikes.

"Too distressing and too disgusting would it be to relate the villainous pain and tortures that they came up with for the helpless women, by whom, after they had bestially abused them (wives in the sight of their husbands, and the maidens in the sight of their fathers), those were considered merciful who did no more than cut their throats. And very certain it is that not in Rome only, but also in the area of Milan that they occupied and oppressed, it sometimes happened that, after tortures being inflicted and money obtained in that way, then someone claiming to be a German or Spanish nobleman would claim to have fallen in love with his host's daughter, say that he would marry her in any event, and then make very earnest efforts to get some money along with her. And whether he got something or got nothing by that ruse, he did not forbear to put, soon after, the father, the mother, the lovely daughter, and the whole entire household to new tortures, to make them tell where any more money was, whether or not there was any. And some did not fail to take the child and bind it to a spit and lay it to the fire to roast, the father and mother looking on. And then begin to talk about a price for the sparing of the child, asking first a hundred ducats, then fifty, then forty, then twenty, then ten, then five, then two, when the poor father had not one left, but these tyrants had them all already. Then would they let the child roast to death. And on top of that, they would in derision, as though they pitied the child, say to the father and the mother, 'Ah, tut-tut, shame on you! What wonder is it if God sends a vengeance among you? What unnatural people you are, who can find it in your hearts to see your own child roasted in front of your face, rather than part with one ducat to deliver it from death.'

"Thus devised these accursed wretches so many different kinds of exquisite cruelties that I think they have taught the devil new torments in hell, that he never knew before, and he will not fail to prove himself a good pupil and surely render them his lesson when they get there—where it is to be feared that many of them are by now. For soon after they had exercised for a while this savage and cruel tyranny in Rome (entering into the holy churches, plundering the holy relics, throwing out the Blessed Sacrament, pulling the chalice from the altar during Mass, killing priests in the church, leaving no kind of cruelty or outrage undone, but from hour to hour staining their hands with blood, and in a way that would have aroused pity or horror in any Turk or Saracen)—

our Lord sent, soon after, such a pestilence among them that he left of them not one-third alive. It is for this purpose that I relate to you this oppressive, wicked behavior of theirs: so that you can perceive by their deeds what good comes of their sect. For as our Savior says, you shall know the tree by the fruit [Mt 7: 16–20]."

8.

The messenger says that the malicious conduct of individuals is not to be imputed to the sect itself, since some in every sect are bad. And the author shows that in the case of the Lutherans, the sect itself is the cause of the malicious conduct that the members engage in.

"Sir," said your friend, "in all sincerity, I neither can nor wish to defend that sect. But yet reason does dictate that one take everything as it is. And if it is bad, it has the less need to be made worse. But as for the malicious, cruel behavior of men of war, that is not, in my opinion, to be imputed to the sect of Luther. For there is no sect so saintly as not to go in for cruelty when they go to war. And, too, some in every sect are bad. And therefore the malicious conduct of those men is not, as it seems to me, to be imputed to the sect."

"It is not," said I, "one and the same thing to be some bad and to be all bad. Those who come into this sect become bad, the whole lot of them. For right away, when this sect started out, the whole flock of such as were infected with it started perpetrating those wicked deeds that I mentioned to you before. And also, though men in war do get savage and cruel, yet never before were there any who went so far there, and especially in such kinds of cruelty as have been, among Christian men in their warfare, always stayed away from, such as the outrages done to the Blessed Sacrament, wherein these beasts were more hot and more busy than would have been the great Turk—and this because their sect is, in a way, even worse than his. Moreover, the unhappy deeds of that

423

sect must needs be imputed to the sect itself, when the doctrine thereof teaches and gives rise to their evil deeds. A Christian man's evil conduct cannot be imputed to his Christianity. For that conduct is contrary to the doctrine and conduct of Christ. But as for the doctrine of this unhappy sect, and the behavior, also, of the beginners of the same, they are such that, as every sensible person well perceives, do teach and give rise to their evil deeds. For what good deed will someone study or strive to do who believes Luther that he has no free will of his own by which he can, with the help of grace, either work or pray? Will he not say to himself that he can sit still and leave God alone? What evil will they care to forbear who believe Luther that God alone, without their will, works all the iniquity that they do themselves? What will he care how long he lives in sin, who believes Luther that he will after this life feel neither well nor ill in body or soul till Judgment Day? Will he not, don't you suppose, bear out what the Welshman said? 'If you give him till that day to pay, by God Davy will have your coat too.' And I say this only by way of illustration. For look his opinions through, and you will find that they plainly direct everyone to wretched living. If they should say that we misconstrue their words, their books are out there and the words plain, and inculcated again and again, so often and so clearly that we cannot mistake them, nor can they by any cloak or pretext defend them.

"And besides that, not only do the rank-and-file members of their sect show the effect and fruit of their doctrine by their abominable behavior, as I have related to you, but also the theologians and archheretics themselves well manifest the holiness of their doctrine by their own conduct. For as they live they teach, and as they teach they live."

9.

The author asserts that it is a great sign that the world is nearly at an end when we see people so far fallen from God that they can stand it to be accepting of this pestilent, insane sect which no people, Christian or heathen, could have tolerated before our day.

"If the world were not nearly at an end, and the fervor of devotion so badly cooled as to be almost quenched among Christian people, it could never have come to pass that so many people should fall to the following of such a beastly sect. For albeit that the Muhammadans, being a sensual and filthy sect, did in a few years draw the great part of the world into it by the selfsame ways which now the Lutherans use—namely, voluptuous living and violence, offering delight to the accepters and death to the refusers—yet there was before this abominable sect never any sect so shameless that its members would keep avowing themselves for Christian folk granting Scripture to be true, and, along with that, so inimically blaspheme and oppugn the church of Christ, the sacraments of Christ, the saints of Christ, the cross of Christ, the mother of Christ, and the holy Body of Christ, so shamefully living and openly professing a bestial manner of life completely contrary to the doctrine and life of Christ. The Arians, the Pelagians, the Manichaeans, and so forth— every band of heretics—began with individuals who, though they wickedly erred in substantial articles of the faith, were nevertheless such that their external fashion of living was so honorable and spiritual in appearance that people felt obliged the better to believe their doctrine was Christian, on account of some spiritual appearance and manner of their Christian living. But now the chieftains of these execrable heresies both teach and practice more sensual and licentious living than ever did Muhammad. Who, though he licenses men to have many wives, yet never taught or allowed his followers to break their chastity promised once and solemnly dedicated to God. Whereas Luther not only directs monks, friars, and nuns to get married, but also, himself being a friar, has married a nun himself and is living with her, under the name of wedlock, in open, incestuous lechery, without anxiety or shame, because he has procured and begotten so many shameful and shameless companions.

"Who could have endured to look in the face any man who should have done thus in Saint Jerome's and Saint Augustine's days? And why speak of Saint Jerome and Saint Augustine? Who was so shameless as to dare do it at any time since Christ's birth, until our wretched day? Or who since Adam's time, among the chosen people of God? And why speak of the chosen people of God? The very pagans and heathens—idolaters—kept their celibacy once it was vowed to their false gods, and chose rather to cut off the members with which they could break it than to stand in jeopardy of breaking it. And in ancient Rome, when the people were pagans, if any vestal virgin (for so they called their nuns) was violated, they not only beat the man to death with rods in the marketplace, and buried the woman alive, but also regarded it as an astonishing aberration and a portent of wrath and indignation of their gods toward their city and empire, and consequently did what they could, with public processions and prayers and sacrifice, to procure the recovery of their gods' favor. So is it not now an astonishing thing to see—given that the celibacy promised once and for all to God, and also to the false idols under the name of God, has always, since the world began, been so highly esteemed, among Christians and heathens, that the breakers thereof have always been, by the common agreement of the whole world, as a thing taught by God to good people and by nature to all people, taken, regarded, and punished as abominable, wicked wretches—is it not, I say, now an astonishing thing to see that in the flock of Christian people, given that by Christ himself, by all his apostles, by all his holy martyrs, confessors, and theologians, by his whole entire church, the whole entire time of these past fifteen hundred years, celibacy has been more highly praised and esteemed than ever it was by any other sect since the world began, we should see now a lewd friar be so bold and so shameless as to marry a nun and stick by this, and still be taken for a Christian man, and, moreover, for a man fit to be the beginner of a sect, whom any honorable man should deign to follow? If our Lord God, whose wisdom is infinite, should have sat and studied to devise a way whereby he might cast in our faces the confusion of our folly, what more effective one could he have found for clearly showing us the shame of our sin than that of allowing us who call ourselves Christian folk to see spring up among us such a rabble as, professing the faith and religion of Christ, do not hesitate to dismiss as worthless all the theologians of Christ's church and rely solely on the authority of Friar Tuck and Mad Marian?"

10.

The author inveighs against this detestable article of this ungodly sect whereby they take away the liberty of people's free will and ascribe everything to destiny.

"Surely, as I say, this world is either, as Saint John puts it, 'totus positus in maligno,' 'all set in malice' [1 Jn 5: 19], that we are so prone to take knowingly so wrong a way, or else it is in an amazing blindness, if we neither can tell from the wicked behavior of the persons that their sect is wicked nor can tell from their doctrine that their sect must make their persons wicked, their heresies being such as you have heard. Whereby anyone who has any faith and any kind of knowledge of Christian belief can quite certainly tell that Luther and all his offspring, with all those who promote and propagate his sect, are very agents of the devil and open enemies to the faith of Christ. And not only to the faith and humanity of Christ our Savior, but also against the Holy Spirit and the Father himself, and utterly against all goodness of the Godhead, in that they wretchedly lay all the weight and blame of our sin to the necessity and constraint of God's ordinance, affirming that we do no sin of ourselves, by any power of our own will, but do it by the compulsion and handiwork of God. And that we do not do the sin ourselves, but that God does the sin in us himself. And thus these wretched heretics, with this blasphemous heresy alone, cast a more scurrilous aspersion on the great majesty of God than ever any one scoundrel cast on another. For who was there ever that blamed all the particular evil deeds of any one man on another, whereas these scoundrels lay to the charge and blame of God all the malice and mischief, from the first misdeed to the last, that ever was wrought or thought by man, woman, or devil. And by this they give wretches great boldness to follow their foul inclinations, as things, according to their opinion, more truly wrought in them by God than the best dispositions are in good people. And that it would therefore be in vain for them to resist their sinful desires. And if they shall be damned, they say it shall yet be long before they feel it. For Luther says that all souls shall sleep and feel nothing, either good or bad, after this life, till Judgment Day. And then they that shall be damned shall be damned, he says, for no deserving by their own deeds, but for such evil deeds as God alone forced and coerced them into and wrought in them himself, using them, in all those evil deeds, only as a passive instrument, as a man hews with a hatchet. And that God shall damn all that shall be damned for his own deeds only, which he himself shall have done in them; and ultimately only for his pleasure, because it was not his pleasure to choose them as he did his chosen people. Whom they say he chose in such a way, before the beginning of the world, that they can never sin."

11.

The messenger says that no matter how Luther and his followers in Germany believe, he yet cannot think that the Lutherans in England, some of whom, he says, have seemed good and honorable, are so mad and unhappy as to believe that everything hangs upon destiny. Whereupon the author states the contrary, and that they are in fact wicked, no matter how good they may seem. And for proof that, regardless of what words they may use to camouflage this, they mean that everything depends solely on destiny, he relates a certain discussion held with a heretic who was reported to the bishop and tried, the author being present, during which discussion the heretic, who was an educated man and a preacher, made many efforts to make it seem that in his evil words he meant but well.

When your friend had heard all this, he said at last that albeit the words of Luther seemed very plainly to go toward the affirming of such opinions, yet the things were so far out of line that it gave him cause to suspect that Luther did not mean them all in as bad a way as his words seem to indicate. And if he did so mean them himself, with others of his flock and kindred in Germany, yet your friend thought that those who favor and follow his sect here in England, some of whom seem quite honorable and far from his manner of living, do not so take his words, or understand them that way, but construe them to some better sense."

"Actually," said I, "they cannot be unaware of his open living in lechery with his lewd lover the nun. And of the fact that all the captains of that company—some formerly Carthusians, some Observants, some of other religious orders, and all now apostate and wedded—live in like manner and direct others to do the same. And on account of this they cannot doubt that their doctrine is bad, unless they themselves accept that way as good. Now, as for their own goodness, you find few that fall into that sect who do not soon after fall into contempt of prayer and fasting and of all good works, under the name of 'rituals.' And if any do otherwise, it is for some intention of blinding the people and keeping themselves in favor for the time being, till they can in the course of time find the opportunity to fashion and frame better to their purpose those who, if they in the beginning showed themselves plainly to, could perhaps not abide to hear them. Whose attitude, and that in these heresies they mean here no better than Luther does himself, I have good knowledge of from experience, and among other things, this that I shall relate to you.

"I recently happened to be present when someone thoroughly versed in the Lutheran books—and, to be honest, unversed neither in holy Scripture nor in secular literature (as I can tell not only from the testimony of other men and the degrees that he had earned at the university, but also from his statements and his writings)—was examined in the presence of quite distinguished, virtuous, and very astute persons. For he was at that time in custody for heresy, because, being educated, and frequently engaged in hearing confessions, and, among many folk, fairly well approved of in his preaching, and thereby growing in good opinion and favor of many good, simple people, he abused all these open and apparent good things to the secret sowing and setting forth of Luther's heresies. And had to that intent not only taught and written, and covertly corrupted several shallow and ignorant persons, but also had bought a great number of the books of Luther, and of Wycliffe, Huss, and Zwingli, and such other heretics, and of many a one book several copies, to be delivered, as he could find occasion, to young undergraduates of the universities—such as he thought, on account of their youth and ignorance, most likely to be easily corrupted. This man, I say, being examined and long keeping himself guarded against any disclosing of the matter, and more ready to go straight to the devil with lying and false forswearing than to have his bad behavior known and confess the truth, at last perceiving the matters (partly by the acknowledgement of other folk, partly by his own handwriting) so much come to light that they could in no way be cloaked, then began somewhat plainly to confess and state not only what he had done for the propagating of that sect, but also, partly, what opinions he and others, his cohorts, had held and were of. Alleging, nevertheless, all the pretexts he could to make it seem that even if the statements which they spoke or wrote were foreign and contrary to right belief, yet the gist of their meaning was not much discrepant from the true faith of Christ's church. However, when he was presented with challenges about that, and saw that he could not so evade them but that, for any pretext he could find, one part of his story always contradicted another, at last he plainly stated their opinions, and brought up, as being on the side of his own defense, as things inducing him thereto, all the texts of Scripture by which they profess to prove their opinions correct. Among which opinions, when he came to the opinion by which they hold that faith alone, by itself, is sufficient, without good works, about this he said in the beginning that by it they meant nothing else than that people should put their faith in God's promises and hope to be saved thereby, and that they should not put their trust in their works, for that would turn them to pride.

"Then it was answered him that he and his cohorts could not mean that. For if they did, then they could not blame the Church as they do, making as though the Church had all this while hidden the true faith from the people, and that they themselves were now being reviled for preaching the Gospel accurately. For if this were their meaning, then they would mean nothing other than what every common preacher of the Church has always preached before Luther's days. For what preacher has not told the people the parable of the poor publican ashamed of his sins, and of the proud Pharisee boasting of his virtues? [See Lk 18:9–14.] Who has not bidden them to do right and, albeit that God will reward them for their good deeds, yet put their trust not in themselves and their own deeds, but in God's goodness? Who has not told them that they should do as God bids them in the Gospel— when they have done all they can do, yet say to themselves, 'We are but unprofitable servants, we have done but our duty'? [See Lk 17:10.] These things and such others the Church has always taught against the putting of a proud trust in our own deeds, because we cannot always accurately judge our own deeds, on account of the blind favor that we bear toward ourselves. And therefore it was said to him, 'If you meant only this, what the Church means, then you would preach only what the Church preaches, and not blaspheme the Church in your sermons, as though you began true preaching of the Gospel, and the Church had up to now preached falsely. And also you must necessarily mean some other thing, since Luther, whose sect you admit to having sided with, writes on this matter far otherwise. For he says straight-out that faith alone, without any good works, does justify us and suffice for our salvation.

"Then he answered that there they meant nothing other than that faith is sufficient alone if someone happens, after he receives faith and Baptism, to die before he has time to do any good works. Then it was said to him that if they should teach this opinion, in such words, as a great, secret mystery newly revealed, and on that basis castigate the Church for misteaching the people, as though the Church taught them to put less trust in God and in faith in Christ than they should, and induced them to put their trust in themselves and their own good works, they then would be conducting themselves in an astonishing way, considering that if they mean nothing other than that, then the Church and they mean entirely the same thing. But they cannot mean that. For then why should they castigate the Church, which does not say the contrary? And also, if they meant no other thing, few words would serve them. They would not need to speak of it so often. For that information can do little good here or anywhere else where folk are christened in their cradles. For either they die before they have time to do good works, and then they are too young to hear that sermon, or else they live and have time to do good works, and then that sermon will not be wholesome for them, that good works are unnecessary and faith suffices by itself, without them. 'And when the people take it as you say it, that faith alone is enough for them, then it is now a transparent cover-up for you to say that you meant not that, but only that faith alone would have been enough for them if they had died in their swaddling clothes.'

"To this he said that they thought also that faith alone, without any good works, does justify a person not only in childhood but at any age. For whenever someone who has been a sinner does repent and amend in his mind with a full faith in the promises of God, he is justified before he ever does any of these good works—almsgiving, fasting, or whatever. For one cannot work well till one is good already. For as Christ says, 'Arbor mala non potest bonum fructum facere,' 'A bad tree cannot bring forth good fruit' [Mt 7:18], and therefore, since good works are good fruits, a bad person cannot work them. Whereby it becomes quite obvious that the person is justified before, by his faith alone, without the works, and then out of that faith grows the good fruit of good works. But faith did justify the person before, and the person was as good before the works as he is after. For his faith did justify him. And as for the works, they are but things that the faith within the person, or the person by the faith, brings forth as the tree brings forth its leaves and cannot do otherwise—faith being in the heart.

"Then it was said to him that in this account he seemed to make the good works to be much like a shadow that the body makes of necessity when it stands in the sun, and is never the better for. And then it was asked him whether one must not, in order for his faith to do him any good, have with it charity and an intention to do good works. 'Yes,' said he, 'that he must, if he is old enough and has enough reasoning capacity.' Then it was answered him that then was all gone what he himself had said before. For then faith alone did not justify the person, but the charity with the intention of good works must, by his own admission, necessarily go with it, or else his faith would justify nothing at all. For if he had no matter how great a faith and no matter how sure a belief in God's promises, yet if he intended to do no good deeds therewith, but perhaps harm, he should have little justification by his faith alone. And therefore it was false, what he had said—that one is no better off for one's good works—when one's good works are so taken and regarded by God that the intending of them, when they are as yet undone, so much works to one's justification that without that intention one cannot be justified. And that other thing he said is also false—that faith alone justifies a person— when he himself is forced to grant that faith without charity and intention of good works cannot justify, which is as much as to say that faith alone cannot justify.

"To this he answered that he had said that faith alone was sufficient, and that faith alone does justify, because if someone had faith, it could not be but that they would work good works. For faith, he said, could never be idle, just as fire must needs burn and give heat. And therefore, just as one may say 'The fire is enough to burn a tree' even though one makes no mention of heat and yet the fire does it by heat, and one may say 'The fire makes me see by night' and yet the fire does it only by the light, so may one say that faith does save us, even though faith does not do it without hope and charity and other virtuous works, because faith always has good hope and charity with it and cannot but work well, any more than the fire could be without heat and light and burn all combustible things that it can reach and remain with.

"Then it was said to him that albeit one might so speak about the fire, yet this thing would not serve their sect. For someone who says fire alone is enough to burn would not disagree with someone who would say the fire could not burn unless it had heat. 'But your sect scorns and castigates the Church because the Church says that faith will not suffice unless it has charity and good works. For else you had no cause in this matter to preach contrary to the Church. Moreover, whereas you say that faith always has good hope with it, that seems not always true. For those who hope that by faith alone they shall be saved without any good works (which is what Lutherans do indeed believe) have a bad hope, and a condemnable one.

" 'Now, whereas you say that you preach faith alone to be sufficient because faith always has charity joined with it—if this is true, why do you not preach as well that charity alone is sufficient, which is as close to the truth as the other?

" 'Now, whereas you base everything on this, that faith always has charity with it, and that it cannot be but that charity (which is actually the thing that specially brings forth good works, much more properly than faith, for faith brings them forth by charity when it is joined therewith, as the Apostle says: "Fides que per dilectionem operatur," "Faith works by charity" [Gal 5: 6])—whereas you say it cannot be but that this charity is always joined to faith, this ground will fail you and make your foundation faulty and all your building fall. The apostle Paul, in many passages of his Epistles, says the contrary thereof. For he says [1 Cor 12: 2–3] that if someone were to have so great a faith that he could by the force of his faith work miracles, and also such a fervent devotedness to the faith that he would give his body to the fire for the defense thereof, yet if he lacked charity, all his faith did not suffice.' "

"In all honesty," said your friend, "he was answered quite admirably. But yet it seems to me he could have said a little something back, in reply to those statements of Saint Paul's, and could well have gotten around them with other statements of his. For where he writes also, to the Galatians [1: 8], that if any angel were to come down from heaven and preach a gospel contrary to the one already being preached, accursed should that angel be, and not believed, he did not in these words affirm, nor did he mean by them, that ever it would be the case, or could be, that any angel would actually do that. For he knew very well that it was impossible that any angel of heaven should come down and say something false. No, he was saying it only by a manner of speaking which is among learned men called 'hyperbole,' for the more forceful making of a point, meaning nothing else but that the gospel which he had preached was the plain, sure, undoubtable truth, against which no one was to be believed. And by the same token, it seems to me, the man whom you speak of could have said that though Saint Paul did say that even if he had so great a faith as to be able to move mountains by it, unless he also had charity it would not serve him, he there meant nothing more than to show the great need there is for having charity, and not that it is possible for faith to exist without charity, any more than he meant that an angel could come down from heaven to preach a false faith. And therefore it still could be quite consistent with the statements of Saint Paul to affirm that faith cannot fail of salvation since it cannot fail of charity. And in all honesty it seems to me that, as that man said, faith cannot be idle but must necessarily work well."

"Actually," said I, "the man fell short of you there, for he did not come up with that gloss. Which, even if he had, would yet not have served him. For between those two texts from Saint Paul there is a big difference. For in the one there is an impossible overstatement and hyperbole, and in the other there is not. For angels of heaven never can come down and teach a false faith. But faith can be severed from charity. And in the one text he intended nothing other than, as you say, to show by that extreme, out-of-bounds statement the undoubtable truth of the faith which he himself had preached. But in the other text his precise purpose was to teach the Corinthians that they should not trust that any gift of nature, or gift of God above nature, or any kind of virtue—almsgiving, faith, or any other—would be able to stand them in good stead without charity. And this he did precisely because he wanted no one to be in such error as to reckon that either excellent intellectual gifts, great labor spent in preaching, great alms spent on poor people, or a very fervent faith could suffice to their salvation if charity was lacking. Against which error he does in such a way ex-

hort them to charity, in avoiding the rancor which by occasion of schisms did arise among them, that he literally *showed*
them that without charity they lost completely the merit of
all their other virtues and graces that God had given them
(intelligence, almsgiving, faith, and all). He showed it by
using for his example his own self, saying that even though
he was a chosen servant and apostle, and even if he were
linguistically on a par with everyone in the whole world and
with angels too, and had all the knowledge that could possibly be had, and the spirit of all prophecy as well, and would
give away all his goods in alms, and had also the whole, full
faith, so greatly that it sufficed to work wonders with, and so
fervently that he would endure being burned for it, yet if he
lacked charity, all this would not serve him.

"So you can see now that your gloss would not have
helped this man. For though no angel could come down and
teach an untruth, and therefore the words that you quote
cannot be otherwise taken than, as you say, to express by way
of overstatement and hyperbole the strength of his conviction on the matter of faith which he was then speaking of,
yet this other text of Saint Paul's, that was brought up against
this heretic that I speak of, as big and strong as the words are,
they yet do plainly prove that the Apostle is saying that faith
can exist without charity—a faith so great that it can suffice
for the doing of great wonders, and so fervent that it can
endure a painful death, and yet, for lack of charity, not sufficient for salvation—and that this can happen as well with
faith as with almsgiving, which the Apostle puts in the same
position. And therefore, whereas that man said, and you
seem to confirm the same, that faith cannot be idle from the
working of good works, the Apostle, to show the contrary,
and that all the works of faith, however good they may seem,
are yet actually bad if they are not wrought with charity,
commends only the faith that works by charity, implying
that all other works of faith are not efficacious. And certainly
faith alone, without charity, can be besides this not only idle,

without the busyness of good works, but also, for lack of good works, it can be utterly dead. And therefore, as was brought up there against that man, the holy apostle James says to those who reckon faith sufficient for salvation without good works, that they are worse than devils [James 2: 18–26]. For he says that the devils do believe, and tremble for fear of God, and that people who by the hope and boldness of their belief think their faith without good works sufficient are worse than devils because they have no fear of God, who threatens them with their suffering the pains of hell unless they do good works. Without which, Saint James for a final conclusion says, the faith is but dead.

"But here it was also said to him, yet again, that though Saint James does say that faith without good works is dead, he should not on that account run to his old gloss and say that therefore he and other Lutherans meant that faith suffices for salvation because they think it cannot be but that it will necessarily bring forth good works, and that therefore, on the contrary side, anyone who has no works has no faith, since a dead faith is no faith, just as a dead man is no man. It was told him that this gloss would not serve him. For Saint James did not mean that the faith that he calls dead for lack of good works is no faith, any more than Saint Paul meant that a widow living in delight and pleasure is no woman, though he said that she is dead even while she goes around alive [1 Tm 5: 6]. No, Saint James meant only that such faith will not benefit them. For Saint James does not deny that such a dead faith as he calls dead because it is unprofitable is yet a real faith indeed, though it is not alive in good works. And thus he likens such a faith that is in a human being to the unprofitable faith that is in a devil. For he says that where such a person presumes upon his faith, the devil has faith as well as that person has it, for the devil does believe the things that we believe.

"To this the man answered that some quite well-educated men were of the opinion that if someone went without working good works, it was a good indication that he had no faith at all, for real faith could not but work; and that the devil had no faith except by an equivocal use of the word. For the real faith is indeed a faith in the promises of God. And the devil is in despair and does not have, nor can have, faith and trust in God's promises.

"Then it was answered him that those 'quite well-educated men' were Luther and Tyndale and their cohorts, who take themselves for better educated than Christ's blessed apostles Saint Paul and Saint James, who in their holy writings affirm fully the contrary. And where they say that the devil has no faith but has the knowledge of the things that we believe and so he does not have faith, there they affirm more than they can prove. For Saint James says they believe, and does not say they know. And he, when he wrote it, knew much better than Luther and Tyndale, too, what kind of perceiving the devils have in the articles of our faith. Just as there are some whereof the devils have, perhaps, not a belief but a certain and sure knowledge, such as Christ's descent into hell and despoiling of their possession, so do they in all likelihood have only belief and opinion in other articles of our faith, without actual knowledge and cognizance. And where those well-educated men Luther and Tyndale say that the devil does not have faith except by an equivocal use of the word—faith being actually, so you say, a faith in the promises of God, whereby Christian people hope to come to heaven, whereas the devils are in despair and can have no such faith in God's promises, nor can hope for or look forward to heaven—these well-educated men who say this are trying to set Saint James straight. For they would have us think that Saint James did speak of faith like someone who did not know what 'faith' means, and who made a mistake by using the word in an equivocal way, calling by the name of 'faith' something that is not in fact faith; whereas in fact Saint James speaks of it as he should, and uses the word in its right signification, and these Lutherans misuse the word out of a malicious intention to deceive uneducated people with equivocation. For whereas 'faith' signifies the belief and firm credence given not only to such things as God promises, but also to every truth that he tells his church, in writing or not, which thing he will have us bound to believe; and whereas in truth the devils, as Saint James says, do believe such things and hold them in a reverent fear, now these heretics would blind us with their equivocation, by which they not only restrict the faith to the promises alone, from all other articles of the faith (many of which are not promises, such as the belief that there is a God, and that there are three Persons, and many other such articles), but also abuse the word 'faith' altogether, turning it slyly from belief into trust, confidence, and hope, and would have it seem as though our faith were nothing else but a sure trust and a faithful hope that we have in God's promises. And this sophistical manipulating of 'faith' is the thing that, as Tyndale makes obvious in his book on obedience, these Lutherans think to deceive the whole world with. They purpose to make people think that 'faith' denotes not belief but hope and trust, and thus to make people think that Saint James did not know what 'faith' meant when he set forth, against those who put their trust as these Lutherans teach us in their faith alone, the comparison between them and devils, who believe as firmly as they. And therefore, to refute Saint James, they would make us believe that our faith is nothing but hope, whereas everyone knows that faith and hope are two distinct virtues, and that hope is not faith but follows faith, in anyone who has hope. For no one can hope for heaven if they do not believe it exists. But on the other hand, a person can, as the devil does, though they believe and even know it exists, yet fall far from all hope of it. And if these Lutherans will defend their heresy by that sophistical gloss, they must then change their article and say no more that faith alone is sufficient, but say rather that *hope*

alone is sufficient. And yet they will then be lying as bla-
tantly as they are now. For hope without charity will but
beguile them.

"After such argumentation the man said that he and the
other Lutherans, when they said that faith alone was sufficient, meant not a dead faith that is without charity and good
works, but a real faith that is alive and works through charity;
and that such faith, he thought, was sufficient. But then it
was answered that neither they nor he could mean that. For
how could they call that thing 'faith alone' that is joined with
charity and good works? Or how can it be that they mean
that faith which through charity works good works, when
they say that it is sufficient alone, without good works, and
that it is, as Luther says, a big sin and sacrilege to try to please
God by good works and not by faith alone? How could they
say that faith alone suffices if they meant that without charity
and good works no faith suffices? For it would be a mad
thing to say that faith alone suffices, without good works,
and to say therewith that without good works faith suffices
not at all. And so it was said to him that therefore, though
they dissemble their contentions when they are examined, it
yet cannot be but that he and other Lutherans, where they
sow their heresy, mean exactly what they say: that folk need
no more but believe, and then however they live will make
no difference. For nothing, says Luther, can damn a Christian, save only lack of belief. For all other sins (if belief and
faith stand fast) are entirely engulfed and swallowed up, he
says, in that faith.

"When this man was with such argumentation (and much
better than I can do or can repeat to you) somewhat sorely
pressed upon, he then came up with another gloss and said
that all they meant was that faith, if it is to suffice for salvation, must needs have with it charity and good works, or else
it is no real faith, just as a dead man is no real man. However,
he said that though it is nothing without good works, yet
when it is joined with good works, all the merit comes of

our faith alone, and no part of it is for our works. So that God gives us heaven for our faith alone, and nothing for our works. For though he does not give it for our faith if we lack good works, yet if we have both, he in his rewarding of our works takes no regard of anything except only our faith. And he said that for this cause they say that faith alone causes our salvation.

"To this it was answered that even if this opinion were correct, it nevertheless would be quite obvious that this is not the thing that they mean. For the statements of Luther and Pomeranus and all the archheretics of that sect are very plain.[10] For they say that it is sacrilege to try to please God by any good works but faith alone. In which case, why should good works be joined to faith? Or why should God exact good works from us? What use are they, if they are in no way pleasing to God? And when Luther says that nothing can damn any Christian except only lack of belief, he is manifestly stating not only that we need no good works with our faith, but also that provided that we have faith, no bad works can hurt us. And so he clearly means that faith alone, without any good works joined thereto, and also with all kinds of bad works joined thereto, is sufficient to save us. 'And therefore if you are of his sect,' it was said to the man, 'you cannot escape the fact that this is your real doctrine, however you disguise it.'

"Then it was further asked him that if their meaning was what he had said, then what was it that moved him and others, his cohorts, to think that in faith and good works

---

[10] Also known by the pen name "Pomeranus," Johann Bugenhagen (1485–1558) was first a canon with the Premonstratensians (the order founded by Saint Norbert in 1120), and then became a Lutheran theologian who helped organize the Lutheran Church in North Germany and Denmark; he also helped Luther with his translation of the Bible, and served as Martin Luther's confessor (*Oxford Dictionary of the Christian Church*, 249–50). Thomas More wrote a powerful letter to Bugenhagen in 1526 in which he addresses the Lutheran controversies at length; the letter was not published until 1568.

joined together, the good works were worth nothing, but that all the merit should be in the faith, and all the credit and reward should be given for the faith, and absolutely nothing for the good works.

"To which he answered that many scriptural texts led them thereto, and especially texts from Saint Paul: 'Fides iustificat,' 'Faith justifies' [see Rom 5:1 and Gal 3:24]; 'Credidit Abraam Deo, et reputatum est ei ad iusticiam,' 'Abraham believed God, and it was credited to him as righteousness' [Rom 4:3]; 'Si ex operibus, habet quidem gloriam, sed non aput Deum,' 'If he was justified by the works, then he did have glory; but not with God' [Rom 4:2]; 'Si ex operibus, Christus pro nobis gratis mortuus est,' 'If we are justified by the works, then Christ died for us for nothing' [Gal 2:21]; 'Gratis redempti estis,' 'You are redeemed for free' [Rom 3:24]. And thereby we can see that our works were no part of the cause. And, moreover, especially these words of Christ our Savior, he said, much moved them to be of that mind, where he says, 'Qui crediderit et baptizatus fuerit, salvus erit,' 'Whoever believes and is baptized will be saved' [Mk 16:16], where Christ requires nothing but faith alone.

"By all these texts, he said, it is clearly shown that all our salvation comes from faith, just as Abraham was justified by faith and not by his works. And that if our good works should be the cause of our salvation, then, as Saint Paul says, Christ died for nothing. For he did not need to die for us if our own works could save us. Nor were we redeemed for free if we are to redeem ourselves with the payment of our own works.

"To this it was answered that those texts and all the others cited for that argument mean nothing other than that, according to the faith of Christ brought into the world by the incarnation and Passion of our blessed Savior, people are no longer bound to the observance of the Mosaic law. And that neither all the Mosaic laws nor all the good works of man could ever of themselves, or without faith, save one man; and that Christ redeemed us for free. For he neither did nor ever will have any recompense from us for the bitter pains taken for us in his blessed Passion. Nor did we ever merit from him that he should do so much for us. Nor was the first faith, or the preaching thereof, or the first justification of man thereby, or the sacrament and fruit of our Baptism, given to the world for any good works that ever the world had wrought, but only of God's sheer, liberal goodness.

"But yet there is not one of those texts, nor any other in all of Scripture, whose meaning is that after the baptism the faith alone will save us without good works, if we live long enough and have enough intelligence to be able to do them. For though it is said by the mouth of our Savior, 'Whoever believes will be saved,' and here he says nothing about any good works, he yet does not mean that whoever believes will be saved without good works if they live long enough to do them. For else why should you not as well say that people will be saved for keeping of the commandments without faith, since Christ says, 'If you want to enter into the kingdom of heaven, keep the commandments' [Mt 19:17]. And says also, 'Do that, and you will have life' [Lk 10:28]. At which time he said not a word about any faith. He says also in holy Scripture, 'Date elemosinam, et omnia munda sunt vobis,' 'Give alms, and all is clean in you' [Lk 11:41]. Which words, 'if people should construe them as sweepingly for the preeminence of almsgiving as you that are of Luther's sect construe those other texts for that of faith, could be given a false interpretation and guise of saying that without faith (or penance either, or any other virtue), almsgiving alone suffices for salvation, no matter how wretchedly we lead our lives otherwise. But if we should say this about almsgiving, we should speak wrongly, as you do when you say it about faith. For just as, even though this is not mentioned in those texts that speak of good works, it is understood that faith must necessarily go with good works if they are to be fruitful, so is it understood that in the case of those who after baptism have the time and intelligence to work well, faith must be accompanied by good works—and by sorrow at heart for lack of good works—if the faith is to be of any benefit to them. For if both good works and final repentance of the lack of good works do fail us (we having had the time and intelligence for them), we are likely to fare much the worse for our faith. And that this is the case we can well know from the texts of holy Scripture, if we put them together and do not take one text, on our side, and disregard another.'

"To this he answered that albeit that these texts put together do prove that faith alone does not suffice without good works (which thing he said that he himself did not deny), yet he said that none of those texts prove anything contrary to this: that when faith and good works are joined together, all the merit still comes from our faith alone, and not at all from our works.

"To which he was answered that even if it were really so that no scriptural texts proved the contrary, yet 'since there is none that says this, and the whole Church says and believes the contrary, what reason do you have to say this, and to give the whole merit to faith, and no part of the reward to good works? And now you have much less reason to do so, when the plain words of Holy Writ are clearly to the contrary. For did not God say to Cain, "If you do well, you will fare well"? [See Gn 4:7.] Does not Christ say about those who do almsgiving, "A good measure, shaken together, heaped and running over, will be poured into your lap"? [See Lk 6:38.] Does not our Lord say that on Judgment Day he will give the kingdom of heaven to those who have given alms of food, drink, clothing, and lodging, because of their charity exercised in those deeds? [See Mt 25:34–36.] Which deeds, though he will not reward them with heaven unless faith went with them, yet if they were wrought in faith, he promises to reward those works, and not the person's faith alone.

This, in fact, is shown by the words of our Savior in the same texts, and by his words in which he said he would on Judgment Day speak to those who had by faith wrought wonders in his name without good works and charity, whom he would then command, "Begone, workers of wickedness," and tell them that he does not know them. From these things, I say, it is quite clear that, be our faith as great as can be, yet if we fail to do good works, our faith will fail to get us into heaven.'

"Then he said, yet again, that faith can never be without good works; that if one has faith, one's faith will not fail or cease to bring forth the fruit of good works, just as the tree brings forth its leaves.

"Then it was answered him that he was driven from that point before, as well by the authority of Saint Paul as by that of Saint James. And also that he well knew that faith or belief is not incompatible with every sin, but only with lack of faith or belief, and thus with other sins it can coexist. Then he said that if people believed surely, he thought they would not sin. For who would sin, said he, if they believed truly and surely that sin would bring them to hell? To which it was answered, 'Whoever believed in accord with your Lutheran faith would never refrain from sinning, since Lutherans believe that no sin could damn them except only lack of belief, and that they need not do any good work, but will be saved no matter how they live for their faith alone. Whereby it becomes quite obvious that you Lutherans have but half a faith. For you believe God only in his promises; in his threats you believe him not at all. However, if one actually believed surely what you would now seem to believe, the truth is that it would keep many a person from sin, but yet not every person. For although there are many who are either the more bold in sin or the more negligent in good virtues because their faith is very faint and feeble, who would if they had a sure and undoubted faith be in such fear of God, and love also, that it would withdraw them from sin and set them on the path of virtue, yet there are also, on the other hand, many whose faith, no matter how strong it was, would still not overcome the obstreperousness of their evil desires. And this would happen sometimes—and does, daily—with people not deeply submerged in wickedness, and folk not out of the faith, either, who yet fall into the breaking of God's commandments by the subtle instigation of the devil, or by the frailty of their own flesh. Of which it seems that the holy Apostle was himself so sorely afraid, for all his faith, that he three times begged God to take the temptation away [2 Cor 12: 7–9]. I cannot see but that Adam believed the words of God, and yet he broke his commandment. And I think that King David did not fall from his faith, though he did fall first into adultery and afterward into murder [2 Sm 11: 2–15]. And some examples have we seen of those who have sought the satisfying of their own malicious minds by ways such that they saw, when they went about it, their own undoubted death before their eyes. And therefore it is but a fiction to say that faith draws always good works with it, and that you Lutherans, when you say that faith is sufficient alone without good works, are speaking thus because it brings always good works with it. For this would be a really silly doctrine, that faith is alone sufficient to save those who have the use of reason without good works, if in those who have the use of reason faith is never without good works.'

"After such objections, he then moved on to another point and said that if our good works and faith are joined, it yet could be clearly shown by Scripture that all the merit was in our faith, and not at all in man's works. For all the works of man, he said, are utterly wicked, as things all spotted with sin. And for that he quoted several scriptural texts, but especially, as the most plain proof, the words of the prophet, 'Omnis iusticia nostra velut pannus menstruate' ['All our righteous deeds are like polluted rags'—Is 64: 6]. 'And since all our works,' he said, 'are spotted and sinful and wicked no matter how good they seem, it must needs follow that all the merit comes of our faith.'

"To this was answered him, 'Look—now, by this, you have somewhat given yourself away unawares and shown your opinion in this matter to be far other than what you said before. For in the glosses that you have used before, you have always said that you, and all the sect of Luther, as far as you knew and thought, believed that faith could not save us, if we had reason, without good works. But you said that faith was enough alone, because it necessarily brought good works with it; and yet all the merit and reward would be due to the faith alone, and not to the good works that it brings forth. And now you say that there are no good works at all; that all our works are utterly wicked. Now, if you think that there are no good works, how can you say what you said before—that you think that faith always brings forth good works? Moreover, those words of the prophet, though they are spoken generally, can be well understood to be verified in by far the greatest part of humankind, though not all, or to refer to the righteousness of human beings as compared with the sovereign righteousness of God. Or to mean that the righteousness of quite good persons is yet badly spotted with sin, because our nature is so frail that we seldom consistently continue for any length of time in good works; the perseverance is interrupted, often spotted, and besprinkled with sin. And about this it is said, "Septies in die cadit iustus, et resurget," "Seven times a day the righteous man falls, and rises again" [Prv 24: 16]. It can also be understood to refer to all the righteousness of one alone, wrought by oneself and one's mere natural powers without the aid and help of special grace. For certainly all such righteousness of ours as is ours alone *is* all spotted and, in effect, all one foul spot, for any beauty that it has in the glorious eye of God. But certainly the holy prophet never meant what Luther and his cohorts would have him seem to be saying: that the grace of God is in all his people so feeble of itself, and of so little force and effect, that no one can with the help of it be able to do one good, virtuous deed. For Luther says straight-out that no one, even if he has the help of God's grace for this, is able to keep and observe the commandments of God. Which blasphemous words seem to imply that both Saint John the Baptist and our blessed Lady also were sinners, and, besides all this, that God would not be able by the aid and help of his grace to make someone keep his commandments, and to keep him out of sin, even if he wanted to.

" 'All the old Fathers who wrote against Pelagius (who held the opinion that the human being is by nature, or at least with the general influence of grace, able and sufficient to do good and meritorious works without help of any special grace toward every good deed itself) disapproved and condemned his doctrine because it sold short the need to have recourse to God, to call for the help of his grace. But you, who hold all our deeds to be utterly wicked even if grace works with them, are two or three times more enemies to grace than the Pelagians were. For whereas they said we could sometimes do good without it, you say we can at no time do any good with it. And so grace, by your account, is a really worthless thing.

" 'Were, then, all the efforts and pains that the apostles took in preaching all wicked and sinful? All the tortures that the martyrs suffered in their passion—altogether sin? All the deeds of charity that Christ shall (as he himself says) reward with everlasting life at the general judgment, are they sin, altogether? Saint Paul reckoned it otherwise. For he confidently said of himself [in 2 Tm 4: 7–8], "Bonum certamen certavi, cursum consummavi, et nunc superest mihi corona iustitiæ," "I have labored and fought a good fight, I have completed my course, now nothing more is lacking for me but the crown of justice." '

"To that he answered that Saint Paul would not say that our deeds were sufficient of themselves, but that all our sufficiency is from God. To which it was answered that this was little to the point. For no more is our faith sufficient of itself, but the sufficiency of it is also from God, in that our Lord with our endeavor gives us grace to believe, and in that it pleases our Lord of his goodness so highly to reward it. For assuredly, just as it is quite true what Saint Paul says, that 'non sunt condigne passiones huius vitæ ad futuram gloriam quæ revelabitur in nobis,' 'all that ever we can suffer in this world is not deserving of the glory to come that shall be shown in us' [Rom 8:18] (for what thing could a poor, wretched creature do or suffer for God in the brief time of this short life, that could by right call for being rewarded everlastingly with such inestimable joy as neither eye has seen nor tongue can express, nor heart can imagine or conceive?), so is it also as true that all the faith we have, or can have, can of its own nature merit heaven as little as, or much less than, our other good deeds can. For what great thing do we do for God, or what great thing could we by right ask of him, because we believe him? As though he were much beholden to us because we deign to trust him! As though his honor hung in our hands, and his reputation would be lost if he were not given credence by us! And therefore, among many foolish statements, as foolish as any heretic ever made, Luther never made a crazier one than what he says about God having need of our faith. For he says that God has no need of our good works, but that he does have need of our faith, and has need for us to believe in him. The truth is that he needs neither our faith nor our works. But since he has determined that he will not save us without both if we possess the capabilities to have both, therefore *we* have need of *both*.

"Now, neither is the one nor the other, nor are both of them together, between them, of their own nature deserving of the reward of heaven. But just as we see that one ounce of gold, of which a weight of ten pounds is not of its own nature worth as much to a human being as one ounce of wheat, and a hundred pounds of which is not of its nature itself worth one scrawny sheep, is yet among humans, by a price set and agreed upon, worth many healthy sheep and many a pound of bread, so has it pleased God, in his liberal goodness, to set as well our faith as our deeds, both of which, of their own nature, would otherwise be quite little in value, at so high a price that no one is able to buy them and pay for them but himself, because we should work them only for him, and have no other paymaster, nor any other customer to sell our wares and our work to, but him alone. Unless we would be so mad, and toward him so cold, that we would sell it to another for less, rather than to him for more. As some do who would sooner travel far off and sell for less than sell to their neighbors at home for more. And as do these foolish hypocrites who, rather than sell their work to God for everlasting enjoyment of heaven, sell it all to the world for the paltry pleasure of the vain praise puffed out of poor mortals' mouths with a whiff of wind.

"To this he said that it was quite true that all our works took their value and price according to their acceptation by God, and as he chose to take them. But he said that God rejected, disapproved, and set at naught all the works of infidels, since they were worked without faith. For 'sine fide impossibile est placere Deo,' 'without faith it is impossible to please God' [Heb 11:6]. And that of his faithful, chosen people, who believe and trust in him, he accepts and approves all the deeds. And that is, said he, well proved by the words of Saint Paul, 'Nihil damnationis est his qui sunt in Christo Iesu' ['There is therefore now no condemnation for those who are in Christ Jesus'—Rom 8:1]. And albeit that in the relating of the conversation had with this man, it may well be that my remembrance may have the order partly wrong—partly, perhaps, be adding to or subtracting from some part of the discussion—yet on this point, I assure you sincerely, there is no kind of change or variance from his opinion. After many evasions, he finally brought it plainly to this point: that he and his cohorts that were of Luther's sect were firmly of this opinion, that they believed that God alone works everything in every person, good works and bad. However, those whom he foreknows to be damned, no works of any kind are profitable to them. For God takes them for bad, no matter how good they are. But, on the other hand, for those whom he has chosen from the beginning and predestinated to glory, all works are good enough. For God accepts them as being quite all right with him, be they bad as can be.

"It was asked him then whether the forsaking of Christ by Peter was all right with Christ and well approved by him. And whether in the case of David, the adultery and the murder were all right with God.

"To which he said that since they were chosen and predestinated, therefore those sins were not imputed to them; and neither are the sins of any such people imputed to them. God, because he has from the beginning chosen them to everlasting bliss, therefore imputes to them no blame for their deeds, but, rather, all the works of a just person (that is to say, said he, of a person predestinated by God to glory) turn him to good, no matter how bad they are. And this, in the end, he showed to be their crystal-clear mind and opinion, for all the cloaks that he had put upon the matter before, to make it seem that they meant in their statements no harm. And there it became quite obvious that he and his cohorts who in their preaching do covertly and craftily propagate the damnable sect of Luther are always hoping and yearning for some other time in which they trust to play openly and boldly the ravenous wolves and devour the sheep and mutilate the whole flock. And in the meantime they are content to play the wily foxes and worry simple souls and poor lambs, as they may catch them straggling from the fold; or to be, rather, like a false sheepdog that would bark only when in sight, and seem to fetch in the sheep, and yet kill a lamb in a corner. People speak of some who bear two faces in one hood. I have never seen any that more truly act out that charade than this species of such preachers. For in preaching to the people, they put a look on their face like they came straight from heaven to teach them a new way, better and truer than the one the Church teaches or has taught this many hundred years. And then to the Church, when they are on trial, they present themselves as poor down-to-earth men, and as though they taught no other way than the Church does. But in the end, when they are well examined, and with much work that falsehood of their cloaked collusion is pulled off, then appears there all the malicious treachery, and what poison they put out under the guise of honey. Such as this man I am telling you about, who, after striving as hard as he could, by many ploys, to make it seem that in preaching that faith alone is sufficient for our salvation and that good works are worth nothing, he had intended nothing not good and consistent with the doctrine of the Church, and that he and his cohorts never meant anything other than what the Church means, yet in the end plainly stated himself that he and his cohorts intend thereby to bring the people ultimately to this position—that everything depends only upon destiny, and that the liberty of the human will serves absolutely no purpose, nor do people's deeds, good or bad, make any difference before God, but in his chosen people nothing displeases him, be it no matter how bad, and in the other group nothing pleases him, be it no matter how good—the very worst and most harmful heresy that ever was thought up; and, on top of that, the most insane. For (as was said to him) if this were true, why would they preach at all? And counsel anyone toward one thing or another? What fruit could come of their exhortation if everything depended on destiny? He was then shown many things for the refutal of this irrational and detestable heresy, and that the texts which he cited did not at all make his point. For as for what he quoted from Saint Paul about there being no condemnation for 'those who are in Christ Jesus,' this means good, faithful folk who live virtuously; and thus, where Saint Paul says that there is no condemnation for those who are in Christ Jesus, there soon follows in that passage, 'those who walk not according to the flesh' [Rom 8: 4]. Meaning, obviously, that there is no one so planted in Christ Jesus but that if he follows the fleshly ways of his sensual appetites, he will be damned, for all his faith in Christ. For else, from this false opinion that God well accepts all the works of those who are predestinate, it would then follow that sin is not sin for them, but only for the other group, whom God has not predestinated. Which would be as much as to say that no one can licitly be wicked, no one licitly do theft or adultery, or licitly be a murderer, or licitly commit perjury, except God's good sons and his special, chosen children.

"Now, where he quoted the words of Saint Paul, 'Quod iustis omnia cooperantur in bonum,' 'With the just, all things work together for their good' [Rom 8: 28], it was said that this meant that all the bad things that people do to them result in good for them, and are for the good the occasion of their merit, as were for Job all the torments by which the devil tested his patience, and as were all the tortures that the pagan tyrants inflicted on the holy martyrs. And sometimes the sin into which a good person is by God's sufferance permitted to fall is for that person an occasion of a greater good, or of the avoiding of a greater sin. The avoiding, for example, of a high spiritual pride into which perhaps the continual course of his virtuous life might by the devil's subtle instigation have brought him, whereas one foul act of lechery has shown him his frailty and brought him into, instead of pride, penance and humility, and has made him run the faster forward in virtue, because he has stopped and sat still a while in sin, and therefore he will run ahead to win back on his track what he before threw himself behind. But it was not meant that ever their sins so worked for their good that they were accepted the more and rewarded the better for their bad deeds. Nor does God remit the sins of his chosen people, or forbear to impute the blame thereof to them, because they are his chosen people. For he accepts folk not for their persons, but for their merits. So, inasmuch as they have sinned, he punishes them as much as others—and sometimes more, because their former good conduct somewhat, by propriety, made them deserve to be by punishment called back to grace, and not be for their guilt too readily cast clean away, just as some others, obdurate in malice and bad habits of sin, deserve to have the grace of God and his calling-on nevermore offered to them, and it is offered to some who will not accept it. God called on David, through the prophet Nathan, and yet punished his offense. Christ looked at Peter after he had forsaken and forsworn him, and Peter therewith took repentance. God looked at Judas—and kissed him, too—and he turned to no amendment. Now, God, from the beginning, before the world was created, foreseeing in his divine prescience (or, rather, in the eternity of his divine nature, beholding in the present) that Peter would repent and Judas would despair, and that the one would take hold of his grace and the other would reject it, accepted and chose the one and not the other, as he would have made the opposite option if he had foreseen in them the opposite outcome."

12.

The author inveighs against that most pestilent sect of these Lutherans, who ascribe salvation and damnation, and all our deeds, to destiny.

"But, now, to say what that heretic, after all his evasions, did finally say—that all who will be saved will be saved only because God from the beginning has chosen them, and because of that choice all their deeds are good, or if they are bad, yet God by reason of his eternal choice takes them as quite all right and imputes no blame to them; and that all other people whom God has created will be damned solely because he did not wish to choose them; and that all their deeds are either wicked or not accepted as good because God

DIALOGUE CONCERNING HERESIES, PART FOUR

did not in the beginning care to choose them; and that he works, both in the one group and in the other, all their deeds himself, alone, and they do nothing there themselves; and thus that God, whose goodness is inestimable, does damn such a huge number of people to intolerable and interminable torments solely for his pleasure, and for his own deeds wrought in them solely by himself—this despicable opinion is, as the King's Highness most virtuously writes in his epistle to Luther, the most abominable heresy that ever was. And assuredly it is so far against all holy Scripture rightly understood, so far against all natural reason, so utterly subversive of all virtue and all good order in the world, so highly blaspheming of the goodness and majesty of Almighty God in heaven, that it is more than a wonder how anyone on earth who has either one spark of intelligence in his head or toward God or man one drop of good will in his heart would not shudder to hear it. For this execrable heresy makes God the cause of all evil; and such a cruel disposition as no tyrant or torturer ever had, they ascribe to the benign nature of Almighty God. For whereas Christ our Savior took upon himself all our sins and of his endless pity bore the punishment of them for our sake, this damnable heresy holds that God is, first of all, so dishonest as to lay on us the weight of and blame for his own wrongdoings (that is, the bad works which, they say, are wrought not by us, but in us by God), and on top of that, they make him out to be so pitiless and cruel that for his own deeds so done, he will take a perpetual delight and pleasure in tormenting us.

"They now turn the antidote of holy Scripture entirely into poison. For once that despicable error was taken for truth, of what use would all of Scripture be? Of what use are the exhortations to good works if people neither do any nor can do any, either of themselves or with the help of grace? Or if any are done by those who are not chosen, and their deeds are not accepted by God because he has not chosen their persons, of what use are the preachings and exhortations to faith, if the hearers have no liberty of their own will by which they can, together with God's grace, work to submit and subdue the rebellion of their reason to the obedience of faith and credence of the word of God? Of what use would be all the dissuasions and warnings and threats in Scripture, by which God calls people away from sin and bad works, if the world were ever of the mind that they believed like Luther, that no one does any bad deed himself, but God does them all himself? And that everyone is either chosen or unchosen. And if we are of the chosen group, no bad deed can damn us. And if we are of the unchosen group, no good deed can do us any good. Whoever thus believes, what do they care what they do, except out of respect for the temporal laws of this world? And, moreover, if their false faith is strong, they attach little importance to those also. For they will think that dying on their bed or on the gallows does not come according to what they deserve, but depends all upon destiny. And therefore all laws they set at naught. And they hold that no one is obliged to obey any, but would be at liberty to believe what they please, and do what they please, just as they say that God does to us not what we deserve, but what he himself pleases.

"Of what use would reason be if we humans had no power of our own toward the direction of our own works, but all our works were brought forth from us without our will— worse than the works are, indeed, out of a brute beast by the inclination of its sensual desire? For ours would be, according to this opinion, brought forth, just as the leaves come out from the tree, or as a stone falls downward, and the smoke upward, by the power of nature, so should, I say, all our deeds, good or bad, ascend or descend by the forceful hand of God, regardless of our intentions. And this those beasts are not ashamed to say when they know, by the experience they have all the time, that when they want to do something, they do it, and when they like, they leave it not done. I do not say by themselves alone, without God. But his assistance is always at hand, if we are willing to work with it, just as the light is present with the sun if we do not willfully choose to shut our eyes and play blind.

"Of what use would all laws be? And what would become of all good order among people, if every disordered wretch could claim that his wicked deed was his destiny?

"If free will serves for nothing, and every man's deed is his destiny, why do these men complain about any man? Unless they will say they do it because it is their destiny to do so. And why, then, will they be angry with those who punish heretics, unless they will say because it is their destiny to be so? For if they will hold them to the beliefs of their own sect and say people do them wrong to burn them for their heresies since it was their destiny to be heretics, then they can be well answered with their own words—as was done to a member of their sect in a good town in Germany. When he had robbed a man and was brought before the judges, he could not deny the deed, but he said it was his destiny to do it and therefore they could not blame him. And they answered him in line with his own doctrine, saying that if it was his destiny to steal, and therefore they must hold him excused, then it was also their destiny to hang him, and therefore he must as well hold them excused right back.

"And undoubtedly among humans these takers-away of free will can never rationally refute that argument. But then the wretches fall to the desperate ways of devils and damned souls. Then they fall to railing and reproving the justice of God, and say that he himself has wrought their evil works, and wrongfully punished them, and cruelly created them to wretchedness. Our mother Eve laid the blame for her sin on the serpent, and God was offended that she did not take on herself her own share. But these wretches excuse themselves and the devils as well, and blame on Almighty God both their own wrongdoings and the devils' too. But surely, whatever they say, they actually are little concerned about hell or about heaven, but would in this world live in lewd liberty and have everyone run wild. And since they see that they cannot get allowance so to do, nor get their sect approved in judgment, they scheme by all the ways they can to get so many to fall into their group that they may be able to turn the world upside down and defend their folly and treacherous heresy by force. And this they call the liberty of the Gospel: to be discharged of all order and of all laws and do what they like, which, be it good, be it bad, is, so they say, nothing but the works of God wrought in them. But they hope that by this means God will in the meantime work in them many merry pastimes. Wherein, if their heresy were ever to be accepted and the world changed thereby, they would find themselves sorely deceived. For the laws and orders among people, with fear of punishment, once taken away, there is no man so strong that he could keep his pleasure long, who would not find a stronger one taking it from him. But after it once came to that point, once the world was thrown into confusion and fallen in a wildness, how long would it be, and what heaps of oppressive evildoings would there befall, before that way was found to set the world in order and peace again?"

13.

The author gives his opinion concerning the burning of heretics, claiming that it is a licit, necessary, and right thing to do, and also pointing out that it is not something procured by the clergy, but only a good and prudent protective measure taken by the secular authorities.

"The fear that these outrages and evildoings will follow upon such sects and heresies," said I to your friend, "together with the experiences that people have had of this in some countries, has been the reason that princes and people have been constrained to punish heresies by terrible death, whereas otherwise more moderate ways would have been taken to deal with them. And therefore here I will say something in answer to the points which you brought up at our first meeting, when you said that many people thought it a heartless, uncharitable way taken by the clergy to put those convicted of heresy sometimes to shame, sometimes to death, and that Christ so much abhorred all such violence that he did not wish any of his flock to fight in any way, neither in the defense of themselves nor in that of anyone else, not so much as in the defense of Christ himself, for which he reproved Saint Peter, but that we should all live like him in endurance and forbearance, this being so much the case that, as you said, folk thought that we should not fight in defense of ourselves against the Turks and infidels.

"These objections are soon answered. For neither do the clergymen do therein any such thing as is being ascribed and imputed to them, nor do the secular authorities either. For although they could with good reason have done this anyway, they yet never in fact would have resorted so heavily to force and violence against heretics if the violent cruelty first used by the heretics themselves against good Catholic folk had not driven good princes to it, for preservation not only of the faith, but also of the peace among their people. For albeit that right after the death of Christ, at the beginning of the Church, many sects and heresies began (as is well evidenced by the Book of Revelation, written by Saint John the Evangelist, and by the Epistles of the apostle Paul), and after that, almost continually, various heresies sprang up in various places (as we plainly see in the history of the Church, by the books of Saint Jerome, Saint Augustine, Saint Eusebius, Saint Basil, Saint Ambrose, Saint Gregory Nazianzen, Saint John Chrysostom, and many other theologians of the Church), yet in all that time, a long space of many years, there was virtually never any punishment inflicted on those heretics other than refutings and disprovings done in disputations, either oral or written, or condemnations of their opinions by synods and councils, or, finally, excommunication and expulsion from Christ's flock; except that sometimes they were put to silence on pain of forfeiture of a certain amount of money.

"But as I said before, if the heretics had never started with the violence, then even if they had used all the ways they could to lure the people by preaching, even if they had thereby done what Luther does now and Muhammad did before—bring into vogue opinions pleasing to the people, giving them license for licentiousness—yet if they had left violence alone, good Christian people would perhaps all the way up to this day have used less violence toward them than they do now. And yet heresy well deserves to be punished as severely as any other sin, since there is no sin that more offends God. However, as long as they refrained from violence, there was little violence done to them. And certainly though God is able against all persecution to preserve and increase his faith among the people, as he did in the beginning, for all the persecution inflicted by the pagans and the Jews, that is still no reason to expect Christian princes to allow the Catholic Christian people to be oppressed by Turks or by heretics worse than Turks."

"By my soul," said your friend, "I wish that all the world were all in agreement to take all violence and compulsion away on all sides, Christian and heathen, and that no one were constrained to believe but as they could be induced to by grace, wisdom, and good words, and then those that would go to God, go on God's name, and those that will go to the devil, the devil go with them."

"Actually," said I, "if it were that way, I yet would little doubt that the good seed being sown among the people would as well come up and be able to save itself as the cockle, and that God would always be stronger than the devil. But yet heretics and heathens are two different cases. For in the case that the Turks, Saracens, and pagans were to allow the Christian faith to be peaceably preached among them, and that we Christians should therefore likewise allow all their religions to be preached among us, and violence be taken away by assent on both the sides, I doubt not at all that the Christian faith would much more increase than decline. And albeit that we would find among us those who would for the licentious liberty of those religions draw to the devil, yet so also would we find among them, I have no doubt, many a thousand that would be happy to leave that bestial pleasure and come to the Christian faith, as in the beginning there did come to Christianity from among the pagans, who lived as hedonistically as the Turks do now. But since violence is used on their side, and Christianity not there allowed to be preached and accepted, those who would now allow that religion to be preached and taught among Christians, and not punish and destroy the doers of that preaching and teaching, are plainly enemies to Christ, since they would be willing to let Christ lose his worship in many souls on this side without anyone being won from the other side to take their place.

"But, now, if violence were withdrawn on that side, then this way that you speak of might perhaps, between Christendom and Turkey or pagans, if the world gave its assent to it and could hold to it, be no bad way. For since we should nothing so much regard as the honor of God and the spreading of the Christian faith and the winning of people's souls to heaven, we would seem to be dishonoring God if we feared that his faith preached among others equally without disturbance would not be able to prosper. And, believing that it would be, we would impair the profit if we were to refuse the condition, when there are many more to be won to Christ on that side than to be lost from him on this side.

"But as for the heretics rising among ourselves and springing from ourselves, they are in no way to be tolerated, but are to be suppressed and overcome at the outset. For by any pact with them, Christendom has nothing to gain. For as many as we allow to fall to them we lose from Christ. And from all of them we could not win to Christ one the more, even if we won them all home again, because they were our own before. And yet, as I said, for all that, from the beginning they were never by any temporal punishment of their bodies at all harshly treated until they began to be violent themselves.

"We read that in the time of Saint Augustine, the great theologian of the Church, the heretics in Africa called the Donatists resorted to force and violence, robbing, beating, torturing, and killing those whom they seized from the true Christian flock, as the Lutherans have done in Germany. For putting a stop to which, that holy man Saint Augustine, who had for a long time with great patience borne and endured their malice, only writing and preaching in refutation of their errors, and not only had done them no temporal harm but also had hindered and opposed others who would have done it, did yet at last, for the peace of good people, both permit and exhort Count Boniface and others to suppress them with force and threaten them with corporal punishment.

"Which way of acting holy Saint Jerome and other virtuous Fathers have in other texts approved. And since that time there have upon necessity—perceived by great outrages committed against the peace and quiet of the people in sundry places of Christendom by heretics rising from a small beginning to a strong and unruly multitude—been devised for them many severe punishments, and in particular death by fire, not only in Italy and Germany, but also in Spain and virtually all parts of Christendom. Among which in England, as a good Catholic realm, it has long been punished by death in fire. And especially in consideration of the fact that in the time of that noble prince of most celebrated memory, King Henry V, when Lord Cobham maintained certain heresies, by that means the number of heretics so grew and increased that within a while, though he himself had fled to Wales, they yet assembled themselves together in a field near London in such a way and in such a number that the king and his nobles had to put on armor in order to suppress them, whereupon they were routed and many of them executed; and after that, Lord Cobham was taken in Wales and burned in London. Then the king, his nobles, and his people, thereupon considering the great peril and jeopardy that the realm was likely to have fallen into on account of those heresies, made at a parliament very good and effective provisions, additional to all such as were made before, for counteraction as well as suppression and severe punishment of any such as should be found guilty thereof and left by the clergy to the secular authorities.

"For here you shall understand that it is not the clergy who endeavor to have them punished by death. It may well be, since we are all human beings and not angels, that some of them may sometimes have too hot a head, or an injudicious zeal, or, perhaps, an irascible and cruel heart, by which they may offend God in the very same deed by which they would otherwise gain great merit. But certainly what the Church law on this calls for is good, reasonable, compassionate, and charitable, and in no way desirous of the death of anyone. For after a first offense the culprit can recant, repudiate by oath all heresies, do such penance for his offense as the bishop assigns him, and in that way be graciously taken back into the favor and graces of Christ's church. But if afterward he is caught committing the same crime again, then he is put out of the Christian flock by excommunication. And because, his being such, his mingling with Christians would be dangerous, the Church shuns him and the clergy give notice of this to the secular authorities—not exhorting the king, or anyone else either, to kill him or punish him, but in the presence of the civil representative, the ecclesiastical official not delivers him but leaves him to the secular authorities, and forsakes him as one excommunicated and removed from the Christian flock. And though the Church will not lightly or hastily take him back, yet at the time of his death, upon his request, with indications of repentance, he is absolved and taken back."

Should heretics be allowed to kill souls?

14.

*The author does some explaining of how it is that the clergy do no
wrong in leaving heretics to the secular jurisdiction, even if their
death follows thereon. And he also claims that it is licit to resist the
Turk and other such infidels, and that rulers are obligated to do so.*

"Indeed," said your friend, "but as I see it the bishop does as
much as kill him when he leaves him to the secular authorities at such a time and place as he knows well he will soon be
burned."

"I will not here enter into the question," said I, "of
whether a priest can for any reason—and if for any, whether
then for heresy—licitly put, or command the putting of,
anyone to death, either by explicit statements or under the
general name of right and justice. In that matter I could not
lack reason, authority, or the example of holy men. But in
this matter that we have in hand, it is sufficient that the
bishop neither does it nor commands it. For I think no
reasonable person will have it that when the heretic, if he was
at large, would with the spreading of his error infect other
folk, the bishop should have such pity on him that he would,
rather than allow other people to punish his body, allow him
to kill other people's souls.

"Indeed," said I, "there are some, as you say, who, out of
either a lofty pretended pity or a feigned regard for the counsels of Christ, would have no one punish any heretic, or
infidel either, not even if they attacked us and did us all the
harm they possibly could. And of this opinion are Luther
and his followers, who among their other heresies hold as an
obvious conclusion that it is not licit for any Christian to
fight against the Turk, or to put up against him any resistance, even if he comes into Christendom with a big army
and strives to destroy everything. For they say that all Christians are bound by the counsels of Christ, according to
which, they say, we are forbidden to defend ourselves, and
that Saint Peter was, as you mentioned, reproved by our
Savior when he struck off Malchus's ear, even though he did

465

it in the defense of his own Master, and the most innocent man that ever was. And in connection with this they claim, as you said in the beginning, that since the time that Christians first resorted to fighting, Christendom has never increased, but has always diminished and declined. So that at this day the Turk has very tightly restricted us and brought it in within a very narrow compass, and will keep making it narrower, they say, as long as we attempt to defend Christendom by the sword. They say that it should be, as in the beginning it was increased, so now continued and preserved only by forbearance and martyrdom. Thus holily speak these godly fathers of Luther's sect, endeavoring to procure that no one would resist the Turk, but would let him win everything. And when it should come to that, then they would, as it seems, win everything back by their forbearance, high virtues, and martyrdom—by which they now cannot manage to resist their bestial sensuality, but instead they break their vows and take to themselves harlots under the name of wives. And whereas they may not fight against the Turk, they rise up in large bands to fight against their fellow Christians. It takes, I trust, no great genius to perceive whom those who hold that opinion are trying to please. And if the Turk happens to come in, there is little doubt as to whose side they will take, and that Christians are likely to find no Turks as cruel as them. What a noble holiness, to abstain out of piety from resisting the Turk, and meanwhile to rise up in rabbles and fight against Christians, and, as that sect has done, destroy many a good religious house, despoil, maim, and kill many a good, virtuous person, and rob, desecrate, and pull down many a goodly church of Christ.

"And now, where they adduce as a proof that God is not pleased with battle made against infidels the losses and diminishment suffered by Christendom since that practice began, they behave as once did an old sage father fool in Kent when several upper-class men had some elderly country folk meet with them to discuss and plan the restoration of Sandwich Harbor. At which time they started out by trying to determine, by discussion and by reports made by the old men from around there, what thing had been the reason that so good a harbor had within such a few years so badly deteriorated, and such sands risen, and such shallow sandbars made therewith, that very small vessels now had a lot of trouble coming in at any kind of tide, whereas a few years before, big ships were accustomed to riding without difficulty. And some laid the blame on Goodwin Sands, and some on the lands reclaimed by various owners on the Isle of Thanet out of the Channel, in which the sea used to encompass the isle and bring the vessels around it, and whose course at the ebb used to scour the harbor, whereas now, the sea being shut out from there, the harbor for lack of such course and scouring was choked up with sand. Thus they alleged, different men, different causes. Then one good old father suddenly stood up and said, 'Y'all gentlemen, say every man what he will, I done marked this here thang good as anyone else. And, by God, I know well 'nuff how it gone bad. For I knowed it when it were good, and I did mark, so I done, when it begun to go bad.' 'And what has hurt it, good father?' said the gentlemen. 'By my faith, sirs,' he said, 'yonder same Tenterden steeple and nothin' else, that, by the Mass, I wish 'twas a nice big fishin' pole.' 'How has the steeple hurt the harbor, good father?' they said. 'Nah, by our Lady, gentlemen,' he said, 'I cain't well tell y'all how, but I well know it did. For, by God, I knowed it to be a good harbor till that there steeple was built, and, by the Mass in honor of our Lady, I done marked it well, it never done good since.'

"And thus intelligently speak these holy Lutherans who, sowing schisms and seditions among Christian people, lay the loss thereof to the fending off of the Turk's invasion and the resisting of his malice, when if they had any sense in their heads, they would instead lay it to the contrary. For when Christian princes did their duty against heretics and infidels, there are histories and monuments enough that witness the manifest aid and help of God in great victories given to good Christian princes by his almighty hand. But on the other hand, ever since the ambition of Christian rulers who desire each other's dominion set them at war and deadly dissension among themselves, whereby while each of them has aspired to the aggrandizing of his own dominion, they have little cared what became of the common corps of Christendom, God, for the punishing of their inordinate appetites, has withdrawn his help and shown that he cares as little, allowing, while they try to eat one another up, the Turk to prosper and to proceed so far that if their blind passions do not look thereto the sooner, he shall not fail (which our Lord forbid) within a short while to swallow them all.

"And although Christ forbade Saint Peter, who was a priest and, under Christ himself, prince of Christ's priests, to fight with the temporal sword toward the hindrance and resistance of his fruitful Passion (on which depended the salvation of humankind), which propensity our Savior had before that time so severely reproved and rebuked in him as to call him Satan for it [Mt 16:23], it is nevertheless completely off-base to claim that in accord with that example, temporal princes should, not with an eye to such spiritual profit but with an allowing of much spiritual harm, let their people be attacked and oppressed by infidels, to their utter undoing, not only temporal, but also, for a great many, perpetual, they being likely of their frailty, for fear of earthly hardship and discomfort, to fall from their faith and renounce their baptism. In which danger our Lord would not have anyone deliberately put himself, and for that reason advised his disciples that if they were persecuted in one city, they should not come forward and foolhardily put themselves in danger of denying him because of inability to endure some intolerable tortures, but should instead flee from there to some other place where they could serve him in peace [Mt 10:23], till he should allow them to fall into a predicament from which there was no way to escape, and then he would have them like mighty champions stand their ground, where they shall not, in such a case, fail of his help.

"Now, although it is true that Christ and his holy apostles exhort everyone to cultivate forbearance and endurance, not requiting an evil deed or putting up any defense against it, but taking endurance further and even returning good for evil, yet neither does this counsel bind us to necessarily, against the nature we all have in common, allow someone to kill us without cause, nor is it meant to deter us from defending someone whom we see innocent and maliciously assaulted and oppressed. In such a situation nature, reason, and God's behest bind, first of all, the ruler to protect his people at risk of himself, as God taught Moses to know himself obliged to kill the Egyptian in defense of the Hebrew [Ex 2: 11–12]. And after that, he obliges everyone to help and defend his good, innocent neighbor against the malice and cruelty of the wrongdoer. For as holy Scripture says, 'He gave commandment to each of them concerning his neighbor' [Sir 17: 14]. God has given everyone charge of his neighbor to keep him from harm of body and soul as much as may lie in his power. [See Lv 19: 18, Lk 10: 27–37, and Rom 15: 2.]

"And for that reason, not only excusable but also commendable is that communal war which every people takes up in the defense of their country against enemies that would invade it, since everyone is fighting not for the defense of himself, out of personal regard for himself, but, out of Christian charity, for the protection and preservation of everyone else. Which reasoning, as much as it holds true with regard to all battles of defense, most especially holds true with regard to the battle by which we defend the Christian countries against the Turks, in that we defend one another from far the more danger and loss, in terms of worldly possessions, bodily harm, and perdition of people's souls.

"And now, if this is licit and obligatory even for every

private citizen, how much more so is it for princes and other rulers? If on pain of losing their souls they may not knowingly allow it to happen that among the people whom they have in governance, anyone takes away anyone else's horse, then how can they without calling down on themselves eternal damnation allow other people, and especially infidels, to come in and disarm and rob and enslave them all? And if they are obligated to provide this defense and cannot do it by themselves, what madness it would be to say that the people may not help them."

15.

On the obligation of rulers to punish heretics, and the fact that gentle treatment helps little with many of them.

"And certainly, just as the rulers are obligated not to allow their people to be attacked by infidels, so are they as gravely obligated not to allow their people to be seduced and corrupted by heretics, since the peril will within a short while grow to as great, with people's souls being withdrawn from God, and their goods lost, and their bodies destroyed, by general sedition, insurrection, and open war, in the interior of their own land. All of which can at the outset be quite easily prevented, by punishment of those few that are the first. Which few well repressed (or, if need so require, utterly uprooted) there will far the fewer be inclined to follow. For if they were handled in a contrary manner and (as you seemed to have in mind at the beginning of our discussion), instead of being punished, treated with persuasion and leniency, and by nice words and rewards brought back home, I am afraid you would then find little fruit in that fashion. For first, given that they fall into heresy through pride, that way would make them prouder, make them think all the more of themselves. And then many more would fall into it, for the purpose of being bribed back out of it. Just as Mamluks and Janissaries around the Turk and sultan have made a practice of having their children baptized for the purpose that, by the renouncing of their faith afterward, these children might be made Mamluks or Janissaries as their fathers were, and may be held in the more esteem and favor with the great Turk, exactly likewise, within a while, if we take that way with heretics, we shall have fresh young fellows first become heretics so that they can afterward be begged and bribed to come back to Christ's faith. I would have them handled not too hastily, but shown little severity and much mercy where the problem proved to be gullibility, and not a proud heart or malice. For about those that are proud and malicious, much has already been found out by experience. For, of a certain type, many who are treated very nicely little change themselves or come to good amendment. I told you myself, and very true it was, about two men who were accused of heresy to the highest-ranking prelate of this realm, and in what a kindly, fatherly manner, and generous also, he dealt with them. And yet what amendment did his gentle and courteous treatment make in their stubborn spirits? Were they not afterward worse than they were before? Did they not conduct themselves in such a way that, after doing a lot of harm, they came a short time later to be publicly convicted? These people are, as you well know, after a first offense customarily received to grace—and truly, for such merits, forgiveness is reward enough. And if they cannot from that warning take warning, then surely, as Saint Paul says, they are not to be trusted often, but are, rather, to be shunned by all good Christian people and removed from the flock [Titus 3: 10–1]. For they are grown so crooked that seldom can they be righted again."

"Indeed," said your friend, "yet, as I said at my first coming to you, if I were worthy to be consulted by the clergy when there was found guilty of heresy a man whom the people hold in high regard because of some great reputation for learning and virtue, I would say that the man should be secretly and soberly admonished, and the matter not publicized among the people. And finally, if these men must of necessity be publicly convicted and corrected in front of the world, then I still would not have them called Lutherans, lest the people who had a good opinion of them should perhaps like Luther the better on account of them; or, if they happen to perceive them as wicked and so take them, then they will perhaps give the less credence to all good men, and think the less of all good preachers thereafter."

"Assuredly," said I, "a certain rule as to what would always be best would be hard to give for such cases. At times there may, perhaps, be joined such honorableness with such repentance that it would not be much amiss to preserve the man's reputation among the people, to whom his perfect change may perchance more than make up for his former error and mistake. But where the contrary will seem appropriate, there I cannot see why we should forbear to call them Lutherans, since it is an old custom to call heretics by the name of the one they follow in their heresy. And also, since Luther's sect is in effect the whole heap of all heresies gathered together, it is now one and the same to call these people Lutherans or to call them heretics, those two words being close to equivalent, Luther teaching almost nothing but heresies, and no heresies being found anywhere, almost, that the Lutherans do not have among them. And since this is so, reason does in my opinion dictate that the name of 'Lutherans' should customarily be brought into people's ears as being as odious as the name of 'heretics.'

"Nor do I see such a great danger that folk will either, because of finding themselves to have been mistaken about someone they had thought virtuous, withdraw their favor and affection from such as are actually good, or fall into favoring Luther's sect because of the high regard they had had for this person whom they now see proved wicked. For this will no one do except those who are either so foolish that they would hate all of Christ's apostles because of the treachery of Judas, or so wicked that they want to have all the world fall into the same sect and be of their own sort."

16.

About simple, uneducated folk who are led astray by the great good opinion that they perhaps have of the learning and way of living of some who teach them errors.

"Indeed," said your friend, "and yet I would think that a lot of pity would be shown now and then in those inquiries. For many an uneducated person, when they hear someone whom they take for knowledgeable, and see such a one as they take for virtuous, commending Luther's way, they are of simpleness and good attitude moved to follow the same."

"Certainly," said I, "there I say not no, but that these things being such, it is a great pity to see many good, simple souls deceived and led out of the right way by the authority of men they regard as both good and knowledgeable, whom they have, by either public sermons or private conversations, perceived to be favorers of that ungodly sect, thinking that men of such erudition and knowledge of Scripture, being also of such virtuous behavior as they seem to be, would never lean to that way unless they knew it to be good. And certainly when it does happen that any simple soul is, by the good opinion that he has of his spiritual leader, led out of the right belief of the faith, thinking the true faith to be that which he sees his leader (whom he reckons both good and knowledgeable) follow and lean to, it is a very piteous thing. And just as that person is less blameworthy and more easily cured, so is that leader doubly damned, as the cause of both his own sin and that of the one who is following him. And very hard is he to amend.

"However, sometimes we deserve with our sin that God, for the punishment of it, allows us to have sorry leaders and bad teachers. And certainly, for the most part, those who are led out of the right way do rather succumb to this out of a sorry lightness of their own minds than because of any great thing that moves them in their leader who teaches them. For we see them as ready to believe a pursemaker, glovemaker, or weaver, who can do nothing but barely read English, as they would be to believe the most intelligent and most learned theologian in a realm. However, no matter how very learned a man is, and no matter how virtuous he seems, we still can with no rationality excuse ourselves if we leave the right belief for the trust that we have in any earthly man. For our belief is taught us by God surely planted in the church of Christ, and the articles of it are not newly begun, but now continued many a hundred years in the great congregation of Christian people, as things certain, sure, and stable, and beyond all question, which no heretic does or can deny, and in the hearts of this congregation are they written by the holy handwork of God. And therefore accursed is anyone who through trust put in any man believes the contrary of any point that the church of Christ is taught by God to believe.

"This faith was taught by Christ, preached by his apostles, written of by his evangelists; and many more things were taught than are written. And this faith would have been taught and firmly established even if nothing had been written. And the articles of this faith had in people's hearts are the just and sure rules of interpretation by which we interpret and understand the holy Scripture that is written. For very sure are we that whoever would interpret any text of holy Scripture in such a way that he would make it seem contrary to any point of this Catholic faith which God has taught his church, he gives Scripture a wrong meaning, and thereby teaches a wrong belief. And as Saint Paul says, accursed would he be even if he was an angel from heaven. And therefore we are not excusable if we believe any man to the contrary of the faith, no matter how good or how knowledgeable he may seem, when we see that he teaches us a wrong way, which we can soon know if we are good Christians and already know the Creed.

"And we can also have a great guess at that if he teaches us secretly, as a confidential mystery, a doctrine that he does not want uttered and declared openly. For commonly such things are they that these heretics teach in a hush-hush way against the faith that all the Church believes.

"Now, I would give this counsel to any uneducated person: When any man whom you hold in high esteem for virtue or knowledge teaches you such things, then consider within yourself the fact that he has neither more virtue nor more knowledge than had Saint Augustine, Saint Jerome, Saint Ambrose, Saint Gregory, Saint Cyprian, Saint John Chrysostom, and many other old Fathers and holy theologians who believed all their days, and died in the belief of, that which you believe already, of which he teaches the contrary. And boldly say so to him. And then if he tries to trick you by saying that those holy theologians believed not as you do but as he says, bring him to the reckoning before some other quite well-educated men. And I dare venture to guarantee that you will find him doubly untruthful. For neither will you find it true, what he told you, nor, besides that, will he hesitate to slander you, saying and even swearing that you have reported him wrongly and that he never told you that."

"Indeed, sir," said your friend, "he will perhaps say that he is possibly on that point to be pardoned, because of the jeopardy that he could fall into by the maintaining of his opinion."

"Pardon him if you wish," said I. "But yet he is not, then, so good as were those good Fathers. For either his way is bad, and then he does bad by teaching it, or if it is good, then he is bad who for any fear forsakes it. For whoever forsakes any truth of Christ's faith forsakes Christ. And then our Savior says that whoever does so will be forsaken by him [Lk 12:9]. And whoever does so is not to be believed like those holy Fathers who have taught us far the contrary. For they did abide by the right faith that they taught, which is, as is evident from their books, the very same faith that we believe. And to such an extent did they abide by it that several of them sustained great persecution for it, and some of them death and martyrdom. So that we would be more than mad if we would not rather send our souls to the souls of those holy Fathers, of whose knowledgeableness, virtue, and salvation we are sure, than throw them away with these folk who, however holy they may seem, yet show themselves evil in that they teach the contrary of such things as those definitely holy theologians taught."

"I wonder, then," said your friend, "why they live so virtuously, fasting and giving their goods in alms, and carrying out other virtuous exercises, both in forbearing the pleasure of the world and also in taking pain in their bodies."

"To this assertion," said I, "our Savior himself responds where he says in the Gospel of Matthew, 'Attendite a falsis prophetis, qui veniunt ad vos in vestimentis ovium, intrinsecus autem sunt lupi rapaces,' 'Beware of the false prophets that come to you in sheep's clothing, and yet inwardly are ravenous wolves' [Mt 7: 15]. For since they by false doctrine endeavor to devour and destroy people's souls, we are sure enough that wolves they are indeed, however sheepish they look. And hypocrites they must needs be, since they are thus denounced by God's own mouth. And well can we perceive that they do not mean well, when they teach badly. And that they teach badly we can well know when we see them teach the contrary of that which God has already taught his whole Church. In which there have been so many holy Fathers, so many learned theologians, and so many blessed martyrs, who so have abided by the faith to the death, that it would be a craziness if we would now, against so many such, believe any false heretic and feigning hypocrite teaching us the contrary.

"As for those holy fathers of our faith, whom their books show to have believed as we believe, we have seen and known their virtuous life well proved by their blessed end, in which our Lord has attested by many a miracle that their faith and their lives have been to his liking. But never yet have we seen any such thing with any of these heretics. Nor even so much as any constancy in their doctrine. No, if they are once found out and examined, we see them always first ready to lie and perjure themselves if that will serve, and when that will not help, but their mendacity and perjury are proved to their faces, then they are ready to abjure and forsake it, as long as that can save their lives. Nor have I ever yet found a one who would not at some point abjure even if he had no intention of keeping his oath. So holy would he be, and so sensible as well, that he would with perjury kill his soul for ever to save his body for a while. For commonly, soon after, those who do this show their true colors again, God of his righteousness not permitting that their false forswearing should benefit them for long."

17.

The author asserts that some who are Lutherans and seem to live holily, and therefore are believed and held in esteem, have in mind a further objective than the one they profess to have, which they will well show if they can ever find their opportunity.

"And as for their conduct, the good appearance whereof is the thing that most blinds us, as much certainty as we have of the godliness of life of our old holy Fathers, whereof the world has written and God has borne witness by many great miracles performed for their sakes, as uncertain are we of these men, with whom we are not always present either, and little also can tell what abominations they may do to some of them secretly. Nor can we even know their intent and purpose that they are bent on, and the cause for which they are for the moment willing to take all the pain.

"Very certain it is that pride is one cause for which they take the pain. For pride is, as Saint Augustine says, the very mother of all heresies. For of a high mind to be in the liking of the people has come into many men so mad a mind, so insane, that they have not cared what pain they took without any other recompense or reward but the idiotic pleasure and delight that they themselves conceive in their hearts when they think how worshipfully people are talking about them.

And they are the devil's martyrs, taking much pain for his pleasure, and his very apes, whom he makes tumble through the hoop of that holiness that puts them to pain without fruit. And even, oftentimes, makes them fail to obtain the vain praise whereof alone they are so proud. For while they delight in thinking how they are taken for holy, they are many times well perceived and taken for the hypocrites that they are.

"But such is this accursed disposition of pride, and so deep does it set in its claws where it catches, that it is hard to pull them out. This pride has before this made some learned men devise new, fictitious notions regarding our faith because they wanted to be singular among the people; men such as Arius, Faustus, Pelagius, and several other old heretics. Whose false opinions have long since been unreservedly condemned by many Church synods and general councils; and now, God be thanked, not only are their opinions quenched, but also all their books are clean gone and vanished quite away, as of before any law was ever made for such books' burning. So that it is well shown to have been solely the work of God that has destroyed those works, which wrought in their times much harm in his church. This disposition of pride not only has made some learned men bring forth new, fictitious notions, but also makes many men of much less than average learning so sorely long to seem far more learned than they are that in order to make the people have them in authority, they devise new sects and schisms to the pleasure of newfangled folk, sparing no pains, for the time being, to propagate their sect with, rewarding their labor with only the delight of beholding what pleasure the people have in their preaching.

"And albeit that this insane pleasure with which the devil inwardly feeds them is the only thing that satisfies and contents some of them, yet there are many, of those that teach ill and appear holy, who are secretly more loose and sensual than they seem. And some also who warily hold back for the time being, but plan on a more liberal lewdness later on. Do you want to see an example of this? Look at Tyndale, who translated the New Testament, who was indeed (as you said in the beginning), before his going over, taken for a man of sober and honorable conduct, and who looked holy and whose preaching was holy, except that it sometimes smelled so badly that he was once or twice examined about it. But yet because he then glossed his words with a better meaning, and said and swore that he meant no harm, folk were willing to take it all for the best. But yet you see that though he feigned himself not to be a Lutheran or to bear any favor to Luther's sect while he was here, yet as soon as he got himself out of here, he got himself to Luther, immediately. And whereas in the translating of the New Testament he concealed and dissembled himself as much as he could, yet when he perceived his cloaked heresies espied and demolished, then he shortly showed himself in his true colors, putting out first his wicked book *Mammona* and afterward his malicious book on obedience. In which books he shows himself so puffed up with the poison of pride, malice, and envy that it is more than a marvel that the skin can hold together. For not only has he sucked out the most poison that he could find through all of Luther's books or take from him by mouth, and spat out all that in these books, but he even has in many things gone much further than his master, running forth so madly, for malice, that he acts as though he did not hear his own voice. He barks against the sacraments much more than Luther. For whereas Luther yet left some confession (and considered his secret confession necessary and profitable) though he set a vile liberty therein, Tyndale takes it away entirely and rails about it and says it was begun by the devil. Which thing undoubtedly would never have prevailed among the people, that folk should themselves reveal their secret sins to another human being, if God had not introduced it himself. Nor could it ever have continued so many hundreds of years without great harm coming of the disclosing of many people's crimes if the Holy Spirit of God had not assisted his holy sacrament, as the King's Highness most judiciously writes.

"Luther also sometimes affirms the existence of purgatory, sometimes doubts it, and sometimes denies it. But Tyndale raises no doubt at all, but denies it as utterly as foolishly, without any basis, cause, or rationale given as to why.

"Concerning the holy Mass, Luther, as mad as he is, was yet never as mad as is Tyndale, who, true to form, so rails about it, in his insane book on obedience, that any good Christian would shudder to read it. And even, writing as he does, is not ashamed to say that the Church will not believe holy Saint Jerome, Saint Augustine, and such others, as though these holy theologians were on his side. Among all of whose writings he will hardly read one page on which he will not find one or another of his abominable heresies refuted. Luther himself was never so shameless as to say that these holy Fathers believed on his side. Rather, because they were against him, he rejected the authority of them all. But what conscience does this Tyndale have, that thus can write to blind, uneducated people with, when he himself well knows both that the holy Fathers all do, unanimously, find that confession-and-absolution is of necessity requisite to our salvation, and that they adduce for themselves, for the further proof of this side of the argument, an abundance of quotes from holy Scripture, which Tyndale would wickedly, solely with railing and jesting against all their wholesome doctrine, drive clean away if he could? He himself also knows that they unanimously teach, and prove by Scripture, too, that there does exist the fire of purgatory—which I wonder why Tyndale fears so little, unless he has fully made up his mind to go straight to hell. They also teach unanimously the great profit of the Mass, and the honor that ought to be done to it, whereas Tyndale teaches people to dishonor it.

"They all teach the venerating of images and relics, and praying to saints, going on pilgrimages, and credence to be given to miracles—of all of which Tyndale teaches the contrary.

"All of them also teach chastity, and preach the high pre-eminence of virginity and widowhood over wedlock, and have always held in abomination the breach of any vow of chastity, whereas Tyndale, teaching the contrary against them all, is here so shameless, and has so little regard for his own conscience, that, seeing that all of them write against him and himself against them all, and that every educated person must needs perceive his shameless audacity here, he yet does not hesitate both to rail against Christ's church for saying what these old holy saints said before and also to say that the Church will not listen to them, whereas he himself sees that the Church and they are saying one and the same thing, and that as well they as the Church loathe and condemn his deadly, damnable heresies.

"Now, I think we need little doubt how he lives, who thus writes. He in all likelihood lives as ill as he teaches; and worse he cannot. But, as I started to say, this Tyndale in the beginning bore forth a fair face, and seemed to the people perhaps an honorable man, as some others perchance do now, whom you speak of, who, when they see their opportunity, will, if they can get tolerated, throw off their masks of hypocrisy and at long last show themselves in their true colors, as he does now.

"I ask you, look at Luther himself. If he had in the beginning said all that he has said since, who could have tolerated him? If he had in the beginning married a nun, would not the people have burned him? And yet now, little by little, he has brought them to be all right with that. And let us not think the contrary, but that of those heretics here who seem so good (if there are any such), we do not yet see their hearts, but shall, if they are upheld a while, see them follow their leader in lewd living, Dr. Luther (with his lover), and see them lure, with the devil's help, good and simple souls so far into wrong ways that eventually they will well like and commend things which now their uncorrupted consciences abhor. And there-fore let all good Christian people knock and break, as holy Scripture counsels, the young children's heads from Babylon against the stone [Ps 137: 8–9]; that is to say, let good Chris-tian folk suspect, abhor, and go after in the beginning all doctrine that is so bad as to be contrary to the faith and teaching of Christ's Catholic Church, which God and his Holy Spirit, both in writing and not, has taught his church, and which has in his church continued from Christ's days up until now, as is quite evident from the good, godly books of all our forefathers the holy theologians of Christ's Church Militant here on earth, now glorious saints in his Church Triumphant in heaven. From whose firm faith joined with good works, which like two wings carried them up to heaven, there shall, unless we are more than mad, no foolish heretic lead us, no matter how saintish he may seem, with any new interpretation of Christ's holy Gospel or of any other part of holy Scripture, which no one with any sense will doubt that those holy, knowledgeable men, illumined with the grace of God, understood much better than the whole pack of these vile heretics. Of all of whom that ever sprang up in Christ's church, the very worst and the most beastly are these Lutherans, as their opinions and their base behavior show. And let us never doubt that all who are of that sect, if any seem good (which very few do), they yet will in the end decline to the like lewd living that their leader and their confreres do, if they can ever (as by God's grace they never shall) mold the people to their own demented delusion. Which dissolute living they are driven to dissemble, because their audience is not yet brought to the point to bear it. They definitely trust to bring this about, and to reshape this realm after the fashion of Switzerland or Saxony and some other parts of Germany, where their sect has already done away with the faith, pulled down the churches, desecrated the temples, put out and despoiled all good religious, joined fri-ars and nuns together in lechery, vilified all saints, blasphemed our blessed Lady, cast down Christ's cross, thrown out the Blessed Sacrament, spurned all good laws, abhorred all good governance, rebelled against all rulers, fallen to fighting among themselves—and slain so many thousands that in many places the land lies virtually deserted and desolate—and finally, which is most abominable of all, put on God the blame for all their own ungodly deeds, taking away the liberty of the human will, ascribing to destiny all our deeds, with all the reward or punishment pursuant upon all our doings, whereby they take away all diligence and good endeavor toward virtue, all withstanding of and striving against vice, all concern about heaven, all fear of hell, all cause for prayer, all desire of devotion, all exhortation to good, all dissuasion from evil, all praise of well-doing, all rebuke of sin, all the laws of the world, all reason among people; they set all wretchedness astir, no one at liberty, and yet everyone to do what he wills, calling it not his will but his destiny, laying their sin to God's ordinance, and their punishment to God's cruelty, and ultimately turning our nature into worse than an animal's, and the goodness of God into worse than the devil. And all this good fruit would a few troublemakers—some out of desire of an unrestrained liberty for an unbridled lewdness, and some out of an arrogant diabolical pride cloaked under a pretext of good zeal and simpleness—undoubtedly bring into this realm if the prince and prelates and the good, faith-filled people did not in the beginning deal with their malice."

18.

The author shows that in the convicting of heretics the clergy could legitimately act with much more severity than they do, and that in fact the clergy now do no more against heretics than what the Apostle counsels and the old holy theologians did.

"For as for the clergy, whom they endeavor to make hated by the false accusation of cruelty, they do no more there than Saint Augustine, Saint Jerome, and other holy Fathers have been wont to do before, and go no further than the Apostle himself advises. For they do no more than, when one heretic, after being warned, will not amend but grows worse, shun him then and expel him from Christ's flock. Which is the very thing that Saint Paul counsels where he writes to Titus, 'Hereticum hominem post primam et secundam correptionem devita' ['As for a man who is factious, after admonishing him once or twice, have nothing more to do with him'—Titus 3:10]. And this is much less, what the clergy do to heretics, than what Saint Peter did to Ananias and Sapphira for a far smaller thing; namely, for their speaking untruthfully and keeping aside a portion of their own money, when they made a show of having brought to the apostles absolutely all of it [Acts 5:1–10]. For though they were not killed by his own hand, it yet is quite evident that God killed them, both of the two, through Saint Peter, his means as governor of his church, as a fearful example for all such as would later break their promise and vow, voluntarily made to God, of themselves or their own goods. Which thing Luther and Tyndale would have everyone do now. Did not Saint Paul write to the Corinthians that they should deliver to the devil that man who had defiled his father's wife [1 Cor 1:1–5], to the punishment of his body, that the spirit might be saved on the day of judgment? What do we say about Hymenaeus and Alexander, about whom he also writes to the Corinthians? 'Hymeneum et Alexandrum tradidi Sathane, ut discant non blasphemare.' 'I have,' says he, 'betaken Hymenaeus and Alexander to the devil, to teach them to quit their blaspheming' [1 Tm 1:20]. In which words we may well learn that Saint Paul, as apostle and spiritual governor in that region, finding the two of them fallen from the faith of Christ into the blaspheming of what they were duty-bound to honor, did cause the devil to torment and punish their bodies, which everyone may well know was no small penalty, and perhaps not without death also. For we find nothing about their amendment. And this corporal punishment Saint Paul gave, as it appears, to heretics; so that if the clergy gave to much more blasphemous heretics than I think the two of them were, much more grief than Saint Paul gave to them, they would be giving it neither without good cause nor without the great authorization and evident example of Christ's blessed apostles. And certainly when our Savior himself calls such heretics wolves cloaked in sheep-skins [Mt 7:15], and would have his shepherds, the gover-nors of his flock, in such manner get rid of them as actual shepherds would get rid of actual wolves [see Acts 20:28–31], there is little doubt that, as an honorable prelate of this realm in his most erudite book says in response to Luther, the prelates of Christ's church ought rather to destroy tem-porally those ravenous wolves than to allow them to worry and devour everlastingly the flock that Christ has committed to their care, and the flock that he himself died in order to save from the wolves' mouths. But, now, even if it is quite evident (which I think it is) that the clergy could in this case rightly take quite drastic measures against heretics, they yet in actuality go no further than the old holy Fathers did in their time, and do no more than the blessed Apostle counsels them to do. No, all the severe punishment of heretics, with which such folk as favor them want so much to render the clergy infamous, is and has been—on account of the great outrages and temporal harms that such heretics have always been wont to do, and the seditious commotions that they are wont to make, besides the far surpassing spiritual hurts that they do to people's souls—devised and executed against them of necessity by good Christian princes and prudent rulers of the secular sphere, because in their wisdom they well perceived that the people would not fail to fall into many grievous and intolerable troubles if such seditious sects of heretics were not by severe punishment repressed in the beginning, and the spark well extinguished before it was allowed to grow to too great a fire."

"Indeed," said your friend, "it is quite evident that the

clergy are not in this matter to be blamed, as many think. For it seems that the severe punishment of heretics is devised not by the clergy, but by civil authorities and good laypeople, and not without great cause."

"Well," said I, "and to the intent that you shall perceive it much the better, and, moreover, believe your own eyes and not my words regarding many things that you have heard from my mouth, we will not part tonight without my having delivered into your hands here more books than you will read through before tomorrow. But so that you will not need to read everything, or lose time searching for what you should see, I have gotten the places ready for you, with rushes between the pages, and notes marked in the margins where the matter is discussed."

So I had someone take into his room a book of decrees, and certain works by Saint Cyprian, Saint Augustine, and some other holy theologians, and along with them a work or two of Luther's, and as many of Tyndale's. And in this wise we went to supper, and on the next day I refrained from speaking with him till near dinnertime. At which meeting of ours he told me that in the decrees, where the rushes lay, especially in *causa 22, questione quinta*, and several of the questions following from there, he had fully seen that the clergy do at this day nothing further for the punishment of heretics than what was done by the old Fathers and holy theologians and saints in times past, as by their own statements there quoted is made clear and obvious. And that as well the clergy in the persecution of heretics licitly could do, as the civil authorities in war against infidels are seriously obligated to do, much more than they now do, or in a long time have done, or, as it seems, even try to do. And, moreover, he said that he had seen of Luther's own statements worse ones than he had ever heard related, and in Tyndale worse yet, in many things, than he saw in Luther himself. And he said that in Tyndale's book on obedience he had found what Tyndale says against miracles and against praying to saints.

"Indeed," said I, "and these two issues caused the two of us a lot of to-do before your going to the university. I wish it had happened that you and I had read through that book of his before. However, I am serious, if you want we shall yet examine one by one his arguments on those points, and consider what weight is in them."

"No, by my word," said your friend, "we shall need now to lose no time there. For as for miracles, he says virtually nothing but that which I alleged against them before: that the miracles were the works of the devil. Except that whereas I said that this *might* perhaps be *said* to be so, he says that in fact it *is* so—and proves it even less than I did. And therefore, as for that statement of his, without better proof it is of little weight."

"Indeed," said I, "Tyndale's statement alone, ascribing all the miracles to the devil, ought not carry much weight among Christian folk against the writings of holy Saint Augustine, Saint Jerome, Saint Ambrose, Saint John Chrysostom, Saint Gregory, and many another holy theologian who wrote of many a great miracle done at holy shrines and saints' relics, done in the public presence of many substantial folk, and several done in their own sight. All of which miracles all of these blessed saints do ascribe to the work of God, and to the honoring of those holy saints who were venerated at those shrines. When, against all of them, Tyndale ascribes them all to the devil, he clearly shows himself as faithful as he would seem—very much in line with the infidelity of those Jews who ascribed Christ's miracles to the devil, saying that he cast out devils by the power of Beelzebub, prince of devils [Lk 11:15]."

"Definitely," said your friend, "and as for what he argues against praying to saints, that is very indefensible."

"It must necessarily," said I, "be indefensible, unless he well gets rid of the miracles. When for this purpose he has nothing to say but to ascribe God's works to the devil, he shows himself driven into a tight spot. For he and his cohorts, as regards miracles, have neither God willing nor the devil able to perform any for the proving of their side. Nor, I trust in God, will they ever."

"Honestly," said your friend, "for discussion of the matter of praying to saints, he is not worth the reading now. For virtually all the main things by which you prove its legitimacy are by him completely unmentioned."

"That is," said I, "no surprise, since he has not heard them."

"Indeed," said your friend. "And of his own creativity he presents arguments for it, such as he pleases, which he sets forth faintly, and then answers so unconvincingly—and his whole entire case, on those points and others, is so plainly confuted by the old holy Fathers—that if I had seen so much before, it would likely have shortened many parts of our long conversation."

"For by my word," said he, "when I well consider both the sides, and read Luther's statements and Tyndale's in some places where you put me the rushes, I cannot but wonder that either any German could approve of the one or any Englishman of the other."

"It is not very surprising to me," said I, "that many well approve of them. For since there is no country lacking plenty of such as are wicked, what wonder is it that depraved folk fall to the favoring of their like? And then, as for such, when their hearts are once fixed upon their blind feelings, a person can with as much fruit preach to a post as reason with them to the contrary. For they do not at all ponder what is reasonably spoken to them, but where their foolish feeling inclines them, that thing they side with, and in that thing they believe, or at least that way they walk and say they believe in it. For in all honesty, that they so believe in actuality, their contentions are so crazy that I do not believe it. And yet they put on a pretense of believing that no one would be able to confute Luther or Tyndale, whereas it seems to me that on these points of their heresies that they thus set forth, there would (if the audience was impartial) be no man more meet to match both of those two in debate than would be mad Collins alone, if he were not of the same sect. For he spouts Scripture in Bedlam as fast as both of them in Germany. And, in all honesty, they both expound it as madly as he.

"And, so help me God, it seems to me that just as mad as any of all those three is anyone who, when they see the right faith of Christ continued in his Catholic Church so many hundred years, and on that side so many glorious martyrs, so many blessed confessors, so many godly virgins; and in all that time, virtue held in honor; fasting, prayer, and alms-giving held in esteem; God and his saints venerated, his sacraments held in reverence, Christian souls tenderly prayed for, religious vows kept and observed, virginity preached and praised, shrines devoutly visited, every kind of good works commended; and they see now suddenly start up a new sect setting forth the complete contrary, destroying Christ's holy sacraments, pulling down Christ's cross, blaspheming his blessed saints, destroying all devotion, forbidding people to pray for their parents' souls, flouting fast days, setting at naught the holy days, pulling down the churches, railing against the Mass, villainously demeaning the Blessed Sacrament, the sacred Body of Christ our Savior; and when they see the one side, and the continuance thereof, so clearly proved by many thousands of miracles, so clearly attested by the virtuous and erudite books of all the old holy theologians, from the apostles' time to our day, and see on the other side a foolish friar and his cohorts without intelligence or grace trying to make us believe that all those holy Fathers never understood the Scripture, but only these beasts that teach us vice as firmly as ever the others taught us virtue; and see on the one side Saint Cyprian, Saint Jerome, Saint Ambrose, Saint Augustine, Saint Basil, Saint John Chrysostom, Saint Gregory, and all the virtuous and learned theologians, one after the other, from the death of Christ and the time of his apostles till now, and see among all these not one priest, monk, or friar that ever did, after making his profession, marry and take a wife, or any allowed to break their vowed celibacy in all their time; and see on the other side no other theologians of this new sect but Friar Luther and his wife, Father Pomeranus and his wife, Friar Huszgen and his wife, Father Carlastadius and his wife, the monk Dom Otho and his wife, Friar Lambert and his wife, and the delirious Collins and the more delirious Tyndale, who says that all priests, monks, and friars must of necessity have wives—as delirious as both of them, I say, would be anyone who would rather send his soul with such a sort as these are than with all those holy saints who ever since Christ's days have testified by their holy handwriting that they died in the same faith that the Church believes in still, and all these fifteen hundred years has believed in, and shall believe in till the world's end. Go there however many heretics out of it, leaving it however small, it yet shall remain and be well known always by the profession of that faith, and those holy sacraments that have continued in it from its beginning, and its holy theologians ever held in honor and reverence, and their acceptance by God incessantly attested by miracles, which not one band out of so many sects of heretics could yet allege for any theologian of theirs, nor ever shall, I think, till the great indignation of God provoked by our sin and wretchedness shall suffer the head of all heretics, Antichrist (of whom these folk are the forerunners), to come into this wretched world, and to work therein such wonders that the sight thereof shall be able to put quite intelligent and good people in great doubt of the truth, seeing false Antichrist proving his preaching by miracles; whereas now, no one either good or intelligent could have any plausible excuse if they were so mad as to believe these mad masters, when they see the principal archheretics among whom, and the first authors of the sect, showing no miracle for the proof of their doctrine, and yet their teaching and their way of life all set upon sin and beastly concupiscence, and thus completely contrary to the doctrine of all the old holy theologians, for whom God has shown and does show so many miracles in his church, which, as I said, shall not fail to be conserved, and his right faith to be preserved in it, despite all the heretics that ever shall spring up, Antichrist and all, and in spite of the devil, the great master of them all, whom Christ shall at the last restrain, and whose idol, Antichrist, he shall destroy with the spirit of his holy mouth, repairing and expanding his church again; and, gathering into it as well the remnant of the Jews as all other religious groups out there around the world, he shall make all folk one flock under himself the Shepherd, and shall deliver to his Father a glorious kingdom of all the saved people from our former father Adam to the last day, from then on to reign in heaven, in joy and bliss unimaginable, one everlasting day with his Father, himself, and the Holy Spirit—whom may it please to send these seditious sects the grace to desist, and the favorers of those factions to amend, and us the grace that, stopping our ears to keep out the false enchantments of all these heretics, we may by the true faith of Christ's Catholic Church so walk with charity in the way of good works in this wretched world that we may be partakers of the heavenly bliss which the blood of God's own Son has bought us unto."

"And this prayer," said I, "serving us for grace, let us now sit down to dinner." Which we did.

And after dinner we departed, he home toward you, and I to the court.

THE END.

With royal privilege,
Year of our Lord 1531, month of May